International Journal on Advances in Telecommunications

2017 vol. 10 nr. 3&4

Printed from e-media with permission by:

Curran Associates, Inc.
57 Morehouse Lane
Red Hook, NY 12571

Some format issues inherent in the e-media version may also appear in this print version.

Printed by Curran Associates, Inc. (2018)

International Academy, Research, and Industry Association (IARIA)
412 Derby Way
Wilmington, DE 19810

Phone: (408) 893-6407
Fax: (408) 527-6351

petre@iaria.org

Additional copies of this publication are available from:

Curran Associates, Inc.
57 Morehouse Lane
Red Hook, NY 12571 USA
Phone: 845-758-0400
Fax: 845-758-2633
Email: curran@proceedings.com
Web: www.proceedings.com

The *International Journal on Advances in Telecommunications* is published by IARIA.
ISSN: 1942-2601
journals site: http://www.iariajournals.org
contact: petre@iaria.org

International Journal on Advances in Telecommunications
Volume 10, Number 3 & 4, 2017

Miguel Arjona Ramirez, São Paulo University, Brasil
Radu Arsinte, Technical University of Cluj-Napoca, Romania
Tulin Atmaca, Institut Mines-Telecom/ Telecom SudParis, France
Mario Ezequiel Augusto, Santa Catarina State University, Brazil
Marco Aurelio Spohn, Federal University of Fronteira Sul (UFFS), Brazil
Philip L. Balcaen, University of British Columbia Okanagan - Kelowna, Canada
Marco Baldi, Università Politecnica delle Marche, Italy
Ilija Basicevic, University of Novi Sad, Serbia
Carlos Becker Westphall, Federal University of Santa Catarina, Brazil
Mark Bentum, University of Twente, The Netherlands
David Bernstein, Huawei Technologies, Ltd., USA
Eugen Borcoci, University "Politehnica"of Bucharest (UPB), Romania
Fernando Boronat Seguí, Universidad Politecnica de Valencia, Spain
Christos Bouras, University of Patras, Greece
Martin Brandl, Danube University Krems, Austria
Julien Broisin, IRIT, France
Dumitru Burdescu, University of Craiova, Romania
Andi Buzo, University "Politehnica" of Bucharest (UPB), Romania
Shkelzen Cakaj, Telecom of Kosovo / Prishtina University, Kosovo
Enzo Alberto Candreva, DEIS-University of Bologna, Italy
Rodrigo Capobianco Guido, São Paulo State University, Brazil
Hakima Chaouchi, Telecom SudParis, France
Silviu Ciochina, Universitatea Politehnica din Bucuresti, Romania
José Coimbra, Universidade do Algarve, Portugal
Hugo Coll Ferri, Polytechnic University of Valencia, Spain
Noel Crespi, Institut TELECOM SudParis-Evry, France
Leonardo Dagui de Oliveira, Escola Politécnica da Universidade de São Paulo, Brazil
Kevin Daimi, University of Detroit Mercy, USA
Gerard Damm, Alcatel-Lucent, USA
Francescantonio Della Rosa, Tampere University of Technology, Finland
Chérif Diallo, Consultant Sécurité des Systèmes d'Information, France
Klaus Drechsler, Fraunhofer Institute for Computer Graphics Research IGD, Germany
Jawad Drissi, Cameron University , USA
António Manuel Duarte Nogueira, University of Aveiro / Institute of Telecommunications, Portugal
Alban Duverdier, CNES (French Space Agency) Paris, France
Nicholas Evans, EURECOM, France
Fabrizio Falchi, ISTI - CNR, Italy
Mário F. S. Ferreira, University of Aveiro, Portugal
Bruno Filipe Marques, Polytechnic Institute of Viseu, Portugal
Robert Forster, Edgemount Solutions, USA
John-Austen Francisco, Rutgers, the State University of New Jersey, USA
Kaori Fujinami, Tokyo University of Agriculture and Technology, Japan
Shauneen Furlong , University of Ottawa, Canada / Liverpool John Moores University, UK
Ana-Belén García-Hernando, Universidad Politécnica de Madrid, Spain
Bezalel Gavish, Southern Methodist University, USA
Christos K. Georgiadis, University of Macedonia, Greece

Adão Silva, University of Aveiro / Institute of Telecommunications, Portugal
Pushpendra Bahadur Singh, MindTree Ltd, India
Mariusz Skrocki, Orange Labs Poland / Telekomunikacja Polska S.A., Poland
Leonel Sousa, INESC-ID/IST, TU-Lisbon, Portugal
Cristian Stanciu, University Politehnica of Bucharest, Romania
Liana Stanescu, University of Craiova, Romania
Cosmin Stoica Spahiu, University of Craiova, Romania
Young-Joo Suh, POSTECH (Pohang University of Science and Technology), Korea
Hailong Sun, Beihang University, China
Jani Suomalainen, VTT Technical Research Centre of Finland, Finland
Fatma Tansu, Eastern Mediterranean University, Cyprus
Ioan Toma, STI Innsbruck/University Innsbruck, Austria
Božo Tomas, HT Mostar, Bosnia and Herzegovina
Piotr Tyczka, ITTI Sp. z o.o., Poland
John Vardakas, University of Patras, Greece
Andreas Veglis, Aristotle University of Thessaloniki, Greece
Luís Veiga, Instituto Superior Técnico / INESC-ID Lisboa, Portugal
Calin Vladeanu, "Politehnica" University of Bucharest, Romania
Benno Volk, ETH Zurich, Switzerland
Krzysztof Walczak, Poznan University of Economics, Poland
Krzysztof Walkowiak, Wroclaw University of Technology, Poland
Yang Wang, Georgia State University, USA
Yean-Fu Wen, National Taipei University, Taiwan, R.O.C.
Bernd E. Wolfinger, University of Hamburg, Germany
Riaan Wolhuter, Universiteit Stellenbosch University, South Africa
Yulei Wu, Chinese Academy of Sciences, China
Mudasser F. Wyne, National University, USA
Gaoxi Xiao, Nanyang Technological University, Singapore
Bashir Yahya, University of Versailles, France
Abdulrahman Yarali, Murray State University, USA
Mehmet Erkan Yüksel, Istanbul University, Turkey
Pooneh Bagheri Zadeh, Staffordshire University, UK
Giannis Zaoudis, University of Patras, Greece
Liaoyuan Zeng, University of Electronic Science and Technology of China, China
Rong Zhao , Detecon International GmbH, Germany
Zhiwen Zhu, Communications Research Centre, Canada
Martin Zimmermann, University of Applied Sciences Offenburg, Germany
Piotr Zwierzykowski, Poznan University of Technology, Poland

International Journal on Advances in Telecommunications
Volume 10, Numbers 3 & 4, 2017

CONTENTS

A Regenerative Detect & Forward Relay Transmission in Linearly Precoded MU-MIMO Downlink

Nobuaki Shimakawa
Dept. of Electrical and Mechanical Engineering
Nagoya Institute of Technology
Nagoya, Japan
E-mail: 28413082@stn.nitech.ac.jp

Yasunori Iwanami
Dept. of Electrical and Mechanical Engineering
Nagoya Institute of Technology
Nagoya, Japan
E-mail: iwanami@nitech.ac.jp

***Abstract*—Recently, Multi-User MIMO (MU-MIMO) downlink system which uses multiple antennas at Base Station (BS) and accommodates multiple users with multiple reception antennas attracts much attention. In MU-MIMO downlink system, by knowing the Channel State Information (CSI) at BS, Inter User Interferences (IUI's) among users are pre-excluded at BS. By increasing the number of transmission antennas assigned to each user, the transmission quality of each user is effectively improved. In MU-MIMO, there exists linear precoding or nonlinear precoding method, but linear precoding is considered more easily implemented and adjusted than nonlinear precoding. In this paper, we aim the coverage extension and the transmission quality improvement by using a regenerative Detect & Forward (DF) relay in MU-MIMO downlink system. We use Block Diagonalization (BD) + Eigen mode transmission (E-SDM) for linear MU-MIMO downlink scheme. By sharing the BD matrix at both BS and DF reiay, the DF relay can demodulate the receive signal with the receive CSI only and can forward the detected signal to each user. At each user, the received signals from BS and DF relay are combined through bit LLR (Log Likelihood Ratio) addition to minimize the BER. With this system configuration and by employing large number of transmission antennas, we have shown the effectiveness of regenerative DF relay through simulations.**

Keywords-MU-MIMO; Block Diagonalization; Eigen mode transmission; Regenerative relay; Detect & Forward.

I. INTRODUCTION

Recently, Multi-User MIMO down link communication systems in which Base Station (BS) can transmit spatially multiplexed signals to multiple users without Inter-User Interference (IUI) are well investigated [1]-[9]. In MU-MIMO downlink system, in order to remove the IUI at BS, the Channel State Information (CSI) of downlink has to be known at BS. By increasing the number of transmission antennas at BS, the channel quality to each user can arbitrary be improved. As representative methods, there exist BD (Block Diagonalization) [4] and Channel Inversion (CI) [5] categorized as linear methods, and DPC (Dirty Paper Coding) [6], THP (Tomlinson-Harashima Precoding) [7] and Vector Perturbation (VP) [8],[9] as nonlinear methods. Although nonlinear methods can achieve greater channel capacity than linear methods, its complexity is higher and the design method is more difficult than linear methods. As for the linear methods, the CI method has the problems of increasing transmission power and limited sum-rate. The BD method consumes a lot of degree of freedom to make the nulls, but it can remove the IUI completely. Also, the BD method matches the Eigen mode transmission (E-SDM; Eigen beam-Space Division Multiplexing) [10] well and is considered as a practical design method. On the other hand, concerning the use of relay in MU-MIMO downlink, increasing the channel capacity by using the relay has been discussed [11],[12]. On the relay transmission in MU-MIMO downlink system, the BD methods are used at BS [13]-[18]. In [13], during the 1st time slot transmission from BS to relay, MU-MIMO is not employed, but during the 2nd time slot from relay to each user, it is used. In [14]-[18], the transmission from BS to relay is done during the 1st time slot, but the direct link from BS to each user during the 1st time slot is not considered.

In this paper, we employed the BD+E-SDM method for the transmission from BS to each user during the 1st time slot. We assume that the DF relay which locates between BS and each user already knows the precoding matrix of BS. By knowing the precoding matrix, the DF relay can demodulate the receive signal with only receive CSI. Accordingly, the BS does not need to assign the transmission antennas to the DF relay and the transmission from BS to DF relay becomes SU (Single-User)-MIMO. During the 2nd time slot, the DF relay transmits the detected signals to each user also with the BD+E-SDM method. At each user, the received signals during the 1st and the 2nd time slots are combined using the bit LLR addition and the combined signal is demodulated. We show the effectiveness of the proposed DF relaying system in MU-MIMO downlink through computer simulations.

The paper is organized as follows. In Section II, the DF relay model in MU-MIMO downlink is introduced. In Section III, we design the downlink transmission during the

TABLE I LIST of PARAMETERS

N_S :Number of transmission antennas of BS
N_u : Number of users
m_i : Number of reception antennas of user i $(i = 1, \cdots, N_u)$
N_D : Total number of reception antennas of all users
M_R : Number of reception antennas of relay
N_R : Number of transmission antennas of relay
$\boldsymbol{C}_{SD}$: Optimum power assignment matrix to each user on SD link
$\boldsymbol{V}_{SD}$: Precoding matrix of E-SDM to each user on SD link
$\boldsymbol{N}_{SD}$: Precoding matrix of BD on SD link
$\boldsymbol{B}_{SDi}$: Block channel matrix of user i on SD link
nl_i : Nullity of user i on SD link
L_{SDi} : Number of transmit streams of user i on SD link

1st and the 2nd time slots. In Section IV, we clarify the BER characteristics through computer simulations. The paper is concluded with Section V with the most important results.

II. DF RELAY MODEL IN MU-MIMO DOWNLINK

The proposed DF relaying model in MU-MIMO downlink system is shown in Figure 1. The Base Station is equipped with N_{S} transmission antennas. There exist total N_{u} users and the user $i\,(=1,\cdots,N_{\mathrm{u}})$ has m_i reception antennas. Thus, there are total $N_{\mathrm{D}}=\sum_{i=1}^{N_{\mathrm{u}}} m_i$ reception antennas at all users. The DF relay, which locates between BS and user terminals, has M_{R} reception and N_{R} transmission antennas. At Base Station, the transmit signal $\boldsymbol{s}=[\boldsymbol{s}_1^T \;\cdots\; \boldsymbol{s}_i^T \;\cdots\; \boldsymbol{s}_{N_{\mathrm{u}}}^T]^T$ to each user is firstly multiplied by the precoding matrix $\boldsymbol{C}_{\mathrm{SD}}$, where $\boldsymbol{C}_{\mathrm{SD}}$ is the optimum power assignment matrix for multiple different modulation streams in E-SDM of each user. The power assignment in E-SDM of each user is done to minimize the BER by using Lagrange multiplier method [10].

Secondary, the precoding matrix $\boldsymbol{V}_{\mathrm{SD}}$ for making the multiple stream transmission using E-SDM is multiplied by $\boldsymbol{C}_{\mathrm{SD}}\boldsymbol{s}$. The transmit signal to user i is expressed as $\boldsymbol{s}_i=[s_i^{(1)} \;\cdots\; s_i^{(L_{\mathrm{SD}i})}]^T$ where $L_{\mathrm{SD}i}$ is the number of modulation streams of user i in E-SDM. The matrix $\boldsymbol{V}_{\mathrm{SD}}$ is expressed as

$$\boldsymbol{V}_{\mathrm{SD}}=\begin{bmatrix}\boldsymbol{V}_{\mathrm{SD1}} & \mathbf{0} & \mathbf{0}\\ \mathbf{0} & \ddots & \mathbf{0}\\ \mathbf{0} & \mathbf{0} & \boldsymbol{V}_{\mathrm{SD}N_{\mathrm{u}}}\end{bmatrix} \quad (1)$$

where the diagonal element $\boldsymbol{V}_{\mathrm{SD}i},\, i=1\sim N_{\mathrm{u}}$ is the precoding matrix of E-SDM for each user. Third, the precoding matrix $\boldsymbol{N}_{\mathrm{SD}}$ for BD is multiplied by $\boldsymbol{V}_{\mathrm{SD}}\boldsymbol{C}_{\mathrm{SD}}\boldsymbol{s}$. The transmit signal from BS is then given by $\boldsymbol{x}=\boldsymbol{N}_{\mathrm{SD}}\boldsymbol{V}_{\mathrm{SD}}\boldsymbol{C}_{\mathrm{SD}}\boldsymbol{s} \;=[x_1 \;\; x_2 \;\; \cdots \;\; x_{N_{\mathrm{S}}}]^T$. During the 1st time slot, the transmit signal $\boldsymbol{x}$ is broadcasted both to user terminals and the DF relay. The precoding matrix $\boldsymbol{N}_{\mathrm{SD}}$ makes the channel matrix $\boldsymbol{H}_{\mathrm{SD}}$ from BS to each user block diagonal. The receive signal vector $\boldsymbol{y}_{\mathrm{SD}}$ at destination users is expressed as

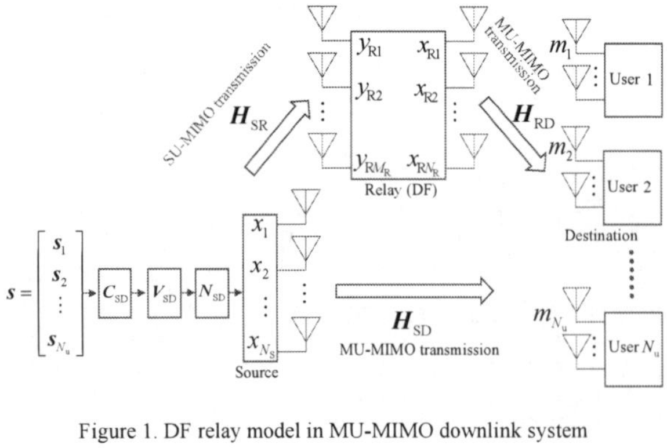

Figure 1. DF relay model in MU-MIMO downlink system

$$\begin{cases}\boldsymbol{y}_{\mathrm{SD}}=\boldsymbol{H}_{\mathrm{SD}}\boldsymbol{x}+\boldsymbol{n}_{\mathrm{SD}}=\boldsymbol{B}_{\mathrm{SD}}\boldsymbol{V}_{\mathrm{SD}}\boldsymbol{C}_{\mathrm{SD}}\boldsymbol{s}+\boldsymbol{n}_{\mathrm{SD}}\\ \boldsymbol{B}_{\mathrm{SD}}=\boldsymbol{H}_{\mathrm{SD}}\boldsymbol{N}_{\mathrm{SD}},\quad \boldsymbol{x}=\boldsymbol{N}_{\mathrm{SD}}\boldsymbol{V}_{\mathrm{SD}}\boldsymbol{C}_{\mathrm{SD}}\boldsymbol{s}\end{cases} \quad (2)$$

$\boldsymbol{B}_{\mathrm{SD}}$ in (2) is the block diagonalized channel matrix and is expressed as

$$\boldsymbol{H}_{\mathrm{SD}}\boldsymbol{N}_{\mathrm{SD}}=\boldsymbol{B}_{\mathrm{SD}}=\begin{bmatrix}\boldsymbol{B}_{\mathrm{SD1}} & \mathbf{0} & \cdots & \mathbf{0}\\ \mathbf{0} & \boldsymbol{B}_{\mathrm{SD2}} & \cdots & \vdots\\ \vdots & \cdots & \ddots & \mathbf{0}\\ \mathbf{0} & \cdots & \mathbf{0} & \boldsymbol{B}_{\mathrm{SD}N_{\mathrm{u}}}\end{bmatrix} \quad (3)$$

where $\boldsymbol{B}_{\mathrm{SD}i},\, i=1,\cdots,N_{\mathrm{u}}$ is the block channel matrix for user i and $\boldsymbol{n}_{\mathrm{SD}}=[\boldsymbol{n}_{\mathrm{SD1}}^T \;\cdots\; \boldsymbol{n}_{\mathrm{SD}i}^T \;\cdots\; \boldsymbol{n}_{\mathrm{SD}N_{\mathrm{u}}}^T]^T$ in (2) is the receive noise vector for each user.

The precoding matrix $\boldsymbol{N}_{\mathrm{SD}}$ for BD is derived as follows. Denoting the channel matrix for user i as $\boldsymbol{H}_{\mathrm{SD}i}(m_i\times N_{\mathrm{S}})$, the entire channel matrix from BS to users is expressed as

$$\boldsymbol{H}_{\mathrm{SD}}=\left[\boldsymbol{H}_{\mathrm{SD1}}^T \;\cdots\; \boldsymbol{H}_{\mathrm{SD}i}^T \;\cdots\; \boldsymbol{H}_{\mathrm{SD}N_{\mathrm{u}}}^T\right]^T \quad (4)$$

We denote the matrix $\tilde{\boldsymbol{H}}_{\mathrm{SD}i}$ in which the channel matrix $\boldsymbol{H}_{\mathrm{SD}i}$ of user i is excluded from the entire channel matrix $\boldsymbol{H}_{\mathrm{SD}}$ as

$$\tilde{\boldsymbol{H}}_{\mathrm{SD}i}=\left[\boldsymbol{H}_{\mathrm{SD1}}^T \;\cdots\; \boldsymbol{H}_{\mathrm{SD}i-1}^T \;\; \boldsymbol{H}_{\mathrm{SD}i+1}^T \;\cdots\; \boldsymbol{H}_{\mathrm{SD}N_{\mathrm{u}}}^T\right]^T \quad (5)$$

with the size of $((N_{\mathrm{D}}-m_i)\times N_{\mathrm{S}})$ [2],[19]. By making the Singular Value Decomposition (SVD) on $\tilde{\boldsymbol{H}}_{\mathrm{SD}i}$, we get

$$\tilde{\boldsymbol{H}}_{\mathrm{SD}i}=\tilde{\boldsymbol{U}}_{\mathrm{SD}i}\tilde{\boldsymbol{\Lambda}}_{\mathrm{SD}i}\left[\tilde{\boldsymbol{V}}_{\mathrm{SD}i}^{(1)} \;\; \boldsymbol{N}_{\mathrm{SD}i}\right]^H \quad (6)$$

where $\boldsymbol{N}_{\mathrm{SD}i}$ is the null space of $\boldsymbol{H}_{\mathrm{SD}i}$ and it orthogonalizes $\boldsymbol{H}_{\mathrm{SD}i'}\,(i'\neq i)$, i.e., $\boldsymbol{H}_{\mathrm{SD}i'}\boldsymbol{N}_{\mathrm{SD}i}=\mathbf{0}\;(i'\neq i)$. By obtaining all the null spaces of every user, the precoding matrix $\boldsymbol{N}_{\mathrm{SD}}$ for BD is evaluated as

$$\boldsymbol{N}_{\mathrm{SD}}=\left[\boldsymbol{N}_{\mathrm{SD1}} \;\cdots\; \boldsymbol{N}_{\mathrm{SD}i} \;\cdots\; \boldsymbol{N}_{\mathrm{SD}N_{\mathrm{u}}}\right] \quad (7)$$

The size of block channel matrix for user i becomes $\boldsymbol{B}_{\mathrm{SD}i}\;(m_i\times n\ell_i)$, where the nullity $n\ell_i$ of the matrix $\tilde{\boldsymbol{H}}_{\mathrm{SD}i}$ is defined by

$$n\ell_i=nullity(\tilde{\boldsymbol{H}}_{\mathrm{SD}i})=N_{\mathrm{S}}-rank(\tilde{\boldsymbol{H}}_{\mathrm{SD}i}) \quad (8)$$

As the rank of $\tilde{\boldsymbol{H}}_{\mathrm{SD}i}$ is given by

$$rank(\tilde{\boldsymbol{H}}_{\mathrm{SD}i})=\min(N_{\mathrm{D}}-m_i,\,N_{\mathrm{S}}) \quad (9)$$

the nullity $n\ell_i$ is expressed as

$$n\ell_i=N_{\mathrm{S}}-rank(\tilde{\boldsymbol{H}}_{\mathrm{SD}i})=N_{\mathrm{S}}-N_{\mathrm{D}}+m_i>0 \quad (10)$$

In E-SDM, the receive weight $\boldsymbol{U}_{\mathrm{SD}i}^H$ which satisfies

$$\boldsymbol{B}_{\mathrm{SD}i}=\boldsymbol{U}_{\mathrm{SD}i}\boldsymbol{\Lambda}_{\mathrm{SD}i}\boldsymbol{V}_{\mathrm{SD}i}^H \quad (11)$$

is multiplied by $\boldsymbol{y}_{\mathrm{SD}i}$ and

$$\begin{aligned}\boldsymbol{z}_{\mathrm{SD}i}&=\boldsymbol{U}_{\mathrm{SD}i}^H\boldsymbol{y}_{\mathrm{SD}i}=\boldsymbol{U}_{\mathrm{SD}i}^H\boldsymbol{B}_{\mathrm{SD}i}\boldsymbol{V}_{\mathrm{SD}i}\boldsymbol{C}_{\mathrm{SD}i}\boldsymbol{s}_i+\boldsymbol{U}_{\mathrm{SD}i}^H\boldsymbol{n}_{\mathrm{SD}i}\\ &=\boldsymbol{\Lambda}_{\mathrm{SD}i}\boldsymbol{C}_{\mathrm{SD}i}\boldsymbol{s}_i+\tilde{\boldsymbol{n}}_{\mathrm{SD}i}\end{aligned} \quad (12)$$

is obtained. As it follows $\boldsymbol{\Lambda}_{\mathrm{SD}i}=diag(\sqrt{d_{\mathrm{SD}i}^{(1)}},\cdots,\sqrt{d_{\mathrm{SD}i}^{(L_{\mathrm{SD}i})}})$ and $\boldsymbol{C}_{\mathrm{SD}i}=diag(\sqrt{\zeta_{\mathrm{SD}i}^{(1)}},\cdots,\sqrt{\zeta_{\mathrm{SD}i}^{(L_{\mathrm{SD}i})}})$, (12) is expanded as

$$\begin{bmatrix}z_{\mathrm{SD}i}^{(1)}\\ \vdots\\ z_{\mathrm{SD}i}^{(L_{\mathrm{SD}i})}\end{bmatrix}=\begin{bmatrix}\sqrt{d_{\mathrm{SD}i}^{(1)}\zeta_{\mathrm{SD}i}^{(1)}}\,s_{\mathrm{SD}i}^{(1)}+\tilde{n}_{\mathrm{SD}i}^{(1)}\\ \vdots\\ \sqrt{d_{\mathrm{SD}i}^{(L_{\mathrm{SD}i})}\zeta_{\mathrm{SD}i}^{(L_{\mathrm{SD}i})}}\,s_{\mathrm{SD}i}^{(L_{\mathrm{SD}i})}+\tilde{n}_{\mathrm{SD}i}^{(L_{\mathrm{SD}i})}\end{bmatrix} \quad (13)$$

where parallel $L_{\mathrm{SD}i}=\min(m_i,n\ell_i)$ AWGN channels independent of each other are obtained.

We assume that the DF relay knows the precoding matrix $N_{SD}V_{SD}C_{SD}$ of BS. Therefore, the BS has to inform $N_{SD}V_{SD}C_{SD}$ to the DF relay before the data transmission starts. The transmission from BS to DF relay during the 1st time slot is done by Single User-MIMO (SU-MIMO) environment. The receive signal $y_{SR} = [y_{R1}\ y_{R2}\ \cdots\ y_{RM_R}]^T$ at DF relay is expressed as

$$y_{SR} = H_{SR}x + n_{SR} = (H_{SR}N_{SD}V_{SD}C_{SD})s + n_{SR} \tag{14}$$

where $n_{SR}\,(M_R \times 1)$ is the receive noise vector at DF relay. The effective channel matrix $H_{SR}N_{SD}V_{SD}C_{SD}$ in (14) is assumed to be known at the DF relay and the demodulation of transmit signal s is done by MMSE (Minimum Mean Squared Error) nulling, MLD (Maximum Likelihood Detection) or Sphere Decoding. This means that the DF relay does not need to inform the channel matrix H_{SR} between BS and DF relay to the BS. The demodulated signal $\hat{s}$ at DF relay is transmitted to each user during the 2nd time slot using MU-MIMO with BD+E-SDM which is the same as in the Source-Destination (SD) link, i.e., the E-SDM is employed for the multiple stream transmission from the DF relay to each user. At each user terminal, the received signals during the 1st and the 2nd time slots are combined using bit LLR addition and demodulated. When the errors are detected at the DF relay through the CRC (Cyclic Redundancy Check), erroneous user does not employ the Relay-Destination (RD) transmission to prevent error propagation, instead the SD link transmission is repeated in the second time slot.

III. DESIGN OF DOWNLINK TRANSMISSION

A. *Transmission during the 1st time slot*

1) *Design of SD Link*

The Source-Destination (SD) link transmission during the 1st time slot is done by using BD+E-SDM. The size of block channel matrix B_{SDi} is given by $m_i \times n\ell_i$ and the number of streams of E-SDM (eigen mode transmission) becomes $L_{SDi}=\min(m_i, n\ell_i)$. When the number of streams is one, BD+E-SDM is referred to as BD+MRT (Maximum Ratio Transmission) [20]. From (10), the nullity $n\ell_i$ of user i can be arbitrary chosen by increasing or decreasing the number of transmission antennas N_S at BS. If the elements of channel matrix H_{SD} follow the i.i.d (independent and identically distributed) complex Gaussian random variables, i.e., if H_{SD} is the MIMO channel matrix of quasi-static flat Rayleigh fading, the diversity order of the first eigen mode stream in E-SDM for the block channel matrix B_{SDi} is given by $m_i \cdot n\ell_i$ [21]. When the minimum number of reception antennas among users is $m_{\min}$, from (10) the nullity $n\ell_{\min}$ of minimum antenna user is given by

$$n\ell_{\min} = N_S - N_D + m_{\min} > 0 \tag{15}$$

Hence, the number of transmission antennas N_S at BS which enables the BD must satisfy

$$N_S > N_D - m_{\min} \tag{16}$$

The nullity $n\ell_i$ of user i other than the minimum antenna user becomes

$$n\ell_i = N_S - N_D + m_i > n\ell_{\min} \tag{17}$$

The size of block channel matrix B_{SDi} of user i is determined as $m_i \times n\ell_i$. In this design method, firstly the nullity $n\ell_{\min}$ of the user which has the minimum number of reception antennas $m_{\min}$ is determined and secondary the nullity $n\ell_i$ of the other user i is derived. The diversity orders of the first eigen mode stream of minimum antenna user and other user i are given by $m_{\min} \cdot n\ell_{\min}$ and $m_i \cdot n\ell_i \geq m_{\min} \cdot n\ell_{\min}$, respectively.

For example, we consider the case where the number of total users is $N_u = 3$, the numbers of reception antennas of three users are $m_1 = 3$, $m_2 = 2$, $m_3 = 1$ respectively, and the total number of reception antennas is $N_D = m_1 + m_2 + m_3 = 6$. In this case, $m_3 = 1$ is minimum and it holds $m_{min} = m_3 = 1$. If the expected diversity order of the first eigen mode stream of user 3 is set to 3, for example, then we obtain $n\ell_{min} = 3/m_{min} = 3/1 = 3$. With these parameters, the total number of transmission antennas at BS N_S is determined as $N_S = n\ell_{min} + N_D - m_{min} = 3 + 6 - 1 = 8$ and the size of block matrix B_{SD3} of user 3 becomes $m_{min} \times n\ell_{min} = 1 \times 3$. Thus, the nullity of user 2 is determined as $n\ell_2 = N_S - N_D + m_2 = 8 - 6 + 2 = 4$, the size of B_{SD2} becomes $m_2 \times n\ell_2 = 2 \times 4$, and the diversity order of the first eigen mode stream of user 2 is given as $m_2 \cdot n\ell_2 = 2 \cdot 4 = 8$. Likewise, the nullity $n\ell_1$ of user 1 is given by $n\ell_1 = N_S - N_D + m_1 = 8 - 6 + 3 = 5$, B_{SD1} becomes $m_1 \times n\ell_1 = 3 \times 5$, and the diversity order of the first eigen mode stream of user 1 is determined as $m_1 \cdot n\ell_1 = 3 \cdot 5 = 15$.

2) *Design of SR Link*

For the Source-Relay (SR) link from BS to DF relay, the precoding for DF relay at BS is not employed. This means no degree of freedom of transmission antennas (number of transmission antennas) at BS is consumed for the SR link. This is because if the transmission antennas at BS are assigned to the DF relay using BD, in the absence of DF relay the assigned transmission antennas to DF relay are of no use. Therefore, the extra transmission antennas are then used for the users to enhance the SD link quality. In this case, the effect of using DF relay does not become obvious compared with the enhanced SD link quality. That is, the DF relay should be employed when the SD link quality is poor and the additional DF relay usage brings the great effect to the overall performance. As the demodulation at DF relay is done by only using receive CSI, the precoding matrix $N_{SD}V_{SD}C_{SD}$ at BS needs to be informed to the DF relay in advance before the data transmission from BS to DF relay starts. The DF relay demodulates the receive signal with MMSE nulling, MLD or Sphere Decoding by using effective channel matrix of $H_{SR}N_{SD}V_{SD}C_{SD}$. So, the SR link transmission is done under SU-MIMO environment and not MU-MIMO. The SR link quality directly affects the subsequent Relay-Destination (RD) link quality very much, because the poor SR link quality causes the error propagation on the RD link. Thus, we must raise the SR link quality as much as possible. To solve this problem, increasing the number of reception antennas at DF relay or increasing the number of transmission antennas at BS is considered. Also at DF relay, MLD or Sphere Decoding with better BER characteristic than MMSE nulling is considered. But when the number of total transmit streams of L from BS to DF relay is large, the exponential increase of complexity in MLD becomes a problem. In such case, we can resort the problem to employ the Sphere Decoding with less complexity or to use the MMSE nulling with far less complexity but degraded performance for demodulating SU-MIMO signals. When the number of reception antennas at DF relay is given by M_{R}, the effective channel matrix for demodulating the transmit signal $\boldsymbol{s}$ at DF relay link becomes $\boldsymbol{H}_{\mathrm{SR}}\boldsymbol{N}_{\mathrm{SD}}\boldsymbol{V}_{\mathrm{SD}}\boldsymbol{C}_{\mathrm{SD}}$ $(M_{\mathrm{R}} \times L)$. Accordingly, to apply MMSE nulling at DF relay it needs $M_{\mathrm{R}} \geq L$. Even though the elements of $\boldsymbol{H}_{\mathrm{SR}}$ are i.i.d. complex Gaussian random variables, the row elements of effective channel matrix $\boldsymbol{H}_{\mathrm{SR}}\boldsymbol{N}_{\mathrm{SD}}\boldsymbol{V}_{\mathrm{SD}}\boldsymbol{C}_{\mathrm{SD}}$ of SR link do not always become i.i.d. complex Gaussian random variables. This channel element correlation deteriorates the BER characteristic of MMSE nulling, MLD (or Sphere Decoding) compared with i.i.d. random variable case. Also, if errors are detected at the DF relay with CRC code, the subsequent RD transmission is not employed for the erroneous users, instead the SD link transmission is repeated using the 2nd time slot. For error free users on SR link, the RD link transmission is done. The received signals at each user during the 1st and 2nd time slots are then combined through the bit LLR addition and the multiple streams to each user are demodulated.

B. *Transmission during the 2nd time slot*

For the Relay-Destination (RD) link transmission during the 2nd time slot, we use BD+MRT or BD+E-SDM, which is the same as in the 1st time slot. In this case, the number of streams to each user on Source-Destination (SD) link does not need to coincide with the one on RD link, because the signal combining between SD link and RD link is done using bit LLR addition. However, the transmission rate (bps/Hz) must be the same between SD link and RD link for the bit LLR combining. We can design the RD link quality as in the SD link. Thus, we can improve the RD link quality by increasing the number of transmission antennas N_{R} at DF relay. As already stated in Section III *A)-2)*, in order to prevent the error propagation in the RD link, we adopt the protocol in which the data from DF relay are only forwarded to each user in case of no error detected at the DF relay. When the error is detected at the DF relay and the RD link is not employed during the 2nd time slot, in order to prevent the degradation of receive signal quality, we repeat the SD link transmission using the vacant 2nd time slot. The signals received in the 1st and 2nd time slots are bit LLR combined and demodulated at each user as mentioned in Section III *A)-2)*.

At each user terminal, each stream of MRT or E-SDM is equivalently represented as the AWGN channel with the positive real gain h. When the received signal in each stream is denoted as r and the corresponding transmitted signal s_l, $l = 0,\cdots,Q-1$ has Q modulation levels, the equivalent AWGN channel of each stream in each user is expressed as

$$r = hs_l + n,\ l = 0,1,\cdots,Q-1 \tag{18}$$

The symbol LLR is the extension of bit LLR and is defined as

$$\lambda_l = \log_e\left\{\frac{p(s_l \mid r)}{p(s_0 \mid r)}\right\} = \log_e\left\{\frac{[p(r\mid s_l)p(s_l)]/p(r)}{[p(r\mid s_0)p(s_0)]/p(r)}\right\} = \log_e\left\{\frac{p(r\mid s_l)}{p(r\mid s_0)}\right\} \tag{19}$$

where we have assumed the priori probabilities are all equal, i.e., $p(s_l) = 1/Q$, $l = 0,1,\cdots,Q-1$. The transition probability density function $p(r\mid s_l)$ is expressed as

$$p(r\mid s_l) = \frac{1}{\sqrt{2\pi}\sigma}\exp\left[-\frac{|r-hs_l|^2}{2\sigma^2}\right] \tag{20}$$

where $\sigma^2 = (1/2)E\{|n|^2\}$. From (19) and (20), it holds

$$\lambda_l = \frac{-|r-hs_l|^2 + |r-hs_0|^2}{2\sigma^2} \tag{21}$$

When the modulation level is $Q = 2$, the symbol LLR coincides with the bit LLR.

The bit LLR is obtained easily from the symbol LLR. When the data bits assigned to a signal point is $(c_1,\cdots,c_k,\cdots,c_N)$, the k-th bit LLR $\lambda(c_k)$ is given by

$$\lambda(c_k) = \log_e\left\{\frac{p(c_k=0\mid r)}{p(c_k=1\mid r)}\right\} = \log_e\left\{\frac{p(c_k=0,r)/p(r)}{p(c_k=1,r)/p(r)}\right\} = \log_e\left\{\frac{\sum_{\{s\mid c_k=0\}} p(s,r)}{\sum_{\{s'\mid c_k=0\}} p(s',r)}\right\} = \log_e\left\{\frac{\sum_{\{s\mid c_k=0\}} p(s)p(r\mid s)}{\sum_{\{s'\mid c_k=0\}} p(s')p(r\mid s')}\right\} \tag{22}$$

where $\{s\mid c_k=0\}$ and $\{s'\mid c_k=1\}$ denote the transmit symbols s and s' with the k-th bit being $c_k = 0$ and $c_k = 1$ respectively. As each bit is generated equally, it holds $p(s) = p(s')$. From (19), we can say

$$p(r\mid s_l) = \exp(\lambda_l)\,p(r\mid s_0) \tag{23}$$

and (22) is expressed as

$$\lambda(c_k) = \log_e\left\{\frac{\sum_{s\mid c_k=0}\exp(\lambda)p(r\mid s_0)}{\sum_{s'\mid c_k=1}\exp(\lambda')p(r\mid s_0)}\right\} = \log_e\left\{\frac{\sum_{\lambda\mid c_k=0}\exp(\lambda)}{\sum_{\lambda'\mid c_k=1}\exp(\lambda')}\right\} \tag{24}$$

where $\lambda\mid c_k = 0$ and $\lambda'\mid c_k = 1$ denote the symbol LLR's of s and s' in which the k-th bits are $c_k = 0$ and $c_k = 1$ respectively. Next, we define the symbol LLR's

$s_\alpha(=s_0-\alpha)$ and $s_\beta(=s_0-j\beta)$ as λ_α and λ_β respectively, where s_α and s_β denotes the transmit signal points displaced by α and $j\beta$ from s_0 respectively. It then holds

$$\lambda_\gamma=\lambda_\alpha+\lambda_\beta \tag{25}$$

where $\gamma=\alpha+j\beta$. By using (25), we do not need to obtain every symbol LLR's when calculating the bit LLR's resulting in simplifying the bit LLR calculation. The bit LLR addition between the 1st time slot and 2nd time slot is done at each user stream and finally the bit decision is made based on the added bit LLR value.

IV. INVESTIGATION OF BER CHARACTERISTICS THROUGH COMPUTER SIMULATIONS

We have checked the BER characteristics of the proposed MU-MIMO downlink transmission using DF relay. The abscissa of BER characteristic is taken as the transmit SNR [22], which is defined as the ratio of transmission power P from BS for a user to the receive noise power σ^2 at each user reception antenna and is given as

$$\left(\frac{S}{N}\right)_{\text{transmit}}=\frac{P}{\sigma^2} \tag{26}$$

where the transmission power P is equal among every user. The channel from BS to each user, the channel from BS to DF relay and the channel from DF relay to each user are all assumed to be quasi-static Rayleigh fading channel. That is, the element h_{ij} of channel matrix $\boldsymbol{H}\,(\boldsymbol{H}_{\text{SD}},\boldsymbol{H}_{\text{SR}},\boldsymbol{H}_{\text{RD}})$ is an i.i.d. complex Gaussian random variable with the variance of $E\{|h_{ij}|^2\}=1$. We consider the distance from BS to each user is equal among users and the DF relay locates at the middle point between BS and users. We also set the power decaying exponent of propagation loss as $\alpha=3.5$ regarding the different distances from BS to DF relay and from BS to users. The BER characteristics in Figure 2~Figure 13 are averaged over N_u users. Thus, the BER shows the average BER among all users.

First, we investigate the case where the number of transmission antennas of BS is $N_{\text{S}}=2$, the number of user terminals $N_{\text{u}}=2$, the number of reception antennas of each user $m_1=m_2=1$, the number of reception antennas of DF relay $M_{\text{R}}=4$, and the number of transmission antennas of DF relay $N_{\text{R}}=2$. We call this as $2\times(4,2)\times(1,1)$ model. In this model, for the SD link during the 1st time slot, BD+MRT scheme is used as the MU-MIMO down link transmission. QPSK modulation is used for each user stream. The BER characteristic is shown in Figure 2. "SD link 2 times w/o relay" means the scheme in which the MU-MIMO transmission on SD link is repeated twice without using the relay. "$2\times(4,2)\times(1,1)$ MMSE" and "$2\times(4,2)\times(1,1)$ MLD" mean the schemes in which the receive signal at DF relay is demodulated using MMSE nulling and using MLD respectively.

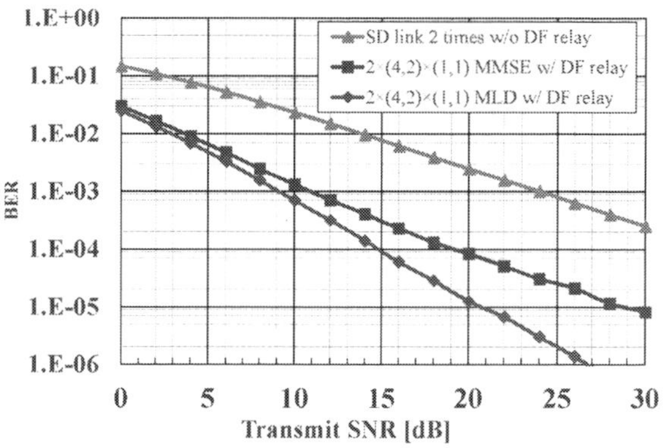

Figure 2. BER characteristics of $2\times(4,2)\times(1,1)$ model (Transmission rate to each user is 2 (bps/Hz).)

From Figure 2, we see that by using the DF relay and by combining the bit LLR's of SD link and RD link signals, the BER characteristic with using DF relay is very much improved compared with the 2 times transmission on SD link without using DF relay. From Figure 2, "SD link 2 times w/o DF relay" shows the BER slope of about $10^{-1}/10\,(\text{dB})$ for the transmit SNR=10~20 (dB) and we see that the diversity order of 1 $(\text{BER}=10^{-1}/10\text{ dB})$ is almost obtained. As stated in Section III. *A)-2)*, as the row elements of channel matrix $\boldsymbol{H}_{\text{SR}}\boldsymbol{N}_{\text{SD}}\boldsymbol{V}_{\text{SD}}\boldsymbol{C}_{\text{SD}}$ on the SR link do not always become independent, the SR link quality is degraded. Accordingly, the diversity order of 2 at each user is not achieved especially when the MMSE nulling is used at the DF relay. However, by using the MLD at DF relay, the SR link quality is improved. So "MLD w/ DF relay" in Figure 2 shows the BER slope of about $10^{-2}/10\,(\text{dB})$ for the transmit SNR=10~20 (dB) and we see that the diversity order of 2 is almost obtained.

Next, we consider the case where the number of transmission antennas at BS is $N_{\text{S}}=4$, the number of users $N_{\text{u}}=2$ and the numbers of reception antennas of each user are $m_1=m_2=1$. Compared with the previous case of $N_{\text{S}}=2$, more transmission antennas are assigned to each user. The numbers of reception and transmission antennas at DF relay are $M_{\text{R}}=4$ and $N_{\text{R}}=4$, respectively. We call this as $4\times(4,4)\times(1,1)$ model. The transmission protocols of SD, SR and RD links are the same as the previous $2\times(4,2)\times(1,1)$ model. The modulation format is QPSK. We show the simulation results in Figure 3. The channel matrix $\boldsymbol{H}_{\text{SD}}$ on SD link is 2×4 and the channel matrix $\tilde{\boldsymbol{H}}_{\text{SD}i}$ in which the channel matrix for user i is excluded from $\boldsymbol{H}_{\text{SD}}$ becomes 1×4 in Figure 3. From (17), the nullity of $\tilde{\boldsymbol{H}}_{\text{SD}i}$ is calculated as $n\ell_i=4-2+1=3,\ (i=1,2)$. The

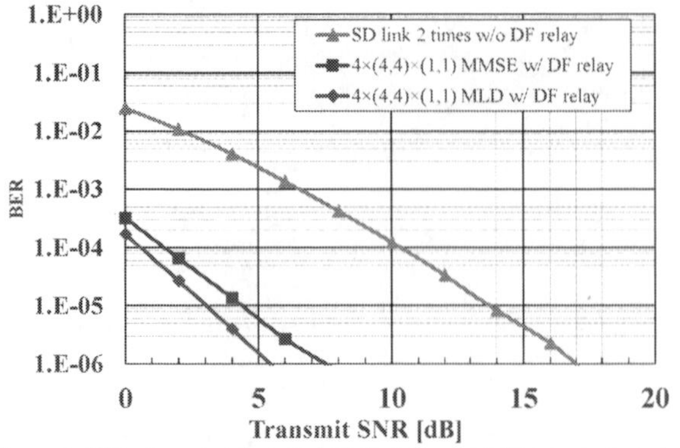

Figure 3. BER characteristics of $4\times(4,4)\times(1,1)$ model (Transmission rate to each user is 2 (bps/Hz).)

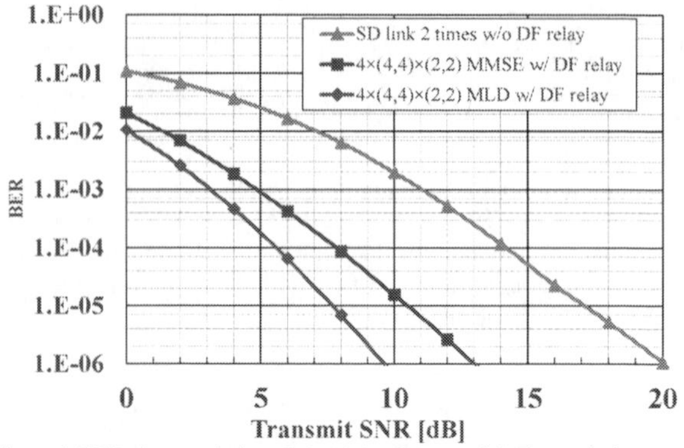

Figure 4. BER characteristics of $4\times(4,4)\times(2,2)$ model (Transmission rate to each user is 4 (bps/Hz) and 16QAM or QPSK is optimally selected to minimize the BER.)

size of block matrix $\boldsymbol{B}_i$ of user i becomes $m_i \times n\ell_i = 1\times 3, (i=1,2)$ and the diversity order of each user stream is given by $m_i \cdot n\ell_i = 3, (i=1,2)$. From Figure 3, "SD link 2 times w/o DF relay" shows the BER slope of about $10^{-3}/10\,(\mathrm{dB})$ for the transmit SNR=5~15 (dB) and we see that the diversity order of 3 is almost obtained. When using the DF relay, we can also expect the diversity order of 3 on the RD link as in the SD link. Thus, if there is no error on the SR link, then we can say the diversity order of 6 is obtained on the BER after the bit LLR addition at each user. As the transmit SNR becomes higher, the errors on SR link decrease and the diversity order of 6 is more easily achievable at high SNR region. But in Figure 3, "MMSE w/ DF relay" shows the BER slope of about $10^{-1}/2\,(\mathrm{dB})$ for the transmit SNR=4~6 (dB) and "MLD w/ DF relay" shows the BER slope of about $10^{-1}/2\,(\mathrm{dB})$ for the transmit SNR=3~5 (dB). So by using DF relay, we know the diversity order of 5 is achieved in this SNR region.

Next, we consider the case where the number of transmission antennas at BS is $N_S = 4$, the number of users $N_u = 2$ and the numbers of reception antennas of each user are $m_1 = m_2 = 2$. The numbers of reception and transmission antennas at DF relay are $M_R = 4$ and $N_R = 4$, respectively. We call this as $4\times(4,4)\times(2,2)$ model. In this case, the optimum modulation formats which minimize the BER characteristics are selected under the constant transmission rate of 4 (bps/Hz) on the SD link. This means one stream transmission with BD+MRT using 16QAM or two stream transmission with BD+E-SDM using two QPSK's is adaptively selected for given $\boldsymbol{H}_{SD}$ [10]. Also, in case of two stream transmission using two QPSK's, the optimum power assignment to the 1st and 2nd eigen mode channels which minimizes the BER is employed [10]. In this two stream transmission, the DF relay needs to know in advance the precoding matrix $\boldsymbol{N}_{SD}$ for BD, the matrix $\boldsymbol{V}_{SD}$ for the eigen mode transmission in E-SDM and the matrix $\boldsymbol{C}_{SD}$ for the power allocation factor to the 1st and 2nd eigen mode channels. Also, in order to make the bit LLR addition at each user, the transmission rate on the RD link must coincide with the one on the SD link. Hence, BD+E-SDM transmission on RD link adopts the same transmission rate as in the SD link. The simulation results are shown in Figure 4. BD+E-SDM scheme is employed on the SD link and the size of block channel matrix for user i becomes $\boldsymbol{B}_i = 2\times 2\ (i=1,2)$ in Figure 4. The transmission to each user is done by one stream transmission with the maximum eigen value using 16QAM or two stream transmission with two different eigen values using two QPSK's. Figure 4 shows the average BER characteristics. In this $4\times(4,4)\times(2,2)$ model, like in Figure 2 and Figure 3, the use of DF relay and the bit LLR addition at each user during the 1st and 2nd time slots improve the diversity order and the BER characteristic when compared with the 2 times transmission on the SD link without using relay.

Next, we consider the case where the number of transmission antennas at BS is $N_S = 6$, the number of users $N_u = 2$ and the numbers of reception antennas of each user are $m_1 = m_2 = 3$. The numbers of reception and transmission antennas at DF relay are $M_R = 6$ and $N_R = 6$, respectively. We call this as $6\times(6,6)\times(3,3)$ model. This model is the extension of previous $4\times(4,4)\times(2,2)$ model. The transmission protocols are the same as the previous $4\times(4,4)\times(2,2)$ model. On the SD link, the size of block channel matrix for user i becomes $\boldsymbol{B}_i = 3\times 3\ (i=1,2)$. For each user, one stream transmission with BD+MRT using 64QAM, two stream transmission with BD+E-SDM using 16QAM and QPSK, or three stream transmission with BD+E-SDM using three QPSK's is adaptively selected for $\boldsymbol{H}_{SD}$ under the constant transmission rate of 6 (bps/Hz). The RD link transmission uses the same bit transmission rate as in the SD link. We show the simulation results in Figure 5. When comparing the BER characteristics at $\mathrm{BER} = 10^{-6}$, "MMSE w/ DF relay" and "MLD w/ DF relay" improve the BER by 5 (dB) and 8 (dB), respectively compared with "SD link 2 times w/o DF relay." We also

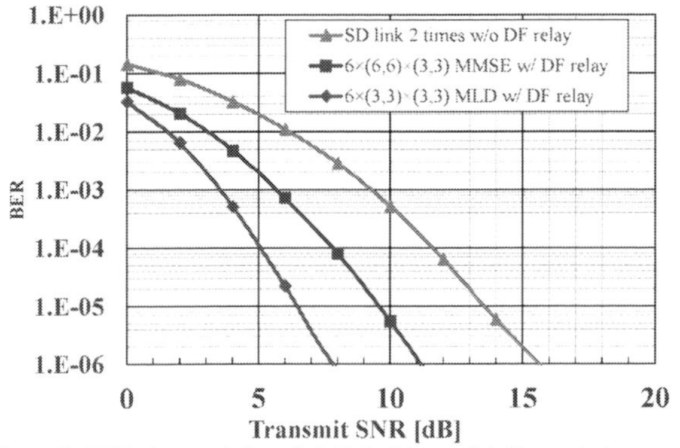

Figure 5. BER characteristics of 6×(6,6)×(3,3) model (Transmission rate to each user is 6 (bps/Hz) and 64QAM, 16QAM or QPSK is optimally selected to minimize the BER.)

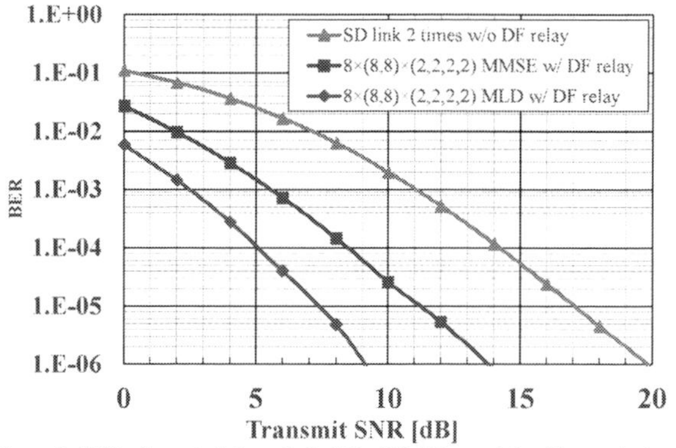

Figure 6. BER characteristics of 8×(8,8)×(2,2,2,2) model (Transmission rate to each user is 4 (bps/Hz) and 16QAM or QPSK is optimally selected to minimize the BER.)

find the slope of BER curve of "MLD w/ DF relay" is steeper than "SD link 2 times w/o DF relay" and know the effectiveness of using DF relay as in the previous cases.

Next, we consider the case where the number of transmission antennas at BS is $N_S = 8$, the number of users $N_u = 4$ and the numbers of reception antennas of each user are $m_1 = m_2 = m_3 = m_4 = 2$. The numbers of reception and transmission antennas at relay are $M_R = 8$ and $N_R = 8$, respectively. We call this as $8\times(8,8)\times(2,2,2,2)$ model. This model is the extension of previous $6\times(6,6)\times(3,3)$ model to $N_u = 4$ users. The transmission protocols are the same as the previous $4\times(4,4)\times(2,2)$ and $6\times(6,6)\times(3,3)$ models. On the SD link, the size of block channel matrix for user i becomes $\boldsymbol{B}_i = 2\times 2$ $(i = 1,2,3,4)$. For each user, one stream transmission with BD+MRT using 16QAM or two stream transmission with BD+E-SDM using two QPSK's is adaptively selected for $\boldsymbol{H}_{SD}$ under the constant transmission rate of 4 (bps/Hz). The RD link transmission uses the same transmission rate as in the SD link. We show the simulation results in Figure 6. In this $8\times(8,8)\times(2,2,2,2)$ model, the demodulation using MLD at relay becomes difficult because the number of searches in MLD becomes $16^4 = 4^8 = 65536$ for the total 4~8 streams from the BS. So instead of using MLD, we employed the Sphere Decoding SE algorithm [23],[24] that can obtain the same Maximum Likelihood (ML) solution as the MLD with far less computational complexity. Like in Figures 2-5, the use of DF relay and the bit LLR addition at each user during the 1st and 2nd time slots improve the diversity order and the BER characteristic compared with the 2 times transmission on SD link without using DF relay. When comparing the BER characteristics at $\mathrm{BER} = 10^{-6}$, "MMSE w/ DF relay" and "MLD w/ DF relay" improve the BER by 6 (dB) and 11 (dB) respectively compared with "SD link 2 times w/o DF relay." We also find the slope of BER curve of "MLD w/ DF relay" is steeper than "SD link 2 times w/o DF relay" and know the effectiveness of using DF relay as

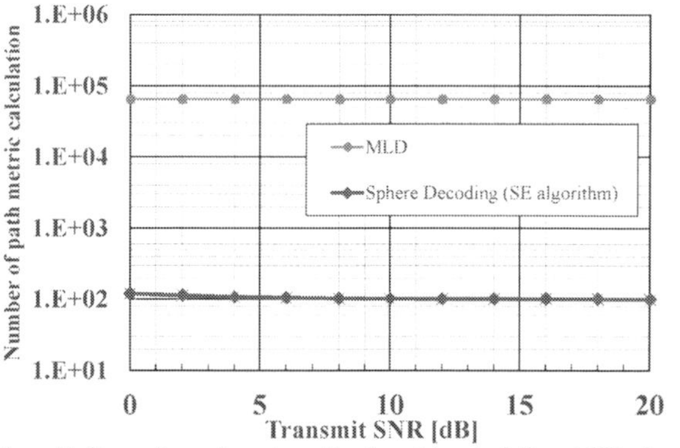

Figure 7. Comparison of number of path metric calculation at DF relay between MLD and Sphere Decoding in 8×(8,8)×(2,2,2,2) model (Transmission rate to each user is 4 (bps/Hz) and 16QAM or QPSK is optimally selected to minimize the BER.)

in the previous cases.

The effect of complexity reduction by using Sphere Decoding (SE algorithm in [23],[24]) in place of MLD at DF relay is shown in Figure 7. When MLD is employed at DF relay, the required number of path metric calculation for 4 users is $16^4 = 65536$, however, by using Sphere Decoding it can be reduced to almost 100 and the large complexity reduction has been achieved. Also, the complexity reduction by Sphere Decoding becomes more prominent at higher transmit SNR.

Next, we consider the case where the number of transmission antennas at BS is $N_S = 6$, the number of users $N_u = 2$ and the numbers of reception antennas of each user are $m_1 = 3, m_2 = 2$. The numbers of reception and transmission antennas at relay are $M_R = 5$ and $N_R = 4$, respectively. We call this as $6\times(5,4)\times(3,2)$ model. On the SD link, the sizes of block channel matrices for user 1 and user 2 become $\boldsymbol{B}_{SD1} = 3\times 4$ and $\boldsymbol{B}_{SD2} = 2\times 3$, respectively. For user 1, one stream transmission with BD+MRT using 64QAM, two stream transmission with BD+E-SDM using

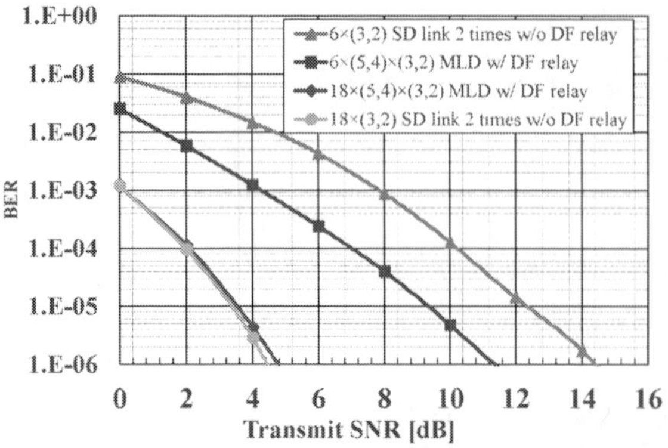

Figure 8. BER characteristics of $6\times(5,4)\times(3,2)$ or $18\times(5,4)\times(3,2)$ model (Transmission rate to user 1 is 6 (bps/Hz) and 64QAM, 16QAM or QPSK is optimally selected to minimize the BER. Transmission rate to user 2 is 4(bps/Hz) and 16QAM or QPSK is optimally selected to minimize the BER.)

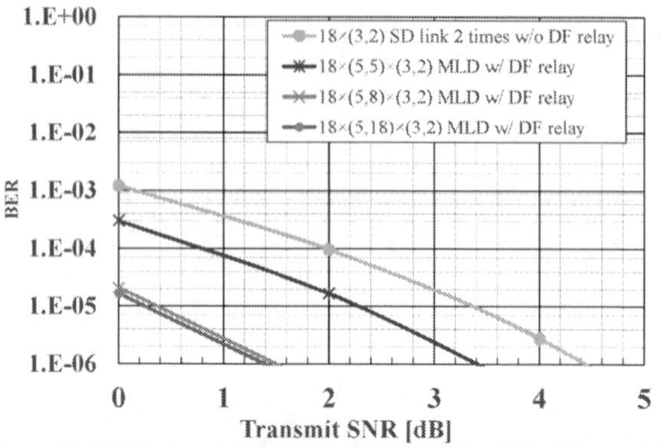

Figure 9. BER characteristics of $18\times(5,5)$ or $(5,8)$ or $(5,18)\times(3,2)$ model (Transmission rate to user 1 is 6 (bps/Hz) and 64QAM, 16QAM or QPSK is optimally selected to minimize the BER. Transmission rate to user 2 is 4(bps/Hz) and 16QAM or QPSK is optimally selected to minimize the BER.)

16QAM and QPSK, or three stream transmission with BD+E-SDM using three QPSK's is adaptively selected for $\boldsymbol{H}_{\text{SD}}$ under the constant transmission rate of 6 (bps/Hz). For user 2, one stream transmission with BD+MRT using 16QAM or two stream transmission with BD+E-SDM using two QPSK's is adaptively selected for $\boldsymbol{H}_{\text{SD}}$ under the constant transmission rate of 4 (bps/Hz). The numbers of reception and transmission antennas at relay is selected as $M_{\text{R}}=5$ and $N_{\text{R}}=4$, respectively and these antenna numbers are minimum required ones. This is because as the numbers of eigen streams for user 1 and user 2 on the SD link are $L_{\text{SD1}}=\min(3,4)=3$ and $L_{\text{SD2}}=\min(2,3)=2$, respectively, the minimum required number of reception antennas at relay should be $M_{\text{R}}=3+2=5$ for making MMSE nulling at relay. From (16) the number of transmission antennas at relay has to satisfy the condition $N_{\text{R}}>N_{\text{D}}-m_{\min}=(m_1+m_2)-\min(m_1,m_2)=5-2=3$ and the minimum number of $N_{\text{R}}=4$ is employed. On the RD link, the sizes of block channel matrices for user 1 and user 2 become $\boldsymbol{B}_{\text{RD1}}=3\times 2$ and $\boldsymbol{B}_{\text{RD2}}=2\times 1$, respectively. For user 1, one stream transmission with BD+MRT using 64QAM or two stream transmission with BD+E-SDM using 16QAM and QPSK is adaptively selected for $\boldsymbol{H}_{\text{RD}}$ under the constant transmission rate of 6 (bps/Hz). For user 2, one stream transmission with BD+MRT using 16QAM is only selected for $\boldsymbol{H}_{\text{RD}}$ under the constant transmission rate of 4(bps/Hz). When the number of transmission antennas at BS is increased, the receive gain of each user on the SD link raises. Accordingly, we increased the number of transmission antennas at BS from $N_{\text{S}}=6$ to $N_{\text{S}}=18$ on this $6\times(5,4)\times(3,2)$ model and compared the BER performance between $6\times(5,4)\times(3,2)$ and $18\times(5,4)\times(3,2)$ models. On the SD link of $18\times(5,4)\times(3,2)$ model, the sizes of block channel matrices for user 1 and user 2 become $\boldsymbol{B}_{\text{SD1}}=3\times 16$ and $\boldsymbol{B}_{\text{SD2}}=2\times 15$, respectively. The numbers of eigen streams on the SD link of user 1 and user 2 become $L_{\text{SD1}}=\min(3,16)=3$ and $L_{\text{SD2}}=\min(2,15)=2$, respectively and these numbers of eigen streams are the same between $6\times(5,4)\times(3,2)$ and $18\times(5,4)\times(3,2)$ models. We show the simulation results in Figure 8. From Figure 8, we know that "$6\times(5,4)\times(3,2)$ MLD w/ DF relay" improves the BER by 2 (dB) at $\text{BER}=10^{-6}$ compared with "$6\times(3,2)$ SD link 2 times w/o DF relay" and the effect of using DF relay is verified. On the other hand, regarding $18\times(5,4)\times(3,2)$ model, we observe that there is almost no BER difference between "$18\times(5,4)\times(3,2)$ MLD w/ DF relay" and "$18\times(3,2)$ SD link 2 times w/o DF relay," thus we could not identify the effectiveness of using DF relay. This is considered that when the number of transmission antennas N_{S} is increased from 6 to 18, the transmission quality of SD link surpasses the RD link and two times transmission on the SD link is enough even though the DF relay is not used.

Next, we increased the number of transmission antennas of DF relay from $N_{\text{R}}=4$ to a larger number on $18\times(5,4)\times(3,2)$ model and examined the effectiveness of using DF relay. When $N_{\text{R}}=5$, the number of eigen streams of user 1 and user 2 on the RD link become $L_{\text{RD1}}=3$ and $L_{\text{RD2}}=2$, respectively and the same pattern of adaptive modulation as the SD link can be employed. We show the simulation results in Figure 9. From Figure 9, we observe that the BER performance of "$18\times(5,5)\times(3,2)$ MLD w/ DF relay" is better than "$18\times(3,2)$ SD link 2 times w/o DF relay" and can verify the effectiveness of using DF relay even when the number of BS antennas is $N_{\text{S}}=18$. When the number of transmission antennas at DF relay N_{R} is further increased, we compared the BER performance between "$18\times(5,8)\times(3,2)$ MLD w/ DF relay" and "$18\times(5,18)\times(3,2)$ MLD w/ DF relay." However, the BER characteristics are almost equal between them and $N_{\text{R}}=8$ seems enough and saturated number for the DF relay.

Next, under the condition of $N_{\text{S}}=18$ and with the same transmission rate, we investigated the required number of

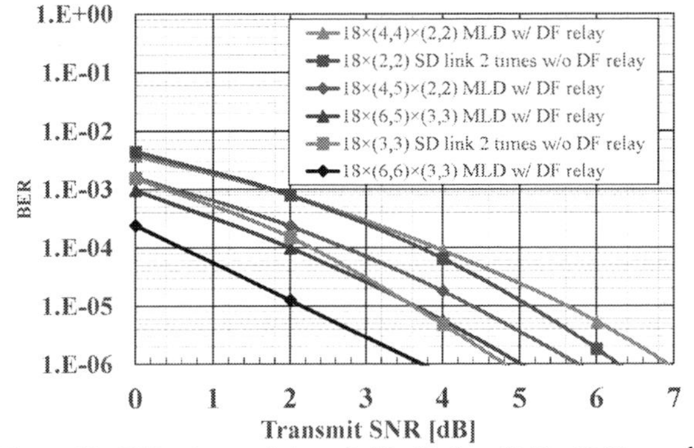

Figure 10. BER characteristics of $18\times(4,4)$ or $(4,5)\times(2,2)$ and $18\times(6,5)$ or $(6,6)\times(3,3)$ model (Transmission rate to user 1 is 6 (bps/Hz) and 64QAM, 16QAM or QPSK is optimally selected to minimize the BER. Transmission rate to user 2 is 4 (bps/Hz) and 16QAM or QPSK is optimally selected to minimize the BER.)

transmission antennas N_R at DF relay to improve the BER performance. We considered $18\times(2,2)$ and $18\times(3,3)$ models on the SD link where two users have equally 2 and 3 reception antennas, respectively. For $18\times(2,2)$ SD link model, the block diagonalized matrix size of user i becomes $\boldsymbol{B}_{\mathrm{SD}i}=2\times16$ $(i=1,2)$ and the number of eigen streams is given by $L_{\mathrm{SD}i}=\min(2,16)=2$ $(i=1,2)$. This means the required number of reception antennas at DF relay is greater than $M_R=2+2=4$ for the MMSE nulling. On the other hand, for $18\times(3,3)$ SD link model, the block diagonalized matrix size of user i becomes $\boldsymbol{B}_{\mathrm{SD}i}=3\times15$ $(i=1,2)$ and the number of eigen streams is given by $L_{\mathrm{SD}i}=\min(3,15)=3$ $(i=1,2)$. This means the required number of reception antennas at DF relay is greater than $M_R=3+3=6$. On the SD link of $18\times(2,2)$, for user 1, one stream transmission with BD+MRT using 64QAM or two stream transmission with BD+E-SDM using 16QAM and QPSK is adaptively selected for $\boldsymbol{H}_{\mathrm{SD}}$ under the constant transmission rate of 6 (bps/Hz). For user 2, one stream transmission with BD+MRT using 16QAM or two stream transmission with BD+E-SDM using two QPSK's is adaptively selected for $\boldsymbol{H}_{\mathrm{SD}}$ under the constant transmission rate of 4 (bps/Hz). On the SD link of $18\times(3,3)$, for user 1, one stream transmission with BD+MRT using 64QAM, two stream transmission with BD+E-SDM using 16QAM and QPSK, or three stream transmission with BD+E-SDM using three QPSK's is adaptively selected for $\boldsymbol{H}_{\mathrm{SD}}$ under the constant transmission rate of 6 (bps/Hz). For user 2, one stream transmission with BD+MRT using 16QAM, two stream transmission with BD+E-SDM using two QPSK's or three stream transmission with BD+E-SDM using QPSK and two BPSK's is adaptively selected for $\boldsymbol{H}_{\mathrm{SD}}$ under the constant transmission rate of 4 (bps/Hz). We show the simulation results in Figure 10. From Figure 10, regarding the $18\times(2,2)$ SD link model, we observe the BER is improved in the order of

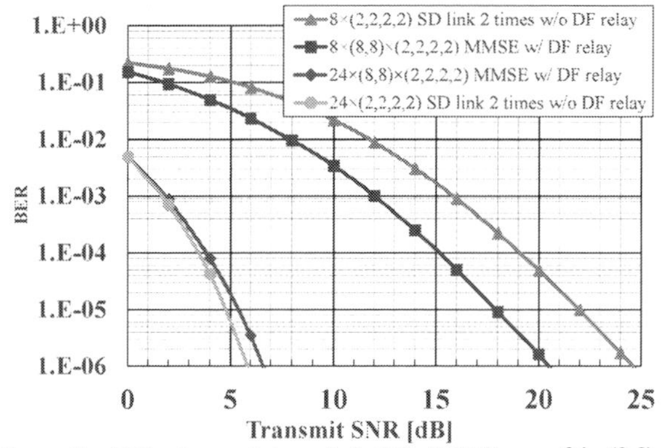

Figure 11. BER characteristics of $8\times(8,8)\times(2,2,2,2)$ or $24\times(8,8)\times(2,2,2,2)$ model (Transmission rate to each user is 6(bps/Hz) and 64QAM, 16QAM or QPSK is optimally selected to minimize the BER.)

"$18\times(4,5)\times(2,2)$ MLD w/ DF relay", "$18\times(2,2)$ SD link 2 times w/o DF relay" and "$18\times(4,4)\times(2,2)$ MLD w/ DF relay." This observation means that $N_R=5$ is required to show the effectiveness of using DF relay rather than $N_R=4$. Regarding the $18\times(3,3)$ SD link model, "$18\times(6,5)\times(3,3)$ MLD w/ DF relay" shows almost the same BER characteristics as "$18\times(3,3)$ SD link 2 times w/o DF relay" and "$18\times(6,6)\times(3,3)$ MLD w/ DF relay" shows the best BER characteristics. Accordingly we can say that minimum $N_R=6$ is needed to show the effectiveness of using DF relay in this case.

Next, we consider the case where the number of transmission antennas at BS is $N_S=8$, the number of users $N_u=4$ and the numbers of reception antennas of each user are $m_1=m_2=m_3=m_4=2$. The numbers of receive and transmission antennas at relay is $M_R=8$ and $N_R=8$, respectively. We call this as $8\times(8,8)\times(2,2,2,2)$ model. This model is the same as the previous Figure 6, but this time we extended the transmission rate from 4 (bps/Hz) to 6 (bps/Hz). On the SD link, the size of block channel matrix for user i becomes $\boldsymbol{B}_i=2\times2$ $(i=1,2,3,4)$. For each user, one stream transmission with BD+MRT using 64QAM or two stream transmission with BD+E-SDM using 16QAM and QPSK is adaptively selected for $\boldsymbol{H}_{\mathrm{SD}}$ under the constant transmission rate of 6 (bps/Hz). The RD link transmission uses the same transmission rate 6 (bps/Hz) as in the SD link. Moreover, regarding on $8\times(8,8)\times(2,2,2,2)$ model, we increased the number of transmission antennas at BS from $N_S=8$ to $N_S=24$. We call this as $24\times(8,8)\times(2,2,2,2)$ model. The size of block diagonalized matrix of user i on the SD link becomes $\boldsymbol{B}_{\mathrm{SD}i}=2\times18$ $(i=1,2,3,4)$ and the number of eigen streams of user i is given by $L_{\mathrm{SD}i}=\min(2,18)=2$ $(i=1,2,3,4)$. Accordingly, the adaptive modulation is the same between $8\times(8,8)\times(2,2,2,2)$ and $24\times(8,8)\times(2,2,2,2)$. We show the simulation results in Figure 11.

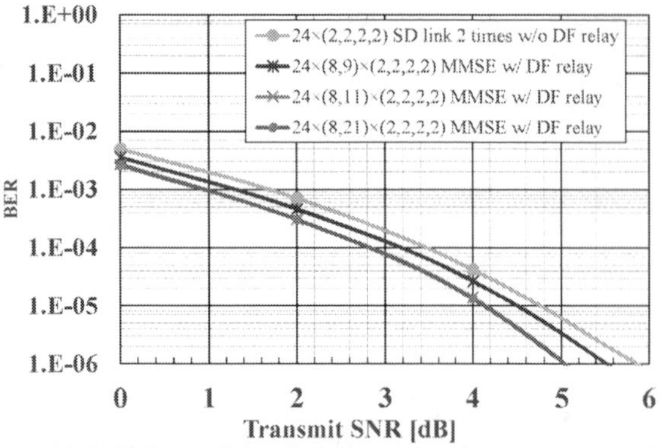

Figure 12. BER characteristics of $24\times(8,9)$ or $(8,11)$ or $(8,21)\times(2,2,2,2)$ model (Transmission rate to each user is 6 (bps/Hz) and 64QAM, 16QAM or QPSK is optimally selected to minimize the BER.)

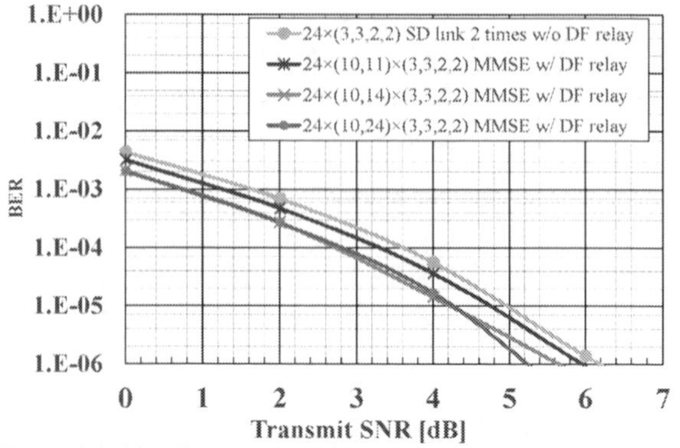

Figure 13. BER characteristics of $24\times(10,11)$ or $(10,14)$ or $(10,24)\times(3,3,2,2)$ model (Transmission rate to each user is 6 (bps/Hz) and 64QAM, 16QAM or QPSK is optimally selected to minimize the BER.)

From Figure 11, the BER of $8\times(8,8)\times(2,2,2,2)$ is superior to "$8\times(2,2,2,2)$ SD link 2 times w/o DF relay" by 4 (dB) at $\mathrm{BER}=10^{-6}$ and we see the effectiveness of using the DF relay. On the other hand, there is almost no BER difference between "$24\times(8,8)\times(2,2,2,2)$ MMSE w/ DF relay" and "$24\times(2,2,2,2)$ SD link 2 times w/o DF relay," and we could not see any effect of using the DF relay in this case. As stated before, this phenomenon comes from the fact that the SD link quality is better than the RD link due to the increased number of transmission antennas $N_S = 24$ at BS.

Next, regarding $24\times(8,8)\times(2,2,2,2)$ model, we increased the number of transmission antennas N_R at DF relay. We show the simulation results in Figure 12. From Figure 12, compared with "$24\times(2,2,2,2)$ SD link 2 times w/o DF relay," the BER is improved by using DF relay. But unlike the cases of "$8\times(2,2,2,2)$ SD link 2 times w/o DF relay" and "$8\times(8,8)\times(2,2,2,2)$ MMSE w/ DF relay" in Figure 11, the effect of using relay is not so large and there is no BER difference between "$24\times(8,11)\times(2,2,2,2)$ MMSE w/ DF relay" and "$24\times(8,21)\times(2,2,2,2)$ MMSE w/ DF relay." From these observations, we know that $N_R = 11$ is the saturated number of transmission antennas at DF relay and when the number of transmission antennas at BS is large such as $N_S = 24$, the effect of using DF relay is limited.

Next, we try to vary the number of reception antennas of each user under the condition that the number of transmission antennas at BS and the transmission rate of each user are unchanged from the previous figure, i.e., $N_S = 24$ and 6 (bps/Hz), respectively. On the SD link, we consider $24\times(3,3,2,2)$ model. The sizes of block diagonalized matrices of SD link are given by $\boldsymbol{B}_{\mathrm{SD}i} = 3\times 17$ $(i=1,2)$ and $\boldsymbol{B}_{\mathrm{SD}i} = 2\times 16$ $(i=3,4)$, respectively. The number of eigen streams of each user becomes $L_{\mathrm{SD}i} = \min(3,17) = 3$ $(i=1,2)$ and $L_{\mathrm{SD}i} = \min(2,16) = 2$ $(i=3,4)$, respectively. For $L_{\mathrm{SD}i} = 3$ $(i=1,2)$, one stream transmission with BD+MRT using 64QAM, two stream transmission with BD+E-SDM using 16QAM and QPSK, or three stream transmission with BD+E-SDM using three QPSK's is adaptively selected for $\boldsymbol{H}_{\mathrm{SD}}$ under the constant transmission rate of 6 (bps/Hz). For $L_{\mathrm{SD}i} = 2$ $(i=3,4)$, one stream transmission with BD+MRT using 64QAM or two stream transmission with BD+E-SDM using 16QAM and QPSK is adaptively selected for $\boldsymbol{H}_{\mathrm{SD}}$ under the constant transmission rate of 6 (bps/Hz). The size of $\boldsymbol{B}_{\mathrm{SD}i} = 3\times 17$ $(i=1,2)$ in $24\times(3,3,2,2)$ model is greater than $\boldsymbol{B}_{\mathrm{SD}i} = 2\times 18$ $(i=1,2,3,4)$ in $24\times(2,2,2,2)$ model. On the other hand, $\boldsymbol{B}_{\mathrm{SD}i} = 2\times 16$ $(i=3,4)$ in $24\times(3,3,2,2)$ model is a little bit less than $\boldsymbol{B}_{\mathrm{SD}i} = 2\times 18$ $(i=1,2,3,4)$ in $24\times(2,2,2,2)$ model. The minimum number of reception antennas at DF relay for MMSE nulling becomes $M_R = 3+3+2+2 = 10$. We show the simulation results in Figure 13. From Figure 13, we see almost the same observations as in Figure 12 and when the number of transmission antennas at BS is large such as $N_S = 24$, the effect of using DF relay is limited.

V. CONCLUSIONS

In this paper, we discussed the improvement of transmission quality when the DF relay is applied to the MU-MIMO down link system with the linear Block Diagonalization plus MRT or E-SDM scheme. By knowing the precoding matrix of BS at DF relay, the DF relay can demodulate the transmit signals from BS with the receive CSI only. As the existence of DF relay does not affect the design of precoding matrix at BS, we can add the DF relay only when the transmission quality between BS and user terminals is insufficient. By adding the DF relay and utilizing the 2nd time slot, we can improve the receive quality or diversity order of each user terminal. We made the designs of SD, SR and RD links during the 1st and the 2nd time slots and verified the effectiveness of using DF relay. Although the SR link quality affects the total BER performance very much, we can utilize the simple MMSE nulling by increasing the number of reception antennas at DF relay to improve the SR link quality. We observed that even though the DF relay is equipped with the minimum number of reception and transmission antennas required, there exists the effect of using DF relay. But by increasing the number of transmission antennas at BS, the SD link quality is improved gradually resulting in the better SD link quality than the relaying SRD link. This large number of transmission antennas at BS finally limits the effect of using DF relay.

ACKNOWLEDGEMENT

This study is supported by the Grants-in-Aid for Scientific Research JP15K06059 of the Japan Society for the Promotion of Science and the Sharp cooperation. The authors also thank Mr. Kentaro Iida for his contributions.

REFERENCES

[1] K. Iida and Y. Iwanami, "A Regenerative Relay Transmission in Linearly Precoded MU-MIMO Downlink," AICT2016, pp. 51-56, May, 2016.

[2] N. Shimakawa and Y. Iwanami, "A Diversity Order Design of Linearly Precoded MU-MIMO Downlink System," IEEE Region 10 Conference (TENCON), pp.1937-1949, Nov. 2016.

[3] H. S Quentin, B. P. Christian, and A. Lee Swindlehurst, M. Hardt, "An introduction to the multi-user MIMO downlink," IEEE Communications Magazine, vol. 42, Issue 10, pp. 60-67, Oct. 2004.

[4] Q. H. Spencer, A. L. Swindlehurst, and M. Haardt, "Zero forcing methods for downlink spatial multiplexing in multiuser MIMO channels," IEEE Trans. Sig. Processing, vol. 52, no. 2, pp. 461-471, Feb.2004.

[5] T. Haustein, C. von Helmolt, E. Jorswieck, V. Jungnickel, and V. Pohl, "Performance of MIMO systems with channel inversion," IEEE 55th VTC Spring, vol. 1, pp. 35 – 39, 2002.

[6] S. Vishwanath, N. Jindal, and A. Goldsmith, "Duality, achievable rates, and sum-rate capacity of MIMO broadcast channels," IEEE Trans. Inform. Theory, vol. 49, no. 10, pp. 2658–2668, Oct. 2003.

[7] V. Stankovic and M. Haardt, "Successive optimization Tomlinson-Harashima precoding (SO THP) for multi-user MIMO systems," IEEE International Conference on Acoustics, Speech, and Signal Processing, Proceedings (ICASSP '05), vol. 3, pp. iii/1117-iii/1120, March 2005.

[8] C. B. Peel, B. M. Hochwald, and A. L. Swindlehurst, "A vector-perturbation technique for near-capacity multi antenna multiuser communication-part I: Channel inversion and regularization," IEEE Trans. Commun., vol. 53, pp. 195-202, Jan. 2005.

[9] C. B. Peel, B. M. Hochwald, and A. L. Swindlehurst, "A vector-perturbation technique for near-capacity multi antenna multiuser communication-part II: perturbation," IEEE Trans. Commun., vol. 53, pp. 195–202, Jan. 2005.

[10] K. Miyashita, T. Nishimura, T. Ohgane, Y. Ogawa, Y. Takatori, and K. Cho, "Eigenbeam-Space Division Multiplexing (E-SDM) in a MIMO Channel," IEICE Technical Report, RCS2002−53, pp. 13−18, May 2002.

[11] H. Sun, S. Meng, Y. Wan, and X. You, "Sum-rate evaluation of multi-user MIMO-relay channel," IEICE Trans. Commun., vol. E-92-B, no. 2, pp. 683-686, Feb. 2009.

[12] K. Nishimori, N. Honma, M. Mizoguchi, "Effectiveness of relay MIMO transmission in an actual outdoor environment," IEICE Technical Report, RCS2008-228, pp. 95-100, March 2009.

[13] K. Fujii and T. Fujii, "Adjacent Cell Interference Reduction Using Multiuser MIMO Relay Station," IEICE Technical Report, RCS2010-164, pp. 31-36, Dec. 2010.

[14] W. Liu, C. Li, J.-D. Li, L. Hanzo, "Block diagonalization-based multiple input multiple output-aided downlink relaying," IET Commun, vol. 6, Iss. 15, pp. 2371-2377, 2012.

[15] L. Liang, W. Xu, X. Dong, "Limited feedback-based multi-antenna relay broadcast channels with block diagonalization," IEEE Trans. Wireless Commun., vol. 12, no. 8, pp. 4092-4101, Aug. 2013.

[16] Y. Tanahashi, Y. Iwanami, R. Yamada, and N. Okamoto, "Study on VP Transmission Schemes for Multiuser MIMO Downlink using Non-Regenerative Relay," IEICE Technical Report, RCS2013-371, pp. 395-400, March 2014.

[17] T. Taniguchi and Y. Karasawa, "An Elementary Study on Node Pair Selection in Relay-Aided Communication System Based on Stable Marriage Problem," IEICE Technical Report, RCS2014-50, pp. 105-108, June 2014.

[18] F. Benkhelifa, A. S. Salem, and M.-S. Alouini, "Sum-Rate Enhancement in Multiuser MIMO Decode-and-Forward Relay Broadcasting Channel With Energy Harvesting Relays," IEEE Journal on Selected Areas in Commun., vol. 34, no. 12, pp. 3675-3683, Dec.2016.

[19] G. Zhang and Y. Iwanami, "A design of communication quality in linearly precoded MU-MIMO downlink system," IEICE Technical Report, RCS2015, March 2016.

[20] T. K. Y. Lo, "Maximum Ratio Transmission," IEEE Trans. Commun.,vol. 47, no. 10, pp. 1458-1461, Oct. 1999.

[21] A. Paulraj, R. Nabar and D. Gore, Introduction to Space Time Wireless Communication, Cambridge University Press, 2008.

[22] J. K. Cavers, "Single-User and Multiuser Adaptive Maximum Ratio Transmission for Rayleigh Channel," IEEE Trans. on Vehicular Technology, vol. 49, No. 6, pp. 2043-2050, Nov. 2000.

[23] Z. Guo and P. Nilsson, "Reduced Complexity Schnorr-Euchner Decoding Algorithms for MIMO systems," IEEE Communication Letters, vol. 8, no. 5, pp. 286-288, May 2004.

[24] B. Shim and I. Kang, "Sphere Decoding with a probabilistic tree pruning," IEEE Transactions on Signal Processing, vol. 56, no. 10, pp. 4867-4878, Oct. 2008.

A Practical Overview of Recursive Least-Squares Algorithms for Echo Cancellation

Camelia Elisei-Iliescu, Constantin Paleologu,
Cristian Stanciu, Cristian Anghel, Silviu Ciochină

University Politehnica of Bucharest, Romania
Email: {pale, cristian, canghel, silviu}@comm.pub.ro

Jacob Benesty

INRS-EMT
University of Quebec, Montreal, Canada
Email: benesty@emt.inrs.ca

Abstract—**Due to its fast convergence rate, the recursive least-squares (RLS) algorithm is very popular in many applications of adaptive filtering. However, the computational complexity of this algorithm represents a major limitation in some applications that involve long filters, like echo cancellation. Moreover, the specific features of this application require good tracking capabilities and double-talk robustness for the adaptive algorithm, which further imply an optimization process on its parameters. In the case of most RLS-based algorithms, the performance can be controlled in terms of two main parameters, i.e., the forgetting factor and the regularization term. In this paper, we outline the influence of these parameters on the overall performance of the RLS algorithm and present several solutions to control their behavior, taking into account the specific requirements of echo cancellation application. The resulting variable forgetting factor RLS (VFF-RLS) and variable-regularized RLS (VR-RLS) algorithms could represent appealing solutions for real-world scenarios, as indicated by simulations performed in the context of both network and acoustic echo cancellation.**

Keywords–Adaptive filters; Echo cancellation; Recursive least-squares (RLS) algorithm; Variable forgetting factor RLS (VFF-RLS); Variable regularized RLS (VR-RLS).

I. INTRODUCTION

The recursive least-squares (RLS) algorithm [1], [2], [3] is one of the most popular adaptive filters. As compared to the normalized least-mean-square (NLMS) algorithm [2], [3], the RLS offers a superior convergence rate especially for highly correlated input signals. Of course, there is a price to pay for this advantage, which is an increase in the computational complexity. For this reason, it is not very often involved in echo cancellation [4], [5], where long filters are required.

In both network and acoustic echo cancellation contexts [4], [5], the basic principle is to build a model of the echo path impulse response that needs to be identified with an adaptive filter, which provides at its output a replica of the echo (that is further subtracted from the reference signal). The main difference between these two applications is the way in which the echo arises. In the network (or electrical) echo problem, there is an unbalanced coupling between the 2-wire and 4-wire circuits which results in echo, while the acoustic echo is due to the acoustic coupling between the microphone and the loudspeaker (e.g., as in speakerphones). However, in both cases, the adaptive filter has to model an unknown system, i.e., the echo path. The system model for echo cancellation is summarized in Section II.

Even if the formulation of the echo cancellation problem is straightforward, its specific features represent a challenge for any adaptive algorithm. There are several issues associated with this application, and they are as follows. First, the echo paths can have excessive lengths in time, e.g., up to hundreds of milliseconds. Consequently, long length adaptive filters are required (hundreds or even thousands of coefficients), influencing the convergence rate of the algorithm. Besides, the echo paths are time-variant systems, requiring good tracking capabilities for the echo canceller. Second, the echo signal is combined with the near-end signal; ideally, the adaptive filter should separate this mixture and provide an estimate of the echo at its output as well as an estimate of the near-end from the error signal. This is not an easy task since the near-end signal can contain both the background noise and the near-end speech; the background noise can be non-stationary and strong while the near-end speech acts like a large level disturbance. Last but not least, the input of the adaptive filter (i.e., the far-end signal) is mainly speech, which is a non-stationary and highly correlated signal that can influence the overall performance of adaptive algorithms.

Different types of adaptive filters have been involved in the context of echo cancellation. The RLS-based algorithms would represent a very appealing choice (especially in terms of the convergence rate), if the computational complexity issue could be overcome. In this paper, we provide a practical overview on several RLS-based algorithms that could be used for echo cancellation, focusing on their key parameters.

It is well known that the performance of the RLS algorithm is mainly controlled by two important parameters, i.e., the forgetting factor and the regularization term. Similar to the attributes of the step-size from the NLMS-based algorithms, the performance of RLS-type algorithms in terms of convergence rate, tracking, misadjustment, and stability depends on the forgetting factor [2], [3]. The classical RLS algorithm uses a constant forgetting factor (between 0 and 1) and needs to compromise between the previous performance criteria. When the forgetting factor is very close to one, the algorithm achieves low misadjustment and good stability, but its tracking capabilities are reduced [6]. A small value of the forgetting factor improves the tracking but increases the misadjustment, and could affect the stability of the algorithm [7]. Motivated by these aspects, a number of variable forgetting factor RLS (VFF-RLS) algorithms have been developed, e.g., [8]–[11] (and references therein).

It should be mentioned that in the context of system identification (like in echo cancellation), where the output of the unknown system is corrupted by another signal (which is usually an additive noise), the goal of the adaptive filter is not to make the error signal goes to zero, because this will introduce noise in the adaptive filter. The objective instead is to recover the "corrupting signal" from the error signal of the adaptive filter after this one converges to the true solution. This was the approach behind the VFF-RLS algorithm proposed in [10], which is analyzed in Section III.

As compared to the forgetting factor, the regularization parameter has been less addressed in the literature. Apparently, it is required in matrix inversion when this matrix is ill conditioned, especially in the initialization stage of the algorithm. However, its role is of great importance in practice, since regularization is a must in all ill-posed problems (like in adaptive filtering), especially in the presence of additive noise [12]–[15]. Consequently, in Section IV, we focus on the regularized RLS algorithm [3]. Following the development from [13], a method to select an optimal regularization parameter is presented, so that the algorithm could behave well in all noisy conditions. Since the value of this parameter is related to the echo-to-noise ratio (ENR), a simple and practical way to estimate the ENR in practice is also presented, which leads to a variable regularized RLS (VR-RLS) algorithm. Also, a low-complexity version of the proposed VR-RLS algorithm is developed, based on the dichotomous coordinate descent (DCD) method [16], [17].

The simulation results (presented in Section V) are performed in the context of both network and acoustic echo cancellation. The results support the theoretical findings and indicate the good performance of these algorithms. Finally, the conclusions are provided in Section VI.

II. System Model for Echo Cancellation

In the context of echo cancellation (Figure 1), the microphone or desired signal at the discrete-time index n is

$$d(n) = \mathbf{x}^T(n)\mathbf{h} + v(n) = y(n) + v(n), \quad (1)$$

where

$$\mathbf{x}(n) = [\ x(n) \quad x(n-1) \quad \cdots \quad x(n-L+1)\ ]^T \quad (2)$$

is a vector containing the L most recent time samples of the zero-mean input (loudspeaker) signal $x(n)$, superscript ^{T} denotes transpose of a vector or a matrix,

$$\mathbf{h} = [\ h_0 \quad h_1 \quad \cdots \quad h_{L-1}\ ]^T \quad (3)$$

is the impulse response (of length L) of the system (from the loudspeaker to the microphone) that we need to identify, and $v(n)$ the zero-mean near-end signal. In case of single-talk (i.e., the near-end speech is absent), $v(n)$ can usually be considered a zero-mean stationary white Gaussian noise signal with the variance $\sigma_v^2 = E\left[v^2(n)\right]$, where $E[\cdot]$ denotes mathematical expectation. The signal $y(n)$ is called the echo in the context of echo cancellation that we want to cancel with an adaptive filter [4], [5].

Then, our objective is to estimate or identify $\mathbf{h}$ with an adaptive filter:

$$\widehat{\mathbf{h}}(n) = \left[\ \widehat{h}_0(n) \quad \widehat{h}_1(n) \quad \cdots \quad \widehat{h}_{L-1}(n)\ \right]^T, \quad (4)$$

in such a way that for a reasonable value of n, we have for the (normalized) misalignment:

$$\frac{\left\|\mathbf{h} - \widehat{\mathbf{h}}(n)\right\|_2^2}{\|\mathbf{h}\|_2^2} \leq \iota, \quad (5)$$

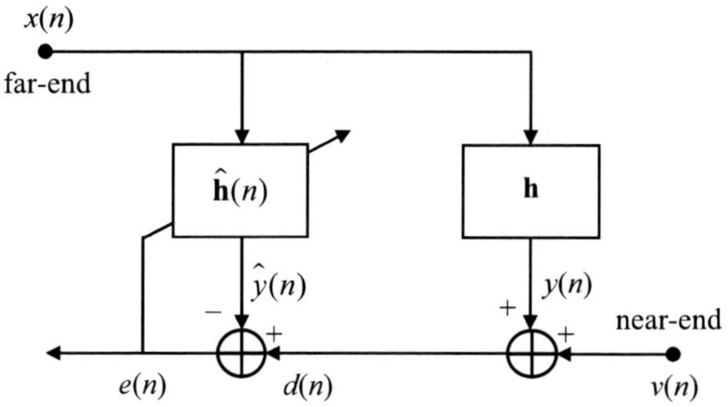

Figure 1. General configuration for echo cancellation.

where ι is a predetermined small positive number and $\|\cdot\|_2$ is the ℓ_2 norm. In this context, the a priori error signal is defined as

$$e(n) = d(n) - \mathbf{x}^T(n)\widehat{\mathbf{h}}(n-1) = d(n) - \widehat{y}(n), \quad (6)$$

where the vector $\widehat{\mathbf{h}}(n-1)$ contains the adaptive filter coefficients at time $n-1$ and $\widehat{y}(n)$ is the output of the adaptive filter.

III. Variable Forgetting Factor RLS Algorithm

The classical RLS algorithm can be immediately deduced from the normal equations, which are

$$\widehat{\mathbf{R}}_{\mathbf{x}}(n)\widehat{\mathbf{h}}(n) = \widehat{\mathbf{r}}_{dx}(n), \quad (7)$$

where

$$\begin{aligned}\widehat{\mathbf{R}}_{\mathbf{x}}(n) &= \sum_{i=1}^{n} \lambda^{n-i}\mathbf{x}(i)\mathbf{x}^T(i) \\ &= \lambda\widehat{\mathbf{R}}_{\mathbf{x}}(n-1) + \mathbf{x}(n)\mathbf{x}^T(n), \quad (8)\\ \widehat{\mathbf{r}}_{\mathbf{x}d}(n) &= \sum_{i=1}^{n} \lambda^{n-i}\mathbf{x}(i)d(i) \\ &= \lambda\widehat{\mathbf{r}}_{\mathbf{x}d}(n-1) + \mathbf{x}(n)d(n), \quad (9)\end{aligned}$$

and the parameter λ is the forgetting factor. According to (1), the normal equations become

$$\sum_{i=1}^{n} \lambda^{n-i}\mathbf{x}(i)\mathbf{x}^T(i)\widehat{\mathbf{h}}(n) = \sum_{i=1}^{n} \lambda^{n-i}\mathbf{x}(i)y(i) + \sum_{i=1}^{n} \lambda^{n-i}\mathbf{x}(i)v(i). \quad (10)$$

For a value of λ very close to 1 and for a large value of n, it may be assumed that

$$\frac{1}{n}\sum_{i=1}^{n} \lambda^{n-i}\mathbf{x}(i)v(i) \approx E\left[\mathbf{x}(n)v(n)\right] = 0. \quad (11)$$

Consequently, taking (10) into account,

$$\begin{aligned}\sum_{i=1}^{n} \lambda^{n-i}\mathbf{x}(i)\mathbf{x}^T(i)\widehat{\mathbf{h}}(n) &\approx \sum_{i=1}^{n} \lambda^{n-i}\mathbf{x}(i)y(i) \\ &= \sum_{i=1}^{n} \lambda^{n-i}\mathbf{x}(i)\mathbf{x}^T(i)\mathbf{h}, \quad (12)\end{aligned}$$

thus $\widehat{\mathbf{h}}(n) \approx \mathbf{h}$ and $e(n) \approx v(n)$. Now, for a small value of the forgetting factor, so that $\lambda^k \ll 1$ for $k \geq n_0$, it can be assumed that

$$\sum_{i=1}^{n} \lambda^{n-i}(\bullet) \approx \sum_{i=n-n_0+1}^{n} \lambda^{n-i}(\bullet).$$

According to the orthogonality theorem [2], [3], the normal equations become

$$\sum_{i=n-n_0+1}^{n} \lambda^{n-i}\mathbf{x}(i)e(i) = \mathbf{0}_{L\times 1},$$

where $\mathbf{0}_{L\times 1}$ denotes a vector with all its L elements equal to zero. This is a homogeneous set of L equations with n_0 unknown parameters, $e(i)$. When $n_0 < L$, this set of equations has the unique solution $e(i) = 0$, for $i = n - n_0 + 1, \ldots, n$, leading to $\widehat{y}(n) = y(n) + v(n)$. Consequently, there is a "leakage" of $v(n)$ into the output of the adaptive filter. In this situation, the signal $v(n)$ is cancelled; even if the error signal is $e(n) = 0$, this does not lead to a correct solution from the system identification point of view. A small value of λ or a high value of L intensifies this phenomenon.

Summarizing, for a low value of λ the output of the adaptive system is $\widehat{y}(n) \approx y(n) + v(n)$, while $\lambda \approx 1$ leads to $\widehat{y}(n) \approx y(n)$. Apparently, for a system identification application, a value of λ very close to 1 is desired; but in this case, even if the initial convergence rate of the algorithm is satisfactory, the tracking capabilities suffer a lot. In order to provide fast tracking, a lower value of λ is desired. On the other hand, taking into account the previous aspects, a low value of λ is not good in the steady-state. Consequently, a VFF-RLS algorithm (which could provide both fast tracking and low misadjustment) can be a more appropriate solution, in order to deal with these aspects.

Let us start the development by writing the relations that define the classical RLS algorithm:

$$\mathbf{k}(n) = \frac{\mathbf{P}(n-1)\mathbf{x}(n)}{\lambda + \mathbf{x}^T(n)\mathbf{P}(n-1)\mathbf{x}(n)}, \quad (13)$$

$$\widehat{\mathbf{h}}(n) = \widehat{\mathbf{h}}(n-1) + \mathbf{k}(n)e(n), \quad (14)$$

$$\mathbf{P}(n) = \frac{1}{\lambda}\left[\mathbf{P}(n-1) - \mathbf{k}(n)\mathbf{x}^T(n)\mathbf{P}(n-1)\right], \quad (15)$$

where $\mathbf{k}(n)$ is the Kalman gain vector, $\mathbf{P}(n)$ is the inverse of the input correlation matrix, and $e(n)$ is the a priori error signal defined in (6). The a posteriori error signal can be defined using the adaptive filter coefficients at time n, i.e.,

$$\varepsilon(n) = d(n) - \mathbf{x}^T(n)\widehat{\mathbf{h}}(n) \quad (16)$$

Using (6) and (14) in (16), it results

$$\varepsilon(n) = e(n)\left[1 - \mathbf{x}^T(n)\mathbf{k}(n)\right]. \quad (17)$$

According to the problem statement, it is desirable to recover the system noise from the error signal. Consequently, it can be imposed the condition:

$$E\left[\varepsilon^2(n)\right] = \sigma_v^2. \quad (18)$$

Using (18) in (17) and taking (13) into account, it finally results

$$E\left\{\left[1 - \frac{\theta(n)}{\lambda(n) + \theta(n)}\right]^2\right\} = \frac{\sigma_v^2}{\sigma_e^2(n)}, \quad (19)$$

where $\theta(n) = \mathbf{x}^T(n)\mathbf{P}(n-1)\mathbf{x}(n)$. In (19), we assumed that the input and error signals are uncorrelated, which is true when the adaptive filter has started to converge to the true solution. We also assumed that the forgetting factor is deterministic and time dependent. By solving the quadratic equation (19), it results a variable forgetting factor

$$\lambda(n) = \frac{\sigma_\theta(n)\sigma_v}{\sigma_e(n) - \sigma_v}, \quad (20)$$

where $E\left[\theta^2(n)\right] = \sigma_\theta^2(n)$. In practice, the variance of the error signal is estimated based on

$$\widehat{\sigma}_e^2(n) = \alpha\widehat{\sigma}_e^2(n-1) + (1-\alpha)e^2(n), \quad (21)$$

where $\alpha = 1 - 1/(KL)$, with $K \geq 1$. Also, the variance of $\theta(n)$ is evaluated in a similar manner, i.e.,

$$\widehat{\sigma}_\theta^2(n) = \alpha\widehat{\sigma}_\theta^2(n-1) + (1-\alpha)\theta^2(n). \quad (22)$$

The estimate of the noise power, $\widehat{\sigma}_v^2$ [which should be used in (20) from practical reasons], can be evaluated in different ways, e.g., [10], [19], [20].

Theoretically, $\sigma_e(n) \geq \sigma_v$ in (20). Compared to the least-mean-square algorithms [where there is the gradient noise, so that $\sigma_e(n) > \sigma_v$], the RLS algorithm with $\lambda(n) \approx 1$ leads to $\sigma_e(n) \approx \sigma_v$. In practice (since power estimates are used), several situations have to be prevented in (20). Apparently, when $\widehat{\sigma}_e(n) \leq \widehat{\sigma}_v$, it could be set $\lambda(n) = \lambda_{\max}$, where $\lambda_{\max}$ is very close or equal to 1. But this could be a limitation, because in the steady-state of the algorithm $\widehat{\sigma}_e(n)$ varies around $\widehat{\sigma}_v$. A more reasonable solution is to impose that $\lambda(n) = \lambda_{\max}$ when

$$\widehat{\sigma}_e(n) \leq \rho\widehat{\sigma}_v, \quad (23)$$

with $1 < \rho \leq 2$. Otherwise, the forgetting factor of the proposed VFF-RLS algorithm is evaluated as

$$\lambda(n) = \min\left[\frac{\widehat{\sigma}_\theta(n)\widehat{\sigma}_v}{\zeta + |\widehat{\sigma}_e(n) - \widehat{\sigma}_v|}, \lambda_{\max}\right], \quad (24)$$

where the small positive constant ζ prevents a division by zero. Before the algorithm converges or when there is an abrupt change of the system, $\widehat{\sigma}_e(n)$ is large as compared to $\widehat{\sigma}_v$; thus, the parameter $\lambda(n)$ from (24) takes low values, providing fast convergence and good tracking. When the algorithm converges to the steady-state solution, $\widehat{\sigma}_e(n) \approx \widehat{\sigma}_v$ [so that the condition (23) is fulfilled] and $\lambda(n)$ is equal to $\lambda_{\max}$, providing low misadjustment. The resulted VFF-RLS algorithm is summarized in Table I. It can be noticed that the mechanism that controls the forgetting factor is very simple and not expensive in terms of multiplications and additions.

IV. Variable Regularized RLS Algorithm

In this section, a different version of the RLS algorithm is presented, which allows us to outline the importance of the regularization parameter. Let us consider the regularized least-squares criterion:

$$J(n) = \sum_{i=0}^{n} \lambda^{n-i}\left[d(i) - \widehat{\mathbf{h}}^T(n)\mathbf{x}(i)\right]^2 + \delta\left\|\widehat{\mathbf{h}}(n)\right\|_2, \quad (25)$$

where λ is the same exponential forgetting factor and δ is the regularization parameter. From (25), the update of the regularized RLS algorithm [3] results in

$$\widehat{\mathbf{h}}(n) = \widehat{\mathbf{h}}(n-1) + \left[\widehat{\mathbf{R}}_{\mathbf{x}}(n) + \delta\mathbf{I}_L\right]^{-1}\mathbf{x}(n)e(n), \quad (26)$$

TABLE I. VFF-RLS algorithm.

Initialization:

$\mathbf{P}(0) = \gamma \mathbf{I}_L$ $(\gamma > 0)$

$\widehat{\mathbf{h}}(0) = \mathbf{0}_{L \times 1}$

$\widehat{\sigma}_e^2(0) = \widehat{\sigma}_\theta^2(0) = 0$

Parameters:

$\alpha = 1 - \frac{1}{KL}$ (with $K > 1$) weighting factor

$\lambda_{\max}$, upper bound of the forgetting factor (very close or equal to 1)

$\zeta > 0$, very small number to avoid division by zero

$\widehat{\sigma}_v^2$, system noise power (estimated)

For time index $n = 1, 2, \ldots$*:*

$e(n) = d(n) - \mathbf{x}^T(n)\widehat{\mathbf{h}}(n-1)$

$\theta(n) = \mathbf{x}^T(n)\mathbf{P}(n-1)\mathbf{x}(n)$

$\widehat{\sigma}_e^2(n) = \alpha\widehat{\sigma}_e^2(n-1) + (1-\alpha)e^2(n)$

$\widehat{\sigma}_\theta^2(n) = \alpha\widehat{\sigma}_\theta^2(n-1) + (1-\alpha)\theta^2(n)$

$$\lambda(n) = \begin{cases} \lambda_{\max}, & \text{if } \widehat{\sigma}_e(n) \le \rho\widehat{\sigma}_v \text{ (where } 1 < \rho \le 2) \\ \min\left[\frac{\widehat{\sigma}_\theta(n)\widehat{\sigma}_v}{\zeta + |\widehat{\sigma}_e(n) - \widehat{\sigma}_v|}, \lambda_{\max}\right], & \text{otherwise} \end{cases}$$

$$\mathbf{k}(n) = \frac{\mathbf{P}(n-1)\mathbf{x}(n)}{\lambda(n) + \theta(n)}$$

$\widehat{\mathbf{h}}(n) = \widehat{\mathbf{h}}(n-1) + \mathbf{k}(n)e(n)$

$$\mathbf{P}(n) = \frac{1}{\lambda(n)}\left[\mathbf{P}(n-1) - \mathbf{k}(n)\mathbf{x}^T(n)\mathbf{P}(n-1)\right]$$

where the matrix $\widehat{\mathbf{R}}_{\mathbf{x}}(n)$ from (8) is an estimate of the correlation matrix of $\mathbf{x}(n)$ at time n, $\mathbf{I}_L$ is the identity matrix of size $L \times L$, and $e(n)$ is the a priori error signal defined in (6). We will assume that the matrix $\widehat{\mathbf{R}}_{\mathbf{x}}(n)$ has full rank, although it can be very ill conditioned. As a result, if there is no noise, regularization is not really required; however, the more the noise, the larger should be the value of δ.

Summarizing, the regularized RLS algorithm is defined by the relations (6), (8), and (26). In the following, we present one reasonable way to find the regularization parameter δ. It can be noticed that the update equation of the regularized RLS can be rewritten as [13]

$$\widehat{\mathbf{h}}(n) = \mathbf{Q}(n)\widehat{\mathbf{h}}(n-1) + \widetilde{\mathbf{h}}(n), \tag{27}$$

where

$$\mathbf{Q}(n) = \mathbf{I}_L - \left[\widehat{\mathbf{R}}_{\mathbf{x}}(n) + \delta\mathbf{I}_L\right]^{-1}\mathbf{x}(n)\mathbf{x}^T(n) \tag{28}$$

and

$$\widetilde{\mathbf{h}}(n) = \left[\widehat{\mathbf{R}}_{\mathbf{x}}(n) + \delta\mathbf{I}_L\right]^{-1}\mathbf{x}(n)d(n) \tag{29}$$

is the correctiveness component of the algorithm, which depends on the new observation $d(n)$. In this context, we can notice that $\mathbf{Q}(n)$ does not depend on the noise signal and $\mathbf{Q}(n)\widehat{\mathbf{h}}(n-1)$ in (27) can be seen as a good initialization of the adaptive filter. In fact, (29) is the solution of the noisy linear system of L equations:

$$\left[\widehat{\mathbf{R}}_{\mathbf{x}}(n) + \delta\mathbf{I}_L\right]\widetilde{\mathbf{h}}(n) = \mathbf{x}(n)d(n). \tag{30}$$

Let us define

$$\widetilde{e}(n) = d(n) - \widetilde{\mathbf{h}}^T(n)\mathbf{x}(n), \tag{31}$$

the error signal between the desired signal and the estimated signal obtained from the filter optimized in (29). Consequently, we could find δ in such a way that the expected value of $\widetilde{e}^2(n)$ is equal to the variance of the noise, i.e.,

$$E\left[\widetilde{e}^2(n)\right] = \sigma_v^2. \tag{32}$$

This is reasonable if we want to attenuate the effects of the noise in the estimator $\widetilde{\mathbf{h}}(n)$.

For the sake of simplicity, let us assume that $x(n)$ is stationary and white. Apparently, this assumption is quite restrictive, even if it was widely used in many developments in the context of adaptive filtering [2], [3]. However, the resulting VR-RLS algorithm will still use the full matrix $\widehat{\mathbf{R}}_{\mathbf{x}}(n)$ and, consequently, it will inherit the good performance feature of the RLS family in case of correlated inputs. In this case and for n large enough (also considering that the forgetting factor λ is on the order of $1 - 1/L$), we have

$$\begin{aligned}\left[\widehat{\mathbf{R}}_{\mathbf{x}}(n) + \delta\mathbf{I}_L\right] &\approx \left[\frac{\sigma_x^2}{1-\lambda} + \delta\right]\mathbf{I}_L \\ &\approx \left[L\sigma_x^2 + \delta\right]\mathbf{I}_L\end{aligned} \tag{33}$$

and $\mathbf{x}^T(n)\mathbf{x}(n) \approx L\sigma_x^2$, where $\sigma_x^2 = E\left[x^2(n)\right]$ is the variance of the input signal. Next, from (1), we can define the echo-to-noise ratio (ENR) as

$$\text{ENR} = \frac{\sigma_y^2}{\sigma_v^2}, \tag{34}$$

where $\sigma_y^2 = E\left[y^2(n)\right]$ is the variance of $y(n)$. Developing (32) and based on the previous approximations, we obtain the quadratic equation:

$$\delta^2 - 2\frac{L\sigma_x^2}{\text{ENR}}\delta - \frac{\left(L\sigma_x^2\right)^2}{\text{ENR}} = 0, \tag{35}$$

with the obvious solution:

$$\begin{aligned}\delta &= \frac{L\left(1 + \sqrt{1 + \text{ENR}}\right)}{\text{ENR}}\sigma_x^2 \\ &= \beta\sigma_x^2,\end{aligned} \tag{36}$$

where

$$\beta = \frac{L\left(1 + \sqrt{1 + \text{ENR}}\right)}{\text{ENR}} \tag{37}$$

is the normalized regularization parameter of the RLS algorithm.

As we can notice from (36), the regularization parameter δ depends on three elements, i.e., the length of the adaptive filter, the variance of the input signal, and the ENR. In most applications, the first two elements (L and σ_x^2) are known, while the ENR can be estimated. Using a proper evaluation of the ENR, the algorithm should own good robustness features against the additive noise.

Let us assume that the adaptive filter has converged to a certain degree, so that we can use the approximation

$$y(n) \approx \widehat{y}(n). \tag{38}$$

Hence,

$$\sigma_y^2 \approx \sigma_{\widehat{y}}^2, \tag{39}$$

where $\sigma_{\widehat{y}}^2 = E\left[\widehat{y}^2(n)\right]$. Since the output of the unknown system and the noise can be considered uncorrelated, (1) can be expressed in terms of power estimates as

$$\sigma_d^2 = \sigma_y^2 + \sigma_v^2, \tag{40}$$

where $\sigma_d^2 = E\left[d^2(n)\right]$. Using (39) in (40), we obtain

$$\sigma_v^2 \approx \sigma_d^2 - \sigma_{\widehat{y}}^2. \tag{41}$$

The power estimates can be evaluated in a recursive manner [similar to (21) and (22)] as

$$\widehat{\sigma}_d^2(n) = \alpha\widehat{\sigma}_d^2(n-1) + (1-\alpha)d^2(n), \tag{42}$$

$$\widehat{\sigma}_{\widehat{y}}^2(n) = \alpha\widehat{\sigma}_{\widehat{y}}^2(n-1) + (1-\alpha)\widehat{y}^2(n). \tag{43}$$

Therefore, based on (39) and (41), an estimation of the ENR is obtained as

$$\widehat{\text{ENR}}(n) = \frac{\widehat{\sigma}_{\widehat{y}}^2(n)}{\left|\widehat{\sigma}_d^2(n) - \widehat{\sigma}_{\widehat{y}}^2(n)\right|}, \tag{44}$$

so that the variable regularization parameter results in

$$\begin{aligned}\delta(n) &= \frac{L\left[1+\sqrt{1+\widehat{\text{ENR}}(n)}\right]}{\widehat{\text{ENR}}(n)}\sigma_x^2 \\ &= \beta(n)\sigma_x^2,\end{aligned} \tag{45}$$

where

$$\beta(n) = \frac{L\left[1+\sqrt{1+\widehat{\text{ENR}}(n)}\right]}{\widehat{\text{ENR}}(n)} \tag{46}$$

is the variable normalized regularization parameter. Consequently, based on (45), we obtain a variable-regularized RLS (VR-RLS) algorithm, with the update:

$$\widehat{\mathbf{h}}(n) = \widehat{\mathbf{h}}(n-1) + \left[\widehat{\mathbf{R}}_{\mathbf{x}}(n) + \delta(n)\mathbf{I}_L\right]^{-1}\mathbf{x}(n)e(n), \tag{47}$$

where $\widehat{\mathbf{R}}_{\mathbf{x}}(n)$ is recursively evaluated according to (8) and $\delta(n)$ is computed based on (42)–(45).

At this point, some practical issues should be outlined. The absolute values in (44) prevent any minor deviations (due to the use of power estimates) from the true values, which can make the denominator negative. The VR-RLS is a non-parametric algorithm, since all the parameters in (44) are available. Also, good robustness against the additive noise variations is expected. The main drawback is due to the approximation in (39). This assumption will be biased in the initial convergence phase or when there is a change of the unknown system. Concerning the initial convergence, we can use a constant regularization parameter δ in the first steps of the algorithm (e.g., in the first L iterations).

However, the VR-RLS algorithm faces two main challenges in terms of computational complexity. The first one is the update of the matrix $\widehat{\mathbf{R}}_{\mathbf{x}}(n)$ from (8), while the second issue is related to the evaluation of the last term from the right-hand side of (47), which contains both the matrix inversion and the product with the input vector.

The complexity of (8) can be greatly reduced taking into account that the vector $\mathbf{x}(n)$ has the time shift property [see (2)] and the matrix $\widehat{\mathbf{R}}_{\mathbf{x}}(n)$ is symmetric. Thus, only the first column of this matrix has to be computed, i.e.,

$$\widehat{\mathbf{R}}_{\mathbf{x}}^{(1)}(n) = \lambda\widehat{\mathbf{R}}_{\mathbf{x}}^{(1)}(n-1) + \mathbf{x}(n)x(n), \tag{48}$$

since the lower-right $(L-1)\times(L-1)$ block of $\widehat{\mathbf{R}}_{\mathbf{x}}(n)$ can be obtained by copying the $(L-1)\times(L-1)$ upper-left block of the matrix $\widehat{\mathbf{R}}_{\mathbf{x}}(n-1)$.

The evaluation of the last term from the right-hand side of (47) is more challenging. In fact, the basic problem can be interpreted in terms of solving the normal equations [3]:

$$\mathbf{R}(n)\widehat{\mathbf{h}}(n) = \widehat{\mathbf{r}}_{\mathbf{x}d}(n), \tag{49}$$

where

$$\mathbf{R}(n) = \widehat{\mathbf{R}}_{\mathbf{x}}(n) + \delta(n)\mathbf{I}_L \tag{50}$$

and $\widehat{\mathbf{r}}_{\mathbf{x}d}(n)$ is defined in (9). As an alternative to the classical approaches [2], [3], the normal equations (49) can be recursively solved using the dichotomous coordinate descent (DCD) method [16]. The basic idea is to express the problem in terms of auxiliary normal equations with respect to increments of the filter weights [17]. In our case, we need to solve

$$\mathbf{R}(n)\triangle\widehat{\mathbf{h}}(n) = \mathbf{p}(n), \tag{51}$$

where $\triangle\widehat{\mathbf{h}}(n)$ is the increment of the filter weights and

$$\mathbf{p}(n) = \lambda\mathbf{r}(n-1) + \mathbf{x}(n)e(n), \tag{52}$$

with $\mathbf{r}(n)$ representing the so-called residual vector associated to the solution [17]. Consequently, following the previous development and the steps presented in [17], the low-complexity version of the proposed VR-RLS algorithm, namely VR-RLS-DCD, is summarized in Table II, where step 6 involves the DCD iterations.

The DCD algorithm [16] is based on coordinate descent iterations with a power of two variable step-size, q. It does not need multiplications or divisions (these operations are simply replaced by bit-shifts), but only additions, so that it is well suited for hardware implementation. In our case, the auxiliary normal equations from step 6 are solved by using the DCD with a leading element [17]. An insightful analysis of this algorithm can be found in [17]. Also, detailed implementation aspects are discussed in [18].

Here, we briefly outline some of the important parameters of the DCD algorithm (using the notation from [17]). First, the parameters H and M_{b} represent the maximum amplitude expected for the values of $\triangle\widehat{\mathbf{h}}(n)$, respectively the number of bits used for their representation. If the value of H is chosen accordingly, the values of the step-size q correspond to the powers of 2 and are associated with the bits comprising the binary representation of each computed value in the solution vector. In this case, any multiplication with q can be replaced by a bit-shift. Second, the parameter N_{u} represents the maximum number of allowed (or "successful") iterations performed for $\triangle\widehat{\mathbf{h}}(n)$ [17]; in practice $N_{\text{u}} \ll L$. The arithmetic complexity of the DCD algorithm is proportional to LN_{u} but using only additions. Consequently, the complexity associated to the matrix inversion is greatly reduced as compared to the classical method [which requires $O(L^3)$ operations] and

TABLE II. VR-RLS-DCD algorithm.

Initialization: $\widehat{\mathbf{h}}(0) = \mathbf{0}$, $\mathbf{r}(0) = \mathbf{0}$, $\widehat{\mathbf{R}}_{\mathbf{x}}(0) = \mathbf{0}_L$

For $n = 1, 2, \ldots$

Step 1: $\widehat{\mathbf{R}}_{\mathbf{x}}(n) = \lambda\widehat{\mathbf{R}}_{\mathbf{x}}(n-1) + \mathbf{x}(n)\mathbf{x}^T(n)$ [using (48)]

Step 2: Compute $\delta(n)$ based on (42)–(45)

Step 3: $\mathbf{R}(n) = \widehat{\mathbf{R}}_{\mathbf{x}}(n) + \delta(n)\mathbf{I}_L$

Step 4: $e(n) = d(n) - \widehat{\mathbf{h}}^T(n-1)\mathbf{x}(n)$

Step 5: $\mathbf{p}(n) = \lambda\mathbf{r}(n-1) + \mathbf{x}(n)e(n)$

Step 6: $\mathbf{R}(n)\Delta\widehat{\mathbf{h}}(n) = \mathbf{p}(n) \Rightarrow \Delta\widehat{\mathbf{h}}(n),\ \mathbf{r}(n)$ (to be solved with DCD iterations [17])

Step 7: $\widehat{\mathbf{h}}(n) = \widehat{\mathbf{h}}(n-1) + \Delta\widehat{\mathbf{h}}(n)$

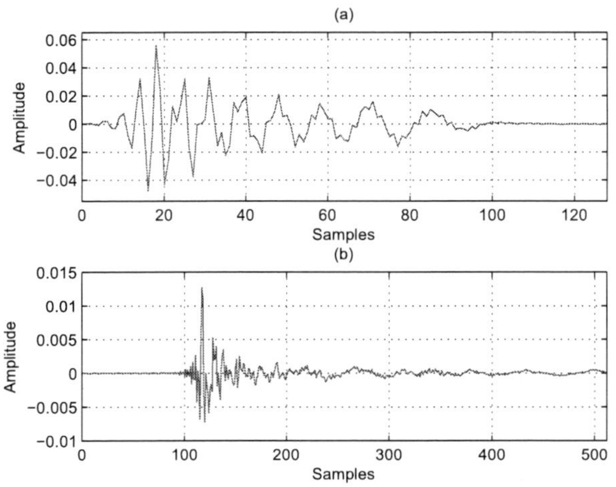

Figure 2. Impulse responses used in simulations.

even to the regular RLS algorithm [2], [3] [which is based on the matrix inversion lemma and needs $O(L^2)$ operations]. Therefore, the DCD-based algorithms are very appealing for real-world applications.

Nevertheless, the RLS-DCD algorithm proposed in [17] uses a constant regularization for $\widehat{\mathbf{R}}_{\mathbf{x}}(0)$, but the influence of this parameter is negligible due to the forgetting factor in the update of the matrix $\widehat{\mathbf{R}}_{\mathbf{x}}(n)$. On the other hand, using a proper estimation of the regularization parameter within the algorithm (i.e., steps 2 and 3 in Table II), the robustness against additive noise can be improved. Thus, the proposed VR-RLS-DCD algorithm owns this robustness feature, but also the low-complexity advantage inherited from the DCD method.

V. Simulation Results

First, let us consider a network echo cancellation scenario, in the framework of G168 Recommendation [21]. The echo path is depicted in Figure 2(a); it is the fourth impulse response (of length $L = 128$) from the above recommendation. The sampling rate is 8 kHz. All adaptive filters used in the experiments have the same length as the echo path. The far-end signal (i.e., the input signal) is a speech signal. The output

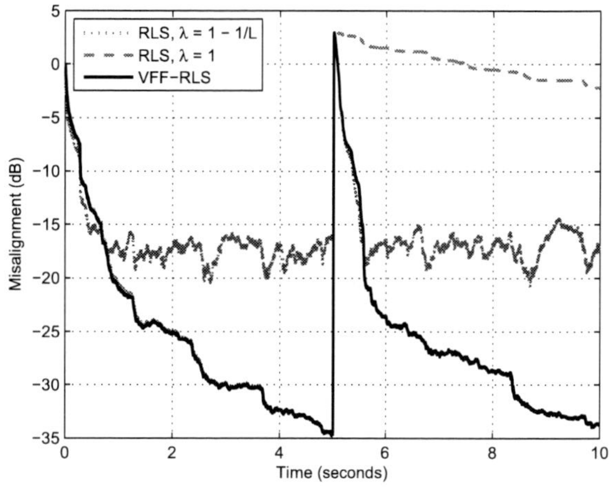

Figure 3. Misalignment of the RLS algorithm (using different constant values of the forgetting factor) and the VFF-RLS algorithm. The input signal is speech, $L = 128$, and ENR = 20 dB. Echo path changes at time 5 seconds.

of the echo path is corrupted by an independent white Gaussian noise with 20 dB ENR. An echo path change scenario is some experiments (in order to evaluate the tracking capabilities of the algorithms), by shifting the impulse response to the right by 8 samples in the middle of simulation. The performance measure is the normalized misalignment (in dB) evaluated as

$$\text{Mis}(n) = 20\log_{10}\frac{\left\|\mathbf{h}(n) - \widehat{\mathbf{h}}(n)\right\|_2}{\|\mathbf{h}(n)\|_2}. \tag{53}$$

In the first experiment, the performance of the VFF-RLS algorithm (presented in Section III) is evaluated, as compared to the classical RLS algorithm defined in (13)–(15), which uses different constant values of the forgetting factor. A single-talk case is considered and the echo path changes in the middle of simulation. It can be noticed in Figure 3 that the VFF-RLS algorithm achieves the same initial misalignment as the RLS with its maximum forgetting factor, but it tracks as fast as the RLS with the smaller forgetting factor. As expected, the classical RLS algorithm using constant forgetting factors has to compromise between these performance criteria, i.e., the larger the value of λ, the better the misalignment level but worse the tracking capability.

Next, the performance of the VR-RLS algorithm (from Section IV) is investigated, as compared to the regularized RLS algorithm defined by the update (26), using different constant values of the regularization parameter. Based on (37), we can determine the values of the optimal normalized regularization parameter of the RLS algorithm for different cases; for example, let us consider two values of the ENR, i.e., 20 dB (the true one) and 0 dB. Using appropriate notation, we obtain $\beta_{20} = 14.14$ and $\beta_0 = 309.01$, respectively. Next, we compare the regularized RLS algorithm using these constant regularization parameters with the VR-RLS algorithm. The constant forgetting factor is set to $\lambda = 1 - 1/(3L)$ for all the algorithms.

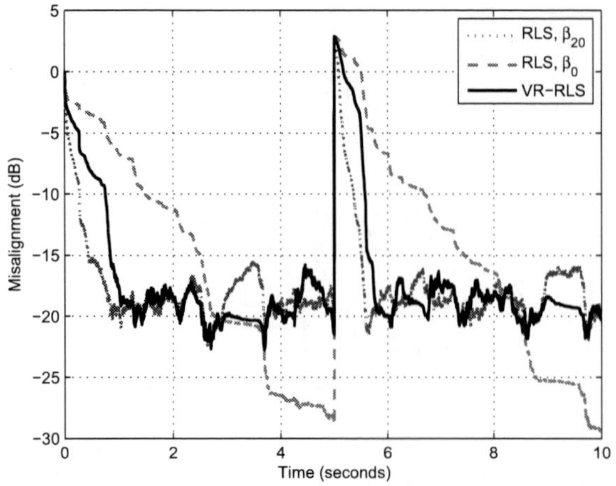

Figure 4. Misalignment of the regularized RLS algorithm (using different constant values of the regularization parameter) and the VR-RLS algorithm. The input signal is speech, $L = 128$, and ENR = 20 dB. Echo path changes at time 5 seconds.

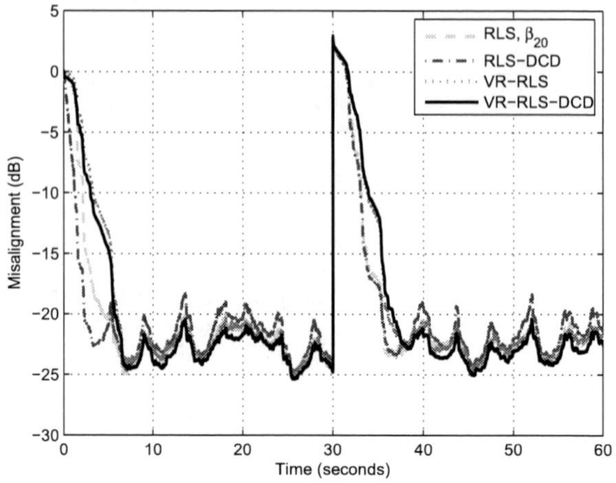

Figure 6. Misalignment of the regularized RLS (using β_{20}), RLS-DCD, VR-RLS, and VR-RLS-DCD algorithms. The input signal is speech, $L = 512$, and ENR = 20 dB. Echo path changes at time 30 seconds.

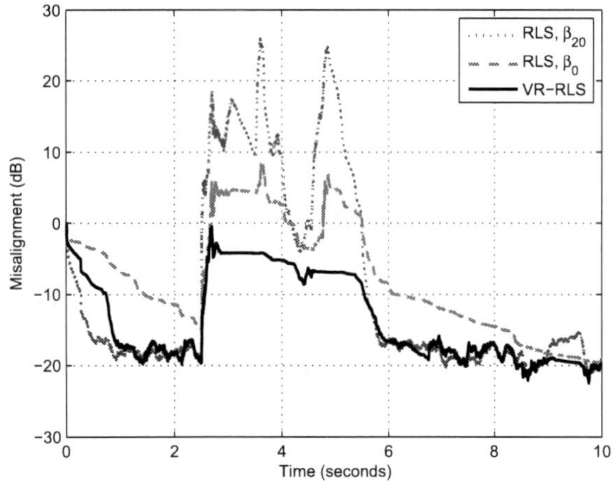

Figure 5. Misalignment of the regularized RLS algorithm (using different constant values of the regularization parameter) and the VR-RLS algorithm. The input signal is speech, $L = 128$, and ENR = 20 dB. Near-end speech appears between time 2.5 and 5 seconds (double-talk scenario).

In Figure 4, a single-talk scenario is considered and an echo path change is introduced in the middle of the simulation. It can be noticed that the VR-RLS algorithm behaves similarly to the RLS algorithm using the constant parameter β_{20}, which is associated to the value of the true ENR. Also, it can be noticed that a larger value of the normalized regularization parameter (β_0) improves the misalignment but affects the convergence rate and tracking.

In Figure 5, a double-talk scenario [4], [5] is considered. The near-end speech appears between time 2.5 and 5 seconds, so that the signal $v(n)$ is now non-stationary, since it contains both noise and speech. It is clear that the VR-RLS algorithm is more robust in this case as compared to the regularized RLS using constant values of β. It should be outlined that we do not use any double-talk detector (DTD) [4], [5] with the VR-RLS algorithm. Therefore, the VR-RLS algorithm owns good robustness features against double-talk, which is an important gain in practice.

The second set of simulations is performed in the context of acoustic echo cancellation [4], [5]. The unknown system, i.e., the echo path, is a measured acoustic impulse response depicted in Figure 2(b). It has 512 coefficients and the same length is used for the adaptive filter ($L = 512$). The output of the echo path is corrupted by a white Gaussian noise with different ENRs, i.e., 20 dB, 10 dB, and 0 dB. Based on (37), we can determine the values of the optimal normalized regularization parameter in these cases. Using appropriate notation, we obtain $\beta_{20} = 56.57$, $\beta_{10} = 221.01$, and $\beta_0 = 1236.07$, respectively. In simulations, we compare the regularized RLS algorithm using these constant regularization parameters with the proposed VR-RLS and VR-RLS-DCD algorithms. Also, the RLS-DCD algorithm [17] is included for comparison, using $N_u = 8$, $M_b = 16$, and $H = 1$ (the same parameters are used in the VR-RLS-DCD algorithm). The forgetting factor is set to $\lambda = 1 - 1/(16L)$ for all the algorithms.

In the first set of experiments, the value of the ENR is set to 20 dB. In Figure 6, an echo path change scenario is simulated in the middle of the experiment, by shifting the impulse response to the right by 25 samples. First, it can be noticed that the VR-RLS and VR-RLS-DCD algorithms behave very similarly and are close to the regularized RLS algorithm using the constant (optimal) parameter β_{20}, which is associated to the value of the ENR. As expected, there is an inherent delay in the initial convergence rate and tracking reaction of the variable-regularized algorithms (as compared to the RLS-DCD algorithm), due to the approximation in (39). In Figure 7, a double-talk scenario is considered; the near-end speech appears between time 27 and 30 seconds. It is clear that the VR-RLS and VR-RLS-DCD algorithms are more robust in

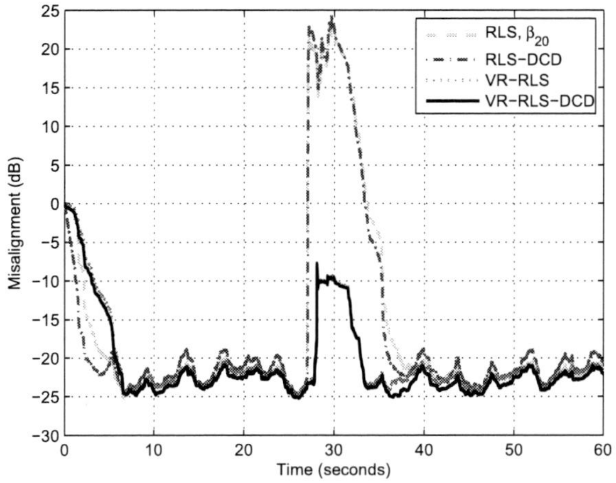

Figure 7. Misalignment of the regularized RLS (using β_{20}), RLS-DCD, VR-RLS, and VR-RLS-DCD algorithms. The input signal is speech, $L = 512$, and ENR = 20 dB. Near-end speech appears between time 27 and 30 seconds (double-talk scenario).

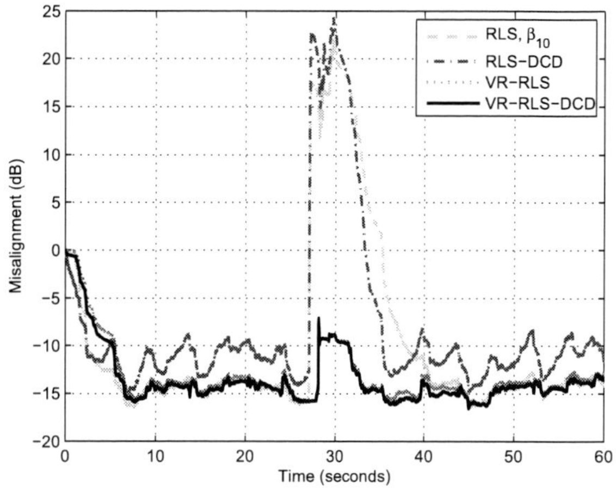

Figure 9. Misalignment of the regularized RLS (using β_{10}), RLS-DCD, VR-RLS, and VR-RLS-DCD algorithms. The input signal is speech, $L = 512$, and ENR = 10 dB. Near-end speech appears between time 27 and 30 seconds (double-talk scenario).

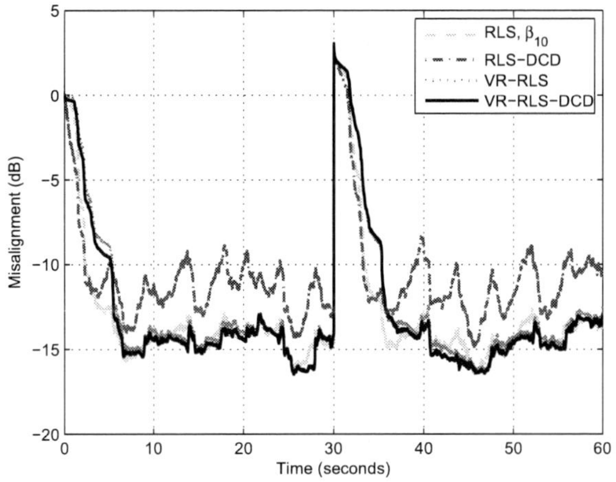

Figure 8. Misalignment of the regularized RLS (using β_{10}), RLS-DCD, VR-RLS, and VR-RLS-DCD algorithms. The input signal is speech, $L = 512$, and ENR = 10 dB. Echo path changes at time 30 seconds.

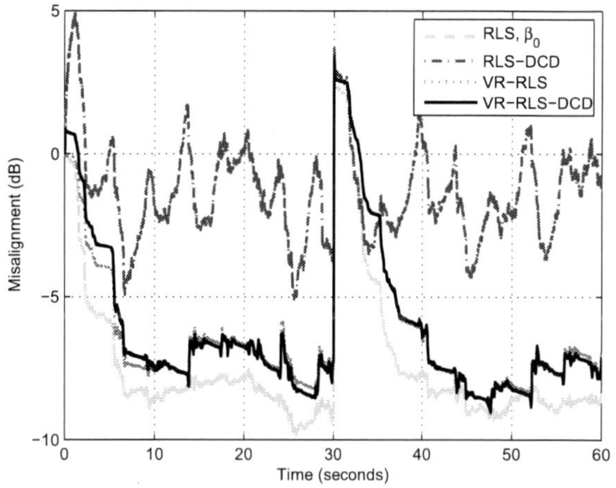

Figure 10. Misalignment of the regularized RLS (using β_0), RLS-DCD, VR-RLS, and VR-RLS-DCD algorithms. The input signal is speech, $L = 512$, and ENR = 0 dB. Echo path changes at time 30 seconds.

this case, since the estimated ENR from (44) also includes the contribution of the near-end signal.

In the second set of experiments, we select a lower ENR value, i.e., 10 dB. In this case, the importance of regularization becomes more apparent. As we can see from Figure 8, the VR-RLS and VR-RLS-DCD algorithms behave similarly to the regularized RLS using the constant (optimal) parameter β_{10}, and outperform the RLS-DCD algorithm (in terms of misalignment). Also, as we can notice in Figure 9, the variable-regularized algorithms are much more robust to double-talk, as compared to their counterparts.

Finally, in the last set of experiments, we consider ENR = 0 dB. As expected, according to the results in Figure 10, the VR-RLS and VR-RLS-DCD algorithms behave now similarly to the regularized RLS using the constant (optimal) parameter β_0, and are much better as compared to the RLS-DCD algorithm. Besides, according to Figure 11, the variable-regularized algorithms outperform by far their counterparts in terms of double-talk robustness.

VI. Conclusions

The RLS algorithms are very appealing due to their fast convergence rate. In this paper, we have focused on the main parameters that control the performance of these algorithms, i.e., the forgetting factor and the regularization term. In order to achieve a better compromise between the performance

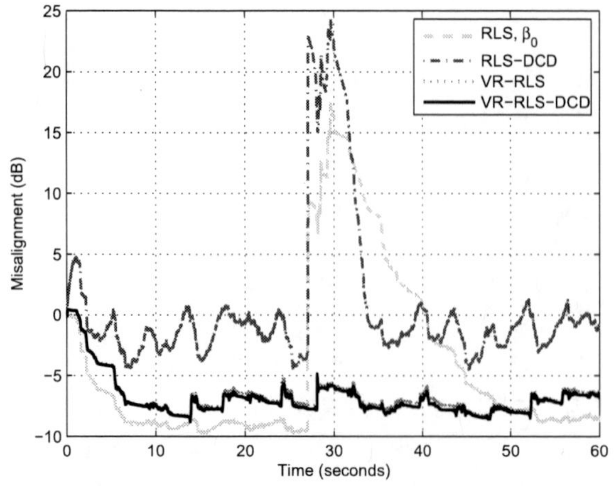

Figure 11. Misalignment of the regularized RLS (using β_0), RLS-DCD, VR-RLS, and VR-RLS-DCD algorithms. The input signal is speech, $L = 512$, and ENR = 0 dB. Near-end speech appears between time 27 and 30 seconds (double-talk scenario).

criteria (i.e., convergence and tracking versus misadjustment and robustness), these parameters could be controlled. In this context, the solutions presented in Sections III and IV led to the VFF-RLS and VR-RLS algorithms, respectively. Also, in Section IV, a low-complexity version of the VR-RLS algorithm was derived, based on the DCD method, namely the VR-RLS-DCD.

The first set of experiments was performed in the context of network echo cancellation. According to the simulation results, the VFF-RLS and VR-RLS algorithms perform very well as compared to their classical counterparts (which use constant values of the key parameters).

The second set of simulations was performed in an acoustic echo cancellation scenario. The results indicate that the VR-RLS and VR-RLS-DCD algorithms own good robustness features against the near-end signal. In other words, the robustness of the algorithm against ENR variations (e.g., like double-talk) can be controlled in terms of the regularization parameter. Moreover, due to its low-complexity feature, the VR-RLS-DCD algorithm could be a reliable candidates for real-world echo cancellation applications.

ACKNOWLEDGMENT

This work was supported by European Space Agency under Grant no. 4000121222/17/NL/CBi and University Politehnica of Bucharest under Grant no. 18/05.10.2017.

REFERENCES

[1] C. Elisei-Iliescu and C. Paleologu, "Recursive least-squares algorithms for echo cancellation – An overview and open issues," in *Proc. ICN*, 2017, pp. 87–91.

[2] S. Haykin, *Adaptive Filter Theory*. Fourth Edition, Upper Saddle River, NJ: Prentice-Hall, 2002.

[3] A. H. Sayed, *Adaptive Filters*. New York, NY: Wiley, 2008.

[4] J. Benesty, T. Gaensler, D. R. Morgan, M. M. Sondhi, and S. L. Gay, *Advances in Network and Acoustic Echo Cancellation*. Berlin, Germany: Springer-Verlag, 2001.

[5] C. Paleologu, J. Benesty, and S. Ciochină, *Sparse Adaptive Filters for Echo Cancellation*. Morgan & Claypool Publishers, 2010.

[6] S. Ciochină, C. Paleologu, J. Benesty, and A. A. Enescu, "On the influence of the forgetting factor of the RLS adaptive filter in system identification," in *Proc. IEEE ISSCS*, 2009, pp. 205–208.

[7] S. Ciochină, C. Paleologu, and A. A. Enescu, "On the behaviour of RLS adaptive algorithm in fixed-point implementation," in *Proc. IEEE ISSCS*, 2003, pp. 57–60.

[8] S. Song, J. S. Lim, S. J. Baek, and K. M. Sung, "Gauss Newton variable forgetting factor recursive least squares for time varying parameter tracking," *Electronics Lett.*, vol. 36, pp. 988–990, May 2000.

[9] S.-H. Leung and C. F. So, "Gradient-based variable forgetting factor RLS algorithm in time-varying environments," *IEEE Trans. Signal Processing*, vol. 53, pp. 3141–3150, Aug. 2005.

[10] C. Paleologu, J. Benesty, and S. Ciochină, "A robust variable forgetting factor recursive least-squares algorithm for system identification," *IEEE Signal Processing Lett.*, vol. 15, pp. 597–600, 2008.

[11] Y. J. Chu and S. C. Chan, "A new local polynomial modeling-based variable forgetting factor RLS algorithm and its acoustic applications," *IEEE/ACM Trans. Audio, Speech, Language Processing*, vol. 23, pp. 2059–2069, Nov. 2015.

[12] P. C. Hansen, *Rank-Deficient and Discrete Ill-Posed Problems: Numerical Aspects of Linear Inversion*. Philadelphia, PA: SIAM, 1998.

[13] J. Benesty, C. Paleologu, and S. Ciochină, "Regularization of the RLS algorithm," *IEICE Trans. Fundamentals*, vol. E94-A, pp. 1628–1629, Aug. 2011.

[14] Y. V. Zakharov and V. H. Nascimento, "Sparse sliding-window RLS adaptive filter with dynamic regularization," in *Proc. EUSIPCO*, 2016, pp. 145–149.

[15] C. Elisei-Iliescu, C. Stanciu, C. Paleologu, J. Benesty, C. Anghel, and S. Ciochină, "Robust variable regularized RLS algorithms," in *Proc. IEEE HSCMA*, 2017, pp. 171–175.

[16] Y. V. Zakharov and T. C. Tozer, "Multiplication-free iterative algorithm for LS problem," *IEE Electronics Lett.*, vol. 40, pp. 567–569, Apr. 2004.

[17] Y. V. Zakharov, G. P. White, and J. Liu, "Low-complexity RLS algorithms using dichotomous coordinate descent iterations," *IEEE Trans. Signal Processing*, vol. 56, pp. 3150–3161, July 2008.

[18] J. Liu, Y. V. Zakharov, and B. Weaver, "Architecture and FPGA design of dichotomous coordinate descent algorithms," *IEEE Trans. Circuits and Systems I: Regular Papers*, vol. 56, pp. 2425–2438, Nov. 2009.

[19] C. Paleologu, S. Ciochină, and J. Benesty, "Variable step-size NLMS algorithm for under-modeling acoustic echo cancellation," *IEEE Signal Processing Lett.*, vol. 15, pp. 5–8, 2008.

[20] M. A. Iqbal and S. L. Grant, "Novel variable step size NLMS algorithms for echo cancellation," in *Proc. IEEE ICASSP*, 2008, pp. 241–244.

[21] *Digital Network Echo Cancellers*, ITU-T Rec. G.168, 2002.

Heterogeneous Migration Paths to High Bandwidth Home Connections - a Computational Approach

Frank Phillipson
TNO,
The Hague, The Netherlands
Email: frank.phillipson@tno.nl

Suzanne de Hoog
Delft University of Technology,
Delft, The Netherlands
Email: suzannedehoog@gmail.com

Theresia van Essen
Delft University of Technology,
Delft, The Netherlands
Email: j.t.vanessen@tudelft.nl

***Abstract*—Most telecom operators have to plan the migration of their existing copper networks to full or hybrid fibre networks, to offer their clients the bandwidth they require. This paper proposes methods to optimise this migration path, heterogeneously per central office area, using geometric models as input. The methods result in a detailed migration path that meets a required bandwidth coverage, installation capacity and/or budget constraint. To solve the optimisation problem in an efficient way, both a problem-based solution method and a simulated annealing approach are tested for scalability of the problem solving. As the data used for the migration path optimisation is in practice hard to gather, the use of geometric modelling is proposed. This modelling approach leads to the optimal migrating path, estimating the total initial investment of a migration step using only two simple parameters per Central Office area.**

***Index Terms*—Access networks; Migration Optimisation; Geometric Models.**

I. Introduction

Broadband internet is becoming a common utility service. Using connected electronic devices in and outside our homes, we use more and more data and demand connectivity 24/7. The used services are asking more bandwidth due to the integration of video into numerous services. Most of the home connections, access networks and systems offered by telecom operators are not prepared for this, because incumbent operators mostly use copper telecommunication networks offering ADSL (Asymmetric Digital Subscriber Line) or VDSL (Very High Bitrate Digital Subscriber Line) techniques as service . Digital subscriber line (DSL) is a family of technologies used to transmit digital data over copper lines. The operators have to make the costly step to Fibre to the Cabinet (FttCab), Fibre to the Curb (FttCurb) or, even more costly, the full step to Fibre to the Home (FttH), Fibre near the home (FntH) or Fibre to the Air (FttA). Bringing the network to the next step we call a migration step, as introduced in [1]. An example of FntH and FttA is a wireless home connection or a Hybrid fibre-wireless (FiWi) access network, where fibre is brought to a location near the homes, e.g., street lights [2], and the remaining distance is covered by WiFi or WiMax [3] [4]. However, in many countries, the roll out of all these fibre connections will take too long to compete with the cable TV operators active in those countries, who can offer the required bandwidth using DOCSIS, Data Over Cable Service Interface Specification, on their Hybrid Fibre Coaxial (HFC) networks at this moment. This urges the operators to take intermediate steps, such as FttCurb, and to think about the optimal migration strategy.

The incumbent telecom operators can choose between various topology types to offer. In this paper, the term 'topology' is used for the way the physical fibres and equipment are designed. It comprises the question where to deploy fibres, where to deploy copper and where the active or passive equipment should be placed. Each topology can run multiple technologies. For example, in the 'Full Copper' topology, the operator offers the services from the Central Office. The operator still can choose to offer ADSL or VDSL (containing here all VDSL based technologies such as VDSL, VDSL2, Vectored VDSL2, Vplus etcetera) technology for this service. In this paper, four topology types are distinguished (see Fig. 1):

1) Full Copper: services are offered from the Central Office (CO) over a copper (twisted pair) cable, using DSL techniques.
2) Fibre to the Cabinet (FttCab): the fibre connection is extended to the cabinet. From the cabinet, the services are offered over the copper cable, using DSL or G.Fast techniques.
3) Hybrid Fibre to the Home (Hybrid FttH): services are offered from a Hybrid FttH Node, which is connected by fibre, close to the customer premises, in the street, or in the building. Here again, VDSL and G.Fast techniques can be offered.
4) Full Fibre to the Home (Full FttH): the fibre connection is brought up to the customer premises.

If the operator starts with a Full Copper topology in a certain area, he has to decide on the next step: bringing the fibre connection all the way to the customers or use an intermediate step, where he brings the fibre closer to the customer, e.g., FttCab. Note that the operator can have a heterogeneous network, where in different areas a different topology is deployed and a different starting position for

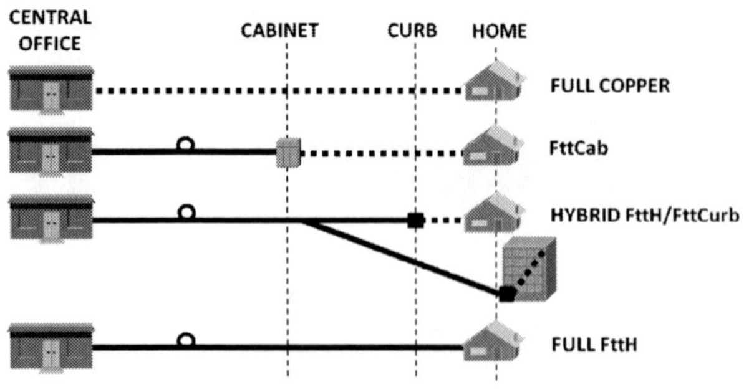

Figure 1. Four topologies.

migration is found. To make in a certain area the decision mentioned before, the operator has to look at the pros and cons of all the options. For example, the deployment of FttCab can be much faster than Full FttH, as it requires less digging, the last part of the connection from the street to the access node in the house does not have to be installed, and it meets the growing bandwidth demand for now and the near future. If, in future, this demand exceeds the supplied bandwidth, the remaining part to the residence can be connected with Full Fibre or using Hybrid Fibre as extra intermediate step. If the demand does not exceed the supplied bandwidth, for example, it reaches some level of saturation, no further migration is needed, saving a lot of investments. However, when Full FttH is the expected final solution, using intermediate steps would incur investment and installation costs that might be lost and not reused.

This decision can be made on strategic level, for a bigger region or a whole country, or more tactical/operational within a region. In this paper, the option that the operator can decide per Central Office area which topology or technology to offer is considered. This means that the operator is offering broadband as a service, instead of offering for example FttH as a service. If an operator decides on the topology or technique per Central Office area and per period (e.g., year), he can develop a detailed migration path that meets, for example, a bandwidth coverage in a larger area. This option is called a heterogeneous optimal migration path in contrast to a homogeneous optimal migration path, where one migration path is used for all Central Office areas within the bigger region. This is the first part where the novelty of this paper is in. Up to now, other papers only considered uniform migration paths or single migration paths.

The second part where this paper is novel, is the data used for the migration path optimisation. To estimate the costs of a topology and the migration from one topology to another topology, for each migration an optimal planning should be made. We propose to solve this by using the geometric modelling, as presented in [5] [6].

Concluding, in this paper, we present a methodology that can be used by operators to design their heterogeneous topology migration path from Full Copper to Full FttH, meeting their business requirements. First, we start with a literature survey on related models in Section II. In Section III, a model is presented to optimise the heterogeneous migration paths, where the complexity of the model is discussed in Section IV. In Section V, a method is presented to gather the input for the migration path optimisation using Geometric models. In Section VI, solution methods are presented in order to get a solution to the problem in reasonable time. Next, in Section VII, the optimisation method is demonstrated by a case study and the scalability of finding a solution is shown by computational results. Finally, in Section VIII, some conclusions are presented.

II. LITERATURE

Migration within telecommunication networks is a topic in many Techno-Economical studies. In these studies, the economic sanity of some choices are investigated. The European projects IST-TONIC [7] and CELTIC-ECOSYS [8] resulted in various upgrade or deployment scenarios for both fixed and wireless telecommunication networks, which was published in [9] and [10]. A major question in these studies is when to make the decision to roll out a FttC/VDSL network or a Full FttH network. Based on demand forecasts, it was shown that it is profitable to start in dense urban areas, wait for five years and then decide to expand it to the other urban areas. With the use of real option valuation, the effect of waiting is rewarded to identify the optimal decision over time. In [11] and [12], the OASE approaches are presented for more in depth analysis of the FttH total cost of ownership (TCO) and for comparing different possible business models both qualitatively and quantitatively.

The work of Casier [13] presents the techno-economic aspects of a fibre to the home network deployment. First, he considers all aspects of a semi-urban roll-out in terms of dimensioning and cost estimation models. Next, the effects of competition are introduced into the analysis.

The work in [14] presents a multi-criteria model aimed at studying the evolution scenarios to deploy new supporting technologies in the access network to deliver broadband services to individuals and small enterprises. This model is based on a state transition diagram, whose nodes characterise a subscriber line in terms of service offerings and supporting technologies. This model was extended for studying the evolution towards broadband services and create the optimal path for broadband network migration. A similar kind of model is presented in [15] and [16], where also an optimal strategy is proposed using a dynamic migration model. They study the best migration path including investments (capital expenditures, CapEx) and operational expenditures (OpEx) and revenues. Several fixed access technologies are considered as intermediate steps. A more recent study [17], proposes several migration strategies for active optical networking from data plane, topology, and control plane perspectives, and investigates their impact on the total cost of ownership. However, these migration strategies are not optimised.

Finally, our own previous work was about the benefits of a migration path as alternative for the direct step from Full Copper to FttH [18], and a Techno-Economic model [19] that can calculate the effect on market share, revenues, costs and earnings of offering different topologies and technologies in access networks (in migration).

As said earlier, all these approaches only consider uniform or single migration paths and do not include the possibility of using geometric models as input.

III. Migration Model

A migration path is here defined as a path from one topology/technique combination to a destination topology/technique, possibly using other topology/technique combinations as intermediate steps. Analogue to [15], we use a figure to clarify the idea, see Fig. 2.

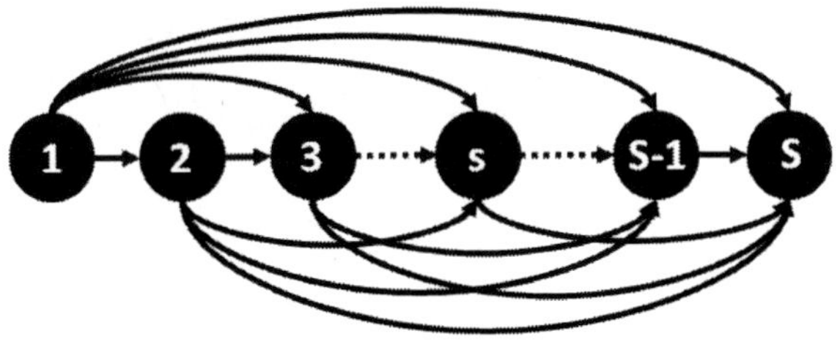

Figure 2. Migration paths.

Each node here is a topology/technique combination. One can choose a path from node 1, typically Full Copper/ADSL, to node S, typically FttH. So examples for the paths are: Full Copper/ADSL to FttH, Full Copper/ADSL to FttCab/VDSL to FttH, Full Copper/ADSL to FttCab/VDSL to FttCurb/G.Fast, etcetera. The focus in this paper is on an area that consists of multiple Central Offices, which is the location of the switching equipment, to which subscriber home and business lines are connected on a local loop, for example, a city or a district. The goal of the operator is to offer in this district a certain bandwidth coverage (per year), given a budget (per year) and possibly other constraints. A bandwidth coverage can be a single value, e.g., 'I want to offer 100 Mb/s in 2017', or a distribution over various bandwidth values in a number of years. An example of this distribution over years is presented in Table I. In the table is stated that in 2018 (at least) 60% of the houses need to have (at least) 100 Mb/s, at least 40% of the houses need to have (at least) 200 Mb/s and (at least) 10% need (at least) 300Mb. The percentages do not add up to 100% as they are exceedance probabilities. If all houses have a connection that offers 500 Mb/s the bandwidth coverage demand is met, obviously.

Now, the problem can be defined as an Integer Programming Problem. The notation that is used is presented in Table II. First, the objective function is defined as:

$$\min \sum_{i\in I}\sum_{j\in I}\sum_{l\in L}\sum_{t\in T} C_{ijl}x_{ijlt}. \quad (1)$$

Table I. Coverage goal.

Year	100 Mb/s	200 Mb/s	300 Mb/s
2018	60%	40%	10%
2021	80%	60%	20%
2024	90%	80%	40%

Table II. Definitions

Notation		Description
I	=	set of topologies/technologies;
L	=	set of locations, here CO areas;
T	=	set of time periods;
D	=	set of distances, e.g.,{200m, 400m, 600m} ;
x_{ijlt}	=	$\begin{cases} 1 & \text{if migration takes place from technology i} \in I \text{ to} \\ & \text{j} \in I \text{ in year } t \in T \text{ for location } l \in L \\ 0 & \text{otherwise} \end{cases}$
y_{ilt}	=	$\begin{cases} 1 & \text{if technology i} \in I \text{ is active on time } t \in T \\ & \text{at location l} \in L \\ 0 & \text{otherwise} \end{cases}$
C_{ijl}	=	migration costs for going from technology $i \in I$ to $j \in I$ at location $l \in L$
H_{ijl}	=	required installation capacity for migrating from technology $i \in I$ to $j \in I$ at location $l \in L$
O_{ilt}	=	operation costs when technology $i \in I$ is active at time $t \in T$ at location $l \in L$
R_{ild}	=	number of houses reached by technology $i \in I$ within distance $d \in D$ for location $l \in L$;
RT_l	=	total number of premises at location $l \in L$;
G_{td}	=	requested percentage of premises to be reached within distance $d \in D$ T time $t \in T$;
B_t	=	maximum budget available for time $t \in T$;
IC_t	=	installation capacity available for time $t \in T$;

This objective function minimises the total costs (CapEx) for the migration under the following constraints:

$$\sum_{i\in I}\sum_{j\in I} x_{ijlt} \leq 1, \ \forall\, t\in T, l\in L \quad (2)$$

$$\sum_{i\in I} y_{ilt} = 1, \ \forall\, l\in L, t\in T \quad (3)$$

$$x_{ijlt} \geq \frac{1}{2}(y_{jlt}-y_{jlt-1}) - \frac{1}{2}(y_{ilt}-y_{ilt-1}) - \frac{1}{2} \quad \forall\, i,j\in I, l\in L, t\in T \quad (4)$$

$$\frac{\sum\limits_{i\in I}\sum\limits_{l\in L} R_{ild}\cdot y_{ilt}}{\sum\limits_{l\in L} RT_l} \geq G_{td}, \ \forall\, t\in T, d\in D \quad (5)$$

$$x_{ijlt}, y_{ilt} \in \{0,1\}, \ \forall\, i,j\in I, l\in L, t\in T \quad (6)$$

This model will be called the base model. Constraint (2) makes sure that there is at most 1 migration step per year per location. Constraint (3) makes sure that each location has exactly 1 topology each year. Constraint (4) creates the migration steps. The right term can only be greater than zero if (and only if) $(y_{jlt}-y_{jlt-1}) = 1$ and $(y_{ilt}-y_{ilt-1}) = -1$, which indicates that there is a transition from technology i to technology j. Constraint (5) makes sure that the required bandwidth is delivered.

An alternative objective function is realised when adding the operational cost, or OpEx. This alters the objective function in:

$$\min \sum_{i\in I}\sum_{j\in I}\sum_{l\in L}\sum_{t\in T} C_{ijl}x_{ijlt} + \sum_{i\in I}\sum_{l\in L}\sum_{t\in T} O_{ilt}y_{ilt} \quad (7)$$

An other alternative model, called the extended model, is the model in which there exists a budget constraint per time period and a constraint for the installation capacity. In this formulation, the budget constraints are hard and the gap between the realised and demanded bandwidth per year is minimised.

$$\min \sum_{t\in T}\sum_{d\in D} \max\left(0, G_{td} - \frac{\sum_{i\in I}\sum_{l\in L} R_{ild}\cdot y_{ilt}}{\sum_{l\in L} RT_l}\right), \quad (8)$$

For the extended model, the following constraints should hold:

$$\begin{aligned}
\sum_{i\in I}\sum_{j\in I} x_{ijlt} &\leq 1, \forall\, l\in I, t\in T && (9)\\
\sum_{i\in I} y_{ilt} &= 1, \forall\, l\in L, t\in T && (10)\\
\frac{1}{2}(y_{jlt}-y_{jlt-1}) - \frac{1}{2}(y_{ilt} -y_{ilt-1}) - \frac{1}{2} &\leq x_{ijlt}, \\
&\quad \forall\, i,j\in I, l\in L, t\in T && (11)\\
\sum_{i\in I}\sum_{j\in I}\sum_{l\in L} c_{ijl}x_{ijlt} &\leq B_t, \forall\, t\in T && (12)\\
\sum_{i\in I}\sum_{j\in I}\sum_{l\in L} h_{ijl}x_{ijlt} &\leq IC_t, \forall\, t\in T && (13)\\
x_{ijlt}, y_{ilt} &\in \{0,1\}, \\
&\quad \forall\, i,j\in I, l\in L, t\in T && (14)
\end{aligned}$$

where (12) and (13) are added as budget and installation capacity constraints. This problem is no longer an ILP, as the objective is not linear. However, it can be linearised by introducing the variable z_{td} with $t\in T, d\in D$. Furthermore, the following constraints for z_{td} are added to the model:

$$\begin{aligned}
z_{td} &\geq 0 && \forall\, d\in D, t\in T \quad (15)\\
z_{td} &\geq G_{td} - \frac{\sum_{i\in I}\sum_{l\in L} R_{ild}\cdot y_{ilt}}{\sum_{l\in L} RT_l} && \forall\, d\in D, t\in T \quad (16)
\end{aligned}$$

As a result, the objective function changes to:

$$\min \sum_{t\in t}\sum_{d\in D} z_{td}. \quad (17)$$

Moreover, z_{td} does not have to be integer. Summarising, the extended model used for creating an optimal solution is:

$$\min \sum_{t\in T}\sum_{d\in D} z_{td} \quad (18)$$

$$\begin{aligned}
\text{s.t.} \sum_{i\in I}\sum_{j\in J}\sum_{l\in L} C_{ijl}x_{ijlt} &\leq B_t, \forall\, t\in T && (19)\\
\sum_{i\in I}\sum_{j\in J}\sum_{l\in L} H_{ijl}x_{ijlt} &\leq IC_t, \forall\, t\in T && (20)\\
\sum_{i\in I}\sum_{j\in J} x_{ijlt} &\leq 1, \forall\, l\in L, t\in T && (21)\\
\sum_{i\in I} y_{ilt} &= 1, \forall\, l\in L, t\in T && (22)\\
\frac{1}{2}(y_{jlt}-y_{jlt-1}) - \frac{1}{2}(y_{ilt} -y_{ilt-1}) - \frac{1}{2} &\leq x_{ijlt}, \\
&\quad \forall\, i,j\in I, l\in L, t\in T && (23)\\
z_{td} &\geq G_{td} - \frac{\sum_{i\in I}\sum_{l\in L} R_{ild}\cdot y_{ilt}}{\sum_{l\in L} RT_l}, \\
&\quad \forall\, d\in D, t\in T && (24)\\
z_{td} &\geq 0, \forall\, d\in D, t\in T && (25)\\
x_{ijlt}, y_{ilt} &\in \{0,1\}, \\
&\quad \forall\, i,j\in I, l\in L, t\in T. && (26)
\end{aligned}$$

IV. COMPLEXITY

In this section, the complexity of the base model and the extended model are discussed and it is shown that both models are NP-hard.

A. Base model

The Single Source Capacitated Facility Location Problem (SSCFLP) is NP-hard and can be reduced to the base model of the Migration of Fibre problem. In this problem, a number of facilities should be located, whereby each customer is fully assigned to a facility at minimum cost, such that the demand of each customer is served and a facility does not supply more than his capacity. This can be described as follows [20]:

$$\min \sum_{i\in Q}\sum_{j\in J} V_{ij}x_{ij} + \sum_{j\in J} F_j y_j \quad (27)$$

$$\begin{aligned}
\text{s.t.} \sum_{j\in J} x_{ij} &= 1 && \forall i\in Q \quad (28)\\
x_{ij} &\leq y_j \\
&&& \forall i\in Q, j\in J \quad (29)\\
\sum_{i\in Q} K_i x_{ij} &\leq S_j y_j && \forall j\in J \quad (30)\\
x_{ij}, y_i &\in \{0,1\} \\
&&& \forall i\in Q, j\in J, \quad (31)
\end{aligned}$$

where I is the set of customers, J is the set of facilities, V_{ij} are the costs for assigning customer $i\in I$ to facility $j\in J$ and F_j are the costs for opening facility $j\in J$. Furthermore,

K_i is the demand of customer $i \in I$ and S_j is the capacity of location $j \in J$. It holds that variable x_{ij} is equal to 1 if customer $i \in I$ is assigned to facility $j \in J$. Otherwise, this variable is equal to 0. The variable y_j is equal to 1 if facility $j \in J$ is opened. Otherwise, this variable is equal to 0.

For the reduction of the SSCFLP to the base problem, firstly, one instance of the base problem is given. Assume there is one location l, one time period $t \in T$ and one distance $d \in D$. By this, the base problem can be reduced to:

$$\min \sum_{i=i_0} \sum_{j \in I} C_{ij} x_{ij} \tag{32}$$

$$\text{s.t.} \sum_{j \in I} x_{ij} \leq 1 \quad \forall\, i = i_0 \tag{33}$$

$$\sum_{j \in I} y_j = 1 \tag{34}$$

$$\frac{1}{2}(y_j - Y_j) - \frac{1}{2}(y_i - Y_i) - \frac{1}{2} \leq x_{ij} \quad \forall i = i_0, j \in I \tag{35}$$

$$\frac{\sum_{j \in I} R_j \cdot y_j}{RT} \geq G \tag{36}$$

$$x_{ij}, y_j \in \{0,1\} \quad \forall\, i = i_0, j \in I. \tag{37}$$

Here, i_0 denotes the start state, namely the combination i of a technology and a topology at time $t = 0$. So, Y_i is equal to 1 for i equal to the technology and topology combination at time period $t = 0$ and zero otherwise. Note that Constraint (5) does not force that $x_{ij} = 1$ for $i = j$ when no migration takes place. However, having $x_{ij} = 1$ for $i = j$ does not affect the objective function, because the migration costs for migrating to the same technology and topology combination i are zero, as there is actually no migration happening. As a result, we can change Constraint (5) to:

$$x_{ij} \geq Y_i + y_j - 1, \qquad \forall\, i = i_0, j \in I. \tag{38}$$

In this equation, it is forced that $x_{ij} = 1$ for $i = j$ when no migration takes place. We know that $Y_{i_0} = 1$, because i_0 is the start state, thus Constraint (38) can be changed to:

$$x_{ij} \geq y_j, \qquad \forall\, i = i_0, j \in I. \tag{39}$$

In the base model, Constraint (33) has got an inequality sign and not an equality sign due to the fact that there is no time period $t = -1$ before the start state, so there is no migration possible from $t = -1$ to $t = 0$, and thus, for the start state $t = 0$ it holds that $x_{ijl0} = 0$ for all $i, j \in I$ and $l \in L$. In the ILP described above, we only have one time period $t \in T$, so we can change the inequality sign in Constraint (33) to an equality sign:

$$\sum_{j \in I} x_{ij} = 1, \qquad \forall\, i = i_0. \tag{40}$$

As a result of Constraint (34) and (40), we can flip the inequality sign in Constraint (38), because this does not affect the relation between the y_j and $x_{i_0 j}$, which should be equal to each other:

$$x_{ij} \leq y_j, \qquad \forall i = i_0, j \in I. \tag{41}$$

From Constraint (34), we know that exactly one technology and topology combination $j \in I$ should be active in the considered time period. We can replace this constraint by adding the following part to the objective function:

$$\sum_{j \in I} U_j y_j, \tag{42}$$

where it holds that $U_j = U$ for all $j \in I$ and $U > \max_{\forall i,j \in I} C_{ij}$. As a result, the ILP becomes:

$$\min \sum_{i=i_0} \sum_{j \in I} C_{ij} x_{ij} + \sum_{j \in I} U_j y_j \tag{43}$$

$$\text{s.t.} \sum_{j \in I} x_{ij} = 1 \quad \forall\, i = i_0 \tag{44}$$

$$x_{ij} \leq y_j \quad \forall\, i = i_0, j \in I \tag{45}$$

$$\frac{\sum_{j \in I} R_j \cdot y_j}{RT} \geq G \tag{46}$$

$$x_{ij}, y_i \in \{0,1\} \quad \forall\, i, j \in I. \tag{47}$$

From Constraint (44), (45) and the fact that only one technology and topology combination $j \in I$ could be active, it follows that we can remove the sum in Constraint (46), by adding $x_{i_0 j}$ at the right side of the inequality sign. This is because it must hold that the active technology and topology combination j after migrating fulfils the bandwidth demand G. This results in the following ILP:

$$\min \sum_{i=i_0} \sum_{j \in I} C_{ij} x_{ij} + \sum_{j \in I} U_j y_j \tag{48}$$

$$\text{s.t.} \sum_{j \in I} x_{ij} = 1 \quad \forall\, i = i_0 \tag{49}$$

$$x_{ij} \leq y_j \quad \forall\, i = i_0, j \in I \tag{50}$$

$$\frac{R_j}{RT} \cdot y_j \geq \sum_{i=i_0} G_i x_{i_0 j} \quad \forall\, j \in I \tag{51}$$

$$x_{ij}, y_i \in \{0,1\} \quad \forall\, i, j \in I, \tag{52}$$

where $G_i = G$ for all $i \in I$.

The values C_{ij}, U_j, $\frac{R_j}{RT}$ and G_i for all $i, j \in I$ correspond to the SSCFLP values V_{ij}, F_j, S_j and K_i for all $i \in Q$ and $j \in J$, respectively. Moreover, i_0 is the set of customers Q and the set of facilities J is equal to the set I of technology and topology combinations. This shows that the SSCFLP is a special case of the base problem and leads to the conclusion that the base problem is at least as hard as the SSCFLP. The SSCFLP is NP-hard [20], and thus, the base problem is also NP-hard.

B. Extended model

The Multiple Constraint Knapsack Problem is NP-hard and can be reduced to the extended model of the Migration of Fibre problem. In this problem, a set of items, each with a weight and value, could be packed once into a knapsack. The objective is to determine which item to include in the knapsack, to maximise the total profit and without exceeding the knapsack constraints. This can be described as follows [21]:

$$\max \sum_{i \in I} P_i y_i \tag{53}$$

$$\text{s.t.} \sum_{i \in I} A_{ji} y_i \leq W_j \quad \forall j \in M \tag{54}$$

$$y_i \in \{0,1\} \quad \forall i \in I, \tag{55}$$

where the sets of items is given by set I and the set of knapsack constraints is given by set M with corresponding capacities W_j with $j \in M$. The required capacity of item i for knapsack constraint j is A_{ji} with $j \in M, i \in I$. The value of item i is denoted by P_i and y_i is equal to 1 if item i is in the knapsack and otherwise this variable is equal to 0.

Similarly, for the reduction of the Multiple Constraint Knapsack problem to the extended problem, firstly, one instance of the extended problem is given. Assume there is one location $l \in L$, one time period $t \in T$ and one distance $d \in D$. By this, the extended model is reduced to:

$$\min \max \left(0, G - \sum_{i \in I} \frac{R_i}{RT} \cdot y_i \right) \tag{56}$$

$$\text{s.t.} \sum_{i \in I} \sum_{j \in I} C_{ij} x_{ij} \leq B \tag{57}$$

$$\sum_{i \in I} \sum_{j \in I} H_{ij} x_{ij} \leq IC \tag{58}$$

$$\sum_{i \in I} \sum_{j \in I} x_{ij} \leq 1 \tag{59}$$

$$\sum_{i \in J} y_i = 1 \tag{60}$$

$$\frac{1}{2}(y_j - Y_{j_0}) - \frac{1}{2}(y_i - Y_{i_0}) - \frac{1}{2} \leq x_{ij} \quad \forall i,j \in I \tag{61}$$

$$x_{ij}, y_i \in \{0,1\} \quad \forall i,j \in I. \tag{62}$$

Again, i_0 denotes again the start state, namely the combination i of a technology and a topology at time $t = 0$. The objective function is a max-min function. However, it is possible to modify the objective function to a maximisation function. Since there is only one location, the objective function can be changed to maximising the bandwidth for this location. The new objective function is defined as:

$$\max \sum_{i \in I} \frac{R_i}{RT} \cdot y_i. \tag{63}$$

Furthermore, the amount of variables can be reduced. This is possible, because there is only one location, one time period and the start state is known. Therefore, x_{ij} can be replaced by y_i. As a result, C_{ij} and H_{ij} are respectively changed to C_i and H_i, and Constraint (59) and (61) become superfluous. Without loss of generality, the equality sign in Constraint (60) can be changed to a "less than or equal to" sign, because the optimal solution will never be $y_i = 0$, for all $i \in I$, due to the used objective function and positive values of $\frac{R_i}{RT}$. Furthermore, it holds that $C_i = 0$ and $H_i = 0$ for $i \in I$ equal to the start state. Summarising, the described instance of the Migration of Fibre problem becomes:

$$\max \sum_{i \in I} \frac{R_i}{RT} \cdot y_i \tag{64}$$

$$\text{s.t.} \sum_{i \in I} C_i y_i \leq B \tag{65}$$

$$\sum_{i \in I} H_i y_i \leq IC \tag{66}$$

$$\sum_{i \in I} y_i \leq 1 \tag{67}$$

$$y_i \in \{0,1\} \quad \forall i \in I. \tag{68}$$

The budget B, installation capacity IC and 1 correspond to the knapsack capacities W_1, W_2 and W_3, respectively. Furthermore, C_i corresponds to A_{1i} for all $i \in I$, H_i corresponds to A_{2i} for all $i \in I$, and A_{3i} is equal to 1 for all $i \in I$. Lastly, $\frac{R_i}{RT}$ is equal to P_i for all i, thus the Multiple Constraint Knapsack problem is a specific case of the extended problem. This leads to the conclusion that the extended problem is at least as hard as the Multiple Constraint Knapsack problem. The Multiple Constraint Knapsack problem is NP-hard [21], thus, the extended problem is also NP-hard.

V. Input from Geometric model

In the previous section, two parameters are used that are not that easy to obtain, namely c_{ijl}, the cost for migrating from technology i to j at location l, and R_{ild}, the number of premises reached by technology i within d meter at location l. To get the value of these parameters, for each migration an optimal planning should be made. We introduce an alternative for this problem by using the outcomes of geometric modelling, as presented in [5] and [6]. This means that we start by a simple set of parameters per (currently) active node: the total cable length (D) and the capacity of this node (n), which equals the number of premises connected. Note that in this section d and D mean something different, using the notation of [6], than in the model of the previous sections. As is shown in [6], from these parameters the geometric density of the premises can be derived. With this geometric density, we can estimate the number of new active locations that a next technology needs in this area to achieve a certain distance coverage, and consequently, the bandwidth coverage. From this number of active elements, the costs of the migration can be estimated. Next, using the same density, also the cable and digging distances to connect those new active elements can be estimated.

To illustrate this approach, think of an area, currently equipped with VDSL2, that contains $n_1 = 1,000$ houses. The given total cable length equals $D_1 = 875,000$ meter. Now, the parameter d, which indicates the house density of the area, expressed in the (average) width of the premises, can be derived by solving (using $s_1 = \sqrt{n_1}$):

$$d = \frac{D_1}{2 \cdot s_1 \cdot \lceil \frac{1}{2} s_1 \rceil \cdot \lfloor \frac{1}{2} s_1 \rfloor}, \tag{69}$$

resulting in $d = 57.7$ for the given example. Let us assume that in the next topology, let us assume V-plus, we want to reach 85% within 400 meters. From [5], we know that the probability distribution of the individual distances of the houses to the active node can be estimated by a Normal distribution $F_{\mu,\sigma}(x)$ with $\mu_2 = \frac{D_2}{n_2}$ and $\sigma_2 = \frac{M-\mu}{2}$. Here M represents the maximum cable distance in the second topology using [6]:

$$M = 2 \cdot \lceil \frac{1}{2} s_2 - 1 \rceil \cdot d + 0.5d, \tag{70}$$

$$s_2 = \sqrt{n_2}, \tag{71}$$

and the total cable length in the second topology

$$D_2 = 2 \cdot d \cdot s_2 \cdot \lceil \frac{1}{2} s_2 \rceil \cdot \lfloor \frac{1}{2} s_2 \rfloor. \tag{72}$$

Now, the question is to choose n_2 such that $F_{\mu(n_2),\sigma(n_2)}(400) = 0.85$. This can be solved numerically and leads to the following values: $n_2 = 100$, $M_2 = 490$, $D_2 = 28800$, $\mu_2 = 290$ and $\sigma_2 = 100$. This means that to meet this requirement of 85% within 400 meter, 10 new nodes (n_1/n_2) should be installed. It takes 28800 meter of digging and (fibre) cable to connect these nodes.

VI. Solution Methods

The time to solve the Migration problem has to be of a reasonable magnitude, regardless of the input of the model. The reason for this is that the telecom operators should be able to run the optimisation model in a few minutes, such that the model can be used in an interactive way. After obtaining a migration plan, the company has to consider whether the migration plan is enforceable. If it is not a feasible plan, they should be able to modify input or requirements and create a new migration plan. Furthermore, in Section IV, it is shown that the Migration of Fibre problem is NP-hard. For these two reasons, heuristic methods are developed to obtain a good solution within an acceptable computation time. A heuristic method is a procedure that is likely to discover a good and feasible solution, but not necessarily an optimal solution. In this chapter, we present the different heuristic solution methods used in this research. The third solution method which is developed, is the optimisation of the base problem and the extended problem per year. Next to these heuristic approaches, the exact solution method is used to create benchmark values.

A. Problem-based heuristic

The first method we used to obtain an good solution in a reasonable computation time, is a heuristic method which is based on the characteristics of the Migration of Fibre problem. The main characteristics of the base problem is the requested bandwidth percentage and the two main characteristics of the extended problem are the budget and the installation capacities. The heuristic starts with a solution in which the technology and topology combination in each year is equal to the start year, i.e., the current situation. The heuristic starts at the first year that has to be upgraded and upgrades the locations with the largest profit. When enough locations are upgraded to meet the constraints for that year, the heuristic continues with the same procedure for the next years. After this, a feasible solution is constructed. In this way, the quality of the solution is guaranteed. Next, we explain how this is implemented for the base and extended problems.

For the implementation of the problem-based heuristic, we distinguish the base problem and the extended problem. For both the problems a total profit matrix is made. For the base problem, the profit is based on the following ratio:

$$\frac{R_{jl}}{C_{ijl}}, \tag{73}$$

where R_{jl} is the matrix containing the mean values over all the distances $d \in D$. For the extended problem, the profit is based on the following ratio:

$$\frac{R_{jl}}{\frac{C_{ijl}}{B_t} + \frac{H_{ijl}}{IC_t}}. \tag{74}$$

By dividing C_{ijl} and H_{ijl} respectively by B_t and IC_t, the influence of the migration costs and required installation capacities are equivalent. Moreover, the profit matrix shows for each possible upgrade per location what the corresponding profit ratio is per year. After this matrix is made, the following steps are performed:

1) Construct a migration schedule in which the technology and topology combinations in each time period are equal to the start time period, i.e., there are no migration upgrades in this schedule.
2) Select the lowest time period $t \in T$ which has not been upgraded yet and which has to be upgraded (base model: requested bandwidth constraint) or which could be upgraded (extended model: there is budget and installation capacity left over).
3) Using the total profit matrix, a profit matrix is made for the current situation. This is a matrix containing

the profits for the selected time period $t \in T$ and the technology and topology combination $i \in I$ of the previous time period $(t-1) \in T$.

4) The upgrade with the highest ratio in the matrix, made in the previous step, is selected and is carried out in the migration schedule. Also the subsequent time periods of this location get the same upgrade.

5a. (Base model) Repeat step 4. until the migration schedule for the selected time period meets the required bandwidth constraint. For the base problem, this is the bandwidth constraint, and in this way, the migration schedule up to the selected time period has became a feasible schedule.

5b. (Extended model) Repeat step 4. until as much locations as possible are upgraded and the solution still meets the budget and installation capacity constraint. In this way, the migration schedule is still a feasible schedule.

6a (Base model) Repeat step 2 until 5, until every time period $t \in T$ is upgraded as much as needed, and then, the migration schedule feasible.

6b (Extended model) Repeat step 2 until 5, until every time period $t \in T$ is upgraded as much as possible, without losing feasibility.

Note that the two last steps of the problem based heuristic are dependent of the type of the model, i.e., the base or extended model. Next to the model-based heuristic, we have also used a meta-heuristic, which is described in the next section.

B. Simulated Annealing

The meta-heuristic used in this research is Simulated Annealing (SA). A meta-heuristic is a general solution method that provides general structures and strategy guidelines for developing a specific heuristic method. SA is a stochastic algorithm which searches for a global optimum and avoids getting stuck in local, non-global optima [22]. It is based on a heating and cooling process and simulates the energy changes in a system subjected to a cooling process until it converges to an equilibrium state.

From an initial solution s_0, the SA algorithm generates a random neighbour during each iteration. A neighbour is a (feasible) solution obtained by performing an operation on the current solution. If this neighbour is a better solution than the current solution, related to the corresponding values of the objective function, the neighbour solution will be accepted and becomes the new current solution. If this is not the case, the neighbour will be accepted with a certain probability, which depends on the current temperature. This probability is the Boltzmann probability:

$$P(\text{acceptance}) = e^{-\frac{|f(s')-f(s)|}{T}}, \quad (75)$$

where $|f(s') - f(s)|$ denotes the difference ΔE between the objective value of the generated neighbour s' and the objective value of the current state s. T denotes the temperature. During each M_{max} iterations of the algorithm, the temperature T decreases, whereby the probability of acceptance also decreases. The probability of acceptance also depends on the quality of the neighbour solution, i.e., the worse the neighbour solution, the lower the chance of acceptance. A cooling schedule $g(T)$ defines for each step r of the algorithm the temperature T_r. Due to the possibility of accepting worse solutions, the algorithm can escape an inferior local minimum. The algorithm stops after a predefined amount of iterations N_{max}. The overview in Algorithm 1 summarises the used steps based on [23].

Algorithm 1: Simulated Annealing algorithm

```
Input: Cooling schedule g(T) and data
s = s_0;
(initial solution)
T = T_max;
(starting temperature)
N = 0;
while N < N_max do
    M = 0;
    while M < M_max do
        Generate a random neighbour s';
        ΔE = f(s') − f(s);
        if ΔE ≤ 0 for minimisation problem or ΔE ≥ 0
         for maximisation problem then
            s = s';
            (accept the neighbour solution);
        else
            Accept s' with probability e^(−|ΔE|/T) ;
            s = s' if s' is accepted ;
        end
        save s' and f(s') if s' is accepted;
        M = M + 1;
        N = N + 1
    end
    T = g(T);
end
Output: Saved solutions s' and corresponding objective
        values f(s')
```

The first step of our implementation of SA is to gain a good initial solution. To create an initial solution, the Problem-Based Heuristic as described in Section VI-A is used. Solutions are presented as a matrix of which the rows illustrate the locations, the columns represent the migrations years and the elements of the matrix represent the technology and topology combination for the corresponding location and year. The technology and topology combinations are ranged from 1 until k, with k the total amount of combinations. Furthermore, combination 1 provides the smallest bandwidth and combination k provides the largest bandwidth.

The objective function for a solution s of the base model is described as:

$$f(s) = \sum_{i \in I} \sum_{j \in I} \sum_{l \in L} \sum_{t \in T} C_{ijl} x_{ijlt}. \quad (76)$$

The objective function for a solution s of the extended model is described as:

$$f(s) = \sum_{t \in T} \sum_{d \in D} \max \left(0, G_{td} - \frac{\sum_{i \in I} \sum_{l \in L} R_{ild} \cdot y_{ilt}}{\sum_{l \in L} RT_l} \right). \quad (77)$$

The goal of Simulated Annealing is to find a solution with the lowest possible objective value. Simulated Annealing also needs a temperature scheme. This scheme defines for each step of the algorithm the temperature T. First, we set an initial temperature T and we define the cooling schedule as:

$$g(T) = \alpha T \text{ , with } 0 < \alpha < 1. \quad (78)$$

We apply this scheme after each βth iteration. Previous research showed that α should be between 0.5 and 0.99 [23]. The stop condition is defined as that the algorithm will stop after γ amount of iterations. In each iteration of the algorithm, a neighbourhood solution will be created, using the current solution. There are three operations possible to create a feasible neighbour solution. First, choose a random number. If the selected number is smaller than $\frac{1}{3}$, then operation 1 is performed, if the number is smaller than $\frac{2}{3}$ and bigger than $\frac{1}{3}$, then operation 2 is performed and otherwise, operation 3 is performed. By operation 1, a location is upgraded in a time period and, if possible, an other location is downgraded in the same time period. By operation 2, a location will be upgraded in a timed period and by operation 3, a location will be downgraded in a time period. The operations are specified as follows:

1) A location is randomly chosen. If the selected location contains already the best possible technology and topology combination in each migration time period, reselect the location randomly, until upgrading in at least one of the migration time periods of this location is possible. Then select a migration time period randomly, where upgrading the technology and topology combination for this location is possible and upgrade the selected location for the selected time period. With upgrading a network, we mean that we add 1 to the corresponding entry in the solution matrix. If needed, some of the following time periods for this location should also be increased by 1, such that the migration steps for the location form a row of non-descending entries.
   If it is possible to downgrade an other location in the selected time period, select randomly an other location and check if it is possible to downgrade this location in the selected time period. With downgrading a network, we mean that we subtract 1 from the corresponding entry. If the technology and topology combination for this location and time period is already as low as possible, then reselect the location randomly. This is repeated until a location is found where a downgrade is still possible in the selected time period and then the location in this time period is downgraded. In addition, if needed, some of the previous time periods for this location should be decreased by 1, such that the migration steps for the location form a row of non-descending entries. If it is not possible to downgrade an other location in the selected time period, no additional steps are performed.
2) A location is randomly chosen. If the selected location contains already the best possible technology and topology combination in each migration time period, reselect the location randomly, until upgrading in at least one of the migration time periods of this location is possible. Then, select a migration time period randomly, where upgrading the technology and topology combination for this location is possible and upgrade the selected location for the selected time period. With upgrading a network, we mean that we add 1 to the corresponding entry in the solution matrix. If needed, some of the following time periods for this location should also be increased by 1, such that the migration steps for the location form a row of non-descending entries.
3) A location is randomly chosen. If the selected location contains already the worst possible technology and topology combination in each migration time period, reselect the location randomly, until downgrading in at least one of the migration time periods of this location is possible. Then, select a migration time period randomly, where downgrading the technology and topology combination for this location is possible and downgrade the selected location for the selected time period. With downgrading a network, we mean that we subtract 1 from the corresponding entry in the solution matrix. If needed, some of the previous time periods for this location should be decreased by 1, such that the migration steps for the location form a row of non-descending entries.

For the extended problem, we added a small extension to operation 2 and 3, to increase the chance of creating a solution which is feasible:

2. Check the feasibility of the adapted solution. If it is infeasible, i.e., it does not meet the budget and/or installation capacity constraint, then also perform operation 3 in the selected time period. In this case, a location is upgraded and an other location is downgraded in the same time period.
3. Check the feasibility of the adapted solution. After operation 3 is performed, i.e., a location is downgraded in a time period, it is possible that the costs for the next time period becomes higher and exceeds the budget for this next time period. If the created neighbour solution is infeasible, i.e., it does not meet the budget and/or installation capacity constraint, then also perform operation 2 in the selected time period. In this case, a location is upgraded and an other location is downgraded

in the same time period.

For the base problem, check if the new solution is feasible, i.e., it meets the bandwidth constraint. For the extended problem, if an extension of operation 2 or 3 is performed, also a check has to be performed: it is checked whether or not the new solution meets the budget and installation capacity constraints. If it does not meet these constraints, the adapted solution is rejected and the procedure of the operation is started again, using the unadapted solution. This is repeated until a solution is found which meets the constraints. We call this adapted solution a neighbour. All the solutions which can be formed by using one of the operations to adapt the current solution, form the neighbourhood of the current solution. Additionally, during each iteration, the neighbour will be compared with the current solution. It will be accepted if it is better than the current solution and otherwise it will be accepted with the Boltzmann probability.

VII. Computational Results

We tested all methods described in the previous section, using the base model and extended model for various test instances. In this section, the results of these methods are presented. First of all, the impact of optimising per year instead of optimising over the total horizon is showed in an example. Next, the heuristics described in section VI are compared to each other, subjected to the accuracy and the computation time of these heuristics for various test instances.

A. Example

First, in this section, an example is presented introducing a small city with 40 cabinets and 18,550 houses, to show the benefit of the optimisation over the total horizon. The current employment is ADSL. The operator has a bandwidth coverage goal, expressed in percentage of the houses that is within a certain distance from the active equipment. The coverage goal is shown in Table III. For example, the goal is to have 70% of the houses within 400 meter in 2021.

TABLE III. Coverage goal.

Year	600m	400m	200m
2018	70%	40%	20%
2021	85%	70%	30%
2024	85%	85%	40%

TABLE IV. Per period optimisation - base model.

Year	ADSL	VDSL	V-plus
2018	23	7	10
2021	17	7	16
2024	5	7	28

TABLE V. Overall optimisation - base model.

Year	ADSL	VDSL	V-plus
2018	25	0	15
2021	18	1	21
2024	8	6	26

Two cases are distinguished. In the first case, the operator tries to meet the distance requirement for each year independently and optimally. This means that the operator optimises the design of each area without knowledge of future networks, topologies and technologies. In the second case, the operator tries to meet the requirements for the total time horizon, by solving the ILP model introduced in Section III. For each cabinet, for each 3-year period, the operator can chose between doing nothing, implementing VDSL and implementing V-plus, each with its own costs and bandwidth consequences. Now, the operator tries to make the decisions such that the total migration costs are minimal, meeting the distance coverage requirements for each period as modelled in the base model of Section III. The used costs for digging and equipment are based on the (Sub-Urban) numbers of [24].

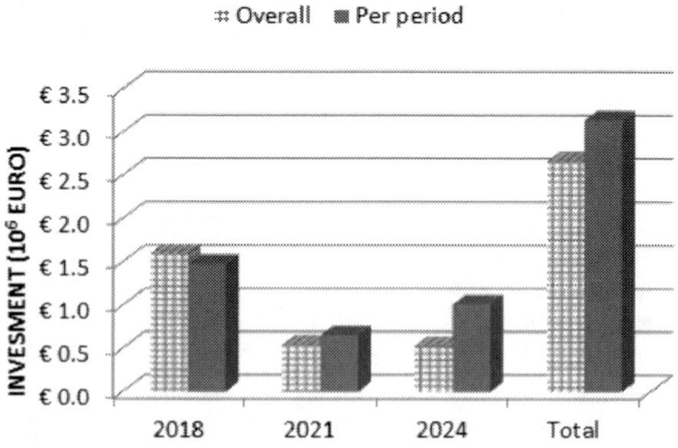

Figure 3. Investment costs.

The result of the optimisation (only using Excel and OpenSolver [25]) of the two cases is depicted in Table IV for the per-period optimisation and Table V for the overall optimisation. In the first year (2018) of the per-period optimisation, more VDSL is chosen, as this is a cheaper solution to meet the 2018 requirements. In the overall optimisation the more expensive choice for V-plus is made, as this is more ready for the future. In the other two stages more or less the same choices are made. This leads to the total overview of costs as depicted in Fig. 3, where the total costs of the overall optimisation are lower, but the costs in the first year are higher. All costs are expressed in Net Present Value, with an average cost of capital of 6%, making the values in the various years comparable.

B. Scalability

To illustrate the scalability of the problem solving, five real life areas containing different amounts of cabinets and houses are selected. The time-span of the migration schedule and the amount of possible technology and topology combinations is the same as in the previous example, respectively three moments in time and three combinations. In Table VI, an overview is given of the characteristics of the areas.

TABLE VI. AREA CHARACTERISTICS

Area	No. of cabinets	No. of houses
A	40	18,550
B	180	58,842
C	496	44,151
D	874	433,092
E	26164	6,352,365

The scalability of the base model and extended model is based on the quality of the optimal solution found by the different solutions methods and the corresponding computation times of these methods. To determine the quality of the provided solution of the methods, first the exact solutions of the base model and extended model for the different areas are calculated. For this, three different solvers are used. The first used solver is 'OpenSolver' in Excel, in combination with COIN-OR [25]. Furthermore, CPLEX Optimizer [26] in combination with MATLAB and the standard solver IntLinProg in MATLAB are used. In Table VII, an overview is given of the computation times using these solvers for the base problem.

TABLE VII. COMPUTATION TIME OF EXACT SOLUTION METHOD FOR THE BASE PROBLEM [SECONDS]

Area	COIN-OR	CPLEX Optimizer	IntLinProg
A	7.5	6.7	110.8
B	36.1	8.3	$>$ 8 days
C	396.3	9.7	$>$ 8 days
D	912.3	15.7	$>$ 8 days
E	$>$ 8 days	12,082.6	$>$ 8 days

TABLE VIII. COMPUTATION TIME OF EXACT SOLUTION METHOD FOR THE EXTENDED PROBLEM [SECONDS]

Area	CPLEX Optimizer
A	28.2
B	17.9
C	37.1
D	111.6
E	24,703.2

The illustrated computation times of the solvers are a combination of the time for building the problem and solving the problem using these solvers. Observe that the NP-hardness of the base model, effects the computation time for area E, using CPLEX Optimizer. This computation time is larger than three hours, which is not an reasonable duration for the telecom operators to obtain a migration schedule. In practise, even more technology and combinations and more migrations periods will be involved, which results in an exponential growing runtime for obtaining an exact solution. In Table VIII, an overview is given of the computation times for extended model using CPLEX Optimizer. This table also shows that the computation time for obtaining a migration schedule for large areas is not acceptable, given the assumptions in the start of this section.

Therefore, to obtain a good solution in a reasonable time, solution methods were developed, as shown in Section VI. These methods are the Problem-based heuristic and Simulated Annealing approaches and, additionally, a per period optimisation, calculating the optimal exact solution per year, sequentially. Simulated Annealing uses the solution of the problem-based heuristic as start solution. The parameters used to simulate the cooling process, based on preliminary results, are illustrated in Table IX for the base model and the extended model.

TABLE IX. BEST PARAMETERS FOR SIMULATED ANNEALING

Area	M_{max}	N_{max}	T_{max}	α
Base model	50	100,000	5,000	0.99
Extended model	50	20,000	0.01	0.95

Preliminary results show that the size of the areas has no effect on the selection of parameters, meaning that the best parameters is only based on the type of model. Now, the solutions of the three methods can be compared with the optimal solution found by CPLEX Optimizer. This is illustrated in Table X for the base model and in Table XI for the extended model.

TABLE X. SOLUTION OF THE HEURISTICS COMPARED TO THE EXACT SOLUTION OF BASE MODEL (COSTS)

Area	Per period opt.	Problem-based	Simulated Annealing
A	23.0%	6.1%	0.9%
B	0.0%	29.9%	12.4%
C	2.4%	30.5%	23.3%
D	0.0%	22.4%	18.5%
E	11.5%	12.1%	10.9%

TABLE XI. SOLUTION OF THE HEURISTICS COMPARED TO THE EXACT SOLUTION OF EXTENDED MODEL (BANDWIDTH)

Area	Per period opt.	Problem-based	Simulated Annealing
A	99.74%	54.57%	98.12%
B	100.00%	83.65%	99.40%
C	99.86%	85.25%	99.69%
D	100.00%	89.89%	99.38%
E	99.94%	76.05%	98.01%

Table X shows that the solution for the base problem in area A, using Simulated Annealing, is 2.6% worse than the exact optimal solution, as found by CPLEX Optimizer. This means that the costs for the migration schedule as found by Simulated Annealing is 2.6% higher than the costs for the migration schedule of the exact solution, as found by CPLEX Optimizer. Table XI shows that the solution for the extended problem in area A, using the problem-based heuristic, has a total realisation of 54.57% of the total realised bandwidth demand of the exact optimal solution, as found by CPLEX Optimizer. Moreover, the 100% of the exact solution is equal to the sum over the minima of the demanded bandwidth and the realised bandwidth per year and distance. Furthermore, these two tables show that the improvement using Simulated Annealing is significantly more effective for the extended model. However, the optimal solutions of Simulated Annealing for both the models are not as good as the optimal solutions of the per period optimisation.

The corresponding computation times of the methods are illustrated in Table XII and Table XIII. Note that the computation time of Simulated Annealing includes the computation time of the problem-based heuristic.

TABLE XII. COMPUTATION TIMES OF THE HEURISTICS FOR THE BASE MODEL [SECONDS]

Area	Per period opt.	Problem-based	Simulated Annealing
A	17.5	8.0	16.6
B	16.3	7.9	40.9
C	19.6	7.7	126.4
D	21.2	9.0	226.3
E	1181.3	694.3	1,242.4

TABLE XIII. COMPUTATION TIMES OF THE HEURISTICS FOR THE EXTENDED MODEL [SECONDS]

Area	Per period opt.	Problem-based	Simulated Annealing
A	26.8	13.1	20.1
B	23.6	10.5	29.2
C	26.8	14.2	39.3
D	29.6	7.2	164.8
E	1,045.7	626.4	1,783.2

Table XII and Table XIII show that the computation time of the problem-based heuristic is the lowest, however, the computation time of the two other methods are also of a reasonable duration. To conclude, combining this with the previous results that the solution of the per year optimisation is significantly better than the solution provided by the problem-based heuristic, the best method to provide a good solution in a reasonable time for the extended model, is the approach of optimising per year. For the base model, this approach can give rather high deviations. Then, for smaller areas, at this moment, the exact solver should be considered.

VIII. CONCLUSION

In this paper, we presented a methodology that can be used by operators to design their heterogeneous topology migration path from Full Copper to (Full) FttH, meeting their business requirements. Heterogeneous means that the operator decides per Central Office area the topology or technique per period (e.g., year), resulting in a detailed migration path that meets a required bandwidth coverage in the larger area. For this, two models were presented. The first, the base problem, minimised the total investment (CapEx) and operational costs (OpEx), such that the bandwidth requirement per period was met. The second, the extended problem, minimised the deviation from this bandwidth requirement meeting a budget constraint per period.

The data used for the migration path optimisation is in practice hard to obtain. For this, the use of geometric modelling was proposed, with which the total CapEx of a migration step can be estimated using only two parameters per Central Office area, namely the total existing cable length and the capacity of this node. The two models were demonstrated in two case studies that showed the gain that can be realised by the migration path optimisation.

To be used in practice, solving bigger instances, two heuristic methods were presented, next to the option to solve the problem per year. Numerical experiments show that an exact optimal solution can be obtained by MIP-solver CPLEX Optimizer up to rather big problems. If for bigger problems the calculation time of the exact solution is experienced to high, a consecutive approach of optimising per year gives the best performance of the heuristic approaches, in the case of the extended problem.

For further research we recommend to look for better performing problem-based heuristics, as we expect them to deliver the best computation times. Furthermore, beside the costs, also the revenues could be taken into account.

REFERENCES

[1] F. Phillipson, "Optimisation of heterogeneous migration paths to high bandwidth home connection," *The Twelfth International Conference on Digital Telecommunication (ICDT)*, 2017.

[2] T. Vos and F. Phillipson, "Dense multi-service planning in smart cities," in *International Conference on Information Society and Smart Cities (ISC 2018)*, 2018.

[3] N. Ghazisaidi, M. Maier, and C. M. Assi, "Fiber-wireless (fiwi) access networks: A survey," *IEEE Communications Magazine*, vol. 47, no. 2, pp. 160–167, 2009.

[4] F. D'Andreagiovanni, F. Mett, and J. Pulaj, "Towards the integration of power-indexed formulations in multi-architecture connected facility location problems for the optimal design of hybrid fiber-wireless access networks," in *OASIcs-OpenAccess Series in Informatics*, vol. 50. Schloss Dagstuhl-Leibniz-Zentrum fuer Informatik, 2016, pp. 1–11.

[5] F. Phillipson, D. Worm, N. Neumann, A. Sangers, and S.-J. Wiarda, "Estimating bandwidth coverage using geometric models," in *Networks and Optical Communications (NOC), 2016 21st European Conference on.* IEEE, 2016, pp. 152–156.

[6] F. Phillipson, "Estimating ftth and fttcurb deployment costs using geometric models with enhanced parameters," in *Networks and Optical Communications-(NOC), 2015 20th European Conference on.* IEEE, 2015, pp. 1–5.

[7] IST-TONIC. Retrieved February 2017. [Online]. Available: cordis.europa.eu/result/rcn/81333_en.html

[8] CELTIC-ECOSYS. Retrieved February 2017. [Online]. Available: www.celticplus.eu/project-ecosys

[9] T. Rokkas, D. Katsianis, and D. Varoutas, "Techno-economic evaluation of FttC/VDSL and FttH roll-out scenarios: Discounted cash flows and real option valuation," *Journal of Optical Communications and Networking*, vol. 2, no. 9, pp. 760–771, 2010.

[10] T. Monath, N. Elnegaard, P. Cadro, D. Katsianis, and D. Varoutas, "Economics of fixed broadband access network strategies," *IEEE Communications Magazine*, vol. 41, no. 9, pp. 132–139, 2003.

[11] S. Verbrugge *et al.*, "Research approach towards the profitability of future FttH business models," in *Proceedings Telecommunications Network Strategy and Planning Symposium (NETWORKS)*, Warshaw, Poland, June 2011, pp. 1–10.

[12] M. Forzati *et al.*, "Next-generation optical access seamless evolution: Concluding results of the european fp7 project oase," *Journal of Optical Communications and Networking*, vol. 7, no. 2, pp. 109–123, 2015.

[13] K. Casier, *Techno-Economic Evaluation of a Next Generation Access Network Deployment in a Competitive Setting*. Universiteit Gent, 2009.

[14] C. Antunes, J. Craveirinha, and J. Clímaco, "Planning the evolution to broadband access networks: A multicriteria approach," *European Journal of Operational Research*, vol. 109, no. 2, pp. 530–540, 1998.

[15] R. Zhao, L. Zhou, and C. Mas Machuca, "Dynamic migration planning towards FttH," in *Telecommunications Network Strategy and Planning Symposium (NETWORKS)*, Warshaw, Poland, September 2010, pp. 1617–1622.

[16] R. R. Reyes, R. Zhao, and C. M. Machuca, "Advanced dynamic migration planning toward ftth," *IEEE Communications Magazine*, vol. 52, no. 1, pp. 77–83, 2014.

[17] K. Wang *et al.*, "Migration strategies for fttx solutions based on active optical networks," *IEEE Communications Magazine*, vol. 54, no. 2, pp. 78–85, 2016.

[18] F. Phillipson, "A cost effective topology migration path towards fibre," *Lecture Notes on Information Theory Vol*, vol. 2, no. 1, 2014.

[19] F. Phillipson, C. Smit-Rietveld, and P. Verhagen, "Fourth generation broadband delivered by hybrid ftth solutiona techno-economic study," *Journal of Optical Communications and Networking*, vol. 5, no. 11, pp. 1328–1342, 2013.

[20] G. Guastraroba and M. Speranza, "A heuristic for bilp problems: The single source capacitated facility location problem," *European Journal of Operational Research*, vol. 238, pp. 428–450, 2014.
[21] A. Fréville, "The multidimensional 0–1 knapsack problem: An overview," *European Journal of Operational Research*, vol. 155, no. 1, pp. 1–21, 2004.
[22] A. Dekkers and E. Aarts, "Global optimization and simulated annealing," *Mathematical programming*, vol. 50, no. 1, pp. 367–393, 1991.
[23] E.-G. Talbi, *Metaheuristics: from design to implementation*. John Wiley & Sons, 2009, vol. 74.
[24] T. Rokkas, "Techno-economic analysis of pon architectures for ftth deployments: Comparison between gpon, xgpon and ng-pon2 for a greenfield operator," in *Telecommunication, Media and Internet Techno-Economics (CTTE), 2015 Conference of*. IEEE, 2015, pp. 1–8.
[25] A. Mason, "Opensolver an open source add-in to solve linear and integer progammes in excel," in *Operations Research Proceedings 2011*, ser. Operations Research Proceedings, D. Klatte, H.-J. Lathi, and K. Schmedders, Eds. Springer Berlin Heidelberg, 2012, pp. 401–406.
[26] CPLEX-Optimizer. Retrieved April 2017. [Online]. Available: https://www.ibm.com/us-en/marketplace/ibm-ilog-cplex

Reliability Evaluation of Erasure Coded Systems

Ilias Iliadis and Vinodh Venkatesan
IBM Research – Zurich
8803 Rüschlikon, Switzerland
Email: ili@zurich.ibm.com, vinodh.iitm@gmail.com

***Abstract*—Replication is widely used to enhance the reliability of storage systems and protect data from device failures. The effectiveness of the replication scheme has been evaluated based on the Mean Time to Data Loss (MTTDL) and the Expected Annual Fraction of Data Loss (EAFDL) metrics. To provide high data reliability at high storage efficiency, modern systems employ advanced erasure coding redundancy and recovering schemes. This article presents a general methodology for obtaining the EAFDL and MTTDL of erasure coded systems analytically for arbitrary rebuild time distributions and for the symmetric, clustered, and declustered data placement schemes. Our analysis establishes that the declustered placement scheme offers superior reliability in terms of both metrics. The analytical results obtained enable the derivation of the optimal codeword lengths that maximize the MTTDL and minimize the EAFDL. It is theoretically shown that, for large storage systems that use a declustered placement scheme, both metrics are optimized when the codeword length is about 60% of the storage system size.**

Keywords–Reliability metric; MTTDL; EAFDL; RAID; MDS codes; Information Dispersal Algorithm; Prioritized rebuild.

I. INTRODUCTION

The reliability of storage systems is affected by data losses due to device and component failures, including disk and node failures. Permanent loss of data is prevented by deploying redundancy schemes that enable data recovery. However, additional device failures that may occur during rebuild operations could lead to permanent data losses. Over the years, several redundancy and recovery schemes have been developed to enhance the reliability of storage systems. These schemes offer different levels of reliability, with varying corresponding overheads due to the additional operations that need to be performed, and different levels of storage efficiencies that depend on the additional amount of redundant (parity) data that needs to be stored in the system [1].

The effectiveness of the redundancy schemes has been evaluated predominately based on the Mean Time to Data Loss (MTTDL) metric. Closed-form reliability expressions are typically obtained using Markov models, with the underlying assumption that the times to component failures and the rebuild times are independent and exponentially distributed [2-14]. Recent work has shown that these results also hold in the practical case of non-exponential failure time distributions. This was achieved based on a methodology for obtaining MTTDL that does not involve any Markov analysis [15]. The MTTDL metric has been used extensively to assess tradeoffs, to compare schemes, and to estimate the effect of various parameters on system reliability [16-20].

To cope with data losses encountered in the case of distributed and cloud storage systems, data is replicated and recovery mechanisms are used. For instance, Amazon S3 is designed to provide 99.999999999% (eleven nines) durability of data over a given year [21]. Similarly, also Facebook [22], LinkedIn [23] and Yahoo! [24] consider the amount of data lost in given periods. To address this issue, a recent work has introduced the Expected Annual Fraction of Data Loss (EAFDL) metric [25]. It has also presented a methodology for deriving this metric analytically in the case of replication-based storage systems, where user data is replicated r times and the copies are stored in different devices. As an alternative to replication, storage systems use advanced erasure codes that provide a high data reliability as well as a high storage efficiency. The use of such erasure codes can be traced back to as early as the 1980s when they were applied in systems with redundant arrays of inexpensive disks (RAID) [2][3]. The RAID-5, RAID-6 and replication-based systems are special cases of erasure coded systems. State-of-the-art data storage systems [26][27] employ more general erasure codes, where the choice of the codes used greatly affects the performance, reliability, and the storage and reconstruction overhead of the system. In this article, we focus on the reliability assessment of erasure coded systems and how the choice of codes affects the reliability in terms of the MTTDL and EAFDL metrics.

The MTTDL of erasure coded systems has been obtained analytically in [28]. It was theoretically shown that the MTTDL of erasure coded systems is practically insensitive to the distribution of the device failure times, but sensitive to the distribution of the device rebuild times. Simulation results confirmed the validity of the theoretical model. In this article, we establish that this also holds for the EAFDL metric. To reduce the amount of data lost, it is imperative to assess not only the frequency of data loss events, which is obtained through the MTTDL metric, but also the amount of data lost, which is expressed by the EAFDL metric [25]. The EAFDL and MTTDL metrics provide a useful profile of the size and frequency of data losses. Accordingly, we present a general framework and methodology for deriving the EAFDL analytically, along with the MTTDL, for erasure coded storage systems. The model developed captures the effect of the various system parameters as well as the effect of various codeword placement schemes, such as clustered, declustered, and symmetric data placement schemes. The results obtained show that the declustered placement scheme offers superior reliability in terms of both metrics. We also investigate the effect of the codeword length and identify the optimal values that offer the best reliability.

The key contributions of this article are the following. We consider the reliability of erasure coded systems that was assessed in our earlier work [1] for deterministic rebuild times. In this study, we extend our previous work by also considering arbitrary rebuild times. We show that the codeword lengths that optimize the MTTDL and EAFDL metrics are similar. Subsequently, we derive the asymptotic analytic expressions for the MTTDL and EAFDL reliability metrics when the number of devices becomes large. We then obtain analytically the optimal codeword lengths corresponding to large storage systems. We establish theoretically that, for large storage systems that use a declustered placement scheme, both metrics are optimized when the codeword length is about 60% of the storage system size.

The remainder of the paper is organized as follows. Section II provides a survey of the relevant literature on erasure coded systems. Section III describes the storage system model and the corresponding parameters considered. Section IV presents the general framework and methodology for deriving the MTTDL and EAFDL metrics analytically for the case of erasure coded systems. Closed-form expressions for the symmetric, clustered, and declustered placement schemes are derived. Section V compares these schemes and establishes that the declustered placement scheme offers superior reliability. Section VI presents a thorough comparison of the reliability achieved by the declustered placement scheme under various codeword configurations. Finally, we conclude in Section VII.

II. Related Work

A comparison between erasure coding and replication in terms of availability in peer-to-peer systems was presented in [29] and [30]. These works established that erasure codes use an order of magnitude less storage than replication for systems with a similar level of reliability. Erasure codes, however, are more demanding as they may require Galois field arithmetic for encoding and decoding. Therefore, to improve the performance of erasure coded systems, new codes as well as new encoding and decoding techniques have been developed (see [31] and references therein).

The study performed in [30] was conducted by considering a dynamic environment where nodes join and leave the system and subsequently trigger data movement. In this context, it was argued that bandwidth, and not spare storage, is most likely the limiting factor for the scalability of peer-to-peer storage systems. Furthermore, not only do erasure codes introduce a higher complexity in the system owing to the encoding and decoding process, but also the entire task of maintaining redundancy in such a dynamic environment becomes more challenging. In contrast to these works that consider the codeword lengths being equal to the number of nodes, our work relaxes this constraint by considering codeword lengths that may be smaller than the number of nodes. This is desirable for performance reasons given that in real storage systems the lengths of the erasure codes used are kept constant and small, whereas the number of nodes grows with the system capacity. In addition, having a smaller code length then allows the use of different placement schemes, some of which enable faster rebuilds and hence a higher reliability for the same erasure code.

In [15],[25],[28],[32] and [33], it was shown that the replica and codeword placements can have a significant impact on reliability. For this reason we also consider and assess the effect of several codeword placement schemes in this article.

TABLE I. NOTATION OF SYSTEM PARAMETERS

Parameter	Definition
n	number of storage devices
c	amount of data stored on each device
l	number of user-data symbols per codeword ($l \geq 1$)
m	total number of symbols per codeword ($m > l$)
s	symbol size
(l, m)	MDS-code structure
k	spread factor of the data placement scheme
b	average reserved rebuild bandwidth per device
X	time required to read (or write) an amount c of data at an average rate b from (or to) a device
$F_X(.)$	cumulative distribution function of X
Y_i	lifetime of the ith device ($i = 1, \ldots, n$)
$F_Y(.)$	cumulative distribution function of Y_i ($i = 1, \ldots, n$)
s_{eff}	storage efficiency of redundancy scheme ($s_{\text{eff}} = l/m$)
U	amount of user data stored in the system ($U = s_{\text{eff}}\, n\, c$)
$\tilde{r}$	minimum number of codeword symbols lost that lead to an irrecoverable data loss ($\tilde{r} = m - l + 1$ and $2 \leq \tilde{r} \leq m$)
$f_X(.)$	probability density function of X ($f_X(.) = F'_X(.)$)
$1/\mu$	mean time to read (or write) an amount c of data at a rate b from (or to) a device ($1/\mu = E(X) = c/b$)
$1/\lambda$	mean time to failure of a storage device ($1/\lambda = E(Y_i)$)

III. Storage System Model

The storage system considered comprises n storage devices (nodes or disks), with each device storing an amount c of data, such that the total storage capacity of the system is $n\,c$. Modern data storage systems use various forms of data redundancy to protect data from device failures. When devices fail, the redundancy of the data affected is reduced and eventually lost. To avoid irrecoverable data loss, the system performs rebuild operations that use the data stored in the surviving devices to reconstruct the temporarily lost data, thus maintaining the initial data redundancy.

A. Redundancy

According to the erasure coded schemes considered, the user data is divided into blocks (or symbols) of a fixed size (e.g., sector size of 512 bytes) and complemented with parity symbols to form codewords. In this article, we consider (l, m) maximum distance separable (MDS) erasure codes, which are a mapping from l user data symbols to a set of m ($> l$) symbols, called a codeword, in such a way that any subset containing l of the m symbols of the codeword can be used to decode (reconstruct, recover) the codeword. The corresponding storage efficiency, s_{eff}, is given by

$$s_{\text{eff}} = \frac{l}{m} . \tag{1}$$

Consequently, the amount of user data, U, stored in the system is given by

$$U = s_{\text{eff}}\, n\, c = \frac{l\, n\, c}{m} . \tag{2}$$

The notation used is summarized in Table I. The parameters are divided according to whether they are independent or derived, and are listed in the upper and the lower part of the table, respectively.

The m symbols of each codeword are stored on m distinct devices, such that the system can tolerate any $\tilde{r} - 1$ device failures, but $\tilde{r}$ device failures may lead to data loss, with

$$\tilde{r} = m - l + 1 . \tag{3}$$

From the preceding, it follows that

$$1 \leq l < m \qquad \text{and} \qquad 2 \leq \tilde{r} \leq m . \tag{4}$$

Examples of MDS erasure codes are the following:

Replication: A replication-based system with a replication factor r can tolerate any loss of up to $r-1$ copies of some data, such that $l = 1$, $m = r$ and $\tilde{r} = r$. Also, its storage efficiency is equal to $s_{\text{eff}}^{(\text{replication})} = 1/r$.
RAID-5: A RAID-5 array comprised of N devices uses an $(N-1, N)$-MDS code, such that $l = N-1$, $m = N$ and $\tilde{r} = 2$. It can therefore tolerate the loss of up to one device, and its storage efficiency is equal to $s_{\text{eff}}^{(\text{RAID-5})} = (N-1)/N$.
RAID-6: A RAID-6 array comprised of N devices uses an $(N-2, N)$-MDS code, such that $l = N-2$, $m = N$ and $\tilde{r} = 3$. It can therefore tolerate a loss of up to two devices, and its storage efficiency is equal to $s_{\text{eff}}^{(\text{RAID-6})} = (N-2)/N$.
Reed–Solomon: It is based on (l, m)-MDS erasure codes.

B. Symmetric Codeword Placement

We consider a placement where each codeword is stored on m distinct devices with one symbol per device. In a large storage system, the number of devices, n, is typically much larger than the codeword length, m. Therefore, there exist many ways in which a codeword of m symbols can be stored across a subset of the n devices. For each device in the system, let its *redundancy spread factor* k denote the number of devices over which the codewords stored on that device are spread [28]. The system effectively comprises n/k disjoint groups of k devices. Each group contains an amount U/k of user data, with the corresponding codewords placed on the corresponding k devices in a distributed manner. Each codeword is placed entirely in one of the n/k groups. Within each group, all $\binom{k}{m}$ possible ways of placing m symbols across k devices are equally used to store all the codewords in that group.

In such a symmetric placement scheme, within each of the n/k groups, the $m-1$ codeword symbols corresponding to the data on each device are *equally* spread across the remaining $k-1$ devices, the $m-2$ codeword symbols corresponding to the codewords shared by any two devices are equally spread across the remaining $k-2$ devices, and so on. Note also that the n/k groups are logical and therefore need not be physically located in the same node/rack/datacenter.

We proceed by considering the clustered and declustered placement schemes, which are special cases of symmetric placement schemes for which k is equal to m and n, respectively. This results in n/m groups for clustered and one group for declustered placement schemes.

1) Clustered Placement: In this placement scheme, the n devices are divided into disjoint sets of m devices, referred to as *clusters*. According to the *clustered* placement, each codeword is stored across the devices of a particular cluster, as shown in Figure 1. In such a placement scheme, it can be seen that no cluster stores the redundancies that correspond to data stored on another cluster. The entire storage system can essentially be modeled as consisting of n/m independent clusters. In each cluster, data loss occurs when $\tilde{r}$ devices fail successively before rebuild operations complete successfully.

2) Declustered Placement: In this placement scheme, all $\binom{n}{m}$ possible ways of placing m symbols across n devices are equally used to store all the codewords in the system, as shown in Figure 1.

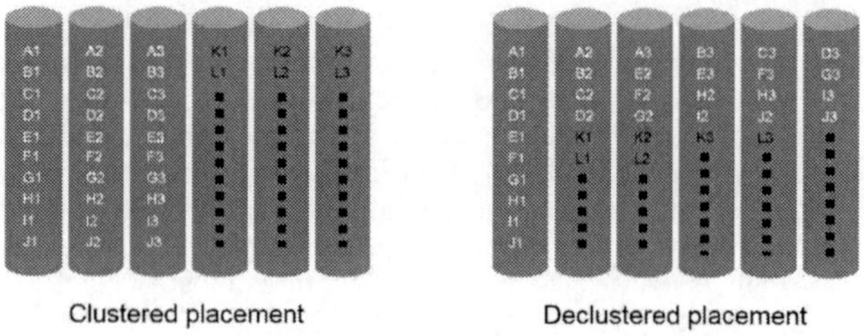

Figure 1. Clustered and declustered placement of codewords of length $m = 3$ on $n = 6$ devices. X1, X2, X3 represents a codeword (X = A, B, C, . . . , L).

These two placement schemes represent the two extremes in which the symbols of the codewords associated with the data stored on a failing device are spread across the remaining devices and hence the extremes of the degree of parallelism that can be exploited when rebuilding this data. For declustered placement, the symbols are spread equally across *all* remaining devices, whereas for clustered placement, the symbols are spread across the smallest possible number of devices.

C. Codeword Reconstruction

When storage devices fail, codewords lose some of their symbols, and this leads to a reduction in data redundancy. The system attempts to maintain its redundancy by reconstructing the lost codeword symbols using the surviving symbols of the affected codewords.

When a declustered placement scheme is used, as shown in Figure 2, spare space is reserved on each device for temporarily storing the reconstructed codeword symbols before they are transferred to a new replacement device. The rebuild bandwidth available on all surviving devices is used to rebuild the lost symbols in parallel. During this process, it is desirable to reconstruct the lost codeword symbols on devices in which another symbol of the same codeword is not already present. A similar reconstruction process is used for other symmetric placement schemes within each group of k devices, except for the clustered placement. When clustered placement is used, the codeword symbols are spread across all $k = m$ devices in each group (cluster). Therefore, reconstructing the lost symbols on the surviving devices of a group will result in more than one symbol of the same codeword on the same device. To avoid this, the lost symbols are reconstructed directly in spare devices as shown in Figure 3. In these reconstruction processes, decoding and re-encoding of data are assumed to be done on the fly and so the time taken for reconstruction is equal to the time taken to read and write the required data to the devices. Alternative methods of reconstruction based on regenerating codes have been proposed as a solution to reduce the amount of data transferred over the storage network during reconstruction (see [34] and references therein). They can, however, result in higher amounts of data being read from the surviving devices and therefore in longer rebuild times. The effect of these methods on the system reliability is outside the scope of this paper and is a subject of further investigation.

1) Exposure Levels and Amount of Data to Rebuild: At time t, let $D_j(t)$ be the number of codewords that have lost j

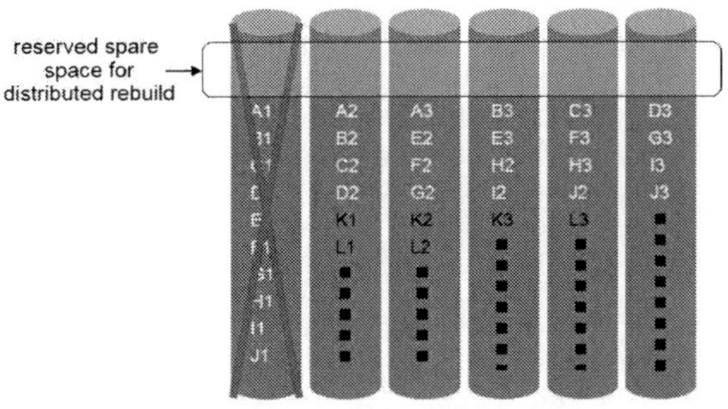

(a) Spare space reserved in each device.

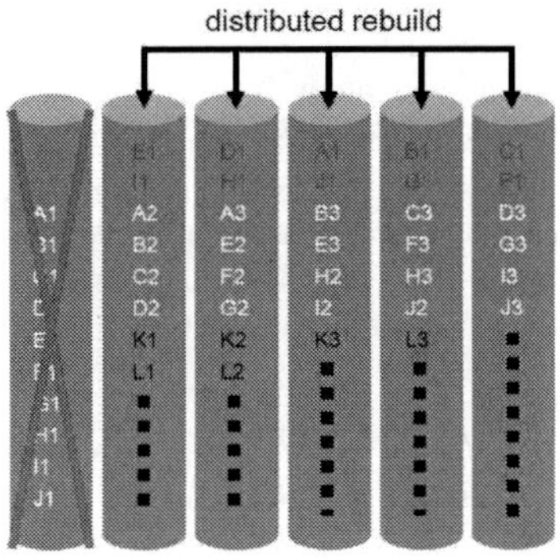

(b) Distributed rebuild.

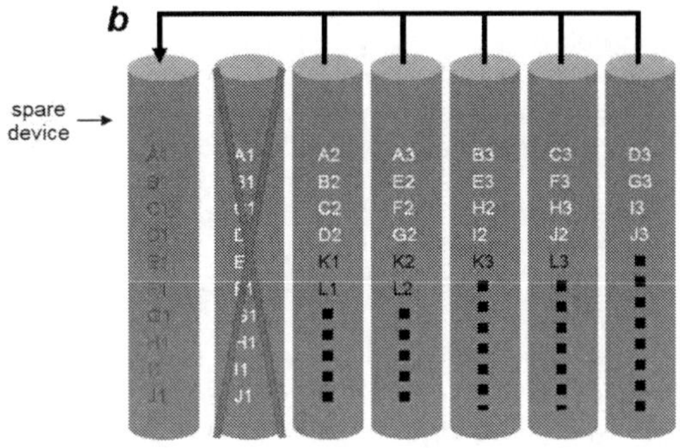

(c) Restoration of data on a spare device.

Figure 2. Rebuild under declustered placement.

symbols, with $0 \leq j \leq \tilde{r}$. The system is at exposure level u $(0 \leq u \leq \tilde{r})$, where

$$u = \max_{D_j(t)>0} j . \quad (5)$$

In other words, the system is at exposure level u if there are codewords with $m-u$ symbols left, but there are no codewords with fewer than $m-u$ symbols left in the system, that is, $D_u(t) > 0$, and $D_j(t) = 0$, for all $j > u$. These codewords are referred to as the *most-exposed* codewords. At $t = 0$, $D_j(0) = 0$, for all $j > 0$, and $D_0(0)$ is the total number of codewords stored in the system. Device failures and rebuild processes cause the values of $D_1(t), \cdots, D_{\tilde{r}}(t)$ to change over time, and when a data loss occurs, $D_{\tilde{r}}(t) > 0$. Device failures cause transitions to higher exposure levels, whereas rebuilds cause transitions to lower ones. Let t_u denote the time of the first transition from exposure level $u-1$ to exposure level u, and

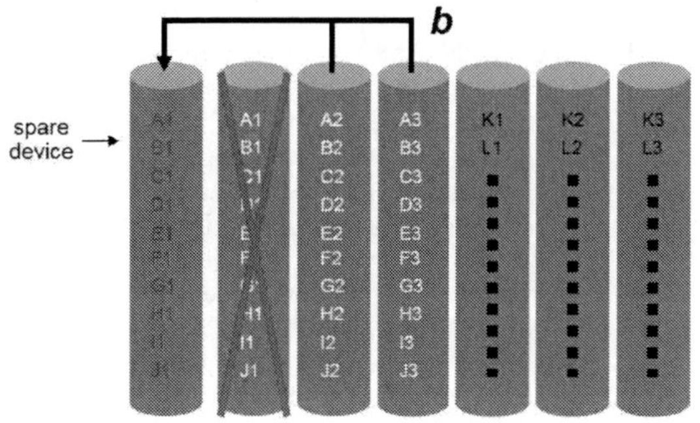

Figure 3. Rebuild under clustered placement.

TABLE II. NOTATION OF SYSTEM PARAMETERS AT EXPOSURE LEVELS

Parameter	Definition
u	exposure level
C_u	number of most-exposed codewords when entering exposure level u
R_u	rebuild time at exposure level u
$P_{u \to u+1}$	transition probability from exposure level u to $u+1$
$\tilde{n}_u$	number of devices at exposure level u whose failure causes an exposure level transition to level $u+1$
α_u	fraction of the rebuild time R_u still left when another device fails causing the exposure level transition $u \to u+1$
V_u	fraction of the most-exposed codewords that have symbols stored on another of the $\tilde{n}_u$ devices
A_u	amount of data corresponding to the C_u symbols ($A_u = C_u\, s$)
b_u	average rate at which recovered data is written at exposure level u

t_u^+ the instant immediately after t_u. Then, the number of most exposed codewords when entering exposure level u, denoted by C_u, $u = 1, \ldots, \tilde{r}$, is given by $C_u = D_u(t_u^+)$.

In Section IV-A1, we will derive the reliability metrics of interest using the direct path approximation, which considers only transitions from lower to higher exposure levels [15][28][32]. This implies that each exposure level is entered only once.

2) Prioritized or Intelligent Rebuild: At each exposure level u, the *prioritized or intelligent* rebuild process attempts to bring the system back to exposure level $u-1$ by recovering one of the u symbols that each of the most-exposed codewords has lost, that is, by recovering a total number of C_u symbols. Let A_u denote the amount of data corresponding to the C_u symbols and let s denote the symbol size. Then, it holds that

$$A_u = C_u\, s . \quad (6)$$

The notation used is summarized in Table II. For an exposure level u $(< \tilde{r})$, A_u represents the amount of data that needs to be rebuilt at that exposure level. In particular, upon the first-device failure, it holds that

$$A_1 = c , \quad (7)$$

which, combined with (6), implies that

$$C_1 = A_1/s = c/s . \quad (8)$$

D. Rebuild Process

During the rebuild process, a certain proportion of the device bandwidth is reserved for data recovery, with b denoting the actual average reserved rebuild bandwidth per device. The average rebuild bandwidth is usually only a fraction of the total bandwidth available at each device; the remainder is used to serve user requests. Let us denote by b_u ($\leq b$) the average rate at which the amount A_u of data that needs to be rebuilt at exposure level u is written to selected device(s). Also, denote the cumulative distribution function of the time X required to read (or write) an amount c of data from (or to) a device by $F_X(.)$ and its corresponding probability density function by $f_X(.)$. The kth moment of X, $E(X^k)$, is then given by

$$E(X^k) = \int_0^\infty t^k f_X(t)dt \ , \quad \text{for } k = 1, 2, \ldots \ . \tag{9}$$

In particular, let us denote by $1/\mu$ the average time required to read (or write) an amount c of data from (or to) a device, given by

$$\frac{1}{\mu} \triangleq E(X) = \frac{c}{b} \ . \tag{10}$$

E. Failure and Rebuild Time Distributions

In this work, we assume that the lifetimes $Y_1, \cdots, Y_n$ of the n devices are independent and identically distributed, with a cumulative distribution function $F_Y(.)$ and a mean of $1/\lambda$. In practice, this assumption is valid when the symbols of a codeword are placed on independently failing devices, for example, on devices located on different nodes/racks/datacenters. An extension of the analysis to also address correlated failures is part of future work. We further consider storage devices with failure time distributions that belong to the large class defined in [15], which includes real-world distributions, such as Weibull and gamma, as well as exponential distributions. The storage devices are *highly reliable* when the ratio of the mean time $1/\mu$ to read all contents of a device (which typically is on the order of tens of hours) to the mean time to failure of a device $1/\lambda$ (which is typically at least on the order of thousands of hours) is small, that is, when

$$\frac{\lambda}{\mu} = \frac{\lambda c}{b} \ll 1 \ . \tag{11}$$

According to [15][28], when the cumulative distribution functions F_Y and F_X satisfy the condition

$$\mu \int_0^\infty F_Y(t)[1 - F_X(t)]dt \ll 1, \quad \text{with } \frac{\lambda}{\mu} \ll 1 \ , \tag{12}$$

the MTTDL reliability metric of replication-based or erasure coded storage systems tends to be insensitive to the device failure distribution, that is, the MTTDL depends only on its mean $1/\lambda$, but not on its density $F_Y(.)$. In [25], it was shown that this also holds for the EAFDL metric in the case of replication-based storage systems and when the rebuild times are deterministic. In this article, we will show that this also holds for the EAFDL metric in the case of erasure coded systems under variable rebuild times.

IV. Derivation of MTTDL and EAFDL

We briefly review the general methodology for deriving the MTTDL and EAFDL metrics presented in [25]. This methodology does not involve any Markov analysis and holds for general failure time distributions, which can be exponential or non-exponential, such as the Weibull and gamma distributions that satisfy condition (12).

At any point in time, the system can be thought to be in one of two modes: normal mode and rebuild mode. During normal mode, all data in the system has the original amount of redundancy and there is no active rebuild process. During rebuild mode, some data in the system has less than the original amount of redundancy and there is an active rebuild process that is trying to restore the lost redundancy. A transition from normal mode to rebuild mode occurs when a device fails; we refer to the device failure that causes this transition as a *first-device* failure. Following a first-device failure, a complex sequence of rebuild operations and subsequent device failures may occur, which eventually leads the system either to an irrecoverable data loss (DL) with probability P_{DL} or back to the original normal mode by restoring initial redundancy, which occurs with probability $1 - P_{DL}$.

Let T be a typical interval of a fully operational period, that is, the time interval from the time t that the system is brought to its original state until a subsequent first-device failure occurs. For a system comprising n devices with a mean time to failure of a device equal to $1/\lambda$, the expected duration of T is given by [25]

$$E(T) = 1/(n\,\lambda) \ , \tag{13}$$

and the MTTDL by

$$\text{MTTDL} \approx \frac{E(T)}{P_{DL}} = \frac{1}{n\,\lambda\,P_{DL}} \ . \tag{14}$$

Let H denote the corresponding amount of data lost conditioned on the fact that a data loss has occurred. The metric of interest, that is, the Expected Annual Fraction of Data Loss (EAFDL), is subsequently obtained as the ratio of the expected amount of data lost to the expected time to data loss normalized to the amount of user data [25]:

$$\text{EAFDL} = \frac{E(H)}{\text{MTTDL} \cdot U} \ , \tag{15}$$

with the MTTDL expressed in years. Let us also denote by Q the unconditional amount of data lost upon a first-device failure. Note that Q is unconditional on the event of a data loss occurring in that it is equal either to H if the system suffers a data loss prior to returning to normal operation or to zero otherwise, that is,

$$Q = \begin{cases} H \ , & \text{if DL} \\ 0 \ , & \text{if no DL} \ . \end{cases} \tag{16}$$

Therefore, the expected amount of data lost, $E(Q)$, upon a first-device failure is given by

$$E(Q) = P_{DL}\,E(H) \ . \tag{17}$$

From (14), (15) and (17), we obtain the EAFDL as follows:

$$\text{EAFDL} \approx \frac{E(Q)}{E(T) \cdot U} = \frac{n\,\lambda\,E(Q)}{U} \ , \tag{18}$$

with $E(T)$ and $1/\lambda$ expressed in years.

A. Reliability Analysis

From (14) and (18), it follows that the derivation of the MTTDL and EAFDL metrics requires the evaluation of P_{DL} and $E(Q)$, respectively. These quantities are derived by considering the direct path approximation [15][28][32], which, under conditions (11) and (12), accurately assesses the reliability metrics of interest [13][14][15][25].

Next, we present the general outline of the methodology in more detail.

1) Direct Path to Data Loss: Consider the direct path of successive transitions from exposure level 1 to $\tilde{r}$. In [15][28][32], it was shown that P_{DL} can be approximated by the probability of the direct path to data loss, $P_{\text{DL,direct}}$, that is,

$$P_{\text{DL}} \approx P_{\text{DL,direct}} = \prod_{u=1}^{r-1} P_{u \to u+1} , \tag{19}$$

where $P_{u \to u+1}$ denotes the transition probability from exposure level u to $u+1$. The above approximation holds when storage devices are highly reliable, that is, it holds for arbitrary device failure and rebuild time distributions that satisfy conditions (11) and (12). In this case, the relative error tends to zero as λ/μ tends to zero [15].

As the direct path to data loss dominates the effect of all other possible paths to data loss considered together, it follows that the amount of data lost H can be approximated by that corresponding to the direct path:

$$H \approx H_{\text{direct}} . \tag{20}$$

Also, from (16) and (20) it follows that

$$Q \approx \begin{cases} H_{\text{direct}} , & \text{if DL follows the direct path} \\ 0 , & \text{otherwise} . \end{cases} \tag{21}$$

Consequently, to derive the amount of data lost, it suffices to proceed by considering the H and Q metrics corresponding to the direct path to data loss.

Note that the amount of data lost, H, is the amount of user data stored in the most-exposed codewords when entering exposure level $\tilde{r}$, which can no longer be recovered and therefore is irrecoverably lost. As the number of these codewords is equal to $C_{\tilde{r}}$ and each of these codewords contains l symbols of user data, it holds that

$$H = C_{\tilde{r}} \, l \, s , \tag{22}$$

and using (6),

$$H = l \, A_{\tilde{r}} . \tag{23}$$

2) Amount of Data to Rebuild and Rebuild Times at Each Exposure Level: We now proceed to derive the conditional values of the random variables of interest given that the system goes through the direct path to data loss. Let R_u denote the rebuild times of the most-exposed codewords at each exposure level in this path, and let α_u be the fraction of the rebuild time R_u still left when another device fails causing the exposure level transition $u \to u+1$. In [35, Lemma 2], it was shown that, for highly reliable devices satisfying conditions (11) and (12), α_u is approximately uniformly distributed between zero and one, that is,

$$\alpha_u \sim U(0,1), \quad u = 1, \ldots, \tilde{r} - 1 . \tag{24}$$

Let $\vec{\alpha}$ denote the vector $(\alpha_1, \ldots, \alpha_{\tilde{r}-1})$, $\vec{\alpha}_u$ the vector $(\alpha_1, \ldots, \alpha_u)$, $\vec{C}_u$ the vector $(C_1, \cdots, C_u)$ and $\vec{A}_u$ the vector $(A_1, \cdots, A_u)$. Clearly, for the rebuild schemes considered, the fraction α_u of the rebuild time R_u still left also represents the expected fraction of the most-exposed codewords not yet recovered upon the next device failure. Therefore, the expected number of most-exposed codewords that are not yet recovered is equal to $\alpha_u \, C_u$. Clearly, the fraction V_u of these codewords that have symbols stored on the newly failed device depends on the codeword placement scheme. Consequently, the expected number of the most-exposed codewords when entering exposure level $u+1$ is given by

$$E(C_{u+1} \,|\, \vec{\alpha}, \vec{C}_u) = V_u \, \alpha_u \, C_u , \quad u = 1, \ldots, \tilde{r} - 1 , \tag{25}$$

with V_u depending only on the placement scheme. Similarly, from (6), it follows that the corresponding expected amount of data that is not yet rebuilt is equal to $\alpha_u \, A_u$. From (25), we deduce that

$$E(A_{u+1} \,|\, \vec{\alpha}, \vec{A}_u) = V_u \, \alpha_u \, A_u , \quad u = 1, \ldots, \tilde{r} - 1 , \tag{26}$$

An expression for the expected amount of data to be rebuilt at each exposure level is given by the following proposition.

Proposition 1: For $u = 2, \ldots, \tilde{r} - 1$, it holds that

$$E(A_u \,|\, \vec{\alpha}_{u-1}) = c \prod_{j=1}^{u-1} V_j \, \alpha_j . \tag{27}$$

Proof: We will prove (27) by induction. For $u = 2$, (27) holds owing to (7) and (26). Suppose that (27) holds for $u = k$, that is,

$$E(A_k \,|\, \vec{\alpha}_{k-1}) = c \prod_{j=1}^{k-1} V_j \, \alpha_j . \tag{28}$$

We will show that (27) also holds for $u = k+1$, that is,

$$E(A_{k+1} \,|\, \vec{\alpha}_k) = c \prod_{j=1}^{k} V_j \, \alpha_j . \tag{29}$$

From (26) it holds that

$$E(A_{k+1} \,|\, \vec{\alpha}, \vec{A}_k) = E(A_{k+1} \,|\, \vec{\alpha}_k, A_k) = V_k \, \alpha_k \, A_k . \tag{30}$$

It also holds that

$$E(A_{k+1} \,|\, \vec{\alpha}_k) = E_{A_k \,|\, \vec{\alpha}_k}[E(A_{k+1} \,|\, \vec{\alpha}_k, \vec{A}_k)] . \tag{31}$$

Substituting (30) into (31) yields

$$E(A_{k+1} \,|\, \vec{\alpha}_k) = E_{A_k \,|\, \vec{\alpha}_k}(V_k \, \alpha_k \, A_k) = V_k \, \alpha_k \, E(A_k \,|\, \vec{\alpha}_k) . \tag{32}$$

Clearly, the number C_k of most-exposed codewords when entering exposure level k and the corresponding amount of data A_k does not depend on the fraction α_k of the rebuild time R_k still left when another device fails causing the exposure level transition $k \to k+1$. It therefore holds that $E(A_k \,|\, \vec{\alpha}_k) = E(A_k \,|\, \vec{\alpha}_{k-1})$, and (32) yields

$$E(A_{k+1} \,|\, \vec{\alpha}_k) = V_k \, \alpha_k \, E(A_k \,|\, \vec{\alpha}_{k-1}) \overset{(28)}{=} c \prod_{j=1}^{k} V_j \, \alpha_j . \tag{33}$$

■

Remark 1: From (27), it follows that the expected amount of data to be rebuilt at each exposure level do not depend on the duration of the rebuild times.

At exposure level 1, according to (7), the amount A_1 of data to be recovered is equal to c. Given that this data is recovered at an average rate of b_1 and that the time required to write an amount c of data at an an average rate of b is equal to X, it follows that the rebuild time R_1 is given by

$$R_1 = \frac{b}{b_1} X . \tag{34}$$

As the rebuild times are proportional to the amount of data to be rebuilt and are inversely proportional to the rebuild rates, it holds that

$$E\left(\frac{R_{u+1}}{R_u} \mid \vec{\alpha}, \vec{A}_u\right) = E\left(\frac{A_{u+1}}{A_u} \mid \vec{\alpha}, \vec{A}_u\right) \frac{b_u}{b_{u+1}} , \; u \geq 1 . \tag{35}$$

Using (26), (35) yields

$$E\left(\frac{R_{u+1}}{R_u} \mid \vec{\alpha}, \vec{A}_u\right) = V_u \, \alpha_u \, \frac{b_u}{b_{u+1}} , \quad u = 1, \ldots, \tilde{r} - 2 , \tag{36}$$

and conditioning on R_u,

$$E(R_{u+1} \mid \vec{\alpha}, \vec{A}_u, R_u) = V_u \, \alpha_u \, \frac{b_u}{b_{u+1}} R_u , \; u = 1, \ldots, \tilde{r} - 2 . \tag{37}$$

The above implies that of all the random variables involved in vectors $\vec{\alpha}$ and $\vec{A}_u$, only a_u and R_u are essential for determining $E(R_{u+1})$. We proceed by considering the mean $1/\mu_u$ of the rebuild time R_u conditioned on α_{u-1} and R_{u-1}:

$$1/\mu_u \triangleq E(R_u \mid R_{u-1}, \alpha_{u-1}), \quad u = 2, \ldots, \tilde{r} - 1 . \tag{38}$$

From (37) and (38), it follows that

$$1/\mu_u = G_{u-1} \, \alpha_{u-1} \, R_{u-1} , \quad \text{for } u = 2, \ldots, \tilde{r} - 1 , \tag{39}$$

where

$$G_u \triangleq \frac{b_u}{b_{u+1}} V_u , \quad u = 1, \ldots, \tilde{r} - 2 . \tag{40}$$

The distribution of R_u, given R_{u-1} and α_{u-1}, could be modeled in several ways. We proceed as in [28] by considering the model B presented in [15], according to which the rebuild time R_u is determined completely by R_{u-1} and α_{u-1} and no new randomness is introduced in the rebuild time at exposure level u, that is,

$$R_u \mid R_{u-1}, \alpha_{u-1} = 1/\mu_u \;\; w.p. 1, \text{ for } u = 2, \ldots, \tilde{r} - 1 , \tag{41}$$

which by virtue of (39) yields

$$R_u = G_{u-1} \, \alpha_{u-1} \, R_{u-1} , \quad \text{for } u = 2, \ldots, \tilde{r} - 1 . \tag{42}$$

Repeatedly applying (42) and using (40) yields

$$R_u = \frac{b_1}{b_u} R_1 \prod_{j=1}^{u-1} V_j \, \alpha_j , \quad u = 1, \ldots, \tilde{r} - 1 . \tag{43}$$

Let $\tilde{n}_u$ be the number of devices at exposure level u whose failure before the rebuild of the most-exposed codewords causes an exposure level transition to level $u+1$. Subsequently, the transition probability $P_{u \to u+1}$ from exposure level u to $u+1$ depends on the duration of the corresponding rebuild time R_u and the aggregate failure rate of these $\tilde{n}_u$ highly reliable devices, and is given by [15]

$$P_{u \to u+1} \approx \tilde{n}_u \, \lambda \, R_u , \quad \text{for } u = 1, \ldots, \tilde{r} - 1 . \tag{44}$$

Conditioning on R_1 and $\vec{\alpha}_{u-1}$, and substituting (43) into (44), yields

$$P_{u \to u+1}(R_1, \vec{\alpha}_{u-1}) \approx \tilde{n}_u \, \lambda \, \frac{b_1}{b_u} \, R_1 \prod_{j=1}^{u-1} V_j \, \alpha_j . \tag{45}$$

Approximate expressions for the probability of data loss, P_{DL}, and the expected amount of data lost, $E(Q)$, are subsequently obtained by the following propositions.

Proposition 2: It holds that

$$P_{\text{DL}} \approx (\lambda \, c)^{\tilde{r}-1} \, \frac{1}{(\tilde{r}-1)!} \, \frac{E(X^{\tilde{r}-1})}{[E(X)]^{\tilde{r}-1}} \prod_{u=1}^{\tilde{r}-1} \frac{\tilde{n}_u}{b_u} \, V_u^{\tilde{r}-1-u} , \tag{46}$$

where $E(X^{\tilde{r}-1})$ is obtained by (9).

Proof: See Appendix A. ■

Proposition 3: It holds that

$$E(Q) \approx l \, c \, (\lambda \, c)^{\tilde{r}-1} \, \frac{1}{\tilde{r}!} \, \frac{E(X^{\tilde{r}-1})}{[E(X)]^{\tilde{r}-1}} \prod_{u=1}^{\tilde{r}-1} \frac{\tilde{n}_u}{b_u} \, V_u^{\tilde{r}-u} , \tag{47}$$

where $E(X^{\tilde{r}-1})$ is obtained by (9).

Proof: See Appendix B. ■

3) Evaluation of $E(H)$: The expected amount $E(H)$ of data lost conditioned on the fact that a data loss has occurred is obtained from (17) as the ratio of $E(Q)$ to P_{DL}. Consequently, using (46) and (47), it follows that

$$E(H) = \frac{E(Q)}{P_{\text{DL}}} \approx \left(\frac{l}{\tilde{r}} \prod_{u=1}^{\tilde{r}-1} V_u\right) c . \tag{48}$$

Remark 2: From (48), it follows that the expected amount of data lost conditioned on the fact that a data loss has occurred does not depend on the duration of the rebuild times.

4) Evaluation of MTTDL *and* EAFDL*:* Substituting (46) into (14) yields

$$\text{MTTDL} \approx \frac{1}{n \, \lambda} \, \frac{(\tilde{r}-1)!}{(\lambda \, c)^{\tilde{r}-1}} \, \frac{[E(X)]^{\tilde{r}-1}}{E(X^{\tilde{r}-1})} \prod_{u=1}^{\tilde{r}-1} \frac{b_u}{\tilde{n}_u} \, \frac{1}{V_u^{\tilde{r}-1-u}} . \tag{49}$$

Substituting (2) and (47) into (18) yields

$$\text{EAFDL} \approx m \, \lambda \, (\lambda \, c)^{\tilde{r}-1} \, \frac{1}{\tilde{r}!} \, \frac{E(X^{\tilde{r}-1})}{[E(X)]^{\tilde{r}-1}} \prod_{u=1}^{\tilde{r}-1} \frac{\tilde{n}_u}{b_u} \, V_u^{\tilde{r}-u} . \tag{50}$$

B. Symmetric Placement

Here, we consider the case where the redundancy spread factor k is in the interval $m < k \leq n$. As discussed in Section III-C2, at each exposure level u, the *prioritized* rebuild process recovers one of the u symbols that each of the C_u most-exposed codewords has lost by reading $m - \tilde{r} + 1$ of the remaining symbols. Thus, there are C_u symbols to be recovered in total, which corresponds to an amount A_u of data. For the symmetric placement discussed in Section III-B, these symbols are recovered by reading $(m - \tilde{r} + 1) C_u$ symbols, which corresponds to an amount $(m - \tilde{r} + 1) A_u$

of data, from the $k-u$ surviving devices in the affected group. Note that these are precisely the devices at exposure level u whose failure before the rebuild of the most-exposed codewords causes an exposure level transition to level $u+1$. Consequently, it holds that

$$\tilde{n}_u^{\text{sym}} = k - u \,. \tag{51}$$

Furthermore, it is desirable to write the recovered symbols to the spare space of these devices in such a way that no symbol is written to a device in which another symbol corresponding to the same codeword is already present. This will ensure that whenever a device fails, no more than one symbol from any codeword is lost. Owing to the symmetry of the symmetric placement, the same amount of data is being read from each of the $\tilde{n}_u$ devices. Similarly, the same amount of data is being written to each of the $\tilde{n}_u$ devices. Consequently, the total average read/write rebuild bandwidth b of each device is split between the reads and the writes, such that the average read rate is equal to $(m-\tilde{r}+1)\,b/(m-\tilde{r}+2)$ and the average write rate is equal to $b/(m-\tilde{r}+2)$. Therefore, the total average write bandwidth, which is also the average rebuild rate b_u, is given by

$$b_u^{\text{sym}} = \frac{\tilde{n}_u}{m-\tilde{r}+2}\, b \,, \quad u = 1, \ldots, \tilde{r}-1 \,. \tag{52}$$

Once all lost codeword symbols have been recovered, they are transferred to a new replacement device.

When the system enters exposure level u, the number of most-exposed codewords that need to be recovered is equal to C_u, $u = 1, \ldots, \tilde{r}$. Upon the next device failure, the expected number of most-exposed codewords that are not yet recovered is equal to $\alpha_u C_u$. Owing to the nature of the symmetric codeword placement, the newly failed device stores codeword symbols corresponding to only a fraction

$$V_u^{\text{sym}} = \frac{m-u}{k-u} \,, \quad u = 1, \ldots, \tilde{r}-1 \,. \tag{53}$$

of these most-exposed, not yet recovered codewords.

Substituting (51), (52), and (53) into (49), (50), and (48), and using (3), yields

$$\text{MTTDL}_k^{\text{sym}} \approx \frac{1}{n\,\lambda}\left[\frac{b}{(l+1)\,\lambda\, c}\right]^{m-l} (m-l)! \, \frac{[E(X)]^{m-l}}{E(X^{m-l})} \prod_{u=1}^{m-l}\left(\frac{k-u}{m-u}\right)^{m-l-u} \,, \tag{54}$$

$$\text{EAFDL}_k^{\text{sym}} \approx \lambda \left[\frac{(l+1)\,\lambda\, c}{b}\right]^{m-l} \frac{m}{(m-l+1)!} \, \frac{E(X^{m-l})}{[E(X)]^{m-l}} \prod_{u=1}^{m-l}\left(\frac{m-u}{k-u}\right)^{m-l+1-u} \,, \tag{55}$$

and

$$E(H)_k^{\text{sym}} \approx \left(\frac{l}{m-l+1}\prod_{u=1}^{m-l}\frac{m-u}{k-u}\right) c \tag{56}$$

$$= \frac{l\,(m-1)!\,(k-m+l-1)!}{(m-l+1)\,(k-1)!\,(l-1)!}\, c \,. \tag{57}$$

Note that for a deterministic rebuild time distribution, for which it holds that $E(X^{m-l}) = [E(X)]^{m-l}$, and for a replication-based system, for which $m = r$ and $l = 1$, (54) and (55) are in agreement with Equations (42.b) and (43.b) of [25], respectively.

Remark 3: From (54), (55), and (56), it follows that $\text{MTTDL}_k^{\text{sym}}$ depends on n, but $\text{EAFDL}_k^{\text{sym}}$ and $E(H)_k^{\text{sym}}$ do not.

Remark 4: From (54), (55), and (56), it follows that, for $m-l=1$, $\text{MTTDL}_k^{\text{sym}}$ does not depend on k, whereas for $m-l>1$, $\text{MTTDL}_k^{\text{sym}}$ is increasing in k. Also, for $m-l \geq 1$, $\text{EAFDL}_k^{\text{sym}}$ and $E(H)_k^{\text{sym}}$ are decreasing in k. Consequently, within the class of symmetric placement schemes considered, that is, for $m < k \leq n$, the $\text{MTTDL}_k^{\text{sym}}$ is maximized and the $\text{EAFDL}_k^{\text{sym}}$ and the $E(H)_k^{\text{sym}}$ are minimized when $k = n$. Also, given that $E(X) = c/b$, the $\text{MTTDL}_k^{\text{sym}}$ and $\text{EAFDL}_k^{\text{sym}}$ depend on the $(m-l)$th moment of the rebuild time distribution, whereas $E(H)_k^{\text{sym}}$ does not depend on the rebuild times. Furthermore, given that $E(X^{m-l}) \geq [E(X)]^{m-l}$, random rebuild times result in lower MTTDL and higher EAFDL values than deterministic rebuild times do.

Approximate expressions for the reliability metrics of interest are given by the following propositions.

Proposition 4: For large values of k, m, l, and $m-l$, the $E(H)^{\text{sym}}$ normalized to c can be approximated as follows:

$$\log\left(E(H)_{\text{approx}}^{\text{sym}}/c\right) \approx \log\left(\frac{(1-h)\,x\,k}{h\,x\,k+1}\sqrt{\frac{1-h}{1-hx}}\right) + k\,V(h,x) \,, \tag{58}$$

where $V(h,x)$ is given by

$$V(h,x) \triangleq \log\left(\frac{x^x\,(1-hx)^{1-hx}}{[(1-h)x]^{(1-h)x}}\right) , \tag{59}$$

h is given by

$$h \triangleq 1 - s_{\text{eff}} = 1 - \frac{l}{m} \tag{60}$$

and x by

$$x \triangleq \frac{m}{k} \,. \tag{61}$$

Proof: See Appendix C. ■

Proposition 5: For large values of k, m, l, and $m-l$, the $\text{MTTDL}^{\text{sym}}$ normalized to $1/\lambda$ can be approximated as follows:

$$\log\left(\lambda\,\text{MTTDL}_{\text{approx}}^{\text{sym}}\right) \approx \log\left(\frac{k}{n}\right) + k^2\,\frac{W(h,x)}{2} + k\,hx\,\log\left(\frac{hx\sqrt{x}\,k\,b}{e\,[(1-h)x\,k+1]\,\lambda\, c}\right) - \frac{1}{8}\left[h(1-x) - \log\left(\frac{1-h}{1-hx}\right)\right] + \log\left(\sqrt{\frac{2\pi hx}{k}}\right) + \log\left(\frac{[E(X)]^{hxk}}{E(X^{hxk})}\right) , \tag{62}$$

where

$$W(h,x) \triangleq hx(1-x) - \log\left(\frac{\left[(1-h)^{(1-h)^2}\,x^{h^2}\right]^{x^2}}{(1-hx)^{(1-hx)^2}}\right) , \tag{63}$$

and h and x are given by (60) and (61), respectively.

Proof: See Appendix D. ■

Proposition 6: For large values of k, m, l, and $m-l$, the $\text{EAFDL}^{\text{sym}}$ normalized to λ can be approximated as follows:

$$\log\left(\text{EAFDL}^{\text{sym}}_{\text{approx}}/\lambda\right) \approx - k^2\,\frac{W(h,x)}{2} + k\left\{hx\,\log\left(\frac{e\,[(1-h)x\,k+1]\,\lambda\,c}{h\sqrt{x}\,k\,b}\right) + \log\left(\frac{(1-hx)^{1-hx}}{(1-h)^{(1-h)x}}\right)\right\} + \frac{1}{8}h(1-x) + \log\left(\frac{1}{hx\,k+1}\sqrt{\frac{x\,k}{2\pi h}}\left(\frac{1-h}{1-hx}\right)^{\frac{3}{8}}\right) + \log\left(\frac{E(X^{hxk})}{[E(X)]^{hxk}}\right), \quad (64)$$

where h, x, and $W(h,x)$ are given by (60), (61), and (63), respectively.

Proof: See Appendix E. ■

C. Clustered Placement

As discussed in Section III-B1, in the clustered placement scheme, the n devices are divided into disjoint sets of m devices, referred to as *clusters*. According to the *clustered* placement, each codeword is stored across the devices of a particular cluster. At each exposure level u, the rebuild process recovers one of the u symbols that each of the C_u most-exposed codewords has lost by reading $m-\tilde{r}+1$ of the remaining symbols. Note that the remaining symbols are stored on the $m-u$ surviving devices in the affected group. As these are precisely the devices at exposure level u whose failure before the rebuild of the most-exposed codewords causes an exposure level transition to level $u+1$, it holds that

$$\tilde{n}_u^{\text{clus}} = m - u\,. \quad (65)$$

The rebuild process in clustered placement recovers the lost symbols by reading $m-\tilde{r}+1$ symbols from $m-\tilde{r}+1$ of the $\tilde{n}_u$ surviving devices of the affected cluster. The lost symbols are computed on-the-fly and written to a spare device using the rebuild bandwidth at an average rate of b. Consequently, it holds that

$$b_u^{\text{clus}} = b\,, \quad u = 1, \ldots, \tilde{r}-1\,. \quad (66)$$

Remark 5: Note that as far as the data placement is concerned, the clustered placement scheme is a special case of a symmetric placement scheme for which k is equal to m. However, its reliability assessment cannot be directly obtained from the reliability results derived in Section IV-B for the symmetric placement scheme by simply setting $k=m$. The reason for that is the difference in the rebuild processes. In the case of a symmetric placement scheme, recovered symbols are written to the spare space of existing devices, whereas in the case of a clustered placement scheme, recovered symbols are written to a spare device. This results in different rebuild bandwidths, which are given by (52) and (66), respectively.

When the system enters exposure level u, the number of most-exposed codewords that need to be recovered is equal to C_u, $u = 1, \ldots, \tilde{r}$. Upon the next device failure, the expected number of most-exposed codewords that have not yet been recovered is equal to $\alpha_u\,C_u$. Clearly, all these codewords have symbols stored on the newly failed device, which implies that

$$V_u^{\text{clus}} = 1\,, \quad u = 1, \ldots, \tilde{r}-1\,. \quad (67)$$

Substituting (65), (66), and (67) into (49), (50), and (48), and using (3), yields

$$\text{MTTDL}^{\text{clus}} \approx \frac{1}{n\,\lambda}\left(\frac{b}{\lambda\,c}\right)^{m-l}\frac{1}{\binom{m-1}{l-1}}\,\frac{[E(X)]^{m-l}}{E(X^{m-l})}\,, \quad (68)$$

$$\text{EAFDL}^{\text{clus}} \approx \lambda\left(\frac{\lambda\,c}{b}\right)^{m-l}\binom{m}{l-1}\frac{E(X^{m-l})}{[E(X)]^{m-l}}\,, \quad (69)$$

and

$$E(H)^{\text{clus}} = \frac{l}{m-l+1}\,c\,. \quad (70)$$

Note that the MTTDL derived in (68) is in agreement with Equation (15) of [28] (with $c/b = 1/\mu$, $E(X) = M_1(G_\mu)$ and $E(X^{m-l}) = M_{m-l}(G_\mu)$). For a RAID-5 array system, for which $n=m=N$ and $l=N-1$, and for a RAID-6 array system, for which $n=m=N$ and $l=N-2$, and for an exponential rebuild time distribution, for which it holds that $E(X^2)/[E(X)]^2 = 2$, Eq. (68) is in agreement with the MTTDL equations reported in [2][3]. Also, for a deterministic rebuild time distribution, for which it holds that $E(X^{m-l}) = [E(X)]^{m-l}$, and for a replication-based system, for which $m=r$ and $l=1$, (68), (69), and (70) are in agreement with Equations (42.a), (43.a), and (39.a) of [25], respectively.

Remark 6: From (68), (69), and (70), and given that $E(X) = c/b$, the $\text{MTTDL}^{\text{clus}}$ and $\text{EAFDL}^{\text{clus}}$ depend on the $(m-l)$th moment of the rebuild time distribution, whereas $E(H)^{\text{clus}}$ does not depend on the rebuild times. Furthermore, given that $E(X^{m-l}) \geq [E(X)]^{m-l}$, random rebuild times result in lower MTTDL and higher EAFDL values than deterministic rebuild times do.

Approximate expressions for the reliability metrics of interest are given by the following propositions.

Proposition 7: For large values of n, m, l, and $m-l$, the $\text{MTTDL}^{\text{clus}}$ normalized to $1/\lambda$ and the $\text{EAFDL}^{\text{clus}}$ normalized to λ can be approximated as follows:

$$\lambda\,\text{MTTDL}^{\text{clus}}_{\text{approx}} \approx \sqrt{\frac{2\pi hx}{(1-h)n}}\left[\left(\frac{hb}{\lambda c}\right)^{h}(1-h)^{1-h}\right]^{xn}\frac{[E(X)]^{hxn}}{E(X^{hxn})}\,, \quad (71)$$

$$\text{EAFDL}^{\text{clus}}_{\text{approx}}/\lambda \approx \frac{1}{h}\sqrt{\frac{1-h}{2\pi hxn}}\left[\left(\frac{hb}{\lambda c}\right)^{h}(1-h)^{1-h}\right]^{-xn}\frac{E(X^{hxn})}{[E(X)]^{hxn}}\,, \quad (72)$$

where

$$x = \frac{m}{n}\,, \quad (73)$$

and h is given by (60).

Proof: From (68) and (69) it follows that

$$\text{MTTDL}^{\text{clus}} \approx \frac{1}{n\lambda}\left(\frac{b}{\lambda c}\right)^{m-l} \frac{(m-1)(m-l)!\,l!}{l\,m!}\,\frac{[E(X)]^{m-l}}{E(X^{m-l})}, \tag{74}$$

and

$$\text{EAFDL}^{\text{clus}} \approx \lambda\left(\frac{\lambda c}{b}\right)^{m-l} \frac{l\,m!}{(m-l+1)(m-l)!\,l!}\,\frac{E(X^{m-l})}{[E(X)]^{m-l}}. \tag{75}$$

Using Stirling's approximation for large values of n,

$$n! \approx \sqrt{2\pi n}\left(\frac{n}{e}\right)^n , \tag{76}$$

(74) and (75) yield

$$\text{MTTDL}^{\text{clus}} \approx \frac{1}{n\,\lambda}\left(\frac{b}{\lambda c}\right)^{m-l} \frac{m-1}{l}\sqrt{\frac{2\pi(m-l)\,l}{m}}\; \frac{(m-l)^{m-l}\,l^l}{m^m}\,\frac{[E(X)]^{m-l}}{E(X^{m-l})} , \tag{77}$$

and

$$\text{EAFDL}^{\text{clus}} \approx \lambda\left(\frac{\lambda c}{b}\right)^{m-l} \frac{l}{m-l+1}\sqrt{\frac{m}{2\pi(m-l)\,l}}\; \frac{m^m}{(m-l)^{m-l}\,l^l}\,\frac{E(X^{m-l})}{[E(X)]^{m-l}} . \tag{78}$$

From (1), (60), and (73), it follows that

$$l = s_{\text{eff}}\,m = (1-h)\,m = (1-h)\,x\,n \tag{79}$$

and

$$m - l = (1 - s_{\text{eff}})\,m = h\,m = h\,x\,n . \tag{80}$$

Substituting (79) and (80) into (77) and (78) yields (71) and (72), respectively. ■

D. Declustered Placement

As discussed in Section III-B, the declustered placement scheme is a special case of a symmetric placement scheme in which k is equal to n. Consequently, for $k = n$, (54), (55), and (56) yield

$$\text{MTTDL}^{\text{declus}} \approx \frac{1}{n\,\lambda}\left[\frac{b}{(l+1)\,\lambda\,c}\right]^{m-l} (m-l)!\; \frac{[E(X)]^{m-l}}{E(X^{m-l})}\prod_{u=1}^{m-l}\left(\frac{n-u}{m-u}\right)^{m-l-u} , \tag{81}$$

$$\text{EAFDL}^{\text{declus}} \approx \lambda\left[\frac{(l+1)\,\lambda\,c}{b}\right]^{m-l} \frac{m}{(m-l+1)!}\; \frac{E(X^{m-l})}{[E(X)]^{m-l}}\prod_{u=1}^{m-l}\left(\frac{m-u}{n-u}\right)^{m-l+1-u} , \tag{82}$$

and

$$E(H)^{\text{declus}} \approx \left(\frac{l}{m-l+1}\prod_{u=1}^{m-l}\frac{m-u}{n-u}\right) c \tag{83}$$

$$= \frac{l\,(m-1)!\,(n-m+l-1)!}{(m-l+1)\,(n-1)!\,(l-1)!}\,c . \tag{84}$$

Note that the MTTDL derived in (81) is in agreement with Equation (16) of [28], with $c/b = 1/\mu$ and $[E(X)]^{m-l}/E(X^{m-l}) = M_1^{m-l}\left(G_{\frac{n-1}{l+1}\mu}\right)/M_{m-l}\left(G_{\frac{n-1}{l+1}\mu}\right)$. Also, for a deterministic rebuild time distribution, for which it holds that $E(X^{m-l}) = [E(X)]^{m-l}$, and for a replication-based system, for which $m = r$ and $l = 1$, (81), (82) and (83) are in agreement with Equations (36.b), (37.b), and (39.b) of [25], respectively.

Remark 7: From (81), (82), and (83), and given that $E(X) = c/b$, it follows that $\text{MTTDL}^{\text{declus}}$ and $\text{EAFDL}^{\text{declus}}$ depend on the $(m-l)$th moment of the rebuild time distribution, whereas $E(H)^{\text{clus}}$ does not depend on the rebuild times. Furthermore, given that $E(X^{m-l}) \geq [E(X)]^{m-l}$, random rebuild times result in lower MTTDL and higher EAFDL values than deterministic rebuild times do.

Approximate expressions for the reliability metrics of interest are given by the following propositions.

Proposition 8: For large values of n, m, l, and $m-l$, the $\text{MTTDL}^{\text{declus}}$ normalized to $1/\lambda$ can be approximated as follows:

$$\begin{aligned}\log\left(\lambda\,\text{MTTDL}^{\text{declus}}_{\text{approx}}\right) \approx\; & n^2\,\frac{W(h,x)}{2} + n\,hx\,\log\left(\frac{hx\sqrt{x}\,n\,b}{e\,[(1-h)x\,n+1]\,\lambda\,c}\right) \\ & - \frac{1}{8}\left[h(1-x) - \log\left(\frac{1-h}{1-hx}\right)\right] + \log\left(\sqrt{\frac{2\pi hx}{n}}\right) \\ & + \log\left(\frac{[E(X)]^{hxn}}{E(X^{hxn})}\right) ,\end{aligned} \tag{85}$$

where h, x, and $W(h,x)$ are given by (60), (73), and (63), respectively.

Proof: Immediate from Proposition 5 by replacing k with n. ■

Proposition 9: For large values of n, m, l, and $m-l$, the $\text{EAFDL}^{\text{declus}}$ normalized to λ can be approximated as follows:

$$\begin{aligned}\log\left(\text{EAFDL}^{\text{declus}}_{\text{approx}}/\lambda\right) \approx\; & -n^2\,\frac{W(h,x)}{2} + n\left\{hx\,\log\left(\frac{e\,[(1-h)x\,n+1]\,\lambda\,c}{h\,\sqrt{x}\,n\,b}\right) + \log\left(\frac{(1-hx)^{1-hx}}{(1-h)^{(1-h)x}}\right)\right\} \\ & + \frac{1}{8}\,h(1-x) + \log\left(\frac{1}{hx\,n+1}\sqrt{\frac{x\,n}{2\pi h}}\left(\frac{1-h}{1-hx}\right)^{\frac{3}{8}}\right) \\ & + \log\left(\frac{E(X^{hxn})}{[E(X)]^{hxn}}\right) ,\end{aligned} \tag{86}$$

where h, x, and $W(h,x)$ are given by (60), (73), and (63), respectively.

Proof: Immediate from Proposition 6 by replacing k with n and using (73). ∎

Proposition 10: For large values of n, m, l, and $m-l$, the $E(H)^{\text{declus}}$ normalized to c can be approximated as follows:

$$\log\left(E(H)^{\text{declus}}_{\text{approx}}/c\right) \approx \log\left(\frac{(1-h)\,x\,n}{h\,x\,n+1}\sqrt{\frac{1-h}{1-hx}}\right) + n\,V(h,x)\,, \quad (87)$$

where h, x, and $V(h,x)$ are given by (60), (73), and (59), respectively.

Proof: Immediate from Proposition 4 by replacing k with n and using (73). ∎

E. Accuracy of Approximations

Here, we assess the accuracy of the approximate reliability expressions derived by the preceding propositions. Regarding the MTTDL measure, we consider the ratio of the approximation $\text{MTTDL}^{\text{clus}}_{\text{approx}}$ given by (71) to $\text{MTTDL}^{\text{clus}}$ given by (68). Note that the ratio $\text{MTTDL}^{\text{clus}}_{\text{approx}}/\text{MTTDL}^{\text{clus}}$ only depends on m and l given that the approximation is obtained by only approximating the term $\frac{1}{\binom{m-1}{l-1}}$ that appears in (68). We also consider the ratio of the approximation $\text{EAFDL}^{\text{clus}}_{\text{approx}}$ given by (72) to $\text{EAFDL}^{\text{clus}}$ given by (69). Note that also this ratio only depends on m and l.

The ratios corresponding to the two reliability measures are shown in Figure 4 as a function of the codeword length for various storage efficiencies. As expected, for any given storage efficiency, for large values of m (and therefore l) the Stirling's approximation is accurate and therefore the ratio of the reliability measures approaches one. But even for small values of m, the ratios are close to one, which implies that the approximations are quite accurate.

Next, we consider the symmetric placement scheme. Regarding the MTTDL measure, we consider the ratio of the approximation $\text{MTTDL}^{\text{sym}}_{\text{approx}}$ given by (62) to $\text{MTTDL}^{\text{sym}}$ given by (81). Note that the ratio $\text{MTTDL}^{\text{sym}}_{\text{approx}}/\text{MTTDL}^{\text{sym}}$ only depends on k, m and l given that the approximation is obtained by only approximating the product $(m-l)!\prod_{u=1}^{m-l}\left(\frac{k-u}{m-u}\right)^{m-l-u}$ that appears in (81). We also consider the ratio of the approximation $\text{EAFDL}^{\text{sym}}_{\text{approx}}$ given by (64) to $\text{EAFDL}^{\text{sym}}$ given by (82) and the ratio of the approximation $E(H)^{\text{sym}}_{\text{approx}}$ given by (58) to $E(H)^{\text{sym}}$ given by (83). Note that also these ratios only depend on k, m and l. The ratios of the three measures are shown in Figures 5, 6 and 7 as a function of the codeword length for various spread factors and storage efficiencies. As expected, for any given storage efficiency, for large values of m (and therefore l) the Stirling's approximation of the $(m-l)!$ term is quite accurate. However, the approximations of the products $\prod_{u=1}^{m-l}\left(\frac{k-u}{m-u}\right)^{m-l-u}$ and $\prod_{u=1}^{m-l}\left(\frac{k-u}{n-u}\right)^{m-l+1-u}$ that appear in the MTTDL and EAFDL expressions in (81) and (82), respectively, result in ratios close to one only for large values of x. For small values of x, they yield ratios that tend to be insensitive as k increases. These ratios, however, still preserve the order of magnitude of the reliability measures. For example, in the case of $k = 200$, $s_{\text{eff}} = 1/2$ and $m = 4$ (which implies that $l = 2$), it holds that $\text{MTTDL}^{\text{sym}}_{\text{approx}}/\text{MTTDL}^{\text{sym}} = 0.913$, with $\text{MTTDL}^{\text{sym}}_{\text{approx}}$ being of the same order as $\text{MTTDL}^{\text{sym}}$ given that $n\,\lambda\,\text{MTTDL}^{\text{sym}}/k = 7.37\times10^{4}$ and $n\,\lambda\,\text{MTTDL}^{\text{sym}}_{\text{approx}}/k = 6.73\times10^{4}$. Also, in the case of $k = 200$, $s_{\text{eff}} = 1/5$ and $m = 5$ (which implies that $l = 1$), it holds that $\text{MTTDL}^{\text{sym}}_{\text{approx}}/\text{MTTDL}^{\text{sym}} = 0.884$, with $\text{MTTDL}^{\text{sym}}_{\text{approx}}$ being of the same order as $\text{MTTDL}^{\text{sym}}$ given that $n\,\lambda\,\text{MTTDL}^{\text{sym}}/k = 3.96\times10^{20}$ and $n\,\lambda\,\text{MTTDL}^{\text{sym}}_{\text{approx}}/k = 3.50\times10^{20}$. Furthermore, for the EAFDL metric it holds that in this case $\text{EAFDL}^{\text{sym}}_{\text{approx}}/\text{EAFDL}^{\text{sym}} = 1.206$, with $\text{EAFDL}^{\text{sym}}_{\text{approx}}$ being of the same order as $\text{EAFDL}^{\text{sym}}$ given that $\text{EAFDL}^{\text{sym}}/\lambda = 1.99\times10^{-31}$ and $\text{EAFDL}^{\text{sym}}_{\text{approx}}/\lambda = 2.40\times10^{-31}$. Consequently, the approximations are quite accurate.

V. Optimal Placement

Here, we identify which of the placement schemes considered offers the best reliability in terms of the MTTDL, EAFDL and $E(H)$ metrics. From Remark 4, it follows that the placement that maximizes MTTDL and minimizes EAFDL and $E(H)$ is either the clustered ($k=m$) or the declustered one ($k=n$). We therefore proceed by comparing these two schemes when $m \neq n$, that is, when $m < n$. This implies that we compare the two schemes when there are at least two clustered groups, that is, when $m \le n/2$, or, by also using (3) and (4), when

$$1 \le l < m \quad \text{and} \quad 1 \le m-l < m \le \frac{n}{2}\,. \quad (88)$$

A. Maximizing MTTDL

From (68) and (81), it follows that

$$\frac{\text{MTTDL}^{\text{declus}}}{\text{MTTDL}^{\text{clus}}} \approx \left(\frac{1}{l+1}\right)^{m-l}(m-l)!\binom{m-1}{l-1}\prod_{u=1}^{m-l}\left(\frac{n-u}{m-u}\right)^{m-l-u}. \quad (89)$$

Remark 8: From (89), it follows that the placement that maximizes MTTDL does not depend on λ, b and c nor on the rebuild time distribution.

Depending on the values of m and l, we consider the following three cases:

1) $m-l=1$: For $m-l=1$, (89) yields

$$\frac{\text{MTTDL}^{\text{declus}}}{\text{MTTDL}^{\text{clus}}} \approx \frac{m-1}{m} < 1\,. \quad (90)$$

2) $m-l=2$: For $m-l=2$, (89) yields

$$\frac{\text{MTTDL}^{\text{declus}}}{\text{MTTDL}^{\text{clus}}} \approx \frac{(m-2)(n-1)}{(m-1)^2} > 1\,, \quad \text{for } n \ge m+2\,. \quad (91)$$

Note that from (88), it holds that $2 < m \le n/2$, which in turn implies that $n > m+2$, and therefore (91) holds.

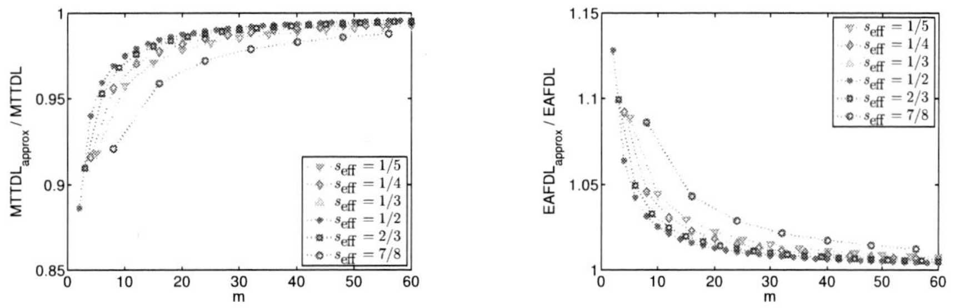

(a) $\text{MTTDL}^{\text{clus}}_{\text{approx}}/\text{MTTDL}^{\text{clus}}$ (b) $\text{EAFDL}^{\text{clus}}_{\text{approx}}/\text{EAFDL}^{\text{clus}}$

Figure 4. Accuracy of approximations for clustered placement vs. codeword length for $s_{\text{eff}} = 1/5, 1/4, 1/3, 1/2, 2/3,$ and $7/8$.

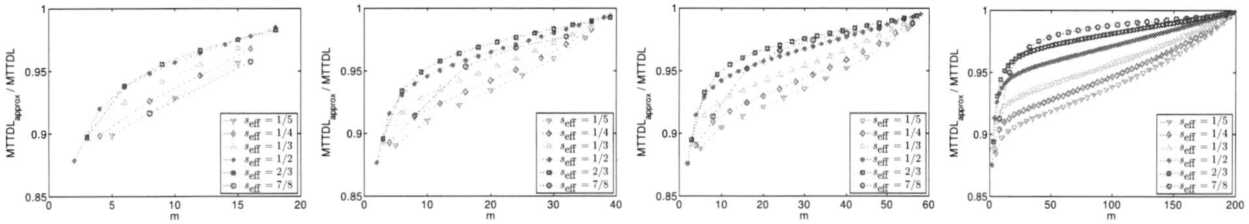

(a) $k = 20$ (b) $k = 40$ (c) $k = 60$ (d) $k = 200$

Figure 5. $\text{MTTDL}^{\text{sym}}_{\text{approx}}/\text{MTTDL}^{\text{sym}}$ ratio vs. codeword length for $s_{\text{eff}} = 1/5, 1/4, 1/3, 1/2, 2/3,$ and $7/8$.

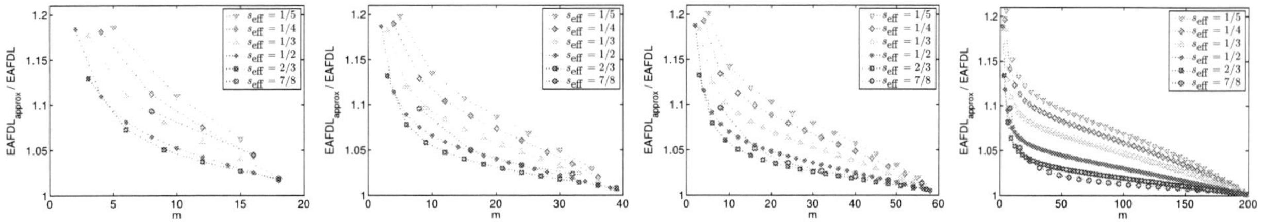

(a) $k = 20$ (b) $k = 40$ (c) $k = 60$ (d) $k = 200$

Figure 6. $\text{EAFDL}^{\text{sym}}_{\text{approx}}/\text{EAFDL}^{\text{sym}}$ ratio vs. codeword length for $s_{\text{eff}} = 1/5, 1/4, 1/3, 1/2, 2/3,$ and $7/8$.

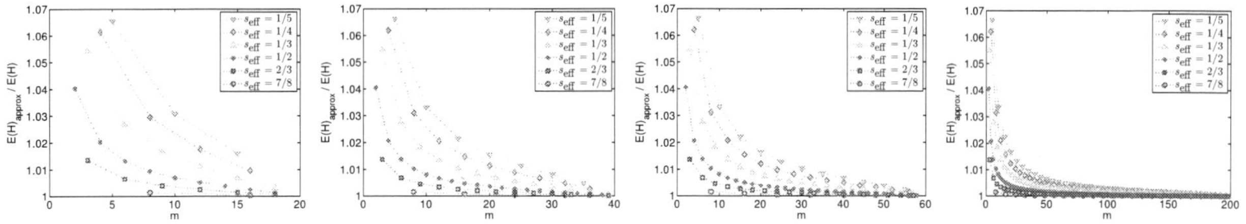

(a) $k = 20$ (b) $k = 40$ (c) $k = 60$ (d) $k = 200$

Figure 7. $E(H)^{\text{sym}}_{\text{approx}}/E(H)^{\text{sym}}$ ratio vs. codeword length for $s_{\text{eff}} = 1/5, 1/4, 1/3, 1/2, 2/3,$ and $7/8$.

3) $m - l \geq 3$: For $m - l \geq 3$, (89) can be written as follows:

$$\frac{\text{MTTDL}^{\text{declus}}}{\text{MTTDL}^{\text{clus}}} \approx \frac{m-1}{l+1} \cdots \frac{l+1}{l+1}\,\frac{l}{l+1}\,\frac{n-m+l+1}{l+1} \left(\frac{n-m+l+2}{l+2}\right)^2 \prod_{u=1}^{m-l-3} \left(\frac{n-u}{m-u}\right)^{m-l-u} . \quad (92)$$

Using (88), (92) yields

$$\begin{aligned} \frac{\text{MTTDL}^{\text{declus}}}{\text{MTTDL}^{\text{clus}}} &> \frac{l}{l+1}\,\frac{n-m+l+1}{l+1}\left(\frac{n-m+l+2}{l+2}\right)^2 \\ &\geq \frac{l}{l+1}\,\frac{l+2}{l+1}\left(\frac{l+3}{l+2}\right)^2 = \frac{l\,(l+3)^2}{(l+1)^2\,(l+2)} \\ &= \frac{2[l^2+2(l-1)+1]}{(l+1)^2\,(l+2)} + 1 > 1 . \end{aligned} \quad (93)$$

Remark 9: From the preceding, it follows that the MTTDL is maximized by the declustered placement scheme, except in the case of $m-l=1$, where it is maximized by the clustered placement scheme.

B. *Minimizing* EAFDL

From (69) and (82), it follows that

$$\frac{\text{EAFDL}^{\text{declus}}}{\text{EAFDL}^{\text{clus}}} \approx (l+1)^{m-l} \, \frac{(l-1)!}{(m-1)!} \prod_{u=1}^{m-l} \left(\frac{m-u}{n-u} \right)^{m-l+1-u} . \tag{94}$$

Remark 10: From (94), it follows that the placement that minimizes EAFDL does not depend on λ, b and c, nor on the rebuild time distribution.

Depending on the value of $\tilde{r}$, we consider the following two cases:

1) $m-l=1$: For $m-l=1$, (94) yields

$$\frac{\text{EAFDL}^{\text{declus}}}{\text{EAFDL}^{\text{clus}}} \approx \frac{m}{n-1} < 1 \, , \quad \text{for } n \geq m+2 \, . \tag{95}$$

Note that from (88), it holds that $2 \leq m \leq n/2$, which in turn implies that $n \geq m+2$, and therefore (95) holds.

2) $m-l \geq 2$: For $m-l \geq 2$, (94) can be written as follows:

$$\frac{\text{EAFDL}^{\text{declus}}}{\text{EAFDL}^{\text{clus}}} \approx \frac{l+1}{m-1} \, \frac{l+1}{m-2} \cdots \frac{l+1}{l} \, \frac{l}{n-m+l} \prod_{u=1}^{m-l-1} \left(\frac{m-u}{n-u} \right)^{m-l+1-u} . \tag{96}$$

Using (88), (96) yields

$$\frac{\text{EAFDL}^{\text{declus}}}{\text{EAFDL}^{\text{clus}}} < \frac{l+1}{n-m+l} \leq \frac{l+1}{(m+1)-m+l} = 1 \, . \tag{97}$$

Remark 11: From the preceding, it follows that the declustered placement scheme minimizes EAFDL for any n, m, l, λ, b, c, and rebuild time distribution.

C. *Minimizing* $E(H)$

From (70) and (83), and using (88), it follows that

$$\frac{E(H)^{\text{declus}}}{E(H)^{\text{clus}}} \approx \prod_{u=1}^{m-l} \frac{m-u}{n-u} < 1 \, . \tag{98}$$

Remark 12: From (98), it follows that for any n, m, l, λ, b, c, and rebuild time distribution, $E(H)$ is minimized by the declustered placement scheme.

D. *Synopsis*

When the codeword length is smaller than the system size ($m < n$), the declustered placement scheme minimizes the expected amount of data lost when a loss occurs, independently of the device capacity c and its reliability characteristics and the mean time to failure expressed by λ, the average reserved rebuild bandwidth b and the resulting rebuild time distribution of X. Also, for $m-l=1$, the clustered placement scheme maximizes the MTTDL, but the declustered placement scheme minimizes the EAFDL. However, for $m-l \geq 2$, the declustered placement scheme maximizes the MTTDL and at the same time minimizes the EAFDL.

Note that the preceding conclusions hold under the assumption that failures are detected instantaneously, which immediately triggers the rebuild process, and the assumption that sufficient network bandwidth is available to support the parallelism of the rebuild process.

VI. Reliability Comparison

Here, we assess the relative reliability of the declustered placement, which according to Remarks 9, 11 and 12 is the optimal one, under various codeword lengths m. We perform a fair comparison by considering systems with the same amount of user data, U, stored under the same storage efficiency, s_{eff}. From (2), it follows that the number of devices n is fixed. Also, from (80), it follows that the parameter h is fixed. Using (79) to express l in terms of h and m in (81), (82), and (83), we obtain

$$\text{MTTDL}^{\text{declus}} \approx \frac{1}{n\,\lambda} \left[\frac{b}{[(1-h)m+1]\,\lambda\,c} \right]^{hm} (hm)! \, \frac{[E(X)]^{hm}}{E(X^{hm})} \prod_{u=1}^{hm} \left(\frac{n-u}{m-u} \right)^{hm-u} , \tag{99}$$

$$\text{EAFDL}^{\text{declus}} \approx \lambda \left[\frac{[(1-h)m+1]\,\lambda\,c}{b} \right]^{hm} \frac{m}{(hm+1)!} \, \frac{E(X^{hm})}{[E(X)]^{hm}} \prod_{u=1}^{hm} \left(\frac{m-u}{n-u} \right)^{hm+1-u} , \tag{100}$$

and

$$E(H)^{\text{declus}} \approx \left(\frac{(1-h)m}{hm+1} \prod_{u=1}^{hm} \frac{m-u}{n-u} \right) c \tag{101}$$

$$= \frac{(1-h)\,m!\,(n-1-hm)!}{(n-1)!\,(hm+1)\,((1-h)m-1))!} \, c \, . \tag{102}$$

As discussed in Section IV-A, the direct-path-approximation method yields accurate results when the storage devices are highly reliable, that is, when the ratio λ/μ of the mean rebuild time $1/\mu$ to the mean time to failure of a device $1/\lambda$ is very small. We proceed by considering systems for which it holds that $\lambda/\mu = \lambda\,c/b = 0.001$ and the rebuild time distribution is deterministic, for which it holds that $E(X^{hm}) = [E(X)]^{hm}$. The combined effect of the number of devices and the system efficiency on the normalized $\lambda\,\text{MTTDL}^{\text{declus}}$ measure is obtained by (99) and shown in Figure 8 as a function of the codeword length. The values for the storage efficiency are chosen to be fractions of the form $z/(z+1)$, $z = 1, \ldots, 7$, such that the first point of each of the corresponding curves is associated with the single-parity $(z, z+1)$-erasure code, and the second point of each of the corresponding curves is associated with the double-parity $(2z, 2z+2)$-erasure code. We observe that the MTTDL increases as the storage efficiency s_{eff} decreases. This is because, for a given m, decreasing s_{eff} implies decreasing l, which in turn implies increasing the parity symbols $m-l$ and consequently improving the MTTDL.

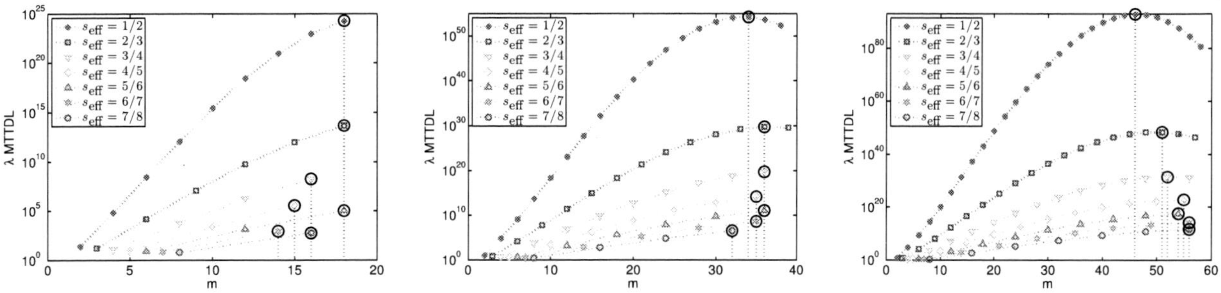

(a) $n = 20$ (b) $n = 40$ (c) $n = 60$

Figure 8. Normalized MTTDL^{declus} vs. codeword length for $s_{\text{eff}} = 1/2, 2/3, 3/4, 4/5, 5/6, 6/7,$ and $7/8$; $\lambda/\mu = 0.001$ and deterministic rebuild times.

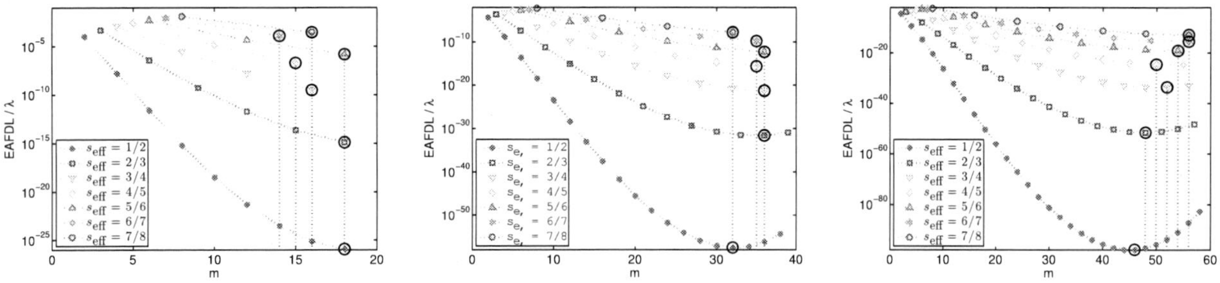

(a) $n = 20$ (b) $n = 40$ (c) $n = 60$

Figure 9. Normalized EAFDL^{declus} vs. codeword length for $s_{\text{eff}} = 1/2, 2/3, 3/4, 4/5, 5/6, 6/7,$ and $7/8$; $\lambda/\mu = 0.001$ and deterministic rebuild times.

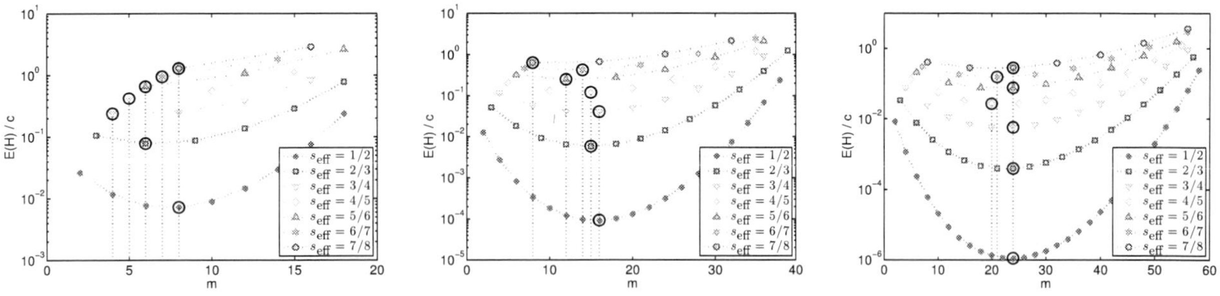

(a) $n = 20$ (b) $n = 40$ (c) $n = 60$

Figure 10. Normalized $E(H)^{\text{declus}}$ vs. codeword length for $s_{\text{eff}} = 1/2, 2/3, 3/4, 4/5, 5/6, 6/7,$ and $7/8$; $\lambda/\mu = 0.001$.

Let us now consider the single-parity codewords, which correspond to the first points of the curves. Note that, according to Remark 9 and (90), the clustered placement scheme yields larger, but of the same order, MTTDL values as the declustered placement does. Consequently, the MTTDL points for the single-parity codewords under a clustered placement scheme are slightly higher than those shown in Figure 8. As s_{eff} increases, so do m and l, which results in a decreasing MTTDL for these codewords. This is due to the fact that as m increases, there are l data symbols, that is, more data symbols associated with each parity. This is in accordance with the results presented in Figure 2 of [28]. We observe that the same applies for the double-parity codewords, which correspond to the second points of the curves.

The combined effect of the number of devices and the system efficiency on the normalized EAFDL$^{\text{declus}}/\lambda$ measure is obtained by (100) and shown in Figure 9 as a function of the codeword length. We observe that the EAFDL increases as the storage efficiency s_{eff} increases. Also, as s_{eff} increases, the EAFDL for the single-parity codewords, which correspond to the first points of the curves, also increases. We observe that the same applies for the double-parity codewords, which correspond to the second points of the curves.

The combined effect of the number of devices and the system efficiency on the normalized $E(H)^{\text{declus}}/c$ measure is obtained by (101) and shown in Figure 10 as a function of the codeword length. We observe that $E(H)$ increases as the storage efficiency s_{eff} increases. Also, as s_{eff} increases, the $E(H)$ for the single-parity codewords, which correspond to the first points of the curves, increases as well. We observe that the same applies for the double-parity codewords, which correspond to the second points of the curves.

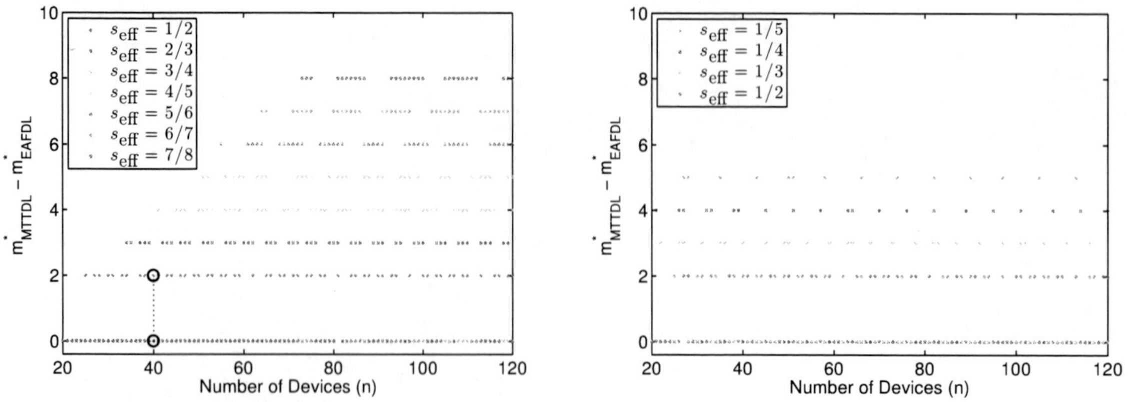

(a) $s_{eff} = 1/2, 2/3, 3/4, 4/5, 5/6, 6/7,$ and $7/8$

(b) $s_{eff} = 1/5, 1/4, 1/3,$ and $1/2$

Figure 11. The difference between m^*_{MTTDL} and m^*_{EAFDL} vs. the number of devices; $\lambda/\mu = 0.001$ and deterministic rebuild times.

We now proceed to identify the optimal codeword length, m^*, that maximizes the MTTDL or minimizes the EAFDL and $E(H)$ for a given storage efficiency. Note that we only consider declustered placements with $m < n$, but not the clustered placement with $m = n$. The optimal codeword length is dictated by two opposing effects on reliability. On the one hand, larger values of m imply that codewords can tolerate more device failures, but on the other hand result in a higher exposure degree to failure as each of the codewords is spread across a larger number of devices. In Figures 8, 9, and 10, the optimal values, m^*, are indicated by the circles, and the corresponding codeword lengths are indicated by the vertical dotted lines. Regarding MTTDL and EAFDL, we observe that for small values of n, it holds that $m^* \approxeq n$, whereas for large values of n it holds that $m^* < n$. It turns out that for $n \geq 60$, the clustered placement scheme with $m = n$ does not result in improved reliability. However, for smaller values of n, that is, for $n < 60$, the clustered placement scheme can improve reliability. For instance, for $n = 20$ and $s_{eff} = 4/5$, the MTTDL is maximized and the EAFDL is minimized by the clustered placement scheme with $m = n$. By comparing Figures 8 and 9, we deduce that in general the optimal codeword lengths m^*_{MTTDL} (for MTTDL) and m^*_{EAFDL} (for EAFDL) are similar and for some values of n even identical. They are, however, significantly larger than those that minimize the $E(H)$, which are shown in Figure 10.

Figure 11 shows the difference between the optimal codeword lengths for MTTDL and EAFDL. It demonstrates that the optimal codeword length for MTTDL is always greater than or equal to that for EAFDL, with the difference being equal either to $z+1$, the denominator of the storage efficiency fraction, or to zero. This implies that the optimal codeword lengths m^*_{EAFDL} for EAFDL are either equal to or slightly lower than and adjacent to the optimal codeword lengths m^*_{MTTDL} for MTTDL. For example, in the case of $n = 40$ and $s_{eff} = 1/2$, Figure 8(b) shows that the maximum value of MTTDL is achieved when the codeword length m is equal to 34, which implies that $m^*_{MTTDL} = 34$. Also, Figure 9(b) shows that the minimum value of EAFDL is achieved when the codeword length m is equal to 32, which implies that $m^*_{EAFDL} = 32$. The value of 32 is adjacent to 34 because when $s_{eff} = 1/2$, m cannot be equal to 33. Consequently, the difference of the optimal codeword lengths for EAFDL and MTTDL is given by 34 – 32 = 2, indicated by a circle in Figure 11. Similarly, for $n = 40$ and $s_{eff} = 2/3$, Figures 8(b) and 9(b) show that both the optimal MTTDL and the optimal EAFDL are obtained when the codeword length is equal to 36, that is, $m^*_{MTTDL} = m^*_{EAFDL} = 36$. In this case, the difference of the optimal codeword lengths for EAFDL and MTTDL is equal to zero, indicated by a circle in Figure 11.

To investigate the behavior of the optimal codeword length, m^*, as the storage system size, n, increases, we proceed by considering the normalized optimal codeword length r^*, namely, the ratio of m^* to n:

$$r^* \triangleq \frac{m^*}{n} . \tag{103}$$

The r^* values for various storage efficiencies and for the MTTDL and EAFDL metrics are shown in Figure 12. From the preceding, it follows that the difference $r^*_{MTTDL} - r^*_{EAFDL}$ of the r^* values for the two metrics is bounded above by $(z+1)/n$, which approaches zero as n increases. Thus, as n increases, the difference $r^*_{MTTDL} - r^*_{EAFDL}$ also approaches zero.

The r^* values for the MTTDL and EAFDL metrics for various values of the storage efficiency s_{eff} and for large values of n are shown in Figures 13 and 14. It turns out that it always holds that $r^*_{EAFDL} \leq r^*_{MTTDL}$ or, equivalently, $m^*_{EAFDL} \leq m^*_{MTTDL}$. We observe that, as n increases, the r^* values tend to decrease. In particular, for a given storage efficiency and as n increases, the r^* values for MTTDL and EAFDL approach a common value, denoted by r^*_∞ and indicated by a small bullet. The r^*_∞ value depends only on s_{eff} and is given by the following proposition.

Proposition 11: As n increases, the r^* values for MTTDL and EAFDL approach r^*_∞ that satisfies the following equation:

$$Q(h, r^*_\infty) = 0 , \tag{104}$$

where

$$Q(h, x) \triangleq hx + \log\left([(1-h)^{(1-h)^2} x^{h^2}]^x (1-hx)^{h(1-hx)} \right) . \tag{105}$$

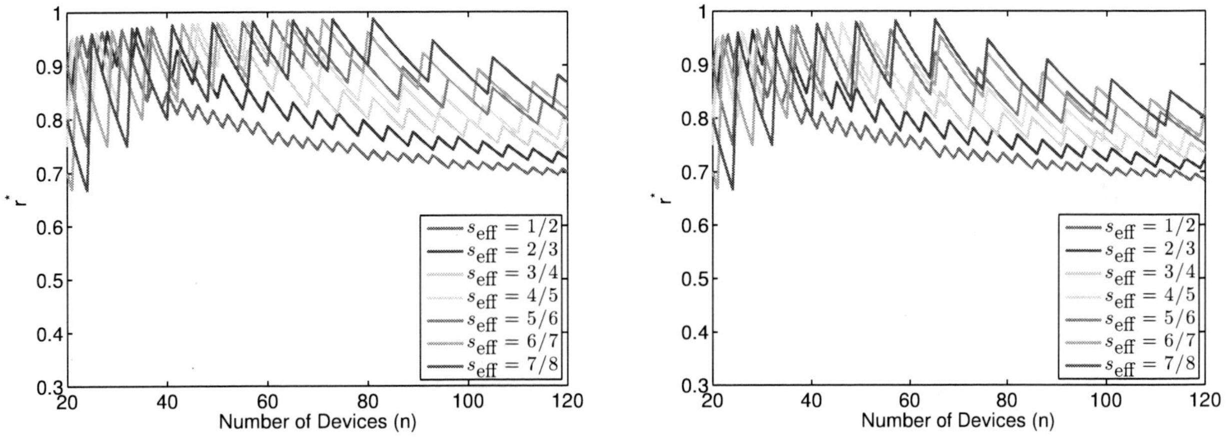

(a) MTTDL (b) EAFDL

Figure 12. r^* vs. number of devices for $s_{\text{eff}} = 1/2, 2/3, 3/4, 4/5, 5/6, 6/7,$ and $7/8$; $\lambda/\mu = 0.001$ and deterministic rebuild times.

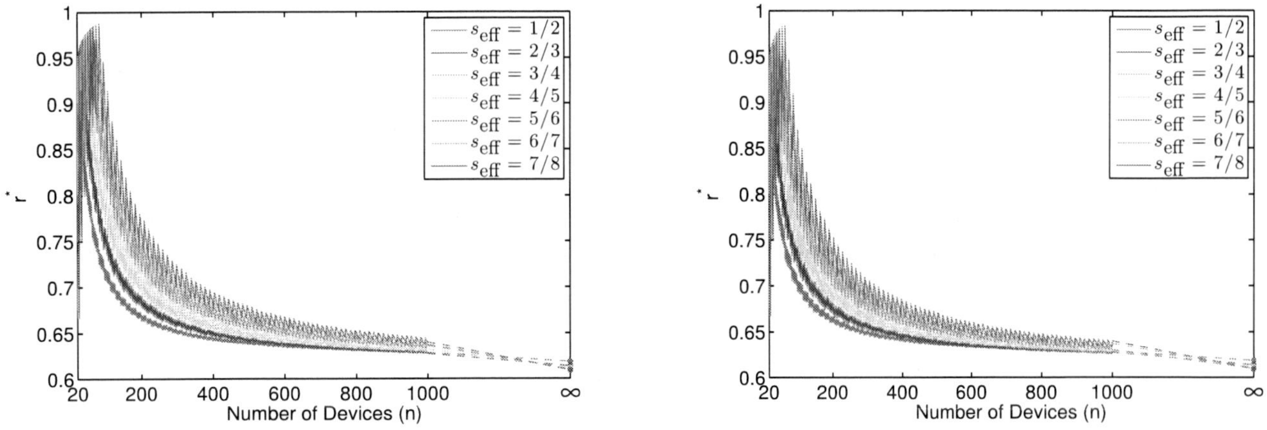

(a) MTTDL (b) EAFDL

Figure 13. r^* vs. number of devices $n \to \infty$, $s_{\text{eff}} = 1/2, 2/3, 3/4, 4/5, 5/6, 6/7,$ and $7/8$; $\lambda/\mu = 0.001$ and deterministic rebuild times.

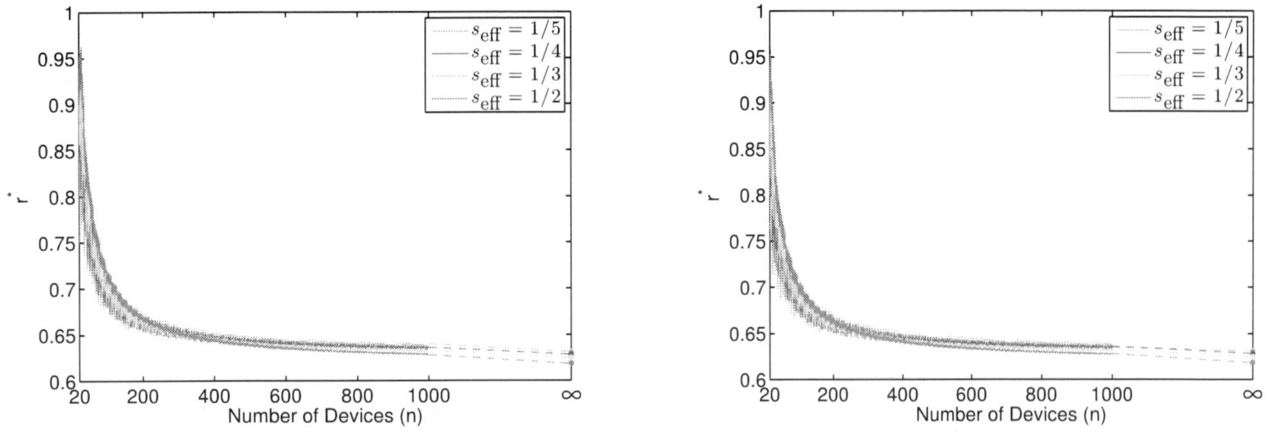

(a) MTTDL (b) EAFDL

Figure 14. r^* vs. number of devices $n \to \infty$, $s_{\text{eff}} = 1/5, 1/4, 1/3,$ and $1/2$; $\lambda/\mu = 0.001$ and deterministic rebuild times.

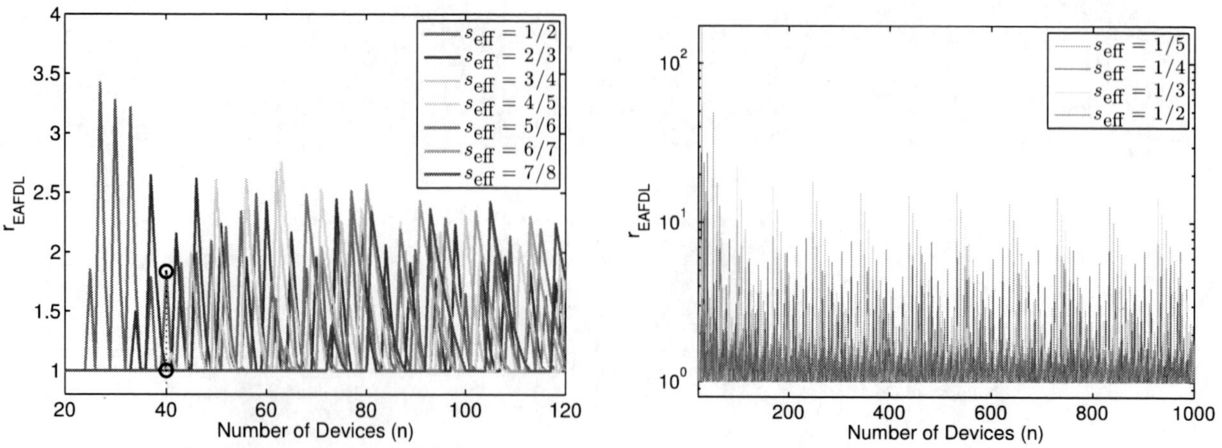

(a) $s_{\mathrm{eff}} = 1/2, 2/3, 3/4, 4/5,\ 5/6, 6/7,$ and $7/8$

(b) $s_{\mathrm{eff}} = 1/5, 1/4, 1/3,$ and $1/2$

Figure 16. The EAFDL efficiency ratio r_{EAFDL} vs. number of devices; $\lambda/\mu = 0.001$ and deterministic rebuild times.

TABLE III. r^*_∞ VALUES FOR VARIOUS s_{eff}

s_{eff}			r^*_∞ MTTDL and EAFDL	r^*_∞ $E(H)$
0	=	0	0.648419	0.5
10^{-4}	=	0.0001	0.648404	0.499795
10^{-3}	=	0.001	0.648265	0.498520
10^{-2}	=	0.01	0.646985	0.490770
10^{-1}	=	0.1	0.637940	0.456298
1/8	=	0.125	0.636043	0.450268
1/7	=	0.142857	0.634788	0.446383
1/6	=	0.166667	0.633224	0.441637
1/5	=	0.2	0.631212	0.435664
1/4	=	0.25	0.628500	0.427826
1/3	=	0.333333	0.624638	0.416889
1/2	=	0.5	0.618499	0.4
2/3	=	0.666667	0.613720	0.387097
3/4	=	0.75	0.611679	0.381625
4/5	=	0.8	0.610543	0.378586
5/6	=	0.833333	0.609818	0.376650
6/7	=	0.857143	0.609316	0.375307
7/8	=	0.875	0.608946	0.374322
$1-10^{-1}$	=	0.9	0.608440	0.372971
$1-10^{-2}$	=	0.99	0.606713	0.368368
$1-10^{-3}$	=	0.999	0.606549	0.367928
$1-10^{-4}$	=	0.9999	0.606532	0.367884
1	=	1	$0.606531 = 1/\sqrt{e}$	$0.367879 = 1/e$

Proof: See Appendix F. ■

The r^*_∞ values corresponding to the MTTDL and EAFDL metrics and to various storage efficiencies are listed in Table III. Note that the r^*_∞ values are in the interval $[e^{-1/2} = 0.606, 0.648]$ and decrease as the storage efficiency s_{eff} increases. In contrast, for small values of n, the r^* values increase as the storage efficiency increases, as shown in Figure 13. For example, for small n, the r^* values corresponding to $s_{\mathrm{eff}} = 1/2$ are smaller than those corresponding to $s_{\mathrm{eff}} = 2/3$. However, for large values of n this is reversed, and for the MTTDL, the first instance that this occurs is for $n = 619$, as shown in Figure 15, with the r^* values being equal to 0.637 and 0.635 (indicated by the circle), respectively. Therefore, in this case, the optimal codeword lengths m^* are equal to 394 and 393, respectively.

Next we examine the increase of the EAFDL metric if

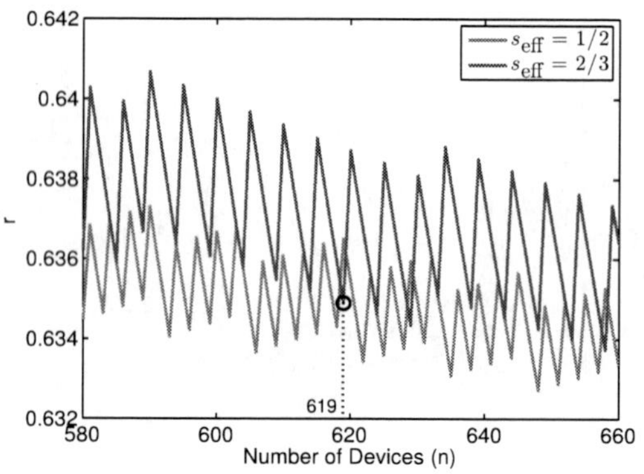

Figure 15. r^* for MTTDL vs. number of devices for $s_{\mathrm{eff}} = 1/2, 2/3$; $\lambda/\mu = 0.001$ and deterministic rebuild times.

instead of the optimal codeword lengths m^*_{EAFDL}, we use the codeword lengths m^*_{MTTDL} that optimize the MTTDL metric. From the preceding, it follows that m^*_{MTTDL} is either equal to m^*_{EAFDL} or adjacent to it, that is, $m^*_{\mathrm{MTTDL}} = m^*_{\mathrm{EAFDL}} + z + 1$. We define the EAFDL *efficiency ratio*, r_{EAFDL}, as the ratio of $\mathrm{EAFDL}(m^*_{\mathrm{MTTDL}})$ to $\mathrm{EAFDL}(m^*_{\mathrm{EAFDL}})$, that is,

$$r_{\mathrm{EAFDL}} \triangleq \frac{\mathrm{EAFDL}(m^*_{\mathrm{MTTDL}})}{\mathrm{EAFDL}(m^*_{\mathrm{EAFDL}})}, \qquad (106)$$

where $\mathrm{EAFDL}(m)$ denotes the EAFDL corresponding to a codeword length m. In the case of $n = 40$ and $s_{\mathrm{eff}} = 1/2$, from the preceding and according to Figure 9(b), it holds that $\mathrm{EAFDL}(m^*_{\mathrm{EAFDL}}) = \mathrm{EAFDL}(32) = 3.08\times10^{-58}$ and $\mathrm{EAFDL}(m^*_{\mathrm{MTTDL}}) = \mathrm{EAFDL}(34) = 5.66\times10^{-58}$, which yields an EAFDL efficiency ratio r_{EAFDL} of 5.66/3.08 = 1.84. This is indicated by a circle in Figure 16(a), which shows the EAFDL efficiency ratio as a function of n. Similarly, in the case of $n = 40$ and $s_{\mathrm{eff}} = 2/3$, from the preceding, it holds that $m^*_{\mathrm{MTTDL}} = m^*_{\mathrm{EAFDL}} = 36$, which implies that $r_{\mathrm{EAFDL}} = 1$, indicated by a circle in Figure 16(a). We observe that for the storage efficiencies considered and as n increases,

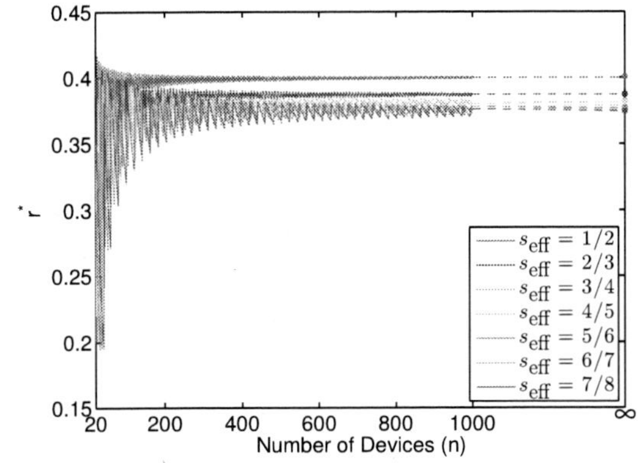

(a) $s_{\text{eff}} = 1/2, 2/3, 3/4, 4/5, 5/6, 6/7$, and $7/8$

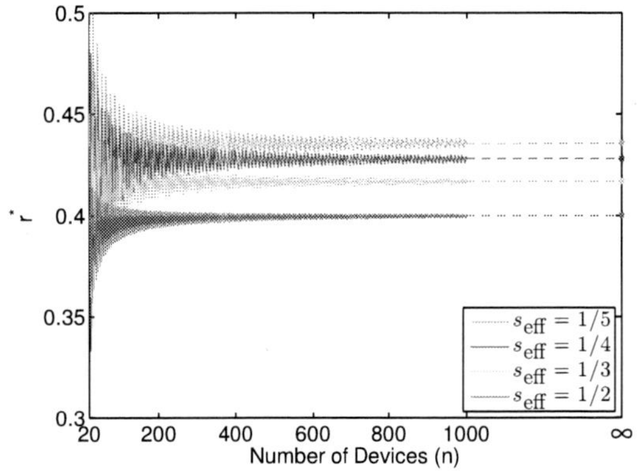

(b) $s_{\text{eff}} = 1/5, 1/4, 1/3$, and $1/2$

Figure 18. r^* for $E(H)$ vs. number of devices $n \to \infty$; $\lambda/\mu = 0.001$.

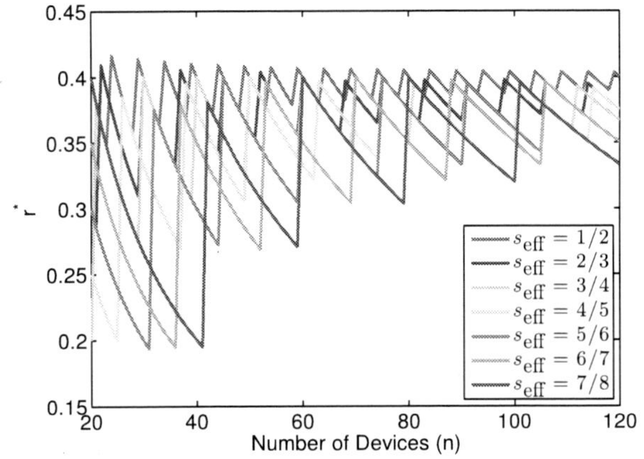

Figure 17. r^* for $E(H)$ vs. number of devices for $s_{\text{eff}} = 1/2, 2/3, 3/4, 4/5, 5/6, 6/7$, and $7/8$; $\lambda/\mu = 0.001$.

the EAFDL efficiency ratios follow a periodic pattern and are always less than a factor of four. This implies that using codewords of length m^*_{MTTDL} yields the maximum possible (optimal) MTTDL and also an EAFDL that is either the optimal one or of the same order as the optimal one. Also, as the storage efficiency decreases, the EAFDL efficiency ratio r_{EAFDL} increases, as shown in Figure 16(b). For any given storage efficiency, r_{EAFDL} follows a periodic pattern and for $s_{\text{eff}} \geq 1/4 = 0.25$, r_{EAFDL} is always less than a factor of 10. Consequently, using codewords of length m^*_{MTTDL} yields an EAFDL that is either the optimal or at most one order of magnitude higher than the optimal one.

Next, we compare the r^* values for the MTTDL and EAFDL metrics shown in Figure 12 with those for the $E(H)$ metric shown in Figure 17. Clearly, the optimal codeword lengths for MTTDL and EAFDL are significantly larger than those that minimize $E(H)$. The r^* values for the $E(H)$ metric for various values of the storage efficiency s_{eff} and for large values of n are shown in Figure 18. The figure indicates that, as n increases, the r^* values oscillate and approach a value denoted by r^*_∞. The r^*_∞ values (indicated by the small bullets) are given by the following proposition,

Proposition 12: As n increases, the r^* values for $E(H)$ approach r^*_∞ given by

$$r^*_\infty = \frac{1}{h + (1-h)^{-\frac{1-h}{h}}} \,, \tag{107}$$

where h is given by (60).

Proof: See Appendix G. ∎

The r^*_∞ values corresponding to the $E(H)$ metric and to various storage efficiencies are listed in Table III. Note that the r^*_∞ values are in the interval $[e^{-1} = 0.368, 0.5]$ and decrease as the storage efficiency s_{eff} increases. By inspecting Figures 13, 14, and 18, it is evident that also in this case the optimal codeword lengths for MTTDL and EAFDL are significantly larger than those that minimize $E(H)$.

Next, we consider a system where the distribution of the rebuild time X is exponential, for which it holds that $E(X^{hm}) = (hm)!\,[E(X)]^{hm}$. According to Remark 2, this only affects the MTTDL and EAFDL metrics, but not the $E(H)$ metric. The combined effect of the number of devices and the system efficiency on the normalized $\lambda\,\text{MTTDL}^{\text{declus}}$ measure is obtained by (99) and shown in Figure 19 as a function of the codeword length. Similarly to the case of deterministic rebuild times, we observe that the MTTDL increases as the storage efficiency s_{eff} decreases. Also, as s_{eff} increases, the MTTDL for the single-parity codewords, which correspond to the first points of the curves, decreases. We observe that the same applies for the double-parity codewords, which correspond to the second points of the curves.

The combined effect of the number of devices and the system efficiency on the normalized $\text{EAFDL}^{\text{declus}}/\lambda$ measure is obtained by (100) and shown in Figure 20 as a function of the codeword length. Similarly to the case of deterministic rebuild times, we observe that the EAFDL increases as the storage efficiency s_{eff} increases. Also, as s_{eff} increases, the EAFDL for the single-parity codewords, which correspond to the first points of the curves, also increases. We observe that the same applies for the double-parity codewords, which correspond to the second points of the curves.

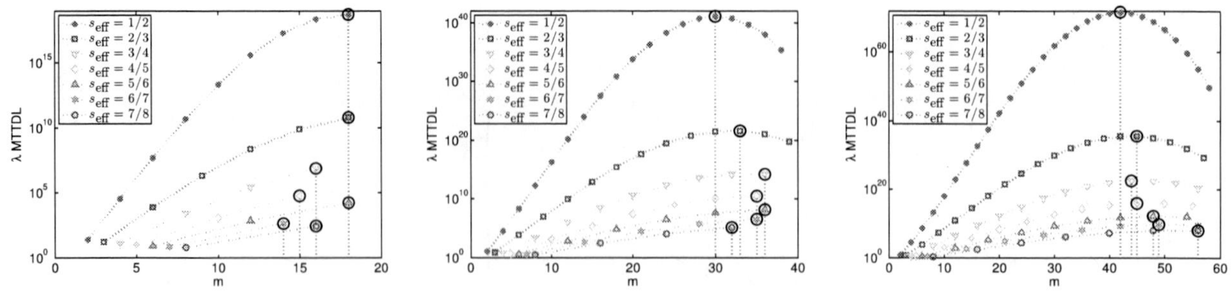

(a) $n = 20$ (b) $n = 40$ (c) $n = 60$

Figure 19. Normalized MTTDL^{declus} vs. codeword length for $s_{\text{eff}} = 1/2, 2/3, 3/4, 4/5, 5/6, 6/7,$ and $7/8$; $\lambda/\mu = 0.001$ and exponential rebuild times.

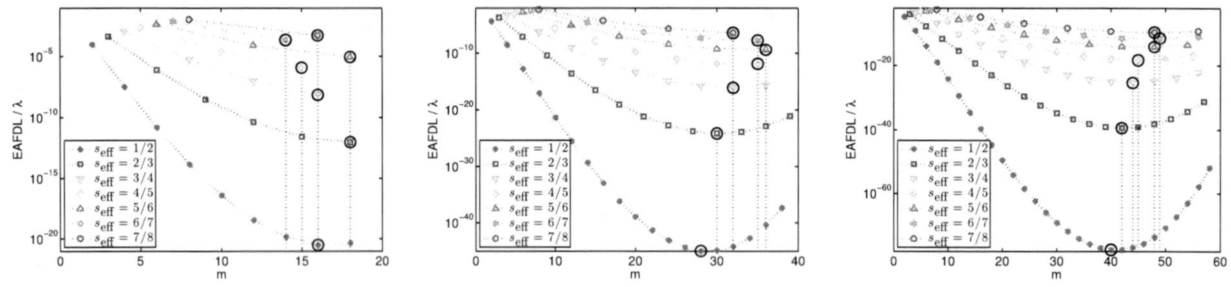

(a) $n = 20$ (b) $n = 40$ (c) $n = 60$

Figure 20. Normalized EAFDL^{declus} vs. codeword length for $s_{\text{eff}} = 1/2, 2/3, 3/4, 4/5, 5/6, 6/7,$ and $7/8$; $\lambda/\mu = 0.001$ and exponential rebuild times.

The optimal codeword lengths, m^*, that maximize the MTTDL or minimize the EAFDL are indicated by the circles and the corresponding vertical dotted lines. The observations regarding the optimal codeword lengths made in the case of deterministic rebuild times also apply here. Note also that, according to Remark 7, $E(H)$ does not depend on the rebuild times, and therefore the optimal codeword lengths that minimize $E(H)$ are those shown in Figure 17 for the case of deterministic rebuild times.

Similarly to the case of deterministic rebuild times, the optimal codeword lengths m^*_{EAFDL} for EAFDL are either equal to or slightly lower than and adjacent to the optimal codeword lengths m^*_{MTTDL} for MTTDL, as demonstrated in Figure 21. The r^* values for the MTTDL and EAFDL metrics for various storage efficiencies are shown in Figure 22. In Appendix F, it is proved that as n increases, and for any storage efficiency, the r^* values for MTTDL and EAFDL approach a common value that is the same as the r^*_∞ value obtained in the case of deterministic rebuild times, which depends on s_{eff} and is listed in Table III.

The EAFDL efficiency ratios r_{EAFDL} as a function of n for various storage efficiencies are shown in Figure 23. We observe that for the storage efficiencies considered and as n increases, the EAFDL efficiency ratios follow a periodic pattern, and for $s_{\text{eff}} \geq 1/4 = 0.25$, they are always less than a factor of 10. By inspecting Figures 16 and 23, we observe that the r_{EAFDL} ratios in the case of exponential rebuild times are smaller than those in the case of deterministic rebuild times.

Figures 24 and 25 show the ratio of the optimal codeword length, m^*_{exp}, for the exponential distribution to the optimal codeword length, m^*_{det}, for the deterministic distribution for various storage efficiencies. We observe that this ratio never exceeds one and approaches one as n increases. This implies that the optimal codeword length for the exponential distribution is in general smaller than the optimal codeword length for the deterministic distribution. This can be intuitively explained as follows. As previously mentioned, larger values of m result in a higher exposure degree to failure as each of the codewords is spread across a larger number of devices. The variation of exponentially distributed rebuild times results in increased vulnerability windows and therefore worse reliability. To reduce the exposure degree to failures, codewords should be spread across a smaller number of devices, which implies a smaller optimal codeword length.

VII. Conclusions

We considered the Mean Time to Data Loss (MTTDL) and the Expected Annual Fraction of Data Loss (EAFDL) reliability metrics of storage systems using advanced erasure codes. A methodology was presented for deriving the two metrics analytically. Closed-form expressions capturing the effect of various system parameters were obtained for arbitrary rebuild time distributions and for the symmetric, clustered, and declustered data placement schemes. We established that the declustered placement scheme offers superior reliability in terms of both metrics. Subsequently, a thorough comparison of the reliability achieved by the declustered placement scheme under various codeword configurations was conducted. The results obtained show that the optimal codeword lengths for MTTDL and EAFDL are similar and, as the system size grows, they are about 60% of the storage system size.

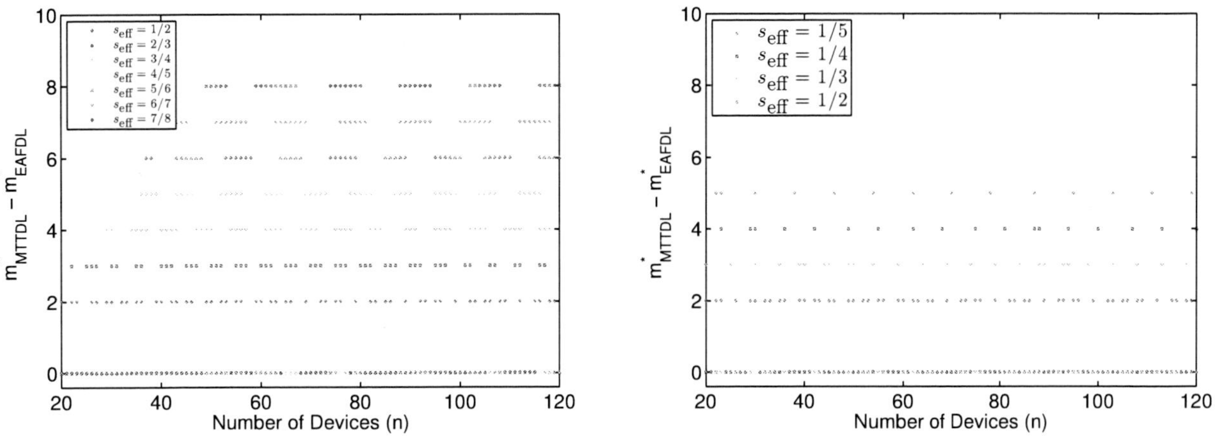

(a) $s_{eff} = 1/2, 2/3, 3/4, 4/5, 5/6, 6/7,$ and $7/8$ (b) $s_{eff} = 1/5, 1/4, 1/3,$ and $1/2$

Figure 21. The difference between m^*_{MTTDL} and m^*_{EAFDL} vs. number of devices; $\lambda/\mu = 0.001$ and exponential rebuild times.

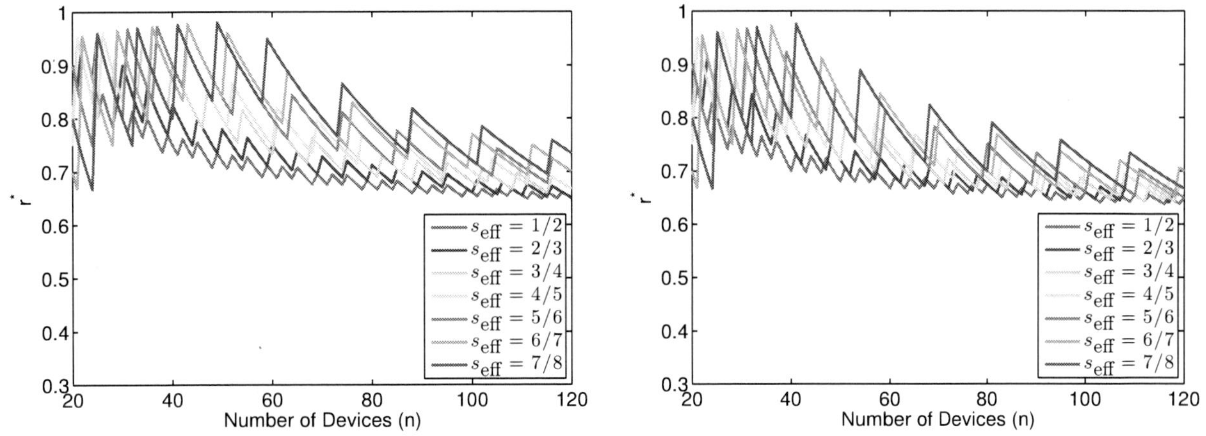

(a) MTTDL (b) EAFDL

Figure 22. r^* vs. number of devices for $s_{eff} = 1/2, 2/3, 3/4, 4/5, 5/6, 6/7,$ and $7/8$; $\lambda/\mu = 0.001$ and exponential rebuild times.

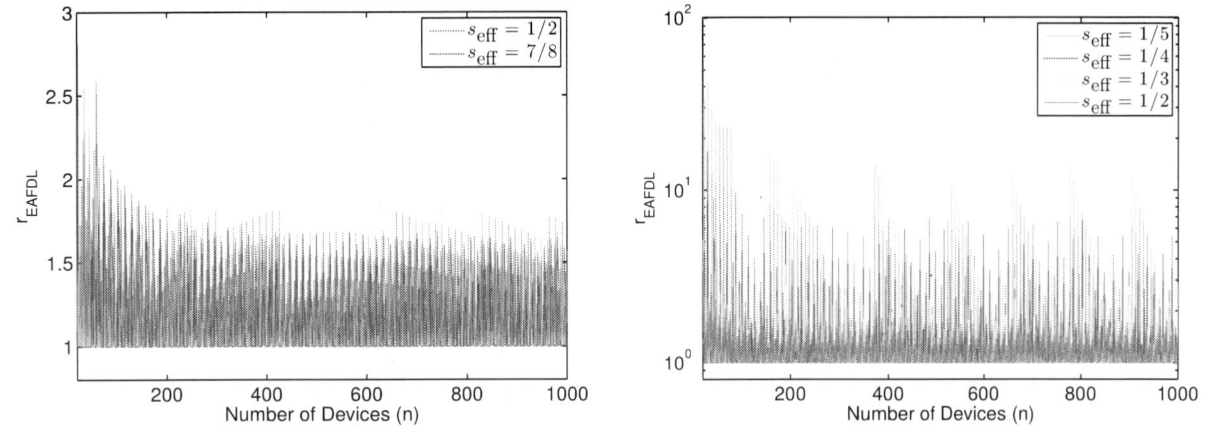

(a) $s_{eff} = 1/2$ and $7/8$ (b) $s_{eff} = 1/5, 1/4, 1/3,$ and $1/2$

Figure 23. The EAFDL efficiency ratio r_{EAFDL} vs. number of devices; $\lambda/\mu = 0.001$ and exponential rebuild times.

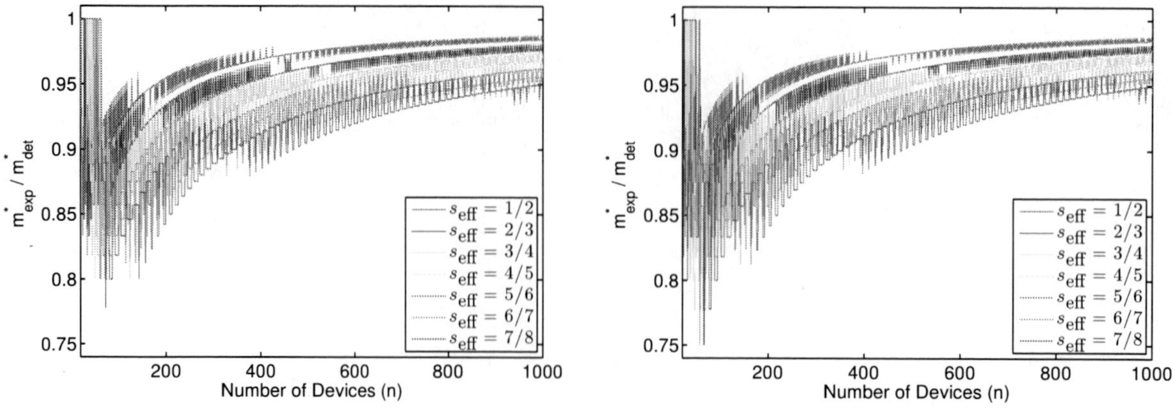

(a) MTTDL

(b) EAFDL

Figure 24. Ratio m^*_{exp} to m^*_{det} vs. number of devices for $s_{\text{eff}} = 1/2, 2/3, 3/4, 4/5,\ 5/6, 6/7,$ and $7/8$; $\lambda/\mu = 0.001$.

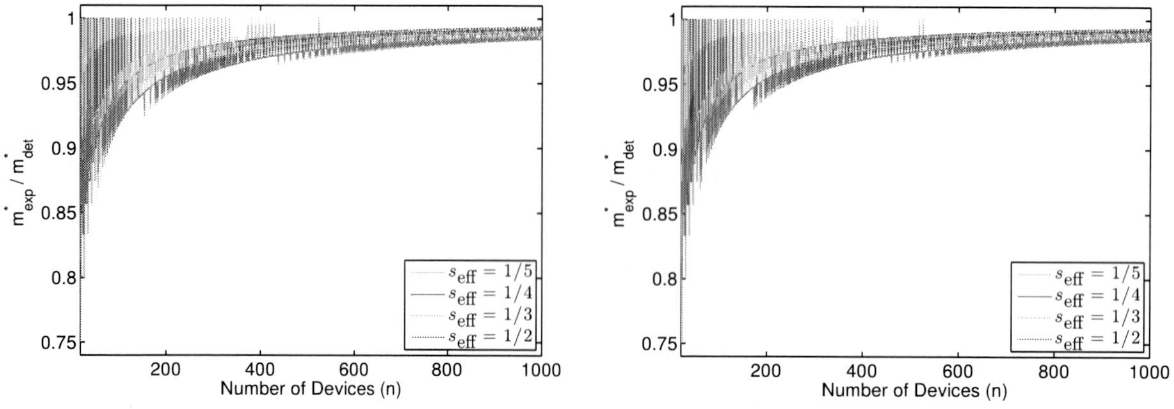

(a) MTTDL

(b) EAFDL

Figure 25. Ratio m^*_{exp} to m^*_{det} vs. number of devices for $s_{\text{eff}} = 1/5, 1/4, 1/3,$ and $1/2$; $\lambda/\mu = 0.001$.

Extending the methodology developed to derive the reliability of erasure coded systems under network rebuild bandwidth limitations and in the presence of unrecoverable latent errors are subjects of further investigation. Also, owing to the parallelism of the rebuild process, the model considered yields very small rebuild times for large system sizes. To take into account the fact that the rebuild times cannot be smaller than the actual failure detection times requires a more sophisticated modeling effort, which is also part of future work.

APPENDIX A
ESTIMATION OF P_{DL}

Proof of Proposition 2.

Consider the direct path $1 \to 2 \to \cdots \to \tilde{r}$ of successive transitions from exposure level 1 to $\tilde{r}$. For ease of reading, we denote the successive transitions from exposure level u to $\tilde{r}$ by $u \to \tilde{r}$. We first evaluate $P_{\text{DL}}(R_1)$, the probability of data loss conditioned on the rebuild time R_1. From (19), and using the fact that α_u does not depend on $R_1, \alpha_1, \cdots, \alpha_{u-1}$, it follows that

$$
\begin{aligned}
P_{\text{DL}}(R_1) &\approx P_{1\to\tilde{r}}(R_1) \\
&= P_{1\to 2}(R_1) P_{2\to\tilde{r}}(R_1) \\
&= P_{1\to 2}(R_1) E_{\alpha_1|R_1}[P_{2\to\tilde{r}}(R_1,\alpha_1)] \\
&= P_{1\to 2}(R_1) E_{\alpha_1}[P_{2\to 3}(R_1,\alpha_1) P_{3\to\tilde{r}}(R_1,\alpha_1)] \\
&= P_{1\to 2}(R_1) E_{\alpha_1}[P_{2\to 3}(R_1,\alpha_1) E_{\alpha_2|R_1,\alpha_1}[P_{3\to\tilde{r}}(R_1,\alpha_1,\alpha_2)]] \\
&= \cdots \\
&= P_{1\to 2}(R_1) E_{\alpha_1}[P_{2\to 3}(R_1,\vec{\alpha}_1) E_{\alpha_2}[P_{3\to 4}(R_1,\vec{\alpha}_2) \cdots \\
&\qquad \cdots E_{\alpha_{\tilde{r}-2}}[P_{\tilde{r}-1\to\tilde{r}}(R_1,\vec{\alpha}_{\tilde{r}-2})] \cdots] \\
&= E_{\vec{\alpha}_{\tilde{r}-2}}[P_{1\to 2}(R_1) P_{2\to 3}(R_1,\vec{\alpha}_1) \cdots P_{\tilde{r}-1\to\tilde{r}}(R_1,\vec{\alpha}_{\tilde{r}-2})] \\
&= E_{\vec{\alpha}_{\tilde{r}-2}}\left[\prod_{u=1}^{\tilde{r}-1} P_{u\to u+1}(R_1,\vec{\alpha}_{u-1})\right] \\
&= E_{\vec{\alpha}_{\tilde{r}-2}}[P_{\text{DL}}(R_1,\vec{\alpha}_{\tilde{r}-2})] ,
\end{aligned}
\tag{108}
$$

where

$$
P_{\text{DL}}(R_1,\vec{\alpha}_{\tilde{r}-2}) \triangleq \prod_{u=1}^{\tilde{r}-1} P_{u\to u+1}(R_1,\vec{\alpha}_{u-1}) , \tag{109}
$$

with

$$P_{1\to 2}(R_1, \vec{\alpha}_0) \triangleq P_{1\to 2}(R_1) \; . \qquad (110)$$

Substituting (45) into (109), and using (44) and (110), yields

$$P_{\rm DL}(R_1, \vec{\alpha}_{\tilde{r}-2}) \approx (\lambda\, b_1\, R_1)^{\tilde{r}-1} \prod_{u=1}^{\tilde{r}-1} \frac{\tilde{n}_u}{b_u} \, (V_u\, \alpha_u)^{\tilde{r}-1-u} \; . \qquad (111)$$

Unconditioning (111) on $\vec{\alpha}_{\tilde{r}-2}$, and given that the elements of $\vec{\alpha}_{\tilde{r}-2}$ are independent random variables approximately distributed according to (24) such that $E(\alpha_u^k) \approx 1/(k+1)$, (108) yields

$$P_{\rm DL}(R_1) \approx (\lambda\, b_1\, R_1)^{\tilde{r}-1} \, \frac{1}{(\tilde{r}-1)!} \prod_{u=1}^{\tilde{r}-1} \frac{\tilde{n}_u}{b_u} \, V_u^{\tilde{r}-1-u} \; . \qquad (112)$$

The probability of data loss $P_{\rm DL}$ is obtained by unconditioning $P_{\rm DL}(R_1)$ on R_1, that is,

$$P_{\rm DL} = E[P_{\rm DL}(R_1)] \; . \qquad (113)$$

Unconditioning (112) on R_1 using (10) and (34), (113) yields (46). ■

Appendix B
Estimation of $E(Q)$

Proof of Proposition 3.

We first evaluate $E(Q|R_1)$, the expected amount of data lost conditioned on the rebuild time R_1. From (21), and considering the direct path $1 \to 2 \to \cdots \to \tilde{r}$ of successive transitions from exposure level 1 to $\tilde{r}$, and using the fact that α_u does not depend on $R_1, \alpha_1, \cdots, \alpha_{u-1}$, it follows that

$$\begin{aligned}
E(Q|R_1) \;&\approx\; P_{1\to 2}(R_1) E(Q|R_1, 1\to 2)\\
&= P_{1\to 2}(R_1) E_{\alpha_1|R_1}[E(Q|R_1, \alpha_1)]\\
&= P_{1\to 2}(R_1) E_{\alpha_1}[P_{2\to 3}(R_1, \alpha_1) E(Q|R_1, \alpha_1, 2\to 3)]\\
&= P_{1\to 2}(R_1) E_{\alpha_1}[P_{2\to 3}(R_1, \alpha_1) E_{\alpha_2|R_1,\alpha_1}[E(Q|R_1, \alpha_1, \alpha_2)]]\\
&= \cdots\\
&= P_{1\to 2}(R_1) E_{\alpha_1}[P_{2\to 3}(R_1, \vec{\alpha}_1) E_{\alpha_2}[P_{3\to 4}(R_1, \vec{\alpha}_2) \cdots\\
&\qquad \cdots P_{\tilde{r}-1\to\tilde{r}}(R_1, \vec{\alpha}_{\tilde{r}-2}) E_{\alpha_{\tilde{r}-1}}(Q|R_1, \vec{\alpha}_{\tilde{r}-1})] \cdots]\\
&= E_{\vec{\alpha}_{\tilde{r}-1}}[P_{1\to 2}(R_1) P_{2\to 3}(R_1, \vec{\alpha}_1) \cdots P_{\tilde{r}-1\to\tilde{r}}(R_1, \vec{\alpha}_{\tilde{r}-2})\\
&\qquad\qquad E(Q|R_1, \vec{\alpha}_{\tilde{r}-1})]\\
&\overset{(20)(21)}{=} E_{\vec{\alpha}_{\tilde{r}-1}}\left[\left(\prod_{u=1}^{\tilde{r}-1} P_{u\to u+1}(R_1, \vec{\alpha}_{u-1})\right) E(H|R_1, \vec{\alpha}_{\tilde{r}-1})\right]\\
&\overset{(109)}{=} E_{\vec{\alpha}_{\tilde{r}-1}}[P_{\rm DL}(R_1, \vec{\alpha}_{\tilde{r}-2})\, E(H|R_1, \vec{\alpha}_{\tilde{r}-1})]\\
&\overset{(23)}{=} E_{\vec{\alpha}_{\tilde{r}-1}}[P_{\rm DL}(R_1, \vec{\alpha}_{\tilde{r}-2})\, E(l\, A_{\tilde{r}}|R_1, \vec{\alpha}_{\tilde{r}-1})]\\
&\overset{\text{Remark 1}}{=} E_{\vec{\alpha}_{\tilde{r}-1}}[P_{\rm DL}(R_1, \vec{\alpha}_{\tilde{r}-2})\, l\, E(A_{\tilde{r}}|\vec{\alpha}_{\tilde{r}-1})]\\
&= E_{\vec{\alpha}_{\tilde{r}-1}}[G(R_1, \vec{\alpha}_{\tilde{r}-1})] \; , \qquad (114)
\end{aligned}$$

where

$$G(R_1, \vec{\alpha}_{\tilde{r}-1}) \;\triangleq\; l\, P_{\rm DL}(R_1, \vec{\alpha}_{\tilde{r}-2})\, E(A_{\tilde{r}}|\vec{\alpha}_{\tilde{r}-1}) \; . \qquad (115)$$

Using (27) and (111), (115) yields

$$G(R_1, \vec{\alpha}_{\tilde{r}-1}) \;\approx\; l\, c\, (\lambda\, b_1\, R_1)^{\tilde{r}-1} \prod_{u=1}^{\tilde{r}-1} \frac{\tilde{n}_u}{b_u} \, (V_u\, \alpha_u)^{\tilde{r}-u} \; . \qquad (116)$$

Unconditioning (116) on $\vec{\alpha}_{\tilde{r}-1}$, and given that the elements of $\vec{\alpha}_{\tilde{r}-1}$ are independent random variables approximately distributed according to (24) such that $E(\alpha_u^k) \approx 1/(k+1)$, (114) yields

$$E(Q|R_1) \approx l\, c\, (\lambda\, b_1\, R_1)^{\tilde{r}-1} \, \frac{1}{\tilde{r}!} \prod_{u=1}^{\tilde{r}-1} \frac{\tilde{n}_u}{b_u} \, V_u^{\tilde{r}-u} \; . \qquad (117)$$

The expected amount of data lost, $E(Q)$, upon a first-device failure is obtained by unconditioning $E(Q|R_1)$ on R_1, that is,

$$E(Q) = E[E(Q|R_1)] \; . \qquad (118)$$

Unconditioning (117) on R_1 using (10) and (34), (118) yields (47). ■

Appendix C
Approximate Derivation of $E(H)^{\rm sym}$

Proof of Proposition 4.

First, we derive an approximation of the product

$$A \triangleq \prod_{j=1}^{m-l} \frac{m-j}{k-j} \; , \qquad (119)$$

which appears in Equation (83). From (60), it follows that $m - l = hm$, as stated by (80). Substituting the preceding into (119), and using (61), yields

$$A = \prod_{j=1}^{hxk} \frac{x - \frac{j}{k}}{1 - \frac{j}{k}} \; , \qquad (120)$$

or equivalently,

$$\log(A) = \sum_{j=1}^{hxk} \log\left(\frac{x - \frac{j}{k}}{1 - \frac{j}{k}}\right) \; , \qquad (121)$$

To evaluate the preceding summation, we first establish the following lemmas.

Lemma 1: For small values of ϵ, that is, when ϵ approaches zero, and for any function $f(y)$, it holds that

$$\epsilon \sum_{j=1}^{\alpha/\epsilon} f(j\epsilon) \approx \int_{\frac{\epsilon}{2}}^{\alpha+\frac{\epsilon}{2}} f(y)\, dy \; , \qquad \forall \alpha \in \mathbb{R} \; . \qquad (122)$$

Proof: The left-hand side of (122) is written as follows:

$$\epsilon \sum_{j=1}^{\alpha/\epsilon} f(j\epsilon) = \sum_{j=1}^{\alpha/\epsilon} f(j\epsilon)\, \epsilon \; . \qquad (123)$$

For small small values of ϵ, the summation in the right-hand side of (123) represents the middle Riemann sum that approximates the definite integral of the $f(y)$ function in the interval $[\epsilon/2, \alpha + \epsilon/2]$, that is,

$$\sum_{j=1}^{\alpha/\epsilon} f(j\epsilon)\, \epsilon \approx \int_{\frac{\epsilon}{2}}^{\alpha+\frac{\epsilon}{2}} f(y)\, dy \; . \qquad (124)$$

□

LEMMA 2: For any functions $f(y)$ and $F(y)$, such that $F(y) = \int f(y)\,dy$, or $F'(y) = f(y)$, and for $\alpha \in \mathbb{R}$ define

$$F^{(1)}(\alpha, z) \triangleq \int_{\frac{z}{2}}^{\alpha+\frac{z}{2}} f(y)\,dy = F\left(\alpha + \frac{z}{2}\right) - F\left(\frac{z}{2}\right). \quad (125)$$

Then it holds that

$$F_z^{(1)}(\alpha, z) = \frac{1}{2}\left[f\left(\alpha + \frac{z}{2}\right) - f\left(\frac{z}{2}\right)\right], \quad (126)$$

and

$$F_{zz}^{(1)}(\alpha, z) = \frac{1}{4}\left[f'\left(\alpha + \frac{z}{2}\right) - f'\left(\frac{z}{2}\right)\right]. \quad (127)$$

Proof: Immediate from the fact that for any $\alpha \in \mathbb{R}$ and function $f(y)$, it holds that $df(\alpha+z/2)/dz = f'(\alpha+z/2)/2$. □

Corollary 1: For $f(y) = \log(x-y)$ and for all $\alpha \in \mathbb{R}$, it holds that

$$F^{(1)}(x, \alpha, z) = \int_{\frac{z}{2}}^{\alpha+\frac{z}{2}} \log(x-y)\,dy = G(x, \alpha, z), \quad (128)$$

where

$$G(x, \alpha, z) \triangleq \log\left(\frac{(x-\frac{z}{2})^{x-\frac{z}{2}}}{(x-\alpha-\frac{z}{2})^{x-\alpha-\frac{z}{2}}}\right) - \alpha. \quad (129)$$

Also,

$$F_z^{(1)}(x, \alpha, z) = G_z(x, \alpha, z) = \frac{1}{2}\log\left(\frac{x-\alpha-\frac{z}{2}}{x-\frac{z}{2}}\right), \quad (130)$$

and

$$F_{zz}^{(1)}(x, \alpha, z) = G_{zz}(x, \alpha, z) = -\frac{\alpha}{4\,(x-\alpha-\frac{z}{2})(x-\frac{z}{2})}. \quad (131)$$

Proof: Equations (128) and (129) are derived from (125) by taking $f(y) = \log(x-y)$ and using the fact that $\int \log(y)\,dy = y\,[\log(y) - 1]$, which in turn implies that $F(y) = \int \log(x-y)\,dy = -(x-y)\,[\log(x-y) - 1]$. Equation (130) is directly obtained from (126), and (131) is obtained from (127) by using the fact that $f'(y) = -1/(x-y)$. □

Note that an approximation of $G(x, \alpha, z)$ for $z \approxeq 0$ can be obtained through its Maclaurin series as follows:

$$G(x, \alpha, z) \approx G(x, \alpha, 0) + G_z(x, \alpha, 0)\,z + \frac{G_{zz}(x, \alpha, 0)}{2}\,z^2, \quad (132)$$

which by virtue of (129), (130), and (131) yields

$$G(x, \alpha, z) \approx \log\left(\frac{x^x}{(x-\alpha)^{x-\alpha}}\right) - \alpha + \frac{1}{2}\log\left(\frac{x-\alpha}{x}\right) z - \frac{\alpha}{8(x-\alpha)x}\,z^2. \quad (133)$$

We now proceed with the evaluation of $\log(A)$. From (122) and (128), it follows that

$$\epsilon \sum_{j=1}^{\alpha/\epsilon} \log\left(\frac{x - j\epsilon}{1 - j\epsilon}\right) = G(x, \alpha, \epsilon) - G(1, \alpha, \epsilon). \quad (134)$$

From (121) and (129), and using (134) with $\epsilon = 1/k$ and $\alpha = hx$, we get

$$\log(A) \approx k\,F\left(x, \frac{1}{2k}\right), \quad (135)$$

where

$$F(x, y) \triangleq \log\left(\frac{(x-y)^{x-y}\,(1-hx-y)^{1-hx-y}}{(1-y)^{1-y}\,[(1-h)x-y]^{(1-h)x-y}}\right). \quad (136)$$

An expression for $\log(A)$ for large values of k, m, l, and $m-l$ can be obtained from (121) and (134) by using approximation (133) with $\epsilon = 1/k$ and $\alpha = hx$ as follows:

$$\log(A) \approx k\,\log\left(\frac{x^x\,(1-hx)^{1-hx}}{[(1-h)x]^{(1-h)x}}\right) + \log\left(\sqrt{\frac{1-h}{1-hx}}\right) - \frac{1}{k}\,\frac{h(1-x)[1+(1-h)x]}{8(1-h)(1-hx)x}. \quad (137)$$

Equation (58) is a direct consequence of (83) and also of (79), (80), (119), and (137), where the third term of the summation in (137) is ignored for large k. ■

APPENDIX D
APPROXIMATE DERIVATION OF MTTDL^{sym}

Proof of Proposition 5.

Using (79) and (80), (81) can be written as follows:

$$\frac{n\,\lambda\,\text{MTTDL}^{\text{sym}}}{k} \approx \frac{1}{k}\left[\frac{b}{[(1-h)xk+1]\,\lambda\,c}\right]^{hxk} (hxk)!\; \frac{[E(X)]^{hxk}}{E(X^{hxk})} \prod_{j=1}^{m-l}\left(\frac{k-j}{m-j}\right)^{m-l-j}. \quad (138)$$

From (138), and using Stirling's approximation (139) for large values of k, with k replaced by hxk, that is

$$(hxk)! \approx \sqrt{2\pi hxk}\,\left(\frac{hxk}{e}\right)^{hxk}, \quad (139)$$

it follows that

$$\log\left(\frac{n\,\lambda\,\text{MTTDL}^{\text{sym}}_{\text{approx}}}{k}\right) \approx \log\left(\sqrt{\frac{2\pi hx}{k}}\right) + hxk\,\log\left(\frac{hxk\,b}{e\,[(1-h)xk+1]\,\lambda\,c}\right) + \log\left(\frac{[E(X)]^{hxk}}{E(X^{hxk})}\right) + \log(B), \quad (140)$$

where B is the product

$$B \triangleq \prod_{j=1}^{m-l}\left(\frac{k-j}{m-j}\right)^{m-l-j}. \quad (141)$$

We now proceed to derive an approximation of the product B. By virtue of (61), (80), and (119), the product B can be written as follows:

$$B = \frac{\prod_{j=1}^{m-l} \left(\frac{m-j}{k-j}\right)^j}{\prod_{j=1}^{m-l} \left(\frac{m-j}{k-j}\right)^{m-l}} = \frac{C}{A^{m-l}} = \frac{C}{A^{hxk}} , \quad (142)$$

where

$$C \triangleq \prod_{j=1}^{m-l} \left(\frac{m-j}{k-j}\right)^j = \prod_{j=1}^{hxk} \left(\frac{x-\frac{j}{k}}{1-\frac{j}{k}}\right)^j . \quad (143)$$

From (142) and (143), it follows that

$$\log(B) = \log(C) - hxk \log(A) \quad (144)$$

and

$$\log(C) = \sum_{j=1}^{hxk} j \log\left(\frac{x-\frac{j}{k}}{1-\frac{j}{k}}\right) . \quad (145)$$

To evaluate the preceding summation, we first establish the following corollary from Lemma 2.

Corollary 2: For $f(y) = y\log(x-y)$ and for all $\alpha \in \mathbb{R}$, it holds that

$$F^{(1)}(x,\alpha,z) = \int_{\frac{z}{2}}^{\alpha+\frac{z}{2}} y\log(x-y)\,dy = R(x,\alpha,z) , \quad (146)$$

where

$$R(x,\alpha,z) \triangleq \frac{1}{2}\log\left(\frac{(x-\frac{z}{2})^{x^2-(\frac{z}{2})^2}}{(x-\alpha-\frac{z}{2})^{x^2-(\alpha+\frac{z}{2})^2}}\right) - \frac{\alpha(2x+\alpha+z)}{4} . \quad (147)$$

Also,

$$F_z^{(1)}(x,\alpha,z) = R_z(x,\alpha,z) = \frac{1}{2}\log\left(\frac{(x-\alpha-\frac{z}{2})^{\alpha+\frac{z}{2}}}{(x-\frac{z}{2})^{\frac{z}{2}}}\right) \quad (148)$$

and

$$F_{zz}^{(1)}(x,\alpha,z) = R_{zz}(x,\alpha,z) = \frac{1}{4}\left[\log\left(\frac{x-\alpha-\frac{z}{2}}{x-\frac{z}{2}}\right) - \frac{\alpha x}{(x-\alpha-\frac{z}{2})(x-\frac{z}{2})}\right] . \quad (149)$$

Proof: Equations (146) and (147) are derived from (125) by taking $f(y) = y\log(x-y)$ and using the fact that $\int y\log(y)\,dy = y^2(2\log(y)-1)/4$, which in turn implies that $F(y) = \int y\log(x-y)\,dy = (x-y)\left[3x+y-2(x+y)\log(x-y)\right]/4$. Equation (148) is directly obtained from (126), and (149) is obtained from (127) by using the fact that $f'(y) = \log(x-y) - y/(x-y)$. □

Note that an approximation of $R(x,\alpha,z)$ for $z \approxeq 0$ can be obtained through its Maclaurin series as follows:

$$R(x,\alpha,z) \approx R(x,\alpha,0) + R_z(x,\alpha,0)\,z + \frac{R_{zz}(x,\alpha,0)}{2}\,z^2 , \quad (150)$$

which by virtue of (147), (148), and (149) yields

$$R(x,\alpha,z) \approx \frac{1}{2}\log\left(\frac{x^{x^2}}{(x-\alpha)^{x^2-\alpha^2}}\right) - \frac{\alpha(2x+\alpha)}{4} + \frac{\alpha}{2}\log(x-\alpha)\,z + \frac{1}{8}\left[\log\left(\frac{x-\alpha}{x}\right) - \frac{\alpha}{(x-\alpha)x}\right] z^2 . \quad (151)$$

We now proceed with the evaluation of $\log(C)$. From (122) and (146), it follows that

$$\epsilon \sum_{j=1}^{\alpha/\epsilon} j \log\left(\frac{x-j\epsilon}{1-j\epsilon}\right) = R(x,\alpha,\epsilon) - R(1,\alpha,\epsilon) . \quad (152)$$

From (121) and (147), and using (152) with $\epsilon = 1/k$ and $\alpha = hx$, we get

$$\log(C) \approx k^2\,\frac{1}{2}\left[hx(1-x) + S\left(x, \frac{1}{2k}\right)\right] , \quad (153)$$

where

$$S(x,y) \triangleq \log\left(\frac{(x-y)^{x^2-y^2}(1-hx-y)^{1-(hx+y)^2}}{(1-y)^{1-y^2}\left[(1-h)x-y\right]^{x^2-(hx+y)^2}}\right) . \quad (154)$$

An expression for $\log(C)$ for large values of k, m, l, and $m-l$ can be obtained from (145) and (152) by using approximation (151) with $\epsilon = 1/k$ and $\alpha = hx$ as follows:

$$\log(C) \approx \frac{k^2}{2}\left[hx(1-x) + \log\left(\frac{x^{x^2}(1-hx)^{1-(hx)^2}}{[(1-h)x]^{(1-h^2)x^2}}\right)\right] + \frac{k}{2}\,hx\log\left(\frac{(1-h)x}{1-hx}\right) + \frac{1}{8}\log\left(\frac{1-h}{1-hx}\right) - \frac{h(1-x)}{8(1-h)(1-hx)} . \quad (155)$$

Substituting (137) and (155) into (144) yields

$$\log(B) \approx \frac{k^2}{2}\left[hx(1-x) - \log\left(\frac{\left[x^{h^2}(1-h)^{(1-h)^2}\right]^{x^2}}{(1-hx)^{(1-hx)^2}}\right)\right] + k\,hx\log(\sqrt{x}) - \frac{1}{8}\left[h(1-x) - \log\left(\frac{1-h}{1-hx}\right)\right] . \quad (156)$$

Equation (62) is a direct consequence of (140) and (156). ■

APPENDIX E
APPROXIMATE DERIVATION OF EAFDL^{sym}

Proof of Proposition 6.

From (15), it follows that

$$\text{EAFDL}/\lambda = \frac{E(H)/c}{\lambda\,\text{MTTDL} \cdot U \cdot c} . \quad (157)$$

Substituting (2) into (157), and using (60), yields

$$\text{EAFDL}/\lambda = \frac{E(H)/c}{\lambda\,\text{MTTDL} \cdot (1-h)\,n} \quad (158)$$

or

$$\log(\text{EAFDL}/\lambda) = \log(E(H)/c) - \log(\lambda\,\text{MTTDL}) - \log((1-h)\,n) . \quad (159)$$

Substituting (58) and (62) into (159), after some manipulations yields (64). ■

APPENDIX F
OPTIMAL CODEWORD LENGTHS FOR MAXIMIZING $\mathrm{MTTDL}^{\mathrm{declus}}$ AND MINIMIZING $\mathrm{EAFDL}^{\mathrm{declus}}$ FOR A LARGE NUMBER OF STORAGE DEVICES, n

Proof of Proposition 11.

We first consider the optimal codeword lengths for maximizing $\mathrm{MTTDL}^{\mathrm{declus}}$. From (103), it holds that

$$r^*_{\mathrm{MTTDL}}(n) = \frac{m^*_{\mathrm{MTTDL}}(n)}{n} = \frac{\arg \max_{1\le m\le n} \mathrm{MTTDL}^{\mathrm{declus}}}{n} . \quad (160)$$

Using (73), the preceding can be written as follows:

$$r^*_{\mathrm{MTTDL}}(n) = \arg \max_{\frac{1}{n}\le x\le 1} \mathrm{MTTDL}^{\mathrm{declus}} \quad (161)$$

or

$$r^*_{\mathrm{MTTDL}}(n) = \arg \max_{\frac{1}{n}\le x\le 1} \log(\lambda\, \mathrm{MTTDL}^{\mathrm{declus}}) \quad (162)$$

or, equivalently,

$$r^*_{\mathrm{MTTDL}}(n) = \arg \max_{\frac{1}{n}\le x\le 1} \left(\frac{2\, \log(\lambda\, \mathrm{MTTDL}^{\mathrm{declus}})}{n^2} \right) . \quad (163)$$

By letting n approach the infinity, we get

$$\begin{aligned} r^*_\infty &= \lim_{n\to\infty} r^*_{\mathrm{MTTDL}}(n) \\ &= \lim_{n\to\infty} \arg \max_{\frac{1}{n}\le x\le 1} \left(\frac{2\, \log(\lambda\, \mathrm{MTTDL}^{\mathrm{declus}})}{n^2} \right) \\ &= \arg \max_{0<x\le 1} \lim_{n\to\infty} \left(\frac{2\, \log(\lambda\, \mathrm{MTTDL}^{\mathrm{declus}})}{n^2} \right) . \end{aligned} \quad (164)$$

Using the approximation obtained in (85), (164) yields

$$r^*_\infty = \arg \max_{0<x\le 1} W(h,x) , \quad (165)$$

provided that for the last term of the summation in (85) it holds that

$$\lim_{n\to\infty} \frac{\log\left(\dfrac{[E(X)]^{hxn}}{E(X^{hxn})} \right)}{n^2} = 0 . \quad (166)$$

Remark 13: It turns out that (166) holds for the cases of deterministic and exponential rebuild time distributions owing to the following lemmas.

LEMMA 3: In the case of deterministic rebuild times, it holds that

$$\log\left(\frac{[E(X)]^{hxn}}{E(X^{hxn})} \right) = 0 . \quad (167)$$

Proof: Equation (167) follows from the fact that in the case of deterministic rebuild times it holds that $E(X^{hxn}) = [E(X)]^{hxn}$. □

LEMMA 4: In the case of exponential rebuild times, it holds that

$$\frac{\log\left(\dfrac{[E(X)]^{hxn}}{E(X^{hxn})} \right)}{n^2} \approx hx \frac{\log\left(\dfrac{hxn}{e}\right)}{n} + \frac{\log(2\pi hxn)}{2\, n^2} . \quad (168)$$

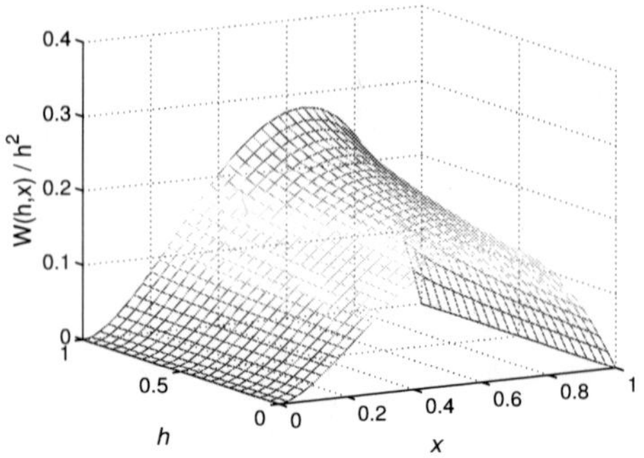

Figure 26. $W(h,x)/h^2$ for h and $x \in [0,1]$.

Proof: In the case of exponential rebuild times, it holds that $E(X^{hxn}) = (hxn)!\,[E(X)]^{hxn}$, which for large n and by virtue of (139), yields

$$\log\left(\frac{[E(X)]^{hxn}}{E(X^{hxn})} \right) \approx \log\left(\sqrt{2\pi hxn} \left(\frac{hxn}{e}\right)^{hxn} \right) . \quad (169)$$

Equation (168) follows directly from (169). □

From (63), it follows that $W(h,x)$ or, equivalently, $W(h,x)/h^2$ are non-negative in $x \in [0,1]$, with $W(h,0) = W(h,1) = 0$, as shown in Figure 26. Consequently, (165) implies that r^*_∞ satisfies the following equation:

$$W_x(h, r^*_\infty) = \left.\frac{dW(h,x)}{dx}\right|_{x=r^*_\infty} = 0 . \quad (170)$$

The derivative of $W(h,x)$ with respect to x can be obtained using the following lemma.

LEMMA 5: For $w(y)$ defined as follows:

$$w(y) = \log\left(f(y)^{g(y)} \right) = \log\left(f^g \right) , \quad (171)$$

it holds that

$$w'(y) = w' = g' \log(f) + g f'/f . \quad (172)$$

Corollary 3: For $v(y)$ defined as follows:

$$v(y) = \log\left(f(y)^{f(y)} \right) = \log\left(f^f \right) , \quad (173)$$

it holds that

$$v'(y) = v' = f' \left(\log(f) + 1 \right) . \quad (174)$$

From (63), it follows that the derivative of $W(h,x)$ with respect to x can be obtained by successively applying (172), which yields

$$W_x(h,x) = -2\, Q(h,x) , \quad (175)$$

where $Q(h,x)$ is given by (105). Thus, r^*_∞ is obtained as the unique root of the equation $Q(h,x) = 0$, with respect to x, in the interval $(0,1]$, that is,

$$Q(h, r^*_\infty) = 0 , \;\; \text{with } r^*_\infty \in (0,1] . \quad (176)$$

The values of r^*_∞ as a function of h are shown in Figure 27.

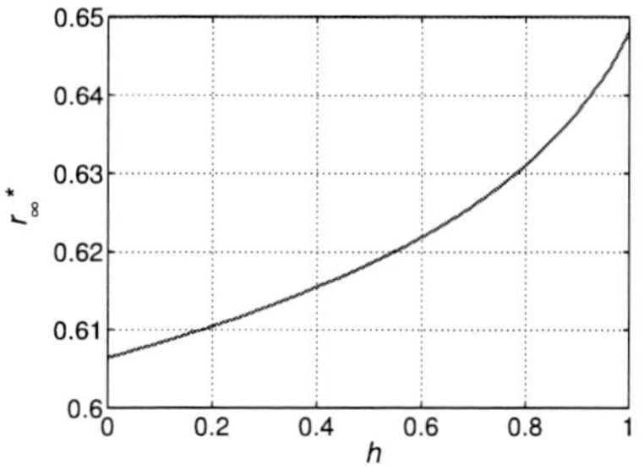

Figure 27. r^*_∞ vs. h for MTTDL and EAFDL.

Remark 14: For $h = 0$, it holds that $Q(0, x) = 0$. To find the root when $h \to 0$, we consider finding the root of the equivalent equation $Q(h, x)/h^2 = 0$. Using L'Hôpital's rule, after some manipulations, we obtain

$$\lim_{h\to 0} \frac{Q(h,x)}{h^2} = x\left(\log(x) + \frac{1}{2}\right) = x\log(\sqrt{e}\,x) \,. \tag{177}$$

Combining (176) and (177) yields

$$r^*_\infty \log(\sqrt{e}\, r^*_\infty) = 0 \,, \quad \text{with } r^*_\infty \in (0, 1]$$
$$\text{or } r^*_\infty = \frac{1}{\sqrt{e}} = 0.606 \,. \tag{178}$$

For $h = 1$, r^*_∞ is obtained as the unique root in $(0, 1]$ of the equation

$$Q(1, x) = x + \log\left(x^x (1-x)^{1-x}\right) = 0 \,, \tag{179}$$

which yields $r^*_\infty = 0.648$.

We now proceed to derive the optimal codeword lengths for maximizing the $\text{EAFDL}^{\text{declus}}$ for large values of n, m, l, and $m - l$. Analogously to (164), it holds that

$$r^*_\infty = \lim_{n\to\infty} r^*_{\text{EAFDL}}(n)$$
$$= \arg\min_{0<x\le 1}\; \lim_{n\to\infty}\left(\frac{2\log(\text{EAFDL}^{\text{declus}}/\lambda)}{n^2}\right) \,. \tag{180}$$

Using the approximation obtained in (86), (180) yields

$$r^*_\infty = \arg\max_{0<x\le 1} W(h, x) \,, \tag{181}$$

provided that for the last term of the summation in (86) the condition given by (166) holds. Given that (181) is the same as (165), we deduce that the r^*_∞ values for EAFDL are the same as those for MTTDL. ■

Appendix G
Optimal Codeword Length for Minimizing $E(H)^{\text{declus}}$ for Large n

Proof of Proposition 12.

From (103), it holds that

$$r^*(n) = \frac{m^*(n)}{n} = \frac{\arg\min_{1\le m\le n} E(H)^{\text{declus}}}{n} \,. \tag{182}$$

Using (73), the preceding can be written as follows:

$$r^*(n) = \arg\min_{\frac{1}{n}\le x\le 1} E(H)^{\text{declus}} \tag{183}$$

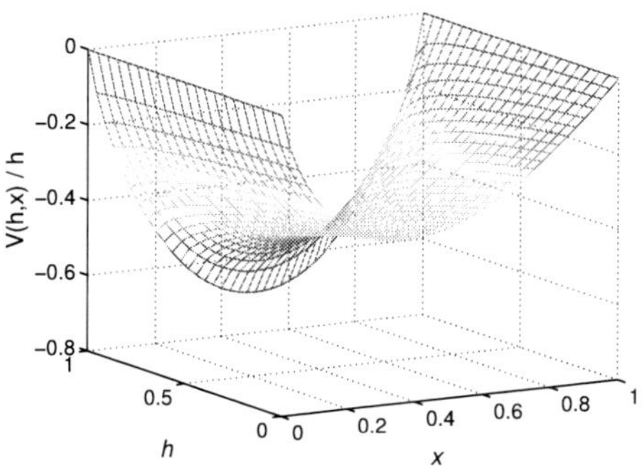

Figure 28. $V(h,x)/h$ for h and $x \in [0, 1]$.

or

$$r^*(n) = \arg\min_{\frac{1}{n}\le x\le 1} \log(E(H)^{\text{declus}}/c) \tag{184}$$

or, equivalently,

$$r^*(n) = \arg\min_{\frac{1}{n}\le x\le 1} \left(\frac{\log(E(H)^{\text{declus}}/c)}{n}\right) \,. \tag{185}$$

By letting n approach the infinity we get

$$r^*_\infty = \lim_{n\to\infty} r^*(n) = \lim_{n\to\infty} \arg\min_{\frac{1}{n}\le x\le 1} \left(\frac{\log(E(H)^{\text{declus}}/c)}{n}\right)$$
$$= \arg\min_{0<x\le 1}\; \lim_{n\to\infty} \left(\frac{\log(E(H)^{\text{declus}}/c)}{n}\right) \,. \tag{186}$$

Using the approximation obtained in (87), (186) yields

$$r^*_\infty = \arg\min_{0<x\le 1} V(h, x) \,. \tag{187}$$

From (59), it follows that $V(h, x)$ or, equivalently, $V(h, x)/h$ are convex in $x \in [0, 1]$, with $V(h, 0) = V(h, 1) = 0$, as shown in Figure 28. Consequently, (187) implies that r^*_∞ satisfies the following equation:

$$V_x(h, r^*_\infty) = \left.\frac{dV(h,x)}{dx}\right|_{x=r^*_\infty} = 0 \,. \tag{188}$$

From (59), it follows that the derivative of $V(h, x)$ with respect to x can be obtained using Corollary 3. By successively applying (174), with $f(x)$ being equal to x, $1 - hx$, and $(1 - h)x$, yields

$$V_x(h, x) = \log\left(\frac{x\,(1-hx)^{-h}}{[(1-h)x]^{1-h}}\right) \,. \tag{189}$$

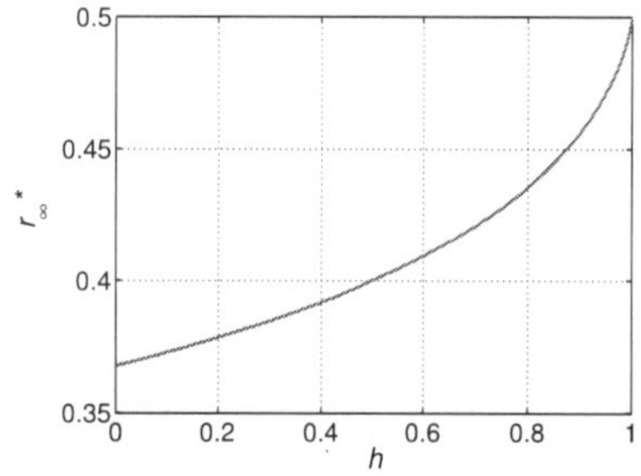

Figure 29. r^*_∞ vs. h for $E(H)$.

From (188) and (189), we deduce that r^*_∞ satisfies the following equation:

$$\log\left(\frac{r^*_\infty\,(1-h\,r^*_\infty)^{-h}}{[(1-h)r^*_\infty]^{1-h}}\right) = 0\,. \qquad (190)$$

Solving (190) for r^*_∞ yields (107), which is shown in Figure 29. ■

REFERENCES

[1] I. Iliadis and V. Venkatesan, "Reliability assessment of erasure coded systems," in Proceedings of the 10th International Conference on Communication Theory, Reliability, and Quality of Service (CTRQ), Apr. 2017, pp. 41–50.

[2] D. A. Patterson, G. Gibson, and R. H. Katz, "A case for redundant arrays of inexpensive disks (RAID)," in Proceedings of the ACM SIGMOD International Conference on Management of Data, Jun. 1988, pp. 109–116.

[3] P. M. Chen, E. K. Lee, G. A. Gibson, R. H. Katz, and D. A. Patterson, "RAID: High-performance, reliable secondary storage," ACM Comput. Surv., vol. 26, no. 2, Jun. 1994, pp. 145–185.

[4] M. Malhotra and K. S. Trivedi, "Reliability analysis of redundant arrays of inexpensive disks," J. Parallel Distrib. Comput., vol. 17, Jan. 1993, pp. 146–151.

[5] W. A. Burkhard and J. Menon, "Disk array storage system reliability," in Proceedings of the 23rd International Symposium on Fault-Tolerant Computing, Jun. 1993, pp. 432–441.

[6] K. S. Trivedi, Probabilistic and Statistics with Reliability, Queueing and Computer Science Applications, 2nd ed. New York: Wiley, 2002.

[7] Q. Xin, E. L. Miller, T. J. E. Schwarz, D. D. E. Long, S. A. Brandt, and W. Litwin, "Reliability mechanisms for very large storage systems," in Proceedings of the 20th IEEE/11th NASA Goddard Conference on Mass Storage Systems and Technologies (MSST), Apr. 2003, pp. 146–156.

[8] T. J. E. Schwarz, Q. Xin, E. L. Miller, D. D. E. Long, A. Hospodor, and S. Ng, "Disk scrubbing in large archival storage systems," in Proceedings of the 12th Annual IEEE/ACM International Symposium on Modeling, Analysis, and Simulation of Computer and Telecommunication Systems (MASCOTS), Oct. 2004, pp. 409–418.

[9] S. Ramabhadran and J. Pasquale, "Analysis of long-running replicated systems," in Proc. 25th IEEE International Conference on Computer Communications (INFOCOM), Apr. 2006, pp. 1–9.

[10] B. Eckart, X. Chen, X. He, and S. L. Scott, "Failure prediction models for proactive fault tolerance within storage systems," in Proceedings of the 16th Annual IEEE International Symposium on Modeling, Analysis, and Simulation of Computer and Telecommunication Systems (MASCOTS), Sep. 2008, pp. 1–8.

[11] K. Rao, J. L. Hafner, and R. A. Golding, "Reliability for networked storage nodes," IEEE Trans. Dependable Secure Comput., vol. 8, no. 3, May 2011, pp. 404–418.

[12] J.-F. Pâris, T. J. E. Schwarz, A. Amer, and D. D. E. Long, "Highly reliable two-dimensional RAID arrays for archival storage," in Proceedings of the 31st IEEE International Performance Computing and Communications Conference (IPCCC), Dec. 2012, pp. 324–331.

[13] I. Iliadis and V. Venkatesan, "An efficient method for reliability evaluation of data storage systems," in Proceedings of the 8th International Conference on Communication Theory, Reliability, and Quality of Service (CTRQ), Apr. 2015, pp. 6–12.

[14] ——, "Most probable paths to data loss: An efficient method for reliability evaluation of data storage systems," Int'l J. Adv. Syst. Measur., vol. 8, no. 3&4, Dec. 2015, pp. 178–200.

[15] V. Venkatesan and I. Iliadis, "A general reliability model for data storage systems," in Proceedings of the 9th International Conference on Quantitative Evaluation of Systems (QEST), Sep. 2012, pp. 209–219.

[16] A. Dholakia, E. Eleftheriou, X.-Y. Hu, I. Iliadis, J. Menon, and K. Rao, "A new intra-disk redundancy scheme for high-reliability RAID storage systems in the presence of unrecoverable errors," ACM Trans. Storage, vol. 4, no. 1, May 2008, pp. 1–42.

[17] A. Thomasian and M. Blaum, "Higher reliability redundant disk arrays: Organization, operation, and coding," ACM Trans. Storage, vol. 5, no. 3, Nov. 2009, pp. 1–59.

[18] K. M. Greenan, J. S. Plank, and J. J. Wylie, "Mean time to meaningless: MTTDL, Markov models, and storage system reliability," in Proceedings of the USENIX Workshop on Hot Topics in Storage and File Systems (HotStorage), Jun. 2010, pp. 1–5.

[19] I. Iliadis, R. Haas, X.-Y. Hu, and E. Eleftheriou, "Disk scrubbing versus intradisk redundancy for RAID storage systems," ACM Trans. Storage, vol. 7, no. 2, Jul. 2011, pp. 1–42.

[20] I. Iliadis and V. Venkatesan, "Rebuttal to 'Beyond MTTDL: A closed-form RAID-6 reliability equation'," ACM Trans. Storage, vol. 11, no. 2, Mar. 2015, pp. 1–10.

[21] "Amazon Simple Storage Service." [Online]. Available: http://aws.amazon.com/s3/ [retrieved: November 2017]

[22] D. Borthakur et al., "Apache Hadoop goes realtime at Facebook," in Proceedings of the ACM SIGMOD International Conference on Management of Data, Jun. 2011, pp. 1071–1080.

[23] R. J. Chansler, "Data availability and durability with the Hadoop Distributed File System," ;login: The USENIX Association Newsletter, vol. 37, no. 1, 2013, pp. 16–22.

[24] K. Shvachko, H. Kuang, S. Radia, and R. Chansler, "The Hadoop Distributed File System," in Proceedings of the 26th IEEE Symposium on Mass Storage Systems and Technologies (MSST), May 2010, pp. 1–10.

[25] I. Iliadis and V. Venkatesan, "Expected annual fraction of data loss as a metric for data storage reliability," in Proceedings of the 22nd Annual IEEE International Symposium on Modeling, Analysis, and Simulation of Computer and Telecommunication Systems (MASCOTS), Sep. 2014, pp. 375–384.

[26] C. Huang et al., "Erasure coding in Windows Azure Storage," in Proceedings of the USENIX Annual Technical Conference (ATC), Jun. 2012, pp. 15–26.

[27] "IBM Cloud Object Storage." [Online]. Available: www.ibm.com/cloud-computing/products/storage/object-storage/how-it-works/ [retrieved: November 2017]

[28] V. Venkatesan and I. Iliadis, "Effect of codeword placement on the reliability of erasure coded data storage systems," in Proceedings of the 10th International Conference on Quantitative Evaluation of Systems (QEST), Sep. 2013, pp. 241–257.

[29] H. Weatherspoon and J. Kubiatowicz, "Erasure coding vs. replication: A quantitative comparison," in Proceedings of the 1st International Workshop on Peer-to-Peer Systems (IPTPS), Mar. 2002, pp. 328–338.

[30] R. Rodrigues and B. Liskov, "High availability in DHTs: Erasure coding vs. replication," in Proceedings of the 4th International Workshop on Peer-to-Peer Systems (IPTPS), Feb. 2005, pp. 226–239.

[31] J. S. Plank and C. Huang, "Tutorial: Erasure coding for storage applications," Slides presented at 11th Usenix Conference on File and Storage Technologies (FAST'13), San Jose, CA, Feb. 2013.

[32] V. Venkatesan, I. Iliadis, C. Fragouli, and R. Urbanke, "Reliability of clustered vs. declustered replica placement in data storage systems," in Proceedings of the 19th Annual IEEE/ACM International Symposium on Modeling, Analysis, and Simulation of Computer and Telecommunication Systems (MASCOTS), Jul. 2011, pp. 307–317.

[33] V. Venkatesan, I. Iliadis, and R. Haas, "Reliability of data storage systems under network rebuild bandwidth constraints," in Proceedings of the 20th Annual IEEE International Symposium on Modeling, Analysis, and Simulation of Computer and Telecommunication Systems (MASCOTS), Aug. 2012, pp. 189–197.

[34] A. G. Dimakis, K. Ramchandran, Y. Wu, and C. Suh, "A survey on network coding for distributed storage," Proc. IEEE, vol. 99, no. 3, Mar. 2011, pp. 476–489.

[35] V. Venkatesan and I. Iliadis, "Effect of codeword placement on the reliability of erasure coded data storage systems," IBM Research Report, RZ 3827, Aug. 2012.

Immersive Video Services at the Edge: an Energy-Aware Approach

Pietro Paglierani
Italtel
Castelletto, Milan, Italy
e-mail: pietro.paglierani@italtel.com

Claudio Meani
Italtel
Castelletto, Milan, Italy
e-mail: claudio.meani@italtel.com

Antonino Albanese
Italtel
Castelletto, Milan, Italy
e-mail: antonino.albanese@italtel.com

Paolo Secondo Crosta
Italtel
Castelletto, Milan, Italy
e-mail: paolosecondo.crosta@italtel.com

Abstract—**To respond to the users' demand for immersive and personalized media services, the 5G and the Multi-access Edge Computing initiatives are proposing novel network architectures. In this context, we present the Video Transcoding Unit (VTU) system, which exploiting the Cloud Enable Radio Access Network proposed by the EU 5G-PPP Sesame project, brings immersive video functionalities to the edge of networks, thus greatly improving User Experience with mobile terminals. A use case is discussed, in which the VTU is deployed in a Stadium or in a large public venue during a Crowded Event, to offer Immersive Video Services. In the proposed architecture, the VTU video processing component can be implemented as a Software-only Virtual Network Function running on different Hardware platforms (X86 or ARM architectures), eventually accelerated by a Graphics Processing Unit. Specific tests are described and discussed and specific Key Performance Indicators are introduced, showing the benefits of the Hardware-accelerated implementation, both in terms of computing performance and of energy efficiency. We believe that the proposed VTU framework significantly advances the state of the art in the provision of video services to the mobile users.**

Keywords-NFV; MEC; 5G; HW acceleration; GPU; Video transcoding.

I. INTRODUCTION

This paper presents an extended and improved version of [1], where we introduced a framework for enhanced video services at the network edge.

The recent worldwide explosion of mobile data traffic in telecommunication networks has been impressive, and this trend will certainly continue in the coming years [2]. The fast spreading of smart terminals and new services based on High-Definition (HD) video have been the main trigger of this explosion, revealing various weaknesses in the architectural and technological approach adopted so far in the design of the traditional mobile network infrastructure [3][4].

The telecommunication market, previously dominated by voice traffic and text messages, is rapidly shifting to completely different and far more complicated scenarios, with millions of connected applications, where even new actors have made their appearance, like machines and "things" (smart home gadgets, vehicles, drones, robots, also including sensors and actuators).

Internet and communication networks have become crucial for any evolutionary process of modern societies and economies. This fact has led to the definition of a new kind of infrastructure based on the "fifth generation" - 5G - architecture, as a response to the requirements coming from the more diverse fields of the future world [3].

5G aims at assuming a fundamental role in the new society; it is not only a simple evolution of previous mobile networks – as was the passage from 3G to 4G - but it stands as a real revolution, able to create the appropriate ecosystem for technical and business innovation [4].

From the technological point of view, 5G will take advantage of the experience coming from the recent convergence of the telecom world with Information Technology (IT). This shift has addressed the necessity coming from Network Operators of lowering general costs, achieving better scalability and reducing the deployment time of new services, and has resulted in a new architectural vision based on Software-Defined Networking (SDN) and Network Function Virtualization (NFV) [5]. 5G will bring the SDN and NFV concepts into the radio communication environment and will use them in a new architectural framework where Multi-access Edge Computing (MEC) will play a major role.

MEC Technology and Architecture concepts are a way to improve both Efficiency and User Experience for a certain number of services. MEC is an ETSI initiative that leverages SDN and NFV principles to push network functions, services and contents to the edge of the mobile network [6].

MEC servers should be directly attached to the base station, but this is not a strict rule because, in this regard, the MEC guidelines are widely open. They provide local computing, storage and networking resources that are virtualized and shared by multiple virtual machines.

Traditionally, all data traffic originating in data centers is forwarded to the mobile core network. The traffic is then routed to a base station that delivers the content to the mobile devices. In the mobile edge scenario, MEC servers take over some or even all of the tasks originally performed in a data center. Being located at the edge, they eliminate the need of routing data through the core network, lowering communication latency. As such, the MEC paradigm can help to reach the severe requirements posed by 5G in terms of throughput, latency, scalability and automation. However, it's important to note that many of the concepts that are at the basis of MEC and the advantages they bring to a broad range of services are valid regardless of 5G technology (in fact MEC concepts can be similarly applied to fixed networks) and can be demonstrated prior to the coming 5G, for instance by using the well-known WIFI access technology. Though, in view of a wireless access solution fully integrated with the core mobile network, many efforts are now being devoted to combine the MEC principles with the 5G architecture.

In this context, the H2020 5GPPP SESAME project [7] has developed a proposal for Cloud-Enabled Radio Access Network (CE-RAN) systems, based on the evolution of the 4G Small Cell (SC), towards the so-called Cloud Enabled Small Cell (CESC). Such a novel architecture, besides improving radio-related capabilities, can also enable the use of Network Functions Virtualization (NFV) and Software Defined Networking (SDN) at the network edge [5][6]. This goal is achieved through the introduction of the so-called Light Data Center, i.e., an aggregated pool of local and virtualized IT resources, including various types of HW accelerating devices, available to a cluster of CESCs. As a consequence, applications can be deployed at the network edge, implemented as Virtual Network Functions running in the Light Data Center, and thus exploiting the HW acceleration capabilities that the Light Data Center can make available.

Many services can benefit from being hosted at the network edge. Several use cases have been defined in the specification of MEC architecture to demonstrate the advantages of the introduced concepts [6]. One of these use cases regards video services in stadiums and/or large public venues, where video signals created during a sport event or a concert are routed to a MEC server responsible for their local distribution, without involving backhaul connection to the core network. The video contents are also stored in this edge platform, and can be locally processed by applications running on the same MEC server, to create new services and improve User Experience.

The possibility to create, share or receive low-latency, high definition video contents, anywhere and with any device, and with real-time interaction with the system, is usually referred to as Immersive Video Service (IVS). Immersive video applications are attracting a lot of interest, but they still remain very critical functionalities, due to the huge needs of compute, storage and networking resources that HD video brings about.

This paper presents the activities carried out by Italtel Research Labs within the H2020 Sesame project, which led to the development of the VTU system for IVSs. Leveraging MEC principles, the VTU Virtual Network Function (VNF) runs in the Light Data Center (as envisioned by the Sesame architecture), and can thus bring several innovative functionalities to the network edge, greatly improving User Experience with mobile terminals. In particular, the VTU can speed up sharing of Video contents, reduce latency and contribute to increasing the battery life of connected devices offloading them from heavy transcoding operations.

This paper shows how the VTU VNF running in the Sesame CESC Light Data Center can fit in a real use case foreseen by 5G and MEC, and enhance it with some novel features. Also, the limitations of a SW-only implementation with respect to a GPU-accelerated one are highlighted and discussed. The paper provides Key Performance Indicators (KPIs), which can effectively summarize the performance of the VTU, both in terms of compute capabilities, and in terms of energy consumption. Such KPIs can be used to select the most appropriate platform for the specific VTU application context.

In the analysis, Intel X86 architectures with and without GPU acceleration, and ARM architectures are considered, and are used to run tests specifically designed to thoroughly characterize the VTU overall performance.

The paper is organized as follows. Section II presents some related work. Section III briefly describes the activities and the outcome of the Sesame project, in particular in terms of its achievements related to the 5G architecture and the CESC concept. Section IV provides a functional description of the overall VTU system. Section V shows a possible use case for the VTU during localized crowded events. Section VI discusses HW acceleration for video functions, and describes different possible approaches, with their pros and cons. Section VII presents the experimental compute performance characterization of VTU, running on different architectures (x86 and ARM), with or without GPU. Finally, Section VIII summarizes the main results of this work.

II. Related Work

The framework proposed in this paper is based on the architectural results achieved in the Sesame project, in particular on the CESC concept. A general overview of the Sesame approach and of the CESC architecture is summarized is in [8][9]. A solution for the placement of processing and storage capabilities close to the users and a discussion of the advantages of hardware accelerators within the Light Data Center is discussed in [10]. Leveraging such concepts, this paper gives a detailed description of a novel software framework to provide enhanced video services at the network edge.

In the proposed framework, the video transcoding capability plays a key role. The subject of real time video transcoding, in contrast to a batch-oriented approach, is addressed in [11] with the proposition of a video transcoding architecture based on a heterogeneous environment. In [12], a NFV-based MEC platform for a traditional distribution service is proposed, showing the advantages of edge computing platforms in term of bandwidth and Quality of Experience, compared to centralized infrastructures located at the network core.

The topic of power consumption for NFV-based multimedia content delivery is faced in [13], which demonstrates that energy efficiency aspects are as important as flexibility and performance in the development of VNFs. However, the video transcoding problem and the use of GPUs to accelerate the most compute-intensive video processing workloads is not addressed.

Previous works carried out by the authors, such as [14][15], were related to GPU utilization in NFV environments, and to hardware and software acceleration at the edge of the network, while [16] and [17] discuss the use of GPUs to accelerate a specific video encoding scheme, namely the google VP8 Video encoder.

The present paper goes beyond such results; in particular, it presents a novel and complete solution for IVS in challenging environments such as crowded events, and provides an energy efficiency analysis of the video transcoding process, comparing the performance of ARM-based and X86-based CPUs. Moreover, it analyzes and highlights the benefits of adding GPU resources, to accelerate video transcoding.

III. The SESAME Cloud Enabled Small Cell

The 5G-PPP is a joint initiative between the European Commission and the European ICT industry, to drive the activities in the development of the 5G ecosystem. The objective is designing and implementing solutions, architectures, technologies and standards for the next generation communication infrastructure.

The European Union has funded 19 research projects under the 5G-PPP Phase 1 program. Among these, the SESAME Project (Grant Agreement No.671596) introduces three innovative elements in 5G:

- The "placement" of network applications at the network edge, leveraging Network Functions Virtualization (NFV) and Edge Cloud Computing.
- The evolution of the SC architecture, which will play a fundamental role in the 5G infrastructure.
- The consolidation of multi-tenancy in communication infrastructures, thus allowing different operators/service providers to share access capacity and edge computing resources.

In particular, the SESAME project aims at evolving the SC architecture, towards the CESC. This way, virtualized compute capabilities and applications are brought to the network edge, based on the NFV paradigm.

A CESC is an enhanced SC that integrates a virtualized execution platform (micro server) equipped with IT resources (RAM, CPU, storage). A simplified model of the CESC architecture is shown in Fig. 1. With these capabilities, a CESC can support novel applications and services at the network edge.

The basic role in the evolution of the SC concept is played by a specific VNF, namely the so-called SC VNF. The SC VNF represents the link between the radio and the cloud domains. In fact, it can intercept and perform encapsulation/de-capsulation of the S1 interface user data between the Long Term Evolution (LTE) base station component (the so-called eNodeB) and the Evolved Packet Core [7][18]. This way, the user data can be processed by standard VNF, running at the edge in the Light Data Center.

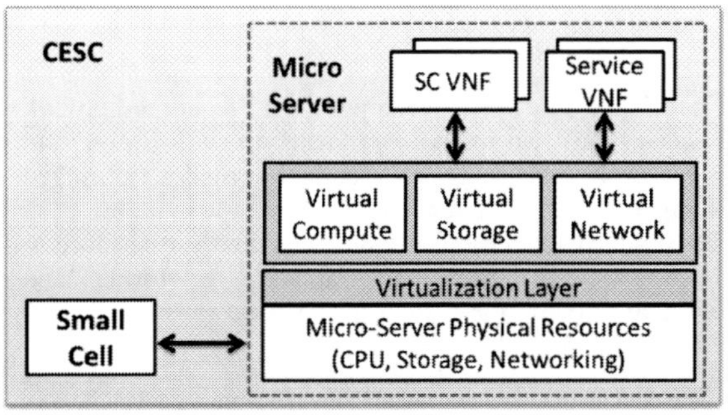

Figure 1. Simplified model of the CESC.

In its basic deployment, the CESC must be able to run the SC VNF, and eventually other VNF, which can run on the low power, low cost IT resources made available to the CESC in its minimal configuration. However, many innovative services, such as IVSs, usually involve compute intensive workloads, which can also require the use of specialized HW accelerators [14][15].

When the basic CESC resources are insufficient to offer the required services, they must be properly enhanced. SESAME proposes the creation of a distributed data center, denominated Light Data Center (Light DC), aimed to enhance the virtualization capabilities and processing power at the network edge.

The Light DC can include HW acceleration devices, such as Graphics Processing Units (GPU), Digital Signal Processors (DSP), and/or Field-Programmable Gate Arrays (FPGA).

Fig. 2 shows a simplified model of the Light DC, where heavy workloads can be offloaded to the additional compute resources. Such resources can be used by VNFs to carry out even compute intensive workloads. However, to offer effective solutions at competitive costs, it is necessary to thoroughly analyze the performance of the proposed VNFs, when executed on the different platforms that can be available at the Light DC.

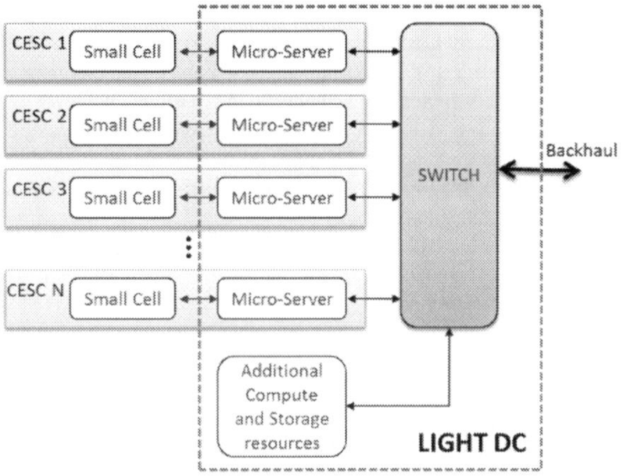

Figure 2. Simplified view of the Light DC Architecture

IV. VTU DESCRIPTION

The VTU framework, developed for IVSs at the network edge, consists of two main components, the VTU VNF and the VTU App. The VTU VNF mainly provides optimized video processing functionalities, which are the main building block to create more complex video services. Furthermore, it can also manage users and groups, by storing and maintaining updated the related information in the so-called VTU User and Group Database.

The VTU App can be downloaded by the users onto their devices; it offers the possibility to register to the VTU system, and create groups of users who can share video contents, exploiting the functionalities made available by the VTU VNF. The main features of the VTU VNF and the VTU App, as well as their interactions, are briefly summarized in the following paragraphs.

A. *The VTU VNF*

The VTU VNF consists of two VNF Components (VNFCs), namely the Media Engine (ME) and the User and Group Database Manager (UGDM). The ME can provide three basic functionalities, which can be summarized as follows:

- Video transcoding capabilities;
- Video streaming capabilities;
- Local storage for video file upload/download.

Besides video, the VTU ME can also perform audio processing, to provide multimedia services to the users. Though, audio processing functions are not as compute intensive as video functions; hence, for the sake of brevity, this paper will focus only on video capabilities. Finally, the VTU ME can also offer system monitoring functionalities, to support the system maintenance process.

The UGDM VNFC, conversely, can handle and store all the needed information about participants of the CE, which have registered to the VTU system.

1) The VTU ME

The VTU ME can convert video streams from one video format to another. Depending on the type of application that should be provided, the source video stream could originate from a file within a storage facility, as well as coming in form of packetized network stream. Moreover, the requested transcoding service could be mono-directional, as in video stream distribution-like applications, or bi-directional, like in videoconferencing (see Fig. 3).

In the VTU ME, the audio and video transcoding capabilities are provided by the Libav library [19], a very popular open source library, which can perform audio/video processing according to a wide set of coding standards. The AVConv tool from Libav is used for performing the conversion between audio and video formats and containers; while it already supports a wide variety of hardware accelerations, native GPU support in encoding tasks is quite limited, experimental and restricted only to H.264 and H.265 standards, exploiting the NVidia NVENC hardware encoder of medium and high level NVidia GPUs [20].

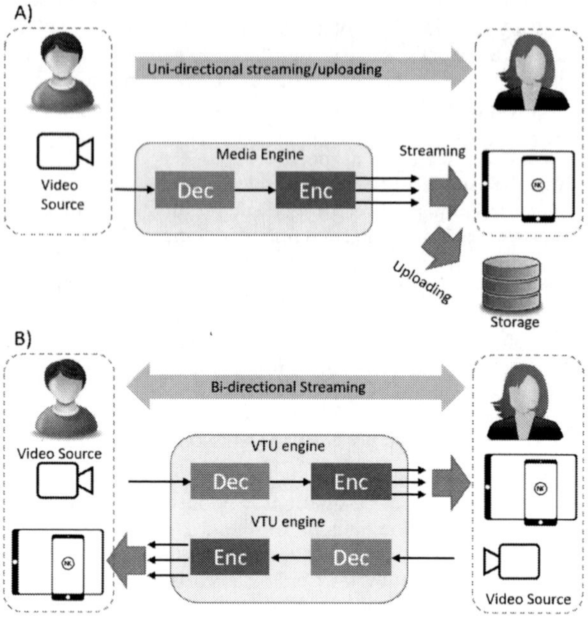

Figure 3. Simplified Media Engine Model A) Unidirectional; B) Bi-directional

To further benefit of HW acceleration, the AVConv tool running in the VTU has been modified so that VP8 video encoding tasks [21] can also exploit the resources eventually offered by off-the-shelf GPUs present in the system. In particular, a proprietary GPU accelerated VP8 video encoder can be used to this end [16][17]. The VTU server can also make use of other software tools, different from the Libav library. For instance, the use of the alternative open source library FFMPEG in place of Libav is not only possible, but also very simple and straightforward.

The VTU ME can support a large set of video codecs, and in particular the most recent and popular ones, such as H.264, H.265 and VP8/VP9 [16][17].

In traditional content delivery systems, the users can receive the video streams they have selected. Conversely, the VTU, through the VTU ME, also gives the users the possibility to originate video contents, and share them within a group, either in real time or as recorded video files in a common storage area.

To implement low-latency, real-time video sharing among the users, two different types of streaming functions have been developed, besides the transcoding function.

The first streaming mode is used to transmitting real-time or pre-recorded video contents from a user to the VTU. This way, an originating user can send contents in real time to the VTU, by means of the Real Time Streaming Protocol (RTSP) [22].

By the second VTU streaming mode, indicated as "broadcasting mode", the VTU can forward any received content to any user in a group. We will say that the video stream sent by the originating user is published by the VTU to the group.

In this case, each user receives a notification from the ME that a video stream is being published. If interested, the receiving user can thus decide to access the originated stream in real-time. For the sake of generality, the originating user can also decide to publish its video stream to all the users registered at the VTU. Thus, the video stream becomes public, and not limited within a group. Video streams published by the users are recorded by the VTU and saved in a distributed storage system, to be shared at a later time.

The broadcasting mode can use different protocols to transmit real-time video contents from the VTU to the users. Besides RTSP, also the Real Time Messaging Protocol (RTMP) and the HTTP Live Streaming (HLS) protocol are available [23][24].

In broadcasting mode, the source originating the video content can also be a video file, stored in the VTU storage system. This way, pre-recorded video contents can be streamed to single users, to an entire group or to all the users. This option can be used, for instance, by event organizers to distribute pre-defined video contents to all the participants to the event.

To facilitate the sharing of pre-recorded video contents among users, the VTU can also provide storage capabilities. Typically, video contents originated by the users are shared through cloud-based applications, which require the transmission of the video file from the user's wireless device to a centralized cloud infrastructure through the core network. Any other interested user can retrieve the video file of interest, by downloading it through the core network. However, during a crowded event, such operations are usually significantly slow or even impossible, due to the high density of users in a relatively small area, who rapidly saturate the backhaul connection to the core network. Preliminary experiments in typical crowded events have shown that the upload of a file of size equal to 100MB at peak hours can take times of the order of tens of minutes. Conversely, the same upload to the local VTU storage system, though accessed through the same WIFI network, can take no longer than 10 to 20 seconds.

Thus, the VTU offers local storage capabilities to groups of users. This way, all the members of a group can locally store or retrieve contents to the group storage area, without accessing the core network through the backhaul connection. In addition, the local storage can be used by event organizers to stream video contents to all the users.

The VTU ME offers a web based interface, dedicated to management and monitoring tasks. Such an interface is available only to system managers, and is accessed through an ad hoc web interface. To monitor the VTU status and performance during service, several metrics are generated and constantly sent at regular and modifiable basis to a user defined network address. Currently, monitoring data generated by the VTU is redirected to a local instance of InfluxDB database, a popular open source database solution, oriented to collecting and managing time-series data [25]; then, such records are graphically arranged and visualized into a browser window by Grafana, a popular dashboard for displaying time series metrics [26]. The collected metrics are related to CPU, GPU (when available), memory, and disk usage; also, encoding performances are captured and visualized, such as the number of transcoded frames per second.

2) The VTU UGDM

The VTU UGDM component collects and continuously monitors relevant information about participants and groups during a crowded event, and stores it into an ad hoc database, the User and Group Database. Any user connecting for the first time to the network during a crowded event can download the VTU App (described in the following sub-section), and register to the system. This way, users are recorded to the VTU framework, and are permanently identified by a suitable randomly generated key, that remains unchanged for the entire duration of the event, combined with the user name and/or nickname. Through the App and interacting with the UGDM, users can then create a group, to share video contents. For each user, the database stores all the relevant information about identity, group belonging, connectivity, and Service Level Agreement, so as to provide to all the users the required type of service. The UGDM component also provides basic security functionalities, such as, for instance, user password management.

B. VTU App

The VTU provides an overall framework that enables IVSs in a simple and straightforward way. Two different types of interfaces are available to the users, to benefit of the services made available by the VTU.

The first interface is based on web services, and is accessible by any browser. However, to improve user experience, a specific VTU App has been developed.

Through the App, the users can interact with the framework. In particular, they can register to the VTU system, as described above. Once registered, the users can create groups, for sharing video contents.

To each group, a shared storage area is assigned, where all the users of the group can read or write video contents. This storage area is private and dedicated to the group. Once the group is created, the users belonging to a specific group can benefit of the functionalities made available by the VTU.

The simplest services accessible through the App include video file exchange and video chatting. In addition, other services can be used, not specifically linked to video functionalities. For instance, geo-location and/or navigation functions can be presently provided combined with augmented-reality-based applications. Though, for the sake of brevity, this type of services will be not further discussed in the following, not being related to video.

C. VTU connectivity

To provide IVSs now, anywhere and with any device, two features play a fundamental role from the connectivity point of view, i.e., bandwidth, and latency, both on the user and on the control plane.

The 5G architecture will provide significant advances related to such parameters. In particular, among the goals of the new 5G network, some are of specific interest for IVSs and crowded events. In fact, the 5G network will enable eMBB (enhanced Mobile Broad Band) types of services, and will consider scenarios with high user device densities (more than 10000 per km square), and low latency. In particular, in the 5G use cases, three latency ranges are considered: high (greater than 50 ms), medium (10-50 ms) and low (1-10ms) [3].

However, the 5G network will start deployment and operations after 2020. Thus, other scenarios must be considered to provide now IVSs. To this end, one solution presently consists in using a WIFI access network to provide the needed connectivity between the VTU App and the VTU VNF. The second option is the use of the CESCs, as discussed in Section III. In this case, the present 4G mobile network architecture can be used, in conjunction with the CESC. A specific solution that can be used to deploy the VTU in a 4G scenario can be found in [10]. Moreover, standardization aspects related to the use of the VTU in 4G and 5G scenario are discussed in [7].

V. The Pervasive Video Use Case

A possible IVS use case can be described by the following two scenarios.

"You're at a stadium, where a football match takes place. Your team scores a goal but you are not in the best position to appreciate it or the action was confusing and you did not realize who scored the goal and how. You would like to have the possibility to watch on your smartphone the most relevant actions from different points of views"

Or:

"You are attending a crowded concert in the front row close to the stage and you want to show to other friends attending the concert far from the stage some videos in real time, picturing the performance in progress. Also, the concert organizers could decide to show on the gigantic main screen a collage of real time videos coming from spectators to give them a more immersive and engaging experience."

In this type of contexts, there is an overwhelming demand for services that give the possibility to the users to have videos on their smartphones or tablets on demand, as services provided, for instance, by the Stadium. Also, the innovative aspect with respect to the traditional Video Content Scenario is that the users are not only the consumers of video contents, but also the generators, with the will to share with other users their video contents.

From the technological perspective, what is needed to implement such type of services is a networking infrastructure featuring a very rapid upload and download of large files, such as HD videos. In addition to that, the possibility to process in a highly effective way video streams is a mandatory function to provide enhanced services. In particular, the capability to adapt the video format to the one required by the users' devices is one of the critical functions needed for this type of service. In fact, video format adaptation, usually referred to as video transcoding, is a compute intensive workload, in particular with high definition video. The VTU, implemented in a MEC environment, thus represents a possible answer to that demand coming from the market. The HW-accelerated transcoding of video streams can help in reducing the computational workload of mobile terminals converting video streams from the uploaded format to one more suitable for the receiving terminal, increasing its battery life.

The whole process of upload, transcoding and download takes place locally in the MEC server (Fig. 4) offloading the backhaul connection towards the core network. This reduces latency and avoids backhaul traffic congestion.

To this end, the MEC server must be equipped with its own high performance storage where all the videos uploaded from the users are kept for a certain amount of time, for instance a week. During this period a suitable application can make them available on demand outside the perimeter of the stadium, e.g., at home. The spectators during a sporting event can then upload many videos and delete them immediately to preserve memory space on their mobile devices, having the possibility to choose at a later time which one to download.

To provide these services, the Stadium or the event organization will then only need to make available the VTU App, to be downloaded on spectators' smartphones.

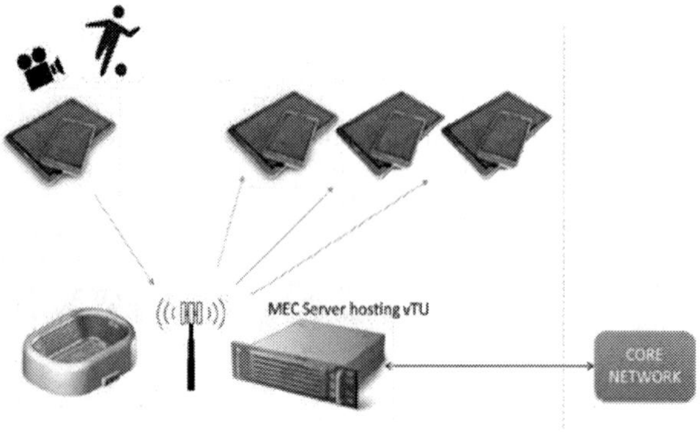

Figure 4. VTU use case: providing low lantency video sevices during localized crowded events leveraging MEC architecture.

VI. VTU And Hardware Acceleration

Although software-only functions can give acceptable performance in many applications, when compute-intensive workloads running at the data plane are of interest, such as those based on video data processing, quite poor results can be obtained. In these cases, to reach the expected performance, it is often necessary to consider a slightly different approach that involves the use of Hardware accelerators. In general, managing HW accelerators and making them transparently available to every VNF goes against the assumption of every virtualized environment, of having a uniform HW platform made of CPU-only computing elements. The presence of HW accelerators bound to a virtual function implies the use of a SW layer that must be HW-aware, thus significantly complicating system management operations and scalability [5][14]. Though, the advantages of HW acceleration can be so preponderant, in particular when performance, latency or Service Level

Agreement (SLA) requirements are challenging, so that not considering them can push a commercial product out of the market. In fact, acceleration is not just related to performance, but also to the reduction of the number of physical servers, footprint, network appliances and power consumption. In short, it can make the difference in the commercial proposition of a product.

A distinctive feature of the VTU is the possibility not only to run on general purpose CPUs but also to exploit the Hardware acceleration provided by a GPU, to improve the compute performance of video codecs. To this end, two different architectural approaches can be used. The first one, also known as "cooperative CPU- GPU" makes use of a GPU to offload the most compute-intensive functions of the video codec (usually, the Motion Estimation block), while the main algorithm is kept running on the CPU. The second approach, conversely, uses full HW implementation of video codecs. Today, various HW versions of the most popular encoding schemes, such as H.264, HEVC, VP8 and VP9, are available [20][21]. The fully HW approach can provide higher compute performance than cooperative CPU-GPU algorithms. However, the HW approach very often lacks the flexibility in service management needed by service operators, thus the cooperative approach is still preferred in many real-life implementations. The VTU can adopt both GPU-accelerated approaches. In fact, it can use the Nvidia NVEnc encoder for the H.264 and H.265 encoding schemes [20]. Also, the CPU-GPU cooperative approach described in [16][17] can be used for the Google open Source VP8 encoder.

VII. VTU Performance

Many tests were carried out to achieve a full performance characterization of the VTU, both for the SW-only version, and the GPU-accelerated one.

The SW-only version of VTU was tested on two different micro servers, based on ARM and INTEL X86 CPUs respectively. The ARM-based micro-server is a NXP commercial evaluation board equipped with a LS2085A processor (with 8x A57 cores @1.8 GHz) and 16GB DDR4 system memory. The INTEL-based server is a commercial platform (GOMA FlexPAC Industrial portable workstation) equipped with an Intel Xeon E5-2630v3 2.4GHz, 8 Core CPU and 64 GB DDR4 RAM.

The GPU-accelerated version of VTU was tested on the same GOMA server, this time equipped with one NVIDIA Quadro M4000 GPU. During all the tests it was verified that the System Memory (RAM) was not completely used, to be sure that the results were not influenced by the different quantity of RAM installed in Intel-based, rather than ARM-based micro-servers.

In the following, only some meaningful results are presented and discussed, for the sake of brevity. In all described tests, the same H.264 Full HD video file (1080x1920 resolution) was used as input. In particular, Fig. 5 shows the results obtained with the VTU featuring the H.264 transcoding (expressed in frames per second) without HW acceleration (SW-only) and with HW acceleration (using a GPU). The processing implies decoding from the input format to the one required as output.

The VTU provided four different video resolutions as output, in four different transcoding tests: VGA (480x640 pixel), HD480 (480x852 pixel), HD720 (720x1280 pixel), HD1080 (1080x1920 pixel). The vertical axis represents the output resolution, while the horizontal axis indicates the achieved output frame-rate in frames per second (fps). The Encoder used in SW-only VTU for H.264 is X264. The Encoder used by the GPU for H.264 and H.265 is NVIDIA NVENC.

Fig. 5 collects the results of the tests achieved with H.264 encoders. Only one session was launched for each test. As one can easily see, the performance for the three HW platforms are very different. In particular, the ARM performance is very poor, to the point that it is not conceivable a utilization in a real-time scenario. The improvement achieved by using the GPU compared to a SW-only solution is remarkable in all cases. This confirms the need of GPU acceleration especially in modern and future scenarios where even higher video resolutions are going to be used. Another important aspect to emphasize is related to the occupation of compute resources during transcoding. Although in SW-only mode CPU resources were completely occupied, (all the CPU cores were running at 100%), using the GPU, both CPU and GPU resources were only partially used. This fact led to a second set of tests in which the multi-session performance was analyzed. In this new set of tests, the focus was on a single case, i.e., H.264 HD1080, launching 2, 4, 8, and 16 concurrent transcoding sessions. The results are reported in Fig. 6 and Fig. 7.

Considering the SW-only implementation (Fig. 6), the performance of each single session decreases with the total number of executing sessions. Again, the ARM performance appears very low, being almost a fourth of the Intel one.

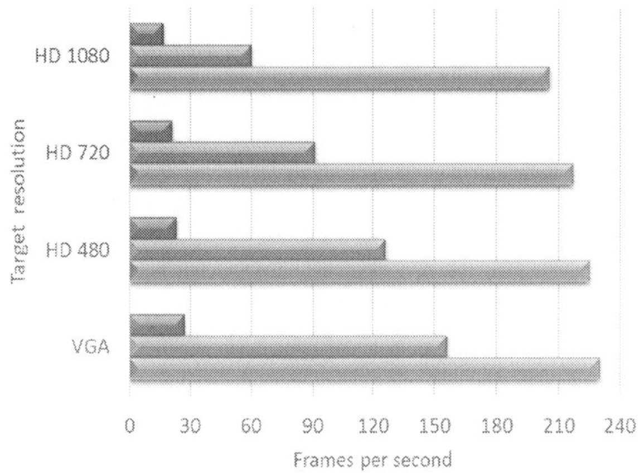

Figure 5. H.264 single session encoding performance (higher is better) measured on three different HW platforms, for different output resolutions.

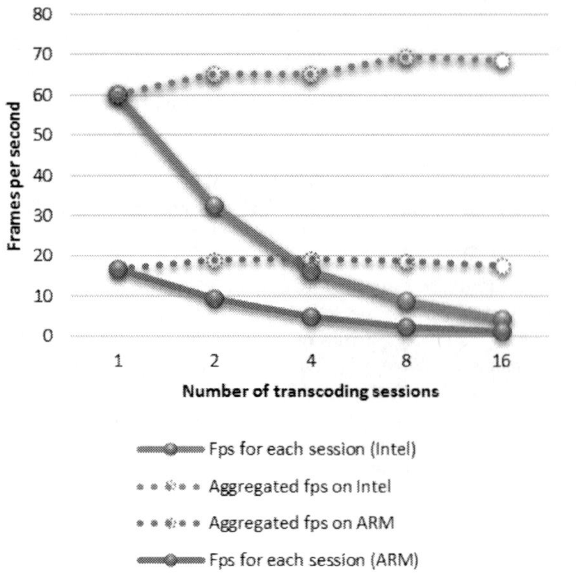

Figure 6. H.264 HD1080 encoding, SW-only, in multi-session transcoding tests (higher is better). Blue lines refer to INTEL, grey to ARM. Performance refers to each single session (solid line) and to aggregated sessions (dotted lines).

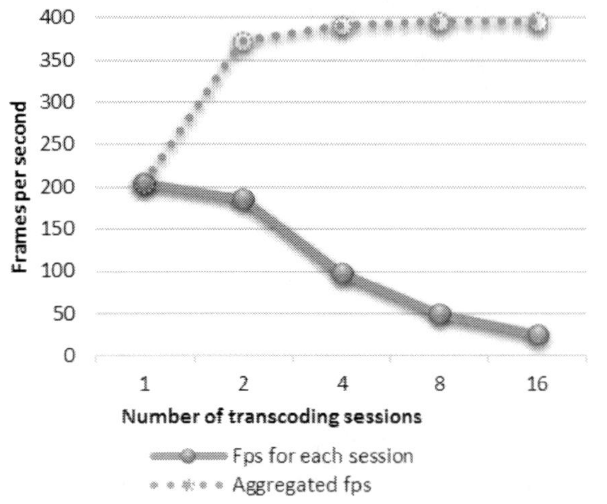

Figure 7. H.264 HD1080 encoding, using a GPU, in multi-session transcoding tests (higher is better). Performance refers to each single session (solid line) and to aggregated sessions (dotted lines).

Comparing the global performance of 1 session to that with 2-4-8-16 concurrent sessions (aggregated fps) the result is very similar as you can see from the dotted lines. This can be easily justified considering that the CPU occupation during the processing is always around 100% also running a single session. The same is not true using the GPU (Fig. 7). In this case the CPU is only partially used because the workload is mainly offloaded to the GPU whose resources are, in turn not fully used (Fig. 8). Using the GPU with 16 concurrent sessions we reach 24.75 fps for each session, for a total of 16x24.75=396 aggregated fps. The 396/69 ratio brings to a 5.7x gain in performance using the GPU respect to a SW-only solution. Furthermore, during the GPU test with 16 transcoding sessions the CPU was running at 70% giving it the possibility to run other tasks. This was not possible with SW-only solution, because in such a case the CPU was always 100% occupied.

It is interesting to analyze what are the power figures of the three HW platforms used to run the tests (multi-session performance). Fig. 9 shows the power consumption, expressed in Watt.

The measures have been carried out in DC, testing the current flowing on the reference voltages of the motherboards (12V, 5V. 3.3V), to the end of excluding the contribution of the main AC-DC power supply and having a more comparable setup between platforms. We used a current clump with a resolution of 0.1A, resulting in a maximum uncertainty of 1.2W (on 12V voltage rail).

As expected, the NXP micro-server exhibits the best results, starting from 31W in idle state and going to 48W when running the VTU application. It is worth noting that 9.5W of the 31W are dedicated to the fans that always run at maximum speed; if the NXP micro server could properly control the fan speed, its power consumption would improve significantly. Regarding the behavior of the Intel platform, with and without GPU, the results could appear unexpected because there are conditions in which the presence of the GPU does not increase the total power consumption, but rather decreases it. This can be explained considering Fig. 8, which shows the percentage of CPU and GPU resources occupied during transcoding (dotted lines). Let us consider, for example, the situation with one session. Intel platform consumes 119W without GPU, and 95W with GPU. However, while w/o GPU the CPU is running at 100% (not reported in the figures), with GPU transcoding requires only 20% of CPU and GPU resources (as in Fig. 8). This is the reason why the power consumption with GPU is in some case even better (lower) than the one w/o GPU.

Comparing the efficiency of the two solutions in term of performance/watt (Fig. 10), we see another important advantage of using the GPU. In fact, in the case of 16 concurrent sessions (H.264-HD1080), the gain in efficiency using Intel + GPU is 5.4x compared to Intel (SW-only). This could be, in some way, expected. Less obvious is the greater efficiency of Intel with respect to ARM (for this particular application).

Finally, Fig. 11 shows the performance of the VTU when the transcoding is made starting from the same input file used so far, but converting it to a H.265 format. This transcoding operation is significantly more complex from the computational point of view than the previous one (H.264), as one can see from the reduced performance respect to Fig. 5. We did not report the ARM performance, because it is too low to be considered. Intel performance is very low too, and the reduction in performance (and efficiency) with respect to the GPU reaches 10x.

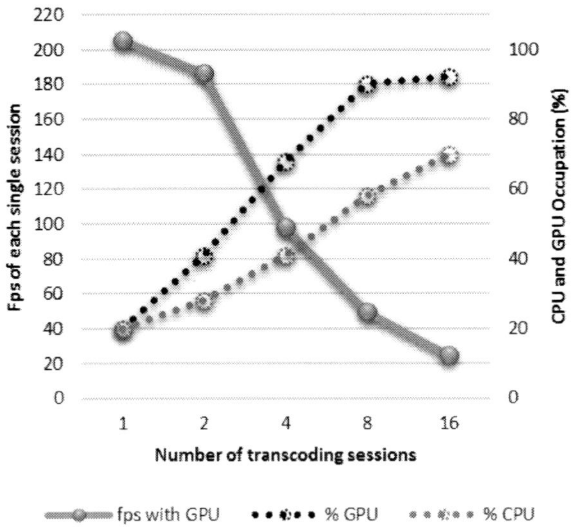

Figure 8. H.264 HD1080 encoding with GPU in multi-session transcoding tests (performance related to each single session) with percentage of CPU and GPU resources utilization.

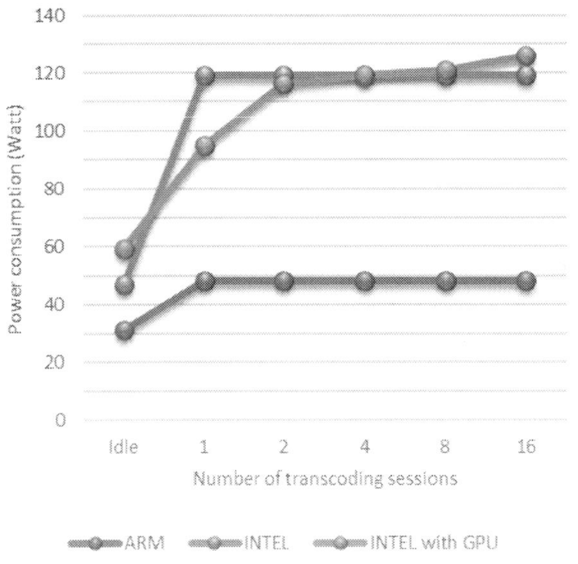

Figure 9. Power consumption (lower is better) of the three HW platforms running the H.264 HD1080 encoding multi-session transcoding tests.

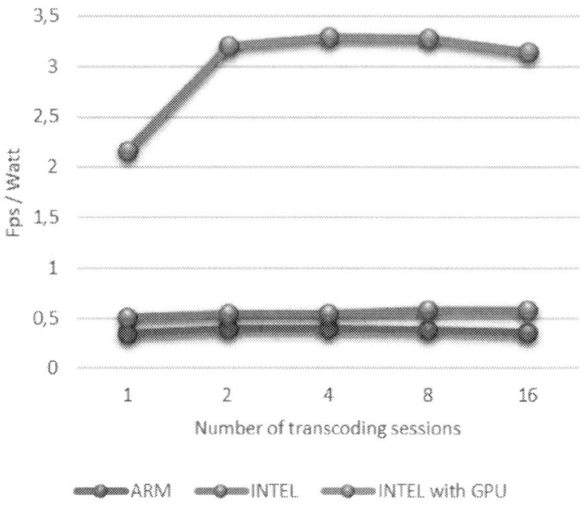

Figure 10. Efficiency of the three HW platforms (expressed in performance/power) for H.264 HD1080 encoding in multi-session transcoding tests (higher is better).

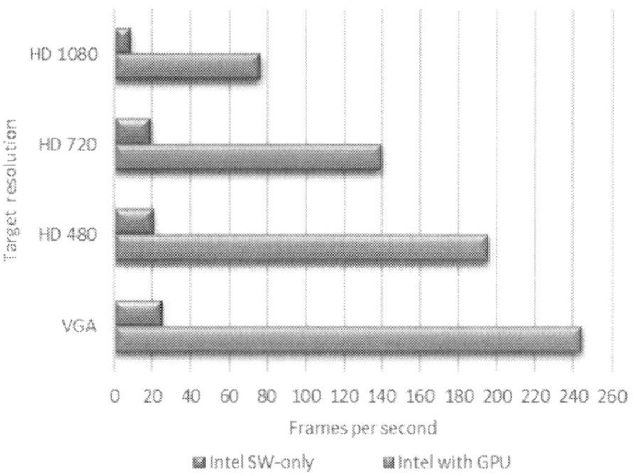

Figure 11. H.265 single session encoding performance (higher is better) measured on two different HW platforms, for different output resolution.

VIII. CONCLUSION

This paper has presented the Video Transcoding Unit (VTU) application, which, leveraging MEC principles, brings high performance video data processing functionalities to the network edge, greatly improving User Experience with mobile terminals. The VTU can be implemented as a SW-only VNF, or be accelerated by a GPU. Specific tests have been reported, showing the clear superiority of the HW-accelerated implementation.

A possible use case has been presented in which the VTU is used in a Stadium or in large public venues during a crowded event like a sporting match or a concert.

In future, we will promote further development of this platform, using it for different video services to deploy at the edge, such as video analytics or augmented reality. In this context, special focus will be on scalability of computing resources, to provide multi-GPU systems for massive, real-time video transcoding.

ACKNOWLEDGMENT

This research received funding from the European Union H2020 Research and Innovation Action under Grant Agreement No.671596 (SESAME project).

The authors are grateful to Mr. Marco Beccari and Mr. Luca Di Muzio who carried out the laboratory tests described in this paper.

REFERENCES

[1] A. Albanese, P. S. Crosta, C. Meani, and P. Paglierani, "GPU-accelerated Video Transcoding Unit for Multi-access Edge Computing Scenarios," SOFTNETWORKING 2017, April 23-27, 2017, Venice, Italy.

[2] CISCO Corporation. The Zettabyte Era: Trends and Analysis. 2017. [Online]. Available from: http://www.cisco.com/c/en/us/solutions/collateral/service-provider/visual-networking-index-vni/vni-hyperconnectivity-wp.html (accessed 13 Nov. 2017).

[3] 5G Infrastructure Public Private Partnership (PPP): The next generation of communication networks will be Made in EU. Digital agenda for Europe. Technical Report, European Commission. February 2014.

[4] NGMN: 5G White paper (2015). [Online]. Available at: https://www.ngmn.org/uploads/media/NGMN_5G_White_Paper_V1_0.pdf (accessed 13 Nov. 2017).

[5] ETSI: ETSI GS NFV-MAN 001 v1.1.1: Network Functions Virtualisation (NFV); Management and Orchestration (2014)

[6] ETSI: Mobile-Edge Computing - Introductory Technical White Paper (2014).

[7] B. Blanco et al., "Technology pillars in the architecture of future 5G mobile networks: NFV, MEC and SDN," Computer Standards & Interfaces, Available online 4 January 2017, ISSN 0920-5489.

[8] White paper. "The SESAME approach for clustered Small Cell deployments: Introducing advanced coordination and service capabilities through a distributed edge data centre," July 2016. [Online]. Available at: http://www.sesame-h2020-5g-ppp.eu/Dissemination.aspx (accessed 13 Nov. 2017).

[9] White paper. "SESAME: An innovative multi-operator enabled Small Cell based infrastructure that integrates a virtualised execution platform for deploying Virtual Network Functions," July 2017. [Online]. Available at: http://www.sesame-h2020-5g-ppp.eu/Dissemination.aspx (accessed 13 Nov. 2017).

[10] Fajardo et al., "Introducing Mobile Edge Computing Capabilities through Distributed 5G Cloud Enabled Small Cells," Mobile Netw Appl (2016) 21: 564. [Online]. Available at: https://doi.org/10.1007/s11036-016-0752-2 (accessed 13 Nov. 2017).

[11] Z. H. Chang, B. F. Jong, W. J. Wong, and M. L. D. Wong, "Distributed Video Transcoding on a Heterogeneous Computing Platform," APCCAS, 25-28 Oct., 2016, Jeju, South Korea.

[12] S. Li et al., "QoE analysis of NFV-based mobile edge computing video application," in 2016 IEEE International Conference on Network Infrastructure and Digital Content (IC-NIDC).

[13] S. Fu, J. Liu, and W. Zhu, "Multimedia Content Delivery with Network Function Virtualization: The Energy Perspective," 2017 IEEE MultiMedia.

[14] P. Paglierani, "High Performance Computing and Network Function Virtualization: A major challenge towards network programmability," 2015 IEEE International Black Sea Conference on Communications and Networking (BlackSeaCom), Constanta, 2015, pp. 137-141.

[15] P. Paglierani et al., "Techniques for providing Software and Hardware Acceleration to VNFs running on the Edge Cloud," EUCNC2017, June 12-15, 2017, Oulu, Finland.

[16] P. Comi et al., "Hardware-accelerated high-resolution video coding in Virtual Network Functions," 2016 European Conference on Networks and Communications (EuCNC), Athens, 2016, pp. 32-36.

[17] P. Paglierani, G. Grossi, F. Pedersini, and A. Petrini, "GPU-based VP8 encoding: Performance in native and virtualized environments," 2016 International Conference on Telecommunications and Multimedia (TEMU), Heraklion, 2016, pp. 1-5.

[18] SESAME D3.1 "CESC Prototype design specifications and initial studies on Self-X and virtualization aspects," June 2016. [Online]. Available at: http://www.sesame-h2020-5g-ppp.eu/Deliverables.aspx (accessed 13 Nov. 2017).

[19] Libav. [Online]. Available at: http://libav.org/documentation/ (accessed 13 Nov. 2017).

[20] NVIDIA NVENC Programming Guide [Online]. Available at: https://developer.nvidia.com/nvenc-programming-guide (accessed 13 Nov. 2017).

[21] WebM Video Hardware RTLs [Online]. Available at: https://www.webmproject.org/hardware/ (accessed 13 Nov. 2017).

[22] IETF RFC7826, "Real-Time Streaming Protocol Version 2.0," [Online]. Available at: https://tools.ietf.org/html/rfc7826 (accessed 13 Nov. 2017).

[23] "Real-Time Messaging Protocol (RTMP) specification," [Online]. Available at: http://www.adobe.com/devnet/rtmp.html (accessed 13 Nov. 2017).

[24] "HTTP Live Streaming (HLS)," [Online]. Available at: https://developer.apple.com/streaming (accessed 13 Nov. 2017).

[25] InfluxData InfluxDB project. [Online]. Available at: http://docs.influxdata.com/influxdb/v1.3/ (accessed 13 Nov. 2017).

[26] Grafana project. [Online]. Available at: http://grafana.org (accessed 13 Nov. 2017).

Experimental Assessment of WiFi Coordination Strategies Using Radio Environment Maps

Rogério Pais Dionísio, Paulo Marques

Escola Superior de Tecnologia
Instituto Politécnico de Castelo Branco
Avenida do Empresário, S/N
6000-767 Castelo Branco, Portugal
Email: (rdionisio,pmarques)@ipcb.pt

Tiago Ferreira Alves, Jorge Miguel Afonso Ribeiro

Allbesmart, Lda
Centro de Empresas Inovadoras
Avenida do Empresário, n.º1
6000-767 Castelo Branco, Portugal
Email: (talves,jribeiro)@allbesmart.pt

***Abstract*—The rapidly increasing popularity of WiFi has created unprecedented levels of congestion in the unlicensed frequency bands, especially in densely populated urban areas. This results mainly because of the uncoordinated operation and the unmanaged interference between WiFi access points. In this context, the main objective of this experiment is to assess the benefit of a coordinated management of radio resources in dense WiFi networks for both 2.4 GHz and 5 GHz bands, using Radio Environment Maps (REM). This experiment has used the w-iLab.t test environment and the portable test-bed provided by iMINDS for indoor scenarios. It was shown that REMs can detect the presence of interfering links on the network (co-channel or adjacent channel interference), and a suitable coordination strategy can use this information to reconfigure Access Points (AP) channel assignment and re-establish the client connection. The coordination strategy almost double the capacity of a WiFi link under strong co–channel interference, from 6.8 Mbps to 11.8 Mbps, increasing the aggregate throughput of the network from 58.7 Mbps to 71.5 Mbps. However, this gain comes with the cost of a relatively high-density network of spectrum sensors, increasing the cost of deployment. The technique of AP hand-off was tested to balance the load form one AP to another, although the aggregate throughput is lower after load balancing. REMs are also capable of detecting coverage holes on the network, and a suitable Radio Resource Management strategy use this information to reconfigure the APs transmit power to re-establish the client connection and increase the throughput of the overloaded AP, at a cost of diminishing the aggregate throughput of the network. The insights coming out from this experiment helped to understand the opportunities and limitations of WiFi coordination strategies in realistic scenarios.**

***Index Terms*—*Radio Environment Map*; *Portable Radio Test-bed*; *Radio Resource Management*; *WiFi*; *Interference Management*; *Load Balancing*.**

I. Introduction

During the last fifteen years, the WiFi technology, as a last mile access to Internet, has experienced global explosion. Nowadays, the WiFi networks carry more traffic to and from end-user's terminals (PCs, tablets, and smartphones) than Ethernet and cellular networks combined. The success of this technology is owed to its introduction in unlicensed spectrum (ISM bands), which has furthermore allowed unprecedented innovation in the wireless technology. However, as the penetration of WiFi continues, the unlicensed bands are becoming overcrowded. Unpredictable user-deployed hot spots (smartphone) are a new source of interference and instability that can undermine the network performance. Moreover, many Internet of Things (IoT) devices also share the unlicensed spectrum with WiFi, which further increases the problem scale.

In fact, interference is a limit factor of WiFi densification; this is a result mainly because of the uncoordinated operation and the unmanaged interference between the WiFi Access Points (AP). In WiFi, each Access Point can only access locally available sensing information within single cell coverage. It cannot access global knowledge on a multi-AP network and the deployment environment, leading to a sub-optimal network configuration.

In this context, the design of the WiFi networks is complex because of the high-density of users and significant variability of capacity requirements that can be strongly dependent on location and time. The variability of the capacity demand can be faced by deploying a dynamic network infrastructure, in which WiFi access points can be switched on and off, can work on different bands, and can tune their coverage range from the network status and QoS requirements.

This paper is organized in five sections. After the introduction, the second section describes the background and the motivation of the work. In Section III, we describe the test-beds and define the setup environment of the experiments. The fourth section presents the experimental results with different measurements and scenarios. Conclusions and future work are drawn in Section V.

II. Background

Recently, we conducted a set of experiments in a pseudo-shielded WiFi test-bed, to assess and verify the benefit of a coordinated approach for interference management in dense WiFi networks on the 2.4 GHz ISM band, which make use of realistic Radio Environment Maps (REM) [1]. Other research work also supports that the REM of the target coverage area is an important input for interference management and coordination strategies [2]; Other studies have recently demonstrated the potential economic value of WiFi coordination in dense indoor experiments [3] or proposed a secured framework to achieve optimal RRM in residential networks, using distributed channel assignment algorithm [4]. Thus, the use of efficient of Radio Resource Management (RRM) strategies, supported by REMs, have emerged as a valid combination to optimize spectrum usage [5].

The REM is a dataset of spectrum occupancy and interference levels computed based on raw spectrum measurements, propagation modeling and spatial interpolation algorithms [6]. Radio Resource Management (RRM) algorithms can use REMs to optimize the overall network performance.

In [1], we experimentally verified that a coordinated approach of the RRM of channel frequency and power, combined with the use of REMs, can increase the performance of WiFi networks in dense deployment scenarios. To extend this study further, the main objective of this experiment is to assess the benefit of a coordinated approach in dense WiFi networks also in the 5 GHz ISM band, using realistic Radio Environment Maps and an implementation-oriented approach in two wireless environments: the pseudo-shielded test-bed w-iLab.t, and a common office building. Besides interference management, we will also verify the potential of REMs for load balancing and hole detection in WiFi networks. An important performance metric is the gain in terms of average throughput, comparing the coordinated approaches with the legacy uncoordinated approach. We are interested in measuring the average capacity gain, when using market available and low-cost spectrum sensors in very dense indoor scenarios. The results of this experiment are very useful from a business perspective and industrial research, to realize if the actual coordination gain is sufficient enough to justify the investment in the sensing and the signaling infrastructure needed to implement a WiFi coordination scheme in realistic scenarios [6].

III. EXPERIMENTAL SETUP AND ARCHITECTURE

This section defines and describes in detail the setup environment. The experiments were divided in two distinct phases:

- Phase 1: Assessment of WiFi coordination in dense indoor scenario using the w-iLab.t test-bed, at 2.4 GHz.
- Phase 2: Assessment of WiFi coordination in dense indoor scenario (two floor building) using a portable test-bed, at 2.4 GHz and 5 GHz.

For each of the two phases, we ran several experiments:

- Intra-network co-channel interference;
- Intra-network adjacent-channel interference;
- Non-overlapping (optimal) channels assignment;
- Channel reallocation triggered by external interferences;
- Load balancing;
- Hole detection.

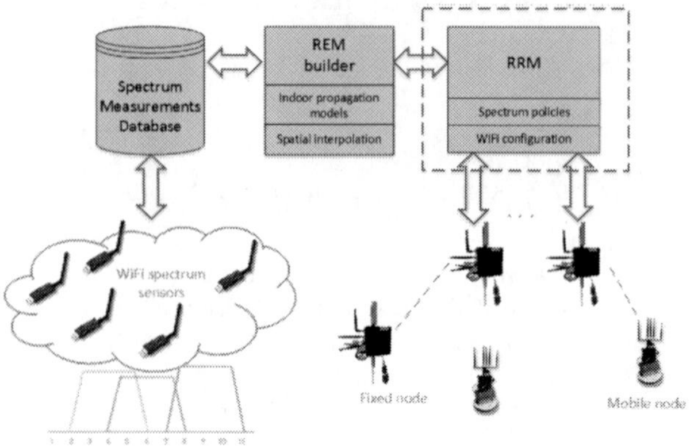

Fig. 1. Generic Setup diagram for the experiment.

A. Setup architecture

The setup diagram of the demonstrator, depicted in Figure 1, encompasses four major components, as briefly explained in the following:

- A network of spectrum sensors (energy detectors) that report spectrum measurements to a database.
- A REM builder module that computes the radio environmental maps based on measurements stored in the spectrum database, the positions/configurations of radio transmitters (AP), indoor propagation models and spatial interpolation algorithms.
- The RRM that optimizes the overall WiFi network in terms of channel and power allocation based on the REM.
- WiFi APs that receive the configuration settings and reports performance metrics to the RRM module.

B. Test-bed and resources allocation

Besides the available WiFi hardware, both portable and w-iLab.t test-bed offers several software tools to setup, control and gather radio measurements. We used the java-based framework jFed [7] to configure the test-bed nodes. jFed is also used to activate nodes, install the Operating System, and SSH into the nodes. OMF6 [8] controls all the experiments, using scripts written with OMF Experiment Description Language (OEDL) [9], which is based on the Ruby programming language. The experiment description with OMF6 is structured in two main steps:

1) First, we declare the resources to be used in the experiment, such as applications, nodes, and related configurations, such as Wi-Fi channels and transmitted power;
2) In the second step, we define the events that triggers the experiment's execution, and the tasks to be executed.

The Iperf traffic generator tool [10] generates data for each link using a client – server configuration. All links parameters are recorded during 100 s for all experiments. This ensures that the radio signals for the links under test are on the air and stable. The measurements data are extracted during the experiment using OML [11]. OML is a stand-alone tool that parses and reports all the measurements to a database (SQLite3 or PostgreSQL) installed on the experiment controller server of the test-bed.

1) Phase 1 – w-iLab.t test-bed: All experiments took place in a shielded environment in the w-iLab.t test-bed (Ghent – Belgium), a cognitive-radio test-bed for remote experimentation [12]. The nodes are installed in an open room (66 m by 21 m) in a grid configuration. Figure 2 shows the testing area and the locations of the nodes, represented by black numbered circles. Each node has one embedded PC (ZOTAC) with two wireless IEEE 802.11 a/b/g/n cards (Spartklan WPEA–110N/E/11n), a spectrum sensor (Wi-Spy USB spectrum analyzer), one Gigabit LAN, and a Bluetooth USB 2.0 Interface and a ZigBee sensor node [13].

We have selected 5 equidistant links in a client – server configuration, represented by a black arrow in Figure 2. The distance between adjacent links is 12 m, and for each link, the distance between the client node and the AP node is 3.6 m. The red arrow represents the interfering link, with a separation of 12.5 m between nodes.

2) Phase 2 – Portable test-bed: The second phase of the experiment took place on a building at the School of Technology – Polytechnic Institute of Castelo Branco. The building is 60 m by 25 m wide. The building is divided in two floors, as depicted in Figure 3(a) (Floor 0) and Figure 3(b) (Floor 1). The walls are 20 cm thick and built with clay bricks and concrete, and the separation floor is made of 50 cm thick reinforced concrete. A staircase give access to both floors as depicted on the bottom left corner of both figures. Each WiFi node has one Intel NUC Embedded PC (NUC), with a wireless IEEE 802.11 a/b/g/n Qualcomm Atheros AR928X (PCI-Express), a spectrum sensor (Wi-Spy USB spectrum analyzer) and one Gigabit LAN interface.

Two radio links were installed on Floor 0:

- Link 2 connects NUC8 (client) and NUC7 (AP). The nodes are located next to the ceiling of a corridor, with Line of Sight (LOS) condition between nodes (Figure 3(a)). The distance between nodes is 8.5 m.
- Link 3 connects NUC6 (client) and NUC3 (AP). As already explained before, NUC6 is located on Floor 0, below NUC3. The dashed line from NUC3 and NUC6 represent the best propagation path between nodes, through the staircase between Floor 0 and Floor 1. The distance between NUC7 and NUC6 is 13.4 m.

Three radio links were installed on Floor 1:

- Link 4 connects NUC1 (client) and NUC2 (AP). The nodes are located on separated rooms with no Line of Sight (NLOS) between nodes (Figure 3(b)). The distance between nodes is 9.6 m.
- Link 1 connects NUC5 (client) and NUC4 (AP). The nodes are located on a corridor with LOS between nodes (Figure 3(b)). The distance between nodes is 9.5 m.
- Link 3 connects NUC6 (client) and NUC3 (AP). NUC6 is located on Floor 0, below NUC3. The dashed line from NUC3 and NUC6 represent the best propagation path between nodes, through the staircase between Floor 0 and Floor 1.

The distance between NUC2 and NUC3 is 12 m.

C. Radio Environment Map builder

The REM is a dataset of spectrum occupancy computed based on raw spectrum measurements, propagation modeling and spatial interpolation algorithms.

There are several methods to compute REMs available on the literature, with different interpolation approaches and based on space and time spectrum measurements. One of the most commonly used methods is the Inverse Distance Weighted Interpolation (IDW) [6]. Despite the "bull's eyes" effect, this method is relatively fast and efficient, and presents good properties for smoothing REM. To decrease the sensitiveness to outlier measurements, we have implemented a modified version of IDW method, which calculates the interpolated values using only the nearest neighbor's points.

To compute the REM, the exact position of each radio node on the w-iLab.t test-bed area is defined as shown in Figure 2. REMs are computed using Matlab to facilitate the integration with the RRM algorithms, also implemented in Matlab.

D. RRM coordinating strategies

The RRM optimizes the overall WiFi network configuration in terms of channel, and power allocation based on the information provided by the REM. The adopted RRM strategies during the experiments are the following [2]:

- Strategy 1: Allocate the WiFi links to disjoint, non-overlapping bands and use minimum possible transmit power for each WiFi link;
- Strategy 2: Optimize the transmit power of multiple WiFi links, when interference is detected.

IV. MEASUREMENTS

After describing the setup architecture and the test-bed resources, we will explain the experimental measurement campaigns. Each set of measurement aims at studying the influence of measurable interference characteristics on the throughput of the WiFi network under study. The process was structured in four steps:

1) Spectrum measurements from the spectrum sensors in all WiFi frequency channels;
2) Compute the REMs based on spectrum measurements and IDW algorithm;
3) Measure and record the throughput of the radio links;
4) Apply the coordination strategy, e.g., reconfigure the channel allocation or the transmitted power of each APs.

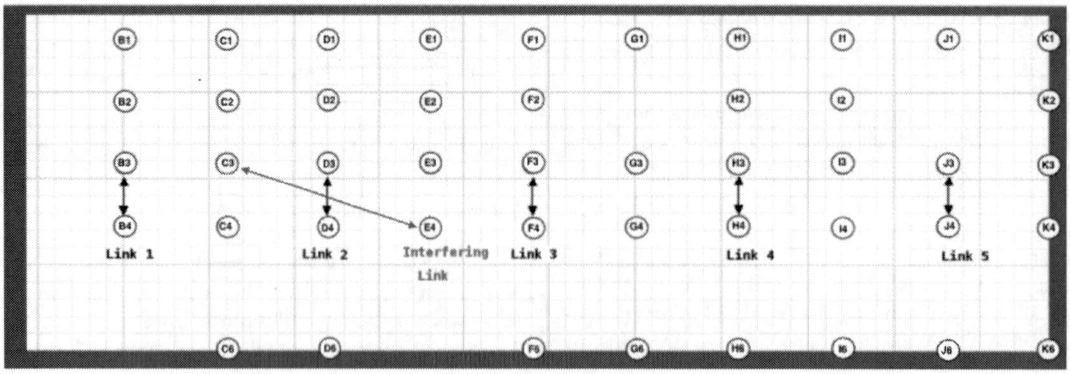

Fig. 2. w-iLab.t test-bed environment (Phase 1): Distance between AP and client is 3.6 m for Links 1, 2, 3, 4 and 5, and 12.5 m for the Interfering Link.

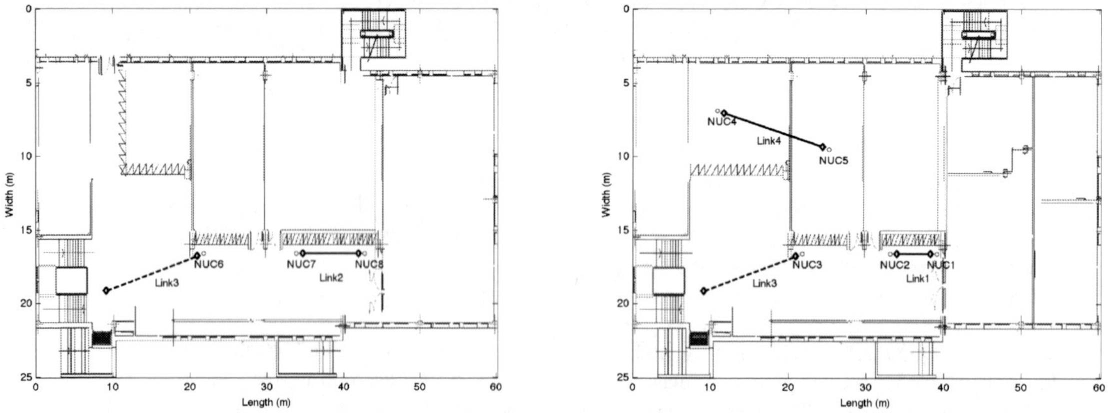

(a) (b)

Fig. 3. Portable test-bed (Phase 2): (a) Floor 0 of the building, with the location of Link 2 (NUC7 and NUC8). Link3, represented with a dashed line, connects NUC6 and NUC3, installed on Floor 1; (b) Floor 1 of the building, with the location of Link 1 (NUC1 and NUC2) and Link 4 (NUC4 and NUC5). Link 3, represented with a dashed line, connects NUC3 and NUC6, located on Floor 0.

A. Phase 1 – w-iLab.t test-bed

1) Estimation of the path-loss propagation model: Having a suitable propagation model is a key element to build good REMs, therefore before running the experiments, we have measured the path loss between the clients and the APs in the w-iLab.t test environment to estimate the propagation model parameters. Since most of the nodes are in Line–of–Sight (LoS) and relatively closed to each other, as shown in Figure 2, we have considered a Free Space Path Loss (FSPL) model:

$$L = n\,(10log_{10}\,(d) + 10log_{10}\,(f)) + 32.45\,(\text{dB}) \qquad (1)$$

Where L is the path loss in dB, d is the distance in meters, f is the frequency in GHz and n is the path loss exponent, which is 2 in the FSPL model. The path-loss measurement process was implemented as follows:

1) Setup one node as an AP with 5 dBm transmit power (P_{Tx}) on WiFi Channel 1 ($f = 2.412$ GHz), and all the other nodes as clients.
2) For each client:
   - Measure the Received Signal Strength Indication (RSSI) of the AP, denoted as P_{Rx}.
   - Measure the distance d between the client and the AP.
3) Setup a different node as AP and the remaining nodes as clients.
4) Repeat steps 1), 2) and 3).

The blue dots on Figure 4 represent the results of the measurement campaign.

Considering Friis transmission equation, $L = P_{Tx}\,(\text{dBm}) - P_{Rx}\,(\text{dBm})$, combined with (1), we compute an estimate of the path loss exponent n [14],

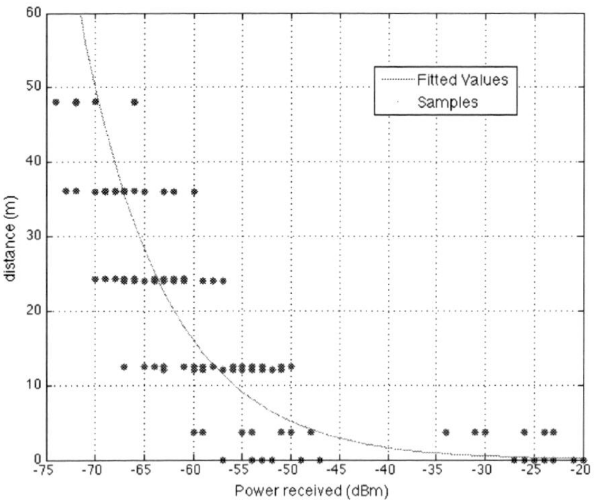

Fig. 4. RSSI measurement campaign (blue dots) and corresponding fitting curve (red line).

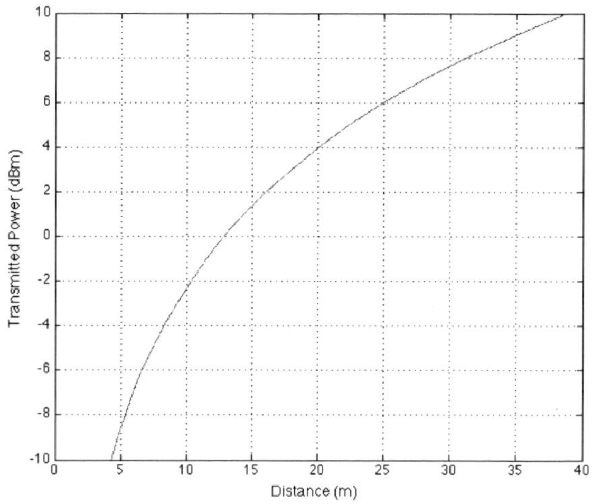

Fig. 5. Transmit power as a function of the distance, for -65 dBm received power baseline.

$$P_{Tx} - P_{Rx} = n\left(10log_{10}\left(d\right) + 10log_{10}\left(f\right)\right) + 32.45 \Leftrightarrow n = \frac{P_{Tx} - P_{Rx} - 32.45}{10log_{10}\left(d\right) + 10log_{10}\left(f\right)} \quad (2)$$

Using (2) with the Fitting Toolbox provided by Matlab and the measured RSSI (P_{Rx}), the value of n was found to be 2.097, with a 95% confidence bounds [2.084, 2.109]. This experimentally determined value corresponds to what we are expecting for a LoS scenario. The red curve in Figure 4 shows the result of the fitting process.

Appropriate AP power levels are essential to maintaining a coverage area, not only to ensure correct (not maximum) amount of power covering an area, but also to ensure that excessive power is not used, which would add unnecessary interference to the radiating area. Transmitted power can be minimized to reduce interference among the APs.

Considering a typical baseline signal strength of -65 dBm for the WiFi received signals coming from adjacent cells, using (1) and n = 2.097, we have computed the optimal transmit power as a function of the distance, as depicted in Figure 5. This study is important to setup the initial APs transmit power to ensure a suitable cell coverage. Considering that 12 m is the separation between adjacent WiFi cells in the experiment set-up (Figure 2), the APs transmit power are set at 0 dBm, unless otherwise noted in the following experiments.

2) Experiment 1 – Assessment of the channel distribution influence on the throughput: The aim of this experiment is to assess the influence of channel distribution on the throughput, and verify the worst-case reference scenario in terms of intra–network co-channel interference, e.g., when all APs assigned to the same channel (Channel 1 – 2.412 GHz).

The average values of the measured throughput for each link and the aggregated throughput of the WiFi network are shown in Table I. As expected, the low values of link's throughput are due to the strong co-channel interference that limits the overall performance of the network. Note that this is a worst-case reference scenario in terms of co-channel interference.

TABLE I. THROUGHPUT RESULTS FOR EXPERIMENT 1.

Experiment 1	Channel Number	Throughput (Mbps) $P_{Tx} = 0$ dBm
Link 1	1	5.25
Link 2	1	4.02
Link 3	1	3.93
Link 4	1	3.86
Link 5	1	5.28
Aggregated Throughput (Mbps)		**22.34**

3) Experiment 2 – Considering non-overlapping channels assignment: With this experiment, all APs are configured with non-overlapping channels: Channel 1 (2.412 GHz), Channel 6 (2.437 GHz) and Channel 11 (2.462 GHz). The measured throughput presented in Table II clearly shows the advantage of using non-overlapping channels in the WiFi planning. With a transmitted power set to 0 dBm on each APs, the measured aggregated throughput is 71.50 Mbps, i.e., more than three times higher than the value in Experiment 1 (22.34 Mbps). However, if the transmitted power P_{Tx} is increased to 5 dBm, the aggregate throughput decreases to 66.05 Mbps, because of the higher co-channel interference between Link 1 and Link 4, and between Link 2 and Link 5. Note that according to [1], with 5 dBm, the APs have 22 m coverage radius. This channel configuration is the baseline scenario for the following measurements of Phase 1.

4) Experiment 3 – Channel reallocation triggered by co-channel interference: The setup for Experiment 3 has the same

TABLE II. THROUGHPUT RESULTS FOR EXPERIMENT 2.

Experiment 2	Channel Number	Throughput (Mbps) $P_{Tx} = 0$ dBm	Throughput (Mbps) $P_{Tx} = 5$ dBm
Link 1	1	13.27	12.16
Link 2	11	11.76	10.50
Link 3	6	21.54	21.56
Link 4	1	12.57	11.18
Link 5	11	12.36	10.65
Aggregated Throughput (Mbps)		**71.50**	**66.05**

TABLE III. THROUGHPUT RESULTS FOR EXPERIMENT 3.

Experiment 3	Channel Number	Throughput (Mbps) P_I=0dBm	Throughput (Mbps) P_I=7dBm	Throughput (Mbps) P_I=15dBm
Before RRM strategy				
Link 1	1	12.12	12.30	12.3
Link 2	**11**	**6.80**	**7.08**	**6.98**
Link 3	6	21.59	21.63	21.61
Link 4	1	11.27	11.23	11.07
Link 5	11	6.88	6.83	6.75
Aggregated Throughput (Mbps)		**58.67**	**58.96**	**58.70**
After RRM strategy				
Link 1	6	13.27	13.12	13.10
Link 2	**1**	**11.76**	**11.62**	**11.56**
Link 3	6	21.53	21.55	21.61
Link 4	11	12.57	12.73	2.70
Link 5	1	12.37	12.41	12.40
Aggregated Throughput (Mbps)		**71.47**	**71.43**	**71.38**

non-overlapping channels allocation as in Experiment 2, with an additional interference Link active at Channel 11, placed next to Link 2, as depicted in Figure 2. Three different interference power levels (P_I) were applied during the experiment $\{0, 7, 15\}$ (dBm). The computed REMs at Channel 11 for different interference link's power are shown in Figure 6(a). The color gradient represents the computed power in dBm for a channel at location (x, y). The location of the nodes is added as an additional layer (black circles). The yellow dots are due the "bull's eye" effect typical of the IDW interpolation algorithm and should be discarded. By observing the REMs, we can detect not only Link 2 and Link 5, but also the extra radio activity coming from the interfering link. Note that the detection of this interfering link will trigger the coordination strategy in the WiFi network.

The results from Table III show an overall network throughput decrease, compared with the results from Experiment 2, mainly due to the interference from the interfering link on Link 2 and Link 5. However, the results indicate that the variation on the power level of the interferer does not have a strong impact on the aggregate throughput.

From the REM information, the coordination strategy reallocates the WiFi channels among the APs, to avoid strong co-channel interference. The REM for Channel 11, depicted in Figure 6(b), shows a clear spatial separation between the interference source and Link 4.

TABLE IV. WEIGHTING FACTOR ACCORDING TO THE FREQUENCY SPACING BETWEEN CHANNELS.

n	**Frequency Spacing (MHz)**	**Weight (dB)**
1	5	0
2	10	-10
3	15	-19.5
4	20	-28
5	25	36.5

Table III shows a significant throughput increase from 58 Mbps to 71 Mbps thanks to the coordination strategy. The aggregate throughput is now close to the values obtained with Experiment 2, i.e., without any interference Link. Once again, the results indicate that the variation on the power level of the interferer does not have a strong impact on the aggregated throughput.

5) Experiment 4 – Channel reallocation triggered by adjacent channel interference: With this experiment, we want to understand how the WiFi network is affected by strong adjacent channel interference and how effective is the coordination strategy under such circumstances. The interfering link is set to operate on Channel 10, while Link 2 uses Channel 11. In the case of adjacent channel interference, the REM generated for channel X must take into account the power received from adjacent channels $X \pm n \in \mathbb{N}$, weighted according to the spectral mask of the filter present at the WiFi receiver [15]. The weighting factors of the transmit mask are listed in Table IV and represented in Figure 7. Note that each WiFi channel is 22 MHz wide, but the channel separation is only 5 MHz. As an example, the power of the 4th adjacent-channel should be reduced by 28 dB to be correctly used in the computation of the REM.

The results from Table V show an overall network throughput decrease, compared with the results obtained from Experiments 3 and 4. This result shows that the first adjacent-channel interference leads to a higher throughput degradation than a co-channel interference (no–interference: 71.5 Mbps, co–channel interference: 58.6 Mbps and adjacent–channel interference: 56.7 Mbps). Once again, the results also indicate that the variation on the power level of the interferer does not have a strong impact on the aggregate throughput.

6) Experiment 5 – Automatic power control to overcome co-channel interference: The aim of this experiment is to understand if automatic power control is a good strategy to overcome co-channel interference. The setup of the network under test has five links using non-overlapping channels, with an additional co–channel interference link in Channel 11. The RRM strategy in this experiment keeps the same channel assignment of each link and increases the power of the victim link (Link 2). The transmitted power increases in steps of 5 dB, from 0 to 15 dBm. The remaining APs of the network under test remains at 0 dBm, and the interfering link is set to transmit 5 dBm in Channel 11. The measured throughput is listed in Table VI.

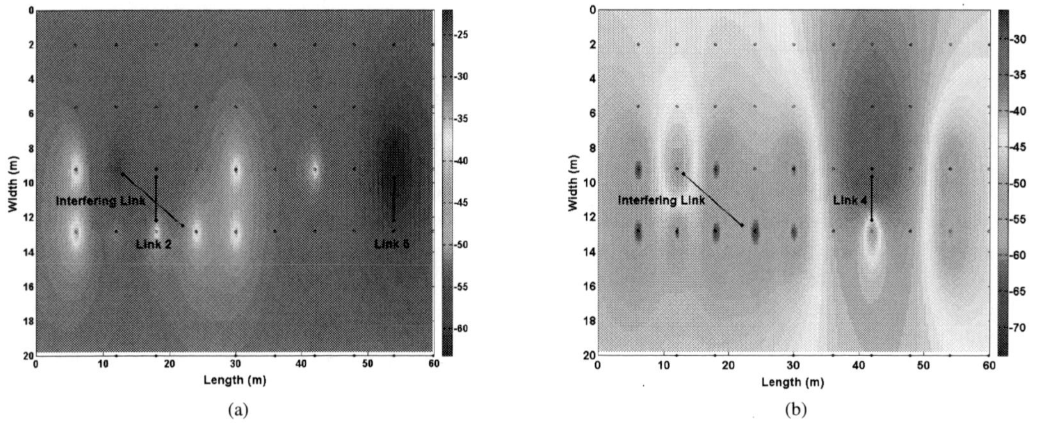

Fig. 6. Measurement 3. (a): REMs with Link 2, Link 5 and Interferer Link at Channel 11 with 0 dBm; (b): REMs with Link 4 and Interferer Link at Channel 11 with 0 dBm. Color bar in dBm.

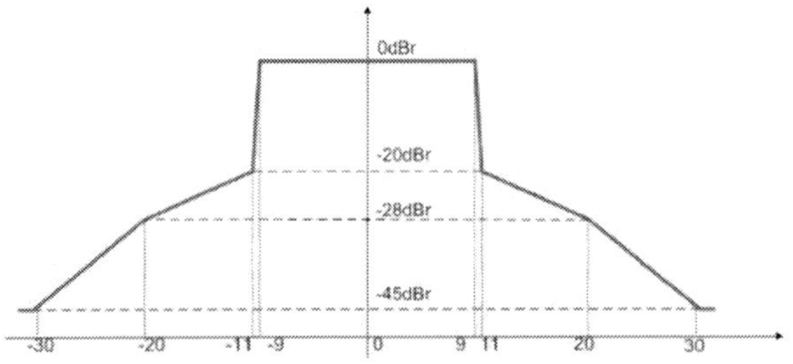

Fig. 7. IEEE transmit mask (IEEE Std. 802.11-2007).

TABLE VI. THROUGHPUT RESULTS FOR EXPERIMENT 5 AFTER AUTOMATIC POWER CONTROL.

Exp. 5	Ch.	Throughput (Mbps) P_2=0dBm	Throughput (Mbps) P_2=5dBm	Throughput (Mbps) P_2=10dBm	Throughput (Mbps) P_2=15dBm
Link 1	6	12.30	12.32	11.47	11.43
Link 2	**11**	**7.08**	**3.84**	**6.88**	**6.97**
Link 3	6	21.63	21.33	21.52	21.39
Link 4	1	11.23	11.12	11.60	11.64
Link 5	11	6.83	9.60	6.90	6.83
Aggregated Throughput (Mbps)		**58.96**	**58.13**	**58.39**	**58.26**

The results suggest that, despite the increase of transmitted power on Link 2, the overall throughput remains low and approximately constant (roughly 58 Mbps), therefore, power increase alone does not overcome the degradation caused by strong co-channel interference. The WiFi coordination strategy investigated in Experiment 3 is much more effective, leading to an aggregated throughput of 71 Mbps.

TABLE V. THROUGHPUT RESULTS FOR EXPERIMENT 4.

Experiment 4	Channel Number	Throughput (Mbps) P_I=0dBm	Throughput (Mbps) P_I=7dBm	Throughput (Mbps) P_I=15dBm
Before RRM strategy				
Link 1	1	12.17	12.23	12.11
Link 2	**11**	**4.63**	**3.84**	**4.04**
Link 3	6	21.37	21.33	21.23
Link 4	1	11.17	11.12	11.27
Link 5	11	7.22	9.60	8.96
Aggregated Throughput (Mbps)		**56.57**	**58.13**	**57.60**
After RRM strategy				
Link 1	6	8.12	8.14	8.16
Link 2	**1**	**7.72**	**7.75**	**7.76**
Link 3	6	21.53	21.51	21.55
Link 4	11	12.08	11.97	12.2
Link 5	1	11.82	11.06	11.16
Aggregated Throughput (Mbps)		**61.13**	**60.43**	**60.83**

B. Phase 2 – Portable test-bed

For the indoor propagation model used to create all REMs, beside the relative position and distance between NUCs, we also consider the following parameters on the algorithm:

- Wall penetration Losses: 5 dBm
- Floor penetration Losses 18 dBm
- Height of each floor: 5 m

All experiences were conducted for both 2.4 GHz and 5 GHz frequency bands.

1) Experiment 1 – Full co-channel interference: In this first experiment, all APs (NUC2, NUC3, NUC4 and NUC7) are configured to transmit at Channel 6 (2.437 GHz). The objective is to have a worst-case reference scenario in terms of co-channel interference, and to verify the influence of walls and floor on the overall performance of the network.

REMs are produced based on the measured RSSI on each client and for each AP. Figure 8 represents the REM computed for Experiment 1, taken at Channel 6 and 17 dBm transmit power. The color gradient represents the computed power in dBm for a channel at location (x, y). The location of the nodes is added as an additional layer (black circles) along with the corresponding link (black lines).

On the first floor (Figure 8(b)), the uniform red color on the REM is the evidence of a high-power level transmitted at Channel 6. The walls between Link 4 and Link 3 or Link 1 have little influence on the propagation of the signal, and cannot avoid co-channel interference. On the other floor (Figure 8(a)), the REM shows the position of the single AP present on that floor (NUC7 - Link 2). The high color contrast suggests that the influence of other APs located on the first floor is low, mainly caused by the presence of a thick floor.

The throughput for each link is computed at different transmitted powers and frequency bands, and the aggregated throughput results are presented in Figure 9 (solid lines). As expected and from the analysis of the REMs, all links from the first floor (Link 1, 3 and 4) are strongly interfering with each other. This effect is more visible when the transmitted power is 17 dBm.

For lower transmit powers, in particular between 0 and 5 dBm, the clients are outside or on the edge of the coverage area of the AP, which cause a low throughput. This is particularly evident for Link 3, as shown in Table VII, with a client on one floor and the AP on the other. This effect is even more evident for the 5 GHz band measurements.

The only link that present good results in the single link located on Floor 0 (Link 2). At 2.4 GHz, this link present higher throughput values, but as the transmit power is increased the throughput decreases due to co-channel interference with the other links. At 5 GHz, where the coverage area is lower for the same transmit power, better throughput results are attained at any transmit power, exception made at 14 dBm, probably due to bad measurement procedures.

2) Experiment 2 – Considering no-overlapping channels assignment: On the second experiment, all APs (NUC2, NUC3, NUC4 and NUC7) are configured with no-overlapping channels and variable transmit power between 0 dBm and 17 dBm. Both 2.4 GHz and 5 GHz frequency bands are tested.

The results shown in Table VIII are consistent with the strategy applied on this experiment, even for Link 3, with a client on one floor and the AP on the other. The increase of the aggregate throughput presented in Figure 9 (dashed lines) reflects the advantage of a coordinated approach. As an example, for the 2.4 GHz frequency band, and compared with the previous Experiment 1, the aggregated throughput has increased from 6.31 Mbps to 49.64 Mbps when transmit power is 17 dBm. For the 5 GHz frequency band and the same transmit power, the aggregated throughput has increased from 28.29 Mbps to 99.77 Mbps.

3) Experiment 3 – Channel reallocation triggered by co-channel interference: Experiment 3 setup is a WiFi network composed by three Links (Links 1, 2 and 3), with a channel distribution following a no-overlapping strategy. Link 4 is used as an external interferer with a constant transmit power of 17 dBm and set to the same frequency channel as Link 3. The objective is to trigger the RRM algorithm to reconfigure the channel distribution, based on REMs.

According the frequency band in use during each experiment, the initial channel distribution is:

- Link 1: Channel 11 or Channel 44
- Link 2: Channel 1 or Channel 36
- Link 3: Channel 6 or Channel 40
- Link 4: Channel 6 or Channel 40 (Interferer)

As an example, from the RSSI measurement on each client, the computed REM at Channel 6 is shown in Figure 10. By observing the REMs on both floors, it is possible to detect not only Link 3 activity on Channel 6, but also the extra radio signal activity coming from the interfering Link 4.

Figure 11 (solid lines) shows the measured throughput for each link at 2.4 GHz and 5 GHz band, when the transmit power of Links 1, 2 and 3 is swept form 0 dBm to 17 dBm. The bold line presents the computed aggregate throughput of

TABLE VII. THROUGHPUT RESULTS FOR EXPERIMENT 1 WITH THE PORTABLE TEST-BED.

Experiment 1 Portable test-bed	Channel Number	Throughput (Mbps) P_I=0dBm	Throughput (Mbps) P_I=8dBm	Throughput (Mbps) P_I=17dBm
2.4 GHz				
Link 1	6	0.16	4.68	2.77
Link 2	6	13.66	4.32	1.59
Link 3	**6**	**0**	**0.45**	**0.58**
Link 4	6	3.98	9.74	1.37
Aggregated Throughput (Mbps)		**56.57**	**19.19**	**6.31**
5 GHz				
Link 1	48	20	0	0
Link 2	48	27.25	27.34	28.27
Link 3	**48**	**0.01**	**0**	**0**
Link 4	48	0	0	0.02
Aggregated Throughput (Mbps)		**47.26**	**27.34**	**28.29**

TABLE VIII. THROUGHPUT RESULTS FOR EXPERIMENT 2 WITH THE PORTABLE TEST-BED.

Experiment 2 Portable test-bed	Channel Number	Throughput (Mbps) P_I=0dBm	Throughput (Mbps) P_I=8dBm	Throughput (Mbps) P_I=17dBm
2.4 GHz				
Link 1	6	0.21	11.37	18.17
Link 2	11	0	16.87	9.63
Link 3	**1**	**0**	**0.06**	**5.69**
Link 4	11	2	11.19	16.15
Aggregated Throughput (Mbps)		**2.21**	**39.49**	**49.64**
5 GHz				
Link 1	36	20.47	29.4	29.5
Link 2	40	0	20.47	29.23
Link 3	**44**	**0.3**	**8.84**	**20.36**
Link 4	48	0	10.39	20.68
Aggregated Throughput (Mbps)		**20.77**	**69.1**	**99.77**

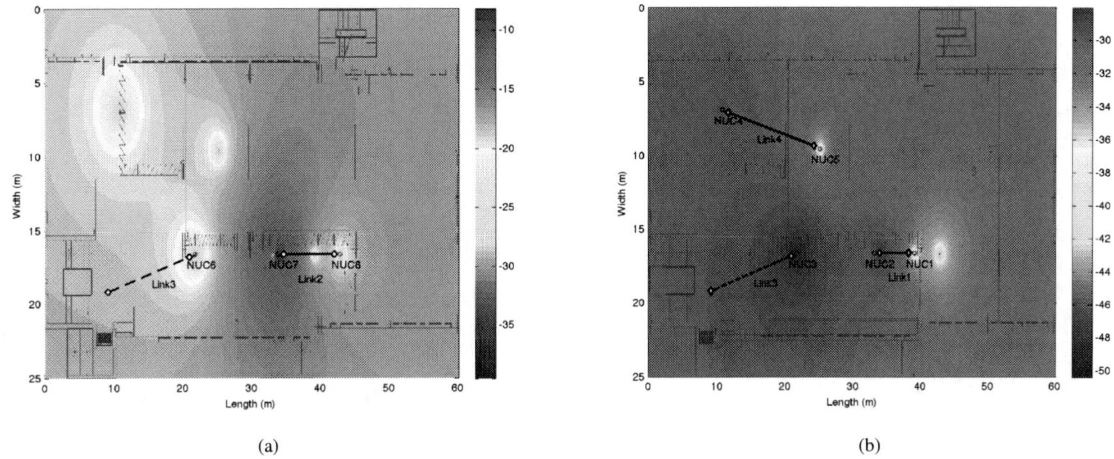

Fig. 8. REMs computed during Experiment 1 for Links 1, 2, 3 and 4, at Channel 6 and 17 dBm transmit power: (a) Floor 0; (b) Floor 1.

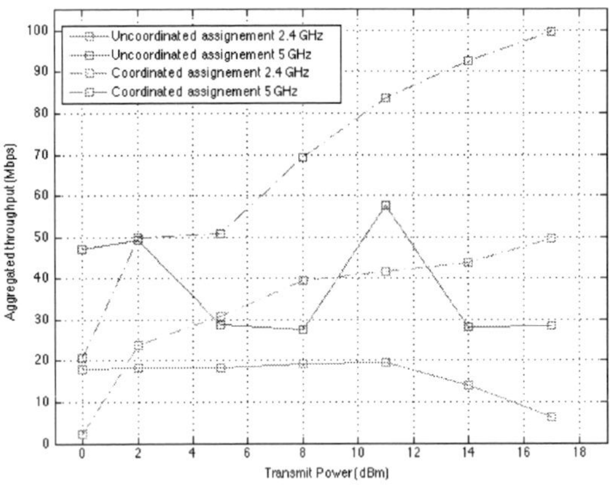

Fig. 9. Aggregated throughput at 2.4 GHz (red lines) and 5 GHz (blue lines) for the uncoordinated approach (solid lines) and coordinated approach (dashed lines).

the network.

As the transmit power increases, so does the aggregated throughput of the network, to a maximum of 19.36 Mbps for 14 dBm (2.4 GHz band) and 67.04 Mbps for 8 dBm transmit power (5 GHz band). As the transmit power increases further, so does the overall co-channel interference of the network mainly at Channel 6 (or 40), causing the throughput to drop.

As shown in Figure 10, the REM allows the detection of the interfering link. With this information, and by setting an appropriate threshold for the minimum throughput on each link, the RRM strategy reallocates the WiFi channels among the APs to avoid the strong co-channel interference. Thus, after the RRM strategy is applied, the network channel reassignment is as follow:

- Link 1: Channel 1 or Channel 36
- Link 2: Channel 6 or Channel 40
- Link 3: Channel 11 or Channel 44
- Link 4: Channel 6 or Channel 40 (Interferer)

After the RRM channel reassignment, throughput measurements shown in Figure 11 have significant increase from 19.36 Mbps to 46.9 Mbps on the 2.4 GHz band, and from 67.94 Mbps to 79.97 Mbps on the 5 GHz band, thanks to the RRM strategy based on REM. The aggregate throughput is now close to the values obtained with Experiment 2, i.e., without any interference Link.

4) Experiment 4 – Hole detection: This experiment is aimed at detecting coverage holes on the network, based on REMs, and implement a RRM algorithm to increase the transmit power of adjacent APs next to the clients with poor or non-existent connection with their former AP. The initial setup consists of 4 NUCs located on Floor 1, with the following configuration:

- NUC2: Access Point 3; Channel 6; 0 dBm transmit power
- NUC5: Access Point 2; Channel 1; 16 dBm transmit power
- NUC4: Access Point 1; Channel 11; 13 dBm transmit power
- NUC3: Client connected to Access Point 2; Channel 1; 17 dBm transmit power

After 100 s, Access Point 2 (Link 1) is disconnected and the client loses connection and the corresponding throughput drops to zero. The RRM algorithm implements a series of actions to ensure that the client reconnects:

- Compute REM of the APs;
- Detect the absence of AP2 transmit signal on Channel 1;
- Increase the transmit power of adjacent Access Points (AP1 and AP3) up to 16 dBm, so the client may discover one or both APs, and connect to one of them.

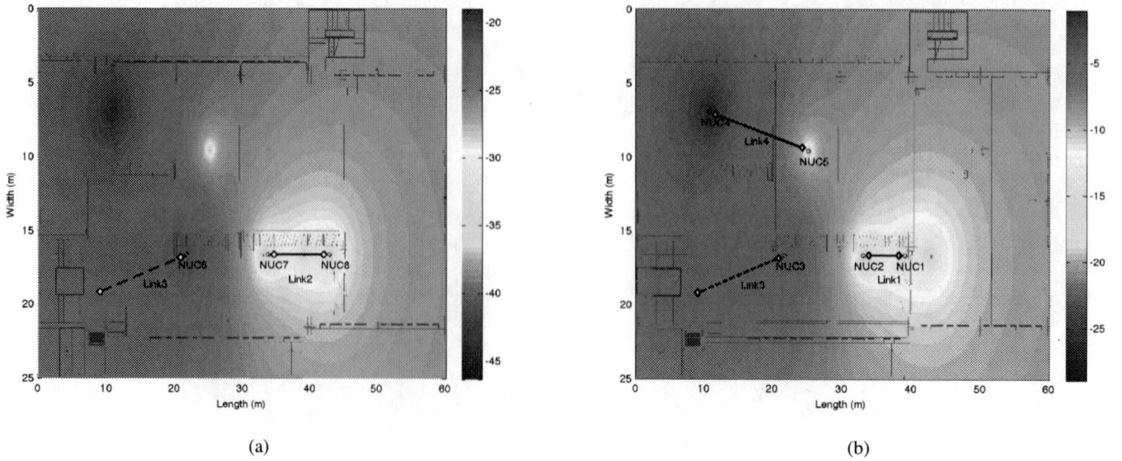

Fig. 10. REMs computed from Experiment 3 with the portable test-bed for Links 3 and 4, at Channel 6 and 17 dBm transmit power: (a) Floor 0; (b) Floor 1.

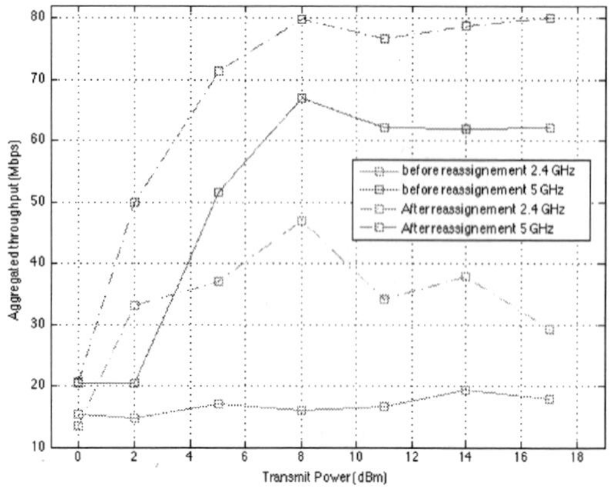

Fig. 11. Aggregated throughput at 2.4 GHz (red lines) and 5 GHz (blue lines) with the presence of an interfence Link, before (solid lines) and after (dashed lines) the coordinated RRM approach.

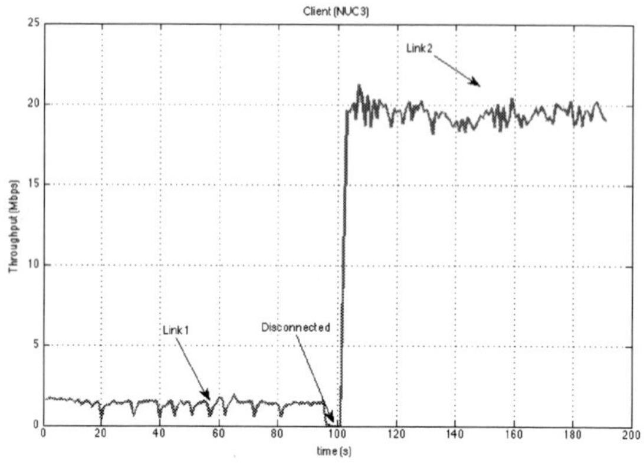

Fig. 12. Throughput of the network client (NUC3) – before (Link 1) and after (Link 2) hole detection.

Compared with the previous state, the RRM decision is to increase the transmit power of adjacent AP1 (NUC4) and AP3 (NUC2) next to the client node with poor or non-existent connection. This action gives to the former Link 1 client the option to select and connect to the best AP available, based on RSSI (AP3 – NUC2 in this experiment). Figure 12 shows the throughput evolution of the client node during the experiment. Initially connected to Link 1, the mean throughput was 1.7 Mbps. After losing connection with AP2, the new connection with AP3 (Link 2) was set with a mean throughput of 19.4 Mbps.

5) Experiment 5 – Characterization of the building floor as a WiFi barrier: In this experiment, the objective is to verify the potential of a building floor as an effective barrier between WiFi Links in a co-channel scenario.

As depicted on Figure 13, the setup consists of two NUCs configured as APs, using the same frequency channel (11 on the 2.4 GHz band or 48 on the 5 GHz band), located on different floor, but on the same vertical alignment. Each AP has two clients connected to it. The floor is made of concrete, 50 cm thick.

From the measurement campaign at 2.4 GHz, the building floor is not efficient in blocking the radio signal from crossing the concrete structure and interfering with the other WiFi link. For Link 1, the power level of the AP located on Floor 0 suffers an attenuation of 10 dB when crossing to Floor 1. For Link 2 AP, located on Floor 1, the signal has no attenuation, when crossing from Floor 1 to Floor 0. However, at 5 GHz, the building floor introduce 20 dB attenuation on both links, when the radio signal crosses the building floor. However, the

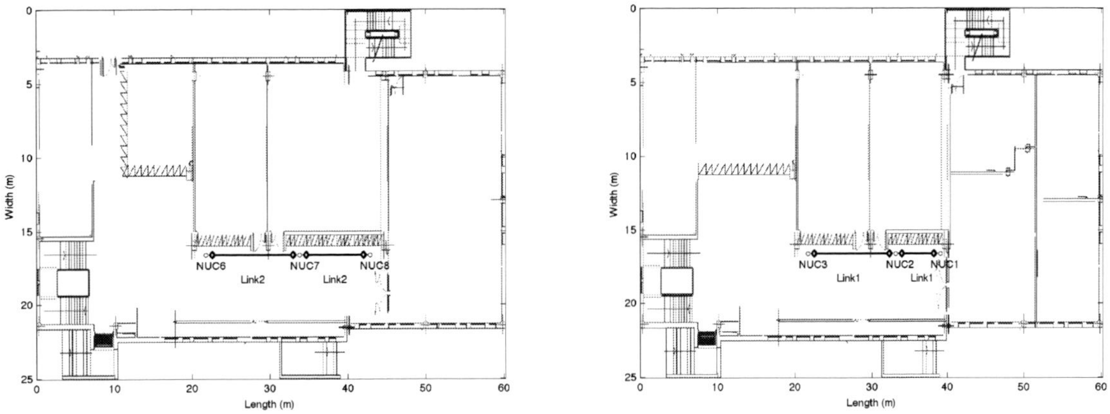

(a) (b)

Fig. 13. Network configuration for Experiment 5 with the portable test-bed. (a) Floor 0 with Link 2 and (b) Floor 1 with Link 1.

signal level from Link 2 is more pronounced than the signal from Link 1 on the other floor.

The aggregated throughput computed and represented on Figure 14 shows that the building floor is not efficient in blocking the radio signal from crossing the concrete structure and interfering with the other WiFi Link at 2.4 GHz. The aggregate throughput decreases from 19.4 Mbps to 3.5 Mbps as the transmit power increases, since co-channel interference between Links becomes stronger. However, Link 2 presents higher throughput, as the co-channel interference from Link 1 is lower.

At 5 GHz, the aggregate throughput increases from 16.7 Mbps to 24.6 Mbps as the transmit power increases, which indicates that co-channel interference between links has diminutive influence on the aggregated throughput. Thus, the presence of concrete walls and floor can be used by the coordination strategy to improve the channel distribution on the 5 GHz band and increase the network capacity.

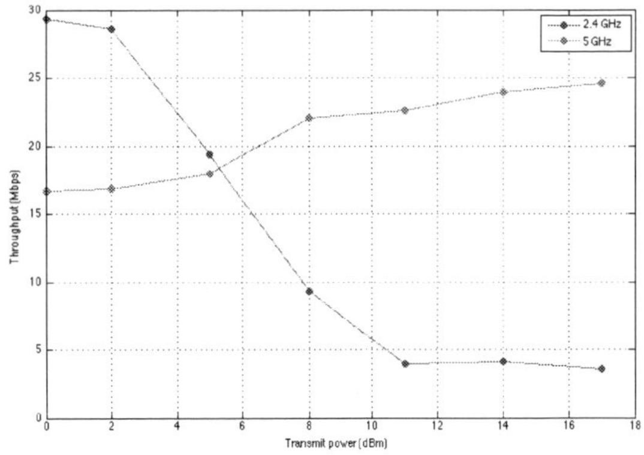

Fig. 14. Throughput of the radio signal crossing through a concrete floor, as a function of the AP transmit power.

V. Conclusion

This paper presented the testing of WiFi coordination strategies that exploits information from Radio Environment Maps, based upon several exploratory measurement campaigns in a pseudo-shielded test-bed environment and in a real environment using a portable test-bed. Several scenarios were tested: Uncoordinated channels assignment, optimal coordination, interference mitigation, automatic power control, hole detection and load balancing.

The overall performance of the WiFi network depends on a smart channel allocation. As an example, for the network under test in the pseudo-shielded test-bed environment, we've got an aggregated throughput of 22.3 Mbps in a full co-channel interference scenario and 71.5 Mbps using a configuration of non-overlapping channels. It was shown that based on the observation of REMs, it is possible to detect the presence of interfering links (co-channel and first adjacent channel). First adjacent-channel interference leads to a higher throughput degradation than a co-channel interference with the same power level (no-interference: 71.5 Mbps, co-channel interference: 58.6 Mbps and adjacent-channel interference: 56.7 Mbps). The coordination strategy that automatically reallocates WiFi channels to avoid channel overlapping is very beneficial (e.g., the aggregated throughput goes from 58.7 Mbps to 71.5 Mbps, the link under interference goes from 6.8 Mbps to 11.8 Mbps). However, in case of strong co-channel interference, the strategy of automatically increase the power level of the victim link, when keeping the same channel allocation, does not bring any gain in terms of measured throughput. With the portable test-bed in a real environment, The RRM that automatically reallocates WiFi channels to avoid channel overlapping from an external interferer is also very beneficial. At 5 GHz, the aggregated throughput goes from 62 Mbps to 79.97 Mbps, the link under interference goes from 3.15 Mbps to 20.7 Mbps.

Moreover, it was shown that a building's concrete floor that separates two WiFi networks using the same channel, act as an effective barrier at 5 GHz, but not on the 2.4 GHz band. Thus, the presence of concrete walls and floor can be used by the coordination strategy to improve the channel distribution and increase the network capacity. Increasing the transmit power on the first case (e.g., 5 GHz band) leads to a higher throughput (from 16.71 Mbps to 24.62 Mbps), while for the second case (e.g., 2.4 GHz band) decreases the aggregate throughput (from 19.36 Mbps to 3.54 Mbps).

For the RRM to be effective, several sensor nodes (energy detectors) are needed to create a REM with enough spatial resolution. The additional hardware required for spectrum sensing, inter–cell signaling and REM building may increase the investment by 50 %, when compared to an uncoordinated WiFi network. However, by implementing a coordinated management of radio resources, the overall throughput in WiFi network was increased more than 200 %, even in the presence of interfering links.

The results coming out from this experiment may have a clear impact in telecommunication companies and WiFi service providers, helping to understand the opportunities and limitations of WiFi coordination strategies in realistic scenarios. We will use the insights form this experiment in dense WiFi outdoor scenarios, to assess the benefit of a coordinate management of radio resources. In particular, WiFi coordination in shopping malls, football stadiums or swimming pool complexes are amongst the most challenging locations to deploy a WiFi network because of the huge crowds in close proximity to each other and the near universal use of smartphones by today's customers and sport fans.

ACKNOWLEDGMENT

The research and development leading to these results has received funding from the European Union's Seventh Programme (FP7) for research, technological development and demonstration under grant agreement N.º 318389 (Fed4FIRE) and the Horizon 2020 Programme under grant agreement N.º 645274 (WiSHFUL).

REFERENCES

[1] R. Dionisio, T. Alves, and J. Ribeiro, "Experimentation with radio environment maps for resources optimisation in dense wireless scenarios," in *7th International Conference on Advances in Cognitive Radio - COCORA 2017*, Apr 2017, pp. 25–30.

[2] L. P. Qian, Y. J. Zhang, and J. Huang, "Mapel: Achieving global optimality for a non-convex wireless power control problem," *IEEE Transactions on Wireless Communications*, vol. 8, no. 3, pp. 1553–1563, March 2009.

[3] D. H. Kang, "Interference Coordination for Low-cost Indoor Wireless Systems in Shared Spectrum," Ph.D. dissertation, KTH, School of Information and Communication Technology (ICT), Communication Systems, CoS, 2014.

[4] S. Zehl, A. Zubow, M. Döring, and A. Wolisz, "ResFi: A secure framework for self organized Radio Resource Management in residential WiFi networks," in *2016 IEEE 17th International Symposium on A World of Wireless, Mobile and Multimedia Networks (WoWMoM)*, June 2016, pp. 1–11.

[5] V. Rakovic, D. Denkovski, V. Atanasovski, and L. Gavrilovska, "Radio resource management based on radio environmental maps: Case of Smart-WiFi," in *2016 23rd International Conference on Telecommunications (ICT)*, May 2016, pp. 1–5.

[6] M. Pesko, T. Jarvonic, A. Kosir, M. Stular, and M. Mohorcic, "Radio Environment Maps: The Survey of Construction Methods," *KSII Transactions on Internet and Information Systems*, vol. 8, no. 11, pp. 3789–3809, November 2014.

[7] iMinds. (2017, November) jFed – Java-based framework for testbed federation. [Online]. Available: http://jfed.iminds.be

[8] (2017, November) OMF–6. [Online]. Available: https://github.com/mytestbed/omf

[9] (2017, November) OEDL – OMF Experiment Description Language. [Online]. Available: http://www.crew-project.eu/portal/oedl-explained

[10] (2017, November) Iperf, The TCP/UDP bandwidth measurement tool. [Online]. Available: http://iperf.fr/

[11] (2017, November) OML. [Online]. Available: https://wiki.confine-project.eu/oml:start

[12] S. Bouckaert, W. Vandenberghe, B. Jooris, I. Moerman, and P. Demeester, *The w-iLab.t Testbed*. Berlin, Heidelberg: Springer Berlin Heidelberg, 2011, pp. 145–154.

[13] (2017, November) w-iLab.t. [Online]. Available: http://doc.ilabt.iminds.be/ilabt-documentation/wilabfacility.html

[14] A. Goldsmith, *Wireless Communications*. Cambridge University Press, 2005.

[15] E. G. Villegas, E. Lopez-Aguilera, R. Vidal, and J. Paradells, "Effect of adjacent-channel interference in ieee 802.11 wlans," in *2007 2nd International Conference on Cognitive Radio Oriented Wireless Networks and Communications*, Aug 2007, pp. 118–125.

A Unified Packet Core Network Architecture and Drone Prototype for ID/Locator Separation

Shoushou Ren, Yongtao Zhang, Shihui Hu
2012, Network Technology Lab, Huawei Technologies Co., Ltd., Beijing, China
E-mail: {renshoushou, zhangyongtao3, hushihui}@huawei.com

Abstract—**In recent years, new Internet applications are raising restrict requirements and great challenges to the Internet. The current IP-based Internet architecture cannot accommodate well with these applications and cannot meet people's demands as before. This is mainly caused by the overloading of Internet protocol (IP) address semantics, namely, an IP address represents not only the location but also the identity of a host. To address this problem, researchers have proposed to replace the IP namespace with separation of namespaces for identities and locators. In this paper, we propose a Unified Packet Core (UPC) network architecture based on Identity Oriented Network (ION) to realize the separation of identities and locators. The UPC architecture also provides a unified access network gateway, which can support hosts to access Internet with multiple Radio Access Technologies. Further, a drone prototype implementation is also designed and described for the validation of the UPC architecture. The prototype realizes the ID-based connection between a moving drone and a fixed stationary endpoint. It is also verified that the ID-based connection can be kept continuous even when the drone moves across different gateways. The prototype shows that the basic idea of ID/Locator separation is a feasible and positive evolution of the current Internet architecture.**
Keywords- ID/Locator separation; Unified Packet Core; identifier; locator; handover.

I. INTRODUCTION

The current Internet architecture which has been built on top of the Internet Protocol (IP) was designed for a very different environment from today's networks. Early versions of the Internet Protocol were designed in the 1970's, at which time the primary application of Internet was a very rudimentary form of messages, like email. After that the landscape of networks has changed dramatically with the development of Internet technologies, and many of the initial Internet architecture tenets have changed too. The decade of 90's and early 2000's witnessed the coming of the mobile era, in which cellular networks have gradually adopted IP as the underlying protocol and merged with the Internet in the 3rd Generation and Long Term Evolution (LTE). From then on, the concept of mobility is well ingrained into the Internet functionality and mobile user equipment (UE) has become a common platform to connect people through rich mobile applications. Today, the 5th Generation Internet is already on the way to be realized, expected to bring more convenience to people's life.

These dramatic changes of Internet are now breeding more and more new applications such as Micro-message, Virtual Reality, Augment Reality [1][2][3], massive Internet of Things [4][5], etc. As these applications are becoming much more sophisticated than ever, more restrict requirements are also being raised and challenging the current Internet. The current Internet architecture, which is IP-based, cannot accommodate well with these applications and cannot meet people's demands as they were expected to in terms of three main aspects.

The first main aspect is the *growing mobility connectivity*. In recent years, communication behavior is swiftly shifting from PC based fixed computing to smartphone and tablets based mobile computing, and mobile data traffic has witnessed an explosion growing [6]. When a UE moves frequently from one place to another, the accessing gateway may also change consequently, which leads to frequently changes of IP address and brings severe problems. *a)* One problem is session interruption caused by frequently changes of IP address. This will further lead to severe packet loss, high latency, and finally cause great impacts on the quality of user experience. In the worst case, it may even interrupt the whole communication and UEs may lost each other. *b)* Another problem caused by the frequently change of IP address is the rapid expansion of routing tables, which brings great pressure on routers with terms of CPU and RAM. The huge size of routing tables can also costs a long time to converge and thus brings great network latency. Both of these issues challenge the scalability of Internet [7][8], while the existing solutions cannot solve these problems well. For example, the GPRS Tunneling Protocol (GTP) needs an anchor at a high position of Internet, bringing traffic roundabout and extra latency [9]. The Distributed Mobility Management (DMM) employs a mobility anchor to allow a mobile node to remain reachable after it has moved to a different network, which cannot overcome the short comings completely [10]. The Mobile IPv6 has the problem of Triangle Routing and high latency [11]. *c)* How to access to heterogeneous networks also remains challenge brought by the growing mobility. Since radio frequency resources are limited, Mobile Network Operators (MNOs) will have to bear more costs due to an increase in the number of cells per unit area. It is foreseen that the future 5G mobile network will become heterogeneous with multi-RATs (Radio Access Technologies) environment, where the existing different RAT cells and wireless LAN networks will be integrated and used [12]. Thus, mobility across heterogeneous access methods, for example from WLAN to LTE/5G network, must be supported. Besides, the IP address of a mobile UE or a fixed end host is now strictly managed by one specific MNO for commercial reasons. The mobility among different

MNOs in heterogeneous networks also remains a challenging issue in the current IP-based Internet.

The second aspect is the *inter-connecting between different applications* on mobile UEs. In most cases, the IP-based connection between two mobile UEs is absolutely driven by mobile applications (like Facebook, Micro-Message, etc.), which are monopolized by different Over-The-Top(OTT) service providers. Since UEs can only be identified by identifiers of different applications on the Application Layer rather than the IP address on the Network Layer, individual UE cannot identify and communicate with each other across different OTT service. For example, a Micro-message user cannot communicate with a Facebook user because they cannot even "see" each other on the Internet. Moreover, when a UE's IP address changes along with its location when it moves, the TCP session/socket with other hosts will be broken down.

The third aspect is the *scale of everything connected*. The past few years has witnessed the rapid development of Internet of Things (IoT) and many new technologies have emerged to realize various IoT applications. Consequently, a massive number of IoT devices are being connected to the Internet progressively, presenting great challenges to the scalability of the Internet by demanding more IP addresses and more space in routing tables. The new features of IoT devices, like various types and complicated access environment, also propose more restrict requirements for the conventional Internet. Moreover, it is also a cruel issue with increased complexity when dealing with non-IP packets generated by some tiny IoT objects.

A common consensus is that these problems are mainly caused by the overloading of Internet protocol (IP) address semantics [13]. That is, an IP address represents not only the location but also the identity of an end host. Therefore, several new schemes, such as the Host Identity Protocol (HIP) [14][15][16] and the Locator/ID Separation Protocol (LISP) [17], have been proposed to replace the IP namespace in today's Internet with a locator namespace and an identity namespace. In these schemes, a locator namespace consists of *locators* that represent the attachment point of hosts in the network, while the identity namespace consists of *identifiers* (ID), also known as endpoint identities (EIDs) that represent unique identities of hosts. When IDs are separated from their network attachment position information, packets destined for IDs are generally forwarded with the default routing method by using the locators as IPs. By decoupling an identifier from its locator, changes of a host's location become transparent to the upper layers above TCP/UDP.

Consider the communication in the ID/Locator separation network between two end hosts, which are called ID hosts. Each host only needs to know the other's ID before the connection is established, since only the ID can tell each other *who* the correspondent host is. While the locator is only used for packet forwarding in the Internet and it may change according to different access gateways. Thus, we call this kind of communication/connection as an ID-based communication/connection. In this paper, we propose a new network architecture called Unified Packet Core (UPC), based on the idea of Identity Oriented networks (IONs) [18]. The UPC architecture provides a unified access network gateway, which can support hosts to access Internet with multiple RATs, including 5G, LTE, WLAN, etc. The UPC architecture can also support ID-based communication between ID hosts. Further, we realize a drone prototype to verify the UPC architecture. In this prototype, a drone and a ground station are used as ID hosts. Each of them is with a unique and fixed ID, while their locators can change according to the access gateways. Our prototype ensures that the drone can establish an ID-based connection with the remote ground station. Moreover, when the drone accesses different gateways, the ID-based connection between the drone and the ground station is continuously maintained even when the drone's locator changes.

The rest of this paper is structured as follows. In Section II, we summary some related works of the ID/Locator separation networks. Then, we introduce the basic framework of the UPC architecture in Section III. Section IV describes the topology of the drone prototype and the main entities in the prototype. Some detail designs are also presented in this section, including the ID packet format, packet encapsulation and decapsulation. In Section V, we show the handover process of the prototype in detail. At last, this paper is concluded in Section VI.

II. RELATED WORKS

Over the past several years, considerable efforts have been made on investigating solutions for the overloading of IP address semantics. Many protocols or architectures have been proposed based on the idea of ID/locator separation and some of them are briefly introduced below.

A. Host Identity Protocol

The Host Identity Protocol (HIP) is a famous protocol which aims to split the locator and the endpoint identifier roles of the IP addresses. HIP uses host identifiers at the host identity layer and IP addresses at the network layer. The identity layer is inserted between the transport layer and the network layer as a shim layer, Briefly, the HIP architecture proposes an alternative to the dual use of IP addresses as "locators" (routing labels) and "identifiers" (endpoint, or host, identifiers). In HIP, public cryptographic keys, of a public/private key pair, are used as host identifiers, to which higher layer protocols are bound instead of an IP address. By using public keys (and their representations) as host identifiers, dynamic changes to IP address sets can be directly authenticated between hosts, and if desired, strong authentication between hosts at the TCP/IP stack level can be obtained [14][15].

HIP does not change the architectural principles of the socket interface and the inserted identity layer is transparent to applications. In addition since it is based in public key identifiers it relies on well-known and proven security mechanisms that provide authentication, confidentiality and message integrity. However, the used cryptographic algorithms, especially those based on asymmetric key pairs, costs much in terms of CPU. HIP may impact user experience when CPU and battery power are limited in mobile devices.

B. The Locator/Identifier Separation Protocol

The Locator/Identifier Separation Protocol (LISP) was originally designed and developed to solve the scalability problem of the routing system proposed by the Routing and Addressing Workshop of Internet Advisory Board. LISP is a network protocol that separates the conventional IP addresses into two new numbering spaces: Endpoint Identifiers (EIDs) and Routing Locators (RLOCs). It provides a set of functions for routers to exchange information used to map from EIDs that are not globally routable to RLOCs. It also defines a mechanism for these LISP routers to encapsulate IP packets addressed with EIDs for transmission across a network infrastructure that uses RLOCs for routing and forwarding.

Three main entities are designed in LISP, namely Ingress Tunnel Routers (ITRs), Egress Tunnel Routers (ETRs), and a mapping system. When an end host in the local LISP site needs to contact a remote end host, it sends a normal (IPv4 or IPv6) packet with the destination EID as destination address. This packet is intercepted by one of the site's ITRs. To forward the packet, the ITR first needs to obtain at least one of the RLOCs of the destination ETR from the mapping system. Then the ITR encapsulates the packet with a LISP header and sends out the packet. The LISP header contains the locator of the ITR and the destination ETR. When the destination ETR receives the packet, it strips the LISP header and forwards it to the destination end host [17].

LISP can be incrementally deployed in the current Internet, while no changes are required to either host protocol stacks or to the "core" of the Internet infrastructure. However, the EID in LISP is actually still IP address. Thus, LISP doesn't works as well as expected with terms of the mobility issue, even though there were relative drafts have been proposed to deal with it.

C. Identity Oriented Network

In order to meet the aforementioned deficiencies and inefficiencies of the current architecture based on IP, our colleagues proposed the Identity Oriented Networks (IONs) based on the idea of Identity and Location separation [18].

Since the concept behind ION is applicable to any underlying network infrastructure, it was proposed to work in a backward compatible manner with the current Internet and didn't intend to change the IP infrastructure. The basic idea of ION is to insert a naming/identifier sub-layer in the protocol stack, generally as an over-layer of IP stack. The ION framework is briefly described in Figure 2 and the details are out of scope for this paper. Since identity and locators are separated, ION expands network layer concept to accommodate ID in the following manner.

- *ID layer* is a distributed function responsible for ID management and authentication services.
- *Mapping system:* An ID/location resolution system is introduced which maintains mappings between a host and its location.

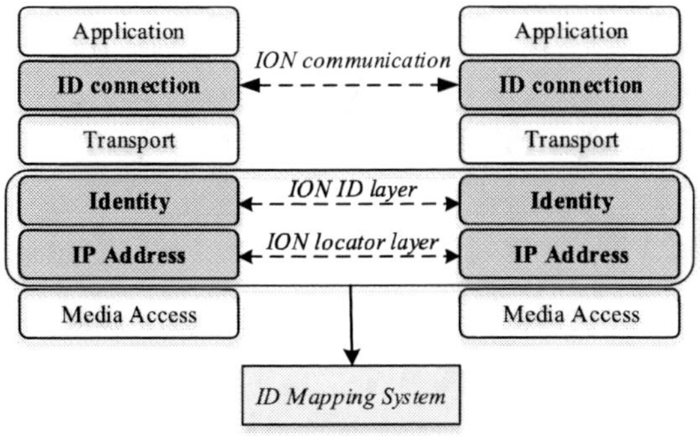

Figure 1. Brief framework of ION.

- *ID based connection:* In order to inter-connect two endpoints independent of network address an ID aware socket connection.

The ID oriented architecture relies on defining the ID of the user and a mapping or binding to the location of the user in order to forward traffic. The ID namespace comprises the whole IPv4 and IPv6 address space to enable it to interoperate with traditional applications, while newer applications can use the newly defined ID. ION architecture enhances traditional network layer with identity awareness. Some advantages ION scheme include: a) communication of non-IP devices such as IoT, b) a smoother and seamless location agnostic mobility and c) cross-silo communication across applications working with same network entities..

III. THE UPC ARCHITECTURE

To fill the gap between the conventional IP-based Internet and the requirements for future networks aforementioned in Section I, we design a Unified Packet Core (UPC) architecture in this section, based on the framework of ION. Compared to the Evolved Packet Core (EPC), the UPC architecture can support ID-based communication by nature and provide a unified core network which allows ID hosts to access the core network via multiple RATs.

Figure 2 shows the overview of the UPC architecture, which consists of mainly three new components, namely the Universal Access Gateway (UAG), the ID-Locator Mapping System (ILMS) and the Inter-Operation Gateway (IOG).

The UAG is the edge access gateway of the UPC architecture. It is extended from the ION gateway and can support multiple radio access technologies, as well as the wired access. The UAG is in charge of locator assignment, locator registration and packets encapsulation/decapsulation. Specifically, when an ID host, such as the drone in the following prototype, is online and tries to access to a UAG for the first time, the UAG assigns to it an IP address as locator. Then the UAG registers the ID/Locator mapping item of the ID host to the mapping system and caches the item until the host leaves. Moreover, the UAG can also perform packet forwarding function as a legacy gateway if a conventional IP host accesses.

Figure 2. Brief architecture of UPC.

The ILMS, which is an extension of the ID mapping system in ION, is another core entity of the UPC. It stores all the ID/Locator mapping items that have been registered. Once an ID host is assigned a locater by its access UAG, the ID/Locator item will be registered or updated to the ILMS. If an ID host wants to communicate with other ID hosts, the accessing UAG can retrieve the demanded locator from its local cache or from the ILMS. The IMLS is designed as a distributed system and independent from all access networks. It helps to realize seamless mobility among heterogeneous networks.

The IoG is a gateway that helps to connect UPC with the legacy network. Besides, the UPC also provide other legacy service such as AAA (Authentication, Authorization and Accounting) service, DHCP (Dynamic Host Configuration Protocol) service (mainly for locator assignment in UPC), Policy routing, etc.

The protocol stack of UPC is shown in Figure 3, which is exactly the same with ION. An ID sub-layer is inserted in the legacy protocol stack, generally as an over-layer of IP stack. On the users' side, hosts are aware of the separation of ID and Locator, and each host is assigned with a global ID. The ID is the only identifies that can represent a host, rather than the legacy IP address, which can only represent the where the host is.

The UPC architecture which can support ID-based communication is a feasible solution to the aforementioned problems. Firstly, with ID/Locator separation, the network are no longer in charge of the mobility management. When a mobile UE moves, the network need not to know WHO the end host is, while it only cares about WHERE the packets should be forwarded according to the UE's locator. Traffic anchors no longer exist in mobility scenario and traffic roundabout can be avoided. Secondly, the core network is decoupled with the access network completely in UPC, which allows seamless roaming in heterogeneous networks. Thirdly, the global ID of hosts enables that an ID host is always on line and reachable at any time. Furthermore, the design of ID can also accommodate well with massive IoT objects. Last but not the least, inserting ID layer also gives new possibilities to change the upper layer by having ID aware applications above the ID layer.

Note that though it is easier to understand and accept the ID/Locator separation protocol stack as designed in Figure 3, there are other options. For example, the ID oriented architecture may also reside directly on the L2 level alternatively, in which case the mapping is between the ID and the L2 layer MAC address. The evolved architecture using ID oriented networks aims at using the IP addressing, but inserting an Identity layer. This also gives new possibilities to change the upper layer by having ID aware applications above the ID layer. Besides, IDs of end hosts may be set before leaving the factories or assigned after that by some organizations and this is out of the scope of this paper.

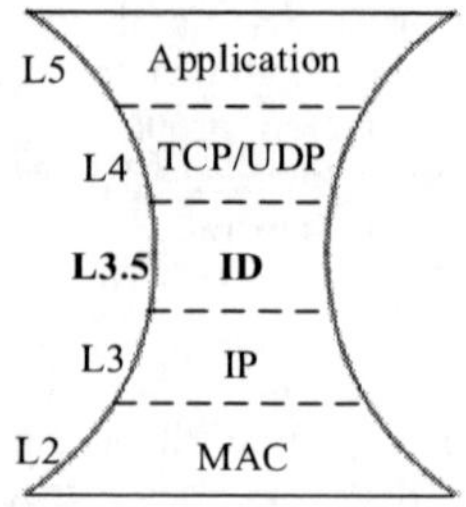

Figure 3. Prototol stack of UPC.

IV. Design of the Drone Prototype

A. Topology

The topology of our drone prototype is depicted in Figure 4, which mainly consists of following five kinds of entities:

- *Drone*: The drone is an ID host with a unique and fixed ID. When it accesses a UAG, a locator will be assigned, which is used to locate where it is. The drone is equipped with a camera for shooting real-time video when flying across different UAGs. It is controlled by a ground station and the video will be transmitted to the ground station via ID-based communication. In this prototype, we use the IPv6 addresses those are with prefix *2F00* as IDs for convenience.
- *UAGs*: Three UAGs are deployed in our prototype and the drone flies randomly in the area covered by the three UAGs.
- *Access Point (AP)*: Traditional APs. The drone access to a UAG via an AP. Only one AP is deployed under each UAG for the case of layer-3 handover [19][20], which will be further explained in the next section.
- *Ground Station (GS)*: the GS, which is also an ID host, is the controller of the drone. It receives and displays the video shot by the drone.
- *ID-Locator Mapping System (ILMS)*: the ID mapping system.
- This prototype aims to achieve the following goals: 1) Realize an ID-based communication between two ID hosts: the drone and the remote GS; 2) When the drone's locator changes while roaming across different UAGs, the ID-based communication could be kept continuous.

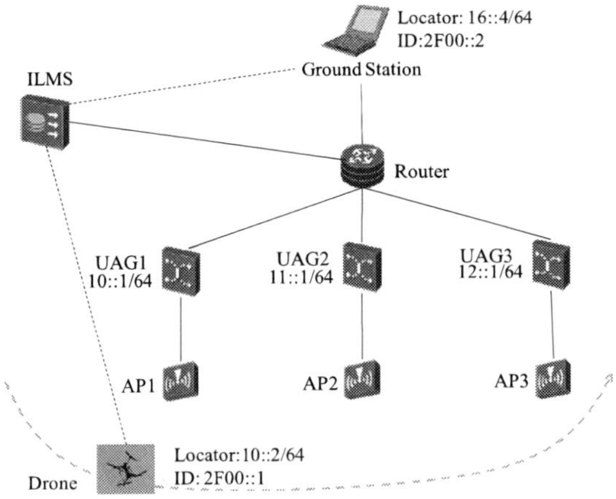

Figure 4. Topology of the drone prototype.

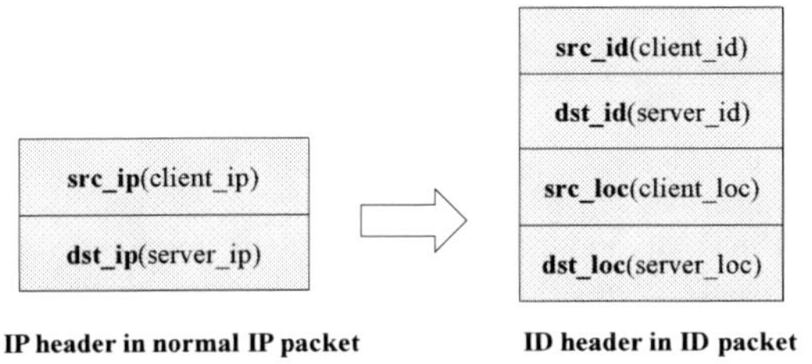

Figure 5. Changes of IP header in ID packet.

B. Packet Format

Packets in an ID-based communication are called ID packets in this prototype, while the traditional packets are called IP packets. As is shown in Figure 5, the format of ID packets in UPC changes accordingly with the protocol stack. The main change in ID packet lies in the IP-layer header. The tuple <*src_ip, dst_ip*> in a normal IP packet is replaced by a new header of tuple <*src_id, dst_id, src_loc, dst_loc*> in the ID packet. In this prototype, the IP address in the normal IP packets has the same meaning with the locator in ID packets.

C. Packet Encapsulation and Decapsulation

In this subsection, we take the drone as an example to show how the ID packets are encapsulated and decapsulated.

- *Packet Encapsulation*

The main encapsulation process of packets in an ID-based communication is depicted in Figure 6.

When a normal packet is generated by the TCP layer at the drone, it will be first checked by an *is_ID()* function to determine whether it belongs to an ID-based communication according to its *src_ip* and *dst_ip*, which can be found in the five-tuple of TCP sockets. If the *src_ip* or *dst_ip* is with IPv6 prefix *2F00*, the packet will be further encapsulated into an ID packet by the *id_out()* function with following steps. *1)* If the *2F00* prefix is detected by the *id_out()* function, the drone firstly tries to get the locator of the GS from local cache, i.e., its own cache and the UAG's cache. *2)* If fails, a request will be sent to the ILMS for the retrieval of GS's locator according to its ID. *3)* Then, the normal packet will be encapsulated according to the format shown in Figure 5. Specifically, the drone's locator, i.e., the *src_loc*, is assigned when it accesses a UAG. The *dst_loc* is retrieved from caches or from the ILMS. Since we use the ipv6 address with prefix *2F00* as id, the *src_id* in id packet is the same with *src_ip* in the normal IP packet, and the *dst_id* in ID packet is the same with *dst_ip* in the normal IP packet. *4)* Now, the original packet has been encapsulated to an ID packet at Layer 3 and it will be sent as normal packets to Layer 2 and then sent out.

Otherwise, If the *2F00* prefix is not detected by the *id_out()*, the packet will be encapsulated as normal IP packet and sent out.

At last, the encapsulated ID packet or normal IP packet will be sent to the access AP and UAG. The access UAG just treats the locator as the normal IP and forwards all packets as usual according to the routing table.

- *Packet Decapsulation*

The decapsulation process of ID packets is shown in Figure 7. Once a packet is received by the hardware of the drone, it will be sent to the IP layer and checked by the *is_ID()* function to determine whether it is an ID packet or not. If the packet is a normal IP packet, it will be sent to the TCP layer directly. Otherwise, it will be treated as an ID packet and further decapsulated by the *id_in()* function. The *id_in()* function strips the locator header, i.e., the *src_loc* and *dst_loc* fields. Then the stripped packet will be further handled as a normal packet.

It should be noted that in this prototype, the ID hosts (i.e., the drone and the GS) are designed to be aware of ID/locator separation. The locator header of ID packets is encapsulated and decapsulated at the drone for realization convenience. In fact, the ID/locator separation network can also be designed as that the hosts are completely unaware of ID/locator separation, in which way the process of packet encapsulation and decapsulation will be embedded into gateways rather than end hosts.

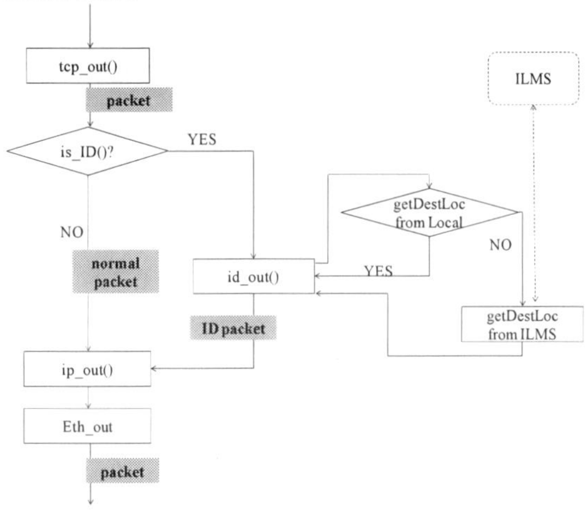

Figure 6. Packet encapsulation process.

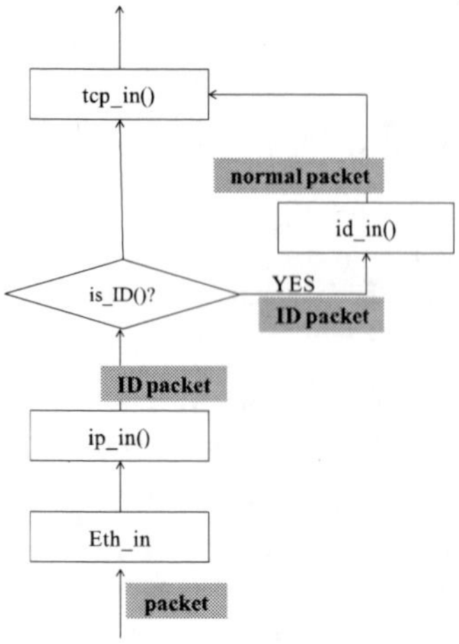

Figure 7. Packet decapsulation process.

V. Handover with Continuous ID-based Connection

In this prototype, we mainly aims to prove that the UPC architecture can realized seamless mobility without session being interrupted when the drone's locator changes. Figure 8 shows the change of data flow in the handover process. The drone was firstly connected to the GS via UAG1, as the dashed green line shows. When the drone moves out of the coverage of AP1, the handover will be handled. When the handover is finished, the drone communicates with the GS via UAG2, which is depicted in the red solid line. During the handover, UAG1 caches the packets those are destined to the drone but still in fly. These packets will further be forwarded to the drone vial UAG2 with an IP tunnel, as the blue dashed line shows.

A. Handover with single Network Interface Card (NIC)

In the first experiment, the drone is equipped with one NIC. When the drone moves out of the range of its access AP, a handover process must be handled. Since the layer-2 handover does not lead to changes of locator, we only consider the layer-3 handover in this prototype. Only one AP is deployed under each UAG for convenience of layer-3 handover. When the drone flies across different APs, its locator changes and a layer-3 handover will be activated.

The detail handover process is shown in Figure 9.

Step 0: the drone, with ID *2F00::1* and locator *10::2* assigned by UAG1, has already established an ID-connection with the GS, whose id is *2F00::2*.

Step 1: Once the signal strength of current AP is lower than a threshold, the handover process will be activated. Then the drone sends a handover notification to UAG1. Upon receiving the notification, UAG1 will send a confirmation to the drone.

Step 2: UAG 1starts to cache packets with *dst_loc* or *dst_ip* equals to the drone's old locator *10::2*.

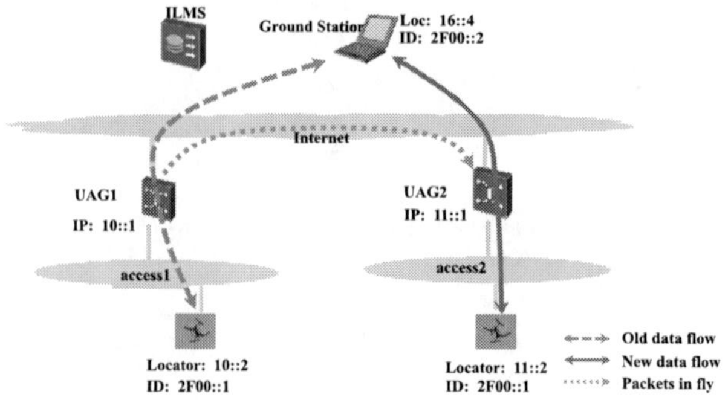

Figure 8. Data flow during the handover.

Step 3: After receiving the confirmation from UAG1, the drone disconnects from the AP under UAG1 and starts to send probe requests on other channels. If success, a new AP will be selected, say AP 2 under UAG2. The drone tries to connect with AP2. If success, the drone will get a new locator *11::2*, which is assigned by UAG2.

Step 4: Then the drone uses the new locator to notify the ILMS and the GS that its locator has changed from *10::2* to *11::2*. The ILMS and the GS then update their mapping item related to ID *2F00::1* and return the confirmation to the drone. At the same time, the drone will also send its new locator to UAG1, notifying UAG1 that it has successfully finished the handover and requests for the cached packets. Upon receiving the notification, UAG1 also sends a confirmation to the drone.

Step 5: With the same ID *2F00::1* and the new locator *11::2*, the drone continues the old ID-based connection with the GS. The packets in fly will also be tunneled to the drone according to its new locator via UAG2.

Though the NIC must change its working channel, which brings interruption on the Physical layer, the session on upper layer is not interrupted. From the view of the GS, the

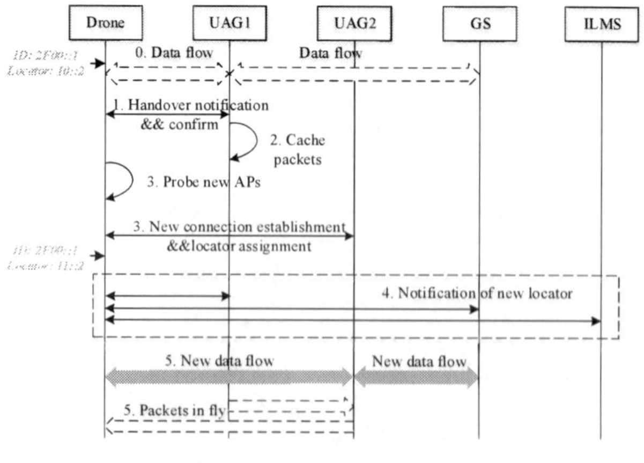

Figure 9. Handover process with single NIC.

corresponding node in the ID-based connection is always the drone with ID 2F00::1 during the handover process. Thus, change of the drone's locator is transparent to the upper layers including TCP/IP, and the ID-based connection can be kept continuous.

B. Seamless Handover with two NICs

To improve the performance of the handover, we then equip the drone with two NICs for another experiment. Two NICs on the drone take turns to perform the function of data transfer and probe. The process is detailed in Figure 10.

Step 0: Initially, the drone is using NIC_1 as the data card to associate with AP1. Locator (*10::2*) of the drone is associated with NIC_1. At this time, NIC_2 is idle and ready for probing other available APs around.

Step 1: When the signal strength of the current AP is lower than the threshold, NIC_2 is waked up to probe new APs.

Step 2: Once a new available AP (say AP2 under UAG2) is discovered and selected, the drone tries to establish new connection with AP2 via NIC2, and NIC2 will be assigned a new locator *11::2* by UAG2 (via AP2).

Step 3: Notifications will be sent to both ILMS and the GS, informing that the current valid locator of the drone is *11::2*. Note that at this time, the drone has two different locators and one unique ID *2F00::1*.

Step 4: The subsequent ID packets, destined to ID *2F00::1*, from the GS to the drone will be forwarded with the destination of new locator *11::2* via UAG2, then finally to the drone. Besides, the connection between NIC_1 and AP1 will be held for a period of time for receiving the packets in fly, which are still forwarded with the old locator *10::2*.

Step 5: At last, the drone disconnects with AP1. Now, NIC2 is in charge of data transfer instead of NIC1, which is idle and waiting for the next handover.

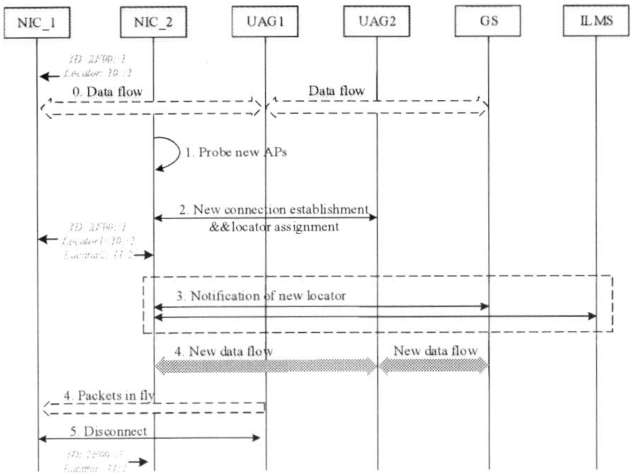

Figure 10. Handover process with two NICs.

During the handover process, since the end hosts of the ID-based connection are always ID 2F00::1 and ID 2F00::2, change of the drone's locator is transparent to the upper layers above including TCP/IP, and the ID-based connection can be kept continuous.

VI. CONCLUSION

In this paper, we proposed a Unified Packet Core architecture based on the Identity Oriented Networks, in which ID is designed as the only identifier of hosts, while the locator is only used for routing and packet forwarding. A relative prototype was also designed to realize the ID-based communication. Some protocol principles are also presented to define the format, as well as encapsulation/decapsulation of id packets. The prototype was proven to be able to support ID-based communication and seamless roaming of ID hosts. As the basic idea of ID/Locator separation is now widely accepted by researchers and Internet organizations such as IETF. This paper shows that this basic idea is a feasible and positive evolution of the current IP-based Internet Protocol.

In the future, there still remains many important issue to be dealt with before the universal deployment of the ID/Locator network architecture. The ID/Locator mapping system, which is at the heart of the ID/Locator network architecture, is the first issue to be considered. An ideal mapping system should be high reliable and with high efficiency. How to design such a mapping system still remains an important problem. Secondly, in order to realize the interoperation among different ID/Locator solutions, a generic control plane is also necessary to be design. Last but not the least, the publication and management of identifiers also needs to be considered carefully. All these issues will be further investigated in our future work.

REFERENCES

[1] S. Ren and Y. Zhang, "A ID/Locator Separation Prototype Using Drone for Future Network," The Tenth International Conference on Communication Theory, Reliability, and Quality of Service (CTRQ), 2017.

[2] Digi-Capital, "Augmented/Virtual Reality to hit $150 billion disrupting mobile by 2020".

[3] "Next Generation Protocols – Market Drivers and Key Scenarios," ETSI White Paper No. 17, http://www.etsi.org/images/files/ETSIWhitePapers/etsi_wp17_Next_Generation_Protocols_v01.pdf

[4] C. Perera, C. H. Liu, S. Jayawardena, and M. Chen, "A survey on internet of things from industrial market perspective," IEEE Access, vol. 2, pp. 1660-1679, 2014.

[5] A. Al-Fuqaha, M.Guizani, M. Mohammadi, M. Aledhari, and M. Ayyash, "Internet of things: A survey on enabling technologies, protocols, and applications," IEEE Communications Surveys & Tutorials, vol. 17, no. 4, pp. 2347-2376, 2015.

[6] "Cisco Visual Networking Index: Global Mobile Data Traffic Forecast Update," 2016–2021 White Paper.

[7] D. Awduche, A. Chiu, A. Elwalid, I. Widjaja, and X. Xiao, "Overview and Principles of Internet Traffic Engineering," IETF Internet Standard, RFC 3272, May 2002.

[8] "BGP Routing Table Analysis Reports," http://thyme.apnic.net/.

[9] "3GPP TS 29.060 General Packet Radio Service (GPRS); GPRS Tunnelling Protocol (GTP) across the Gn and Gp interface," 2013.

[10] H. Chan, Ed., X. Wei, J. Lee, S. Jeon, A. Petrescu, et al., "Distributed Mobility Anchoring," IETF Internet Draft, July 2017.

[11] R. Koodli, Ed., "Fast Handovers for Mobile IPv6", IETF Internet Standard, RFC4086, July 2005.

[12] "NGMN 5G White Paper," 2015.

[13] D. Meyer, L. Zhang, and K. Fall, "Report from the IAB Workshop on Routing and addressing," IETF Internet Standard, RFC4984, September 2007.

[14] R. Moskowitz and P. Nikander, "Host Identity Protocol (HIP) Architecture," IETF Internet Standard, RFC 4423, May 2006.

[15] R. Moskowitz, P. Nikander, P. Jokela, and T. Henderson, "Host Identity Protocol, IETF Internet Standard," RFC5201, April 2008.

[16] T. R Henderson, J. M. Ahrenholz, and J. H. Kim, "Experience with the host identity protocol for secure host mobility and multihoming," In IEEE Wireless Communications and Networking, pp. 2120-2125, 2003.

[17] D. Farinacci, V. Fuller, D. Meyer, and D.Lewis, "The Locator/ID Separation Protocol (LISP)," IETF Internet Standard, RFC6830, January 2013.

[18] https://www.iaria.org/conferences2016/filesAICT16/AICT_Keynote_May_2016_Padma_V5.0.pdf

[19] D. Johnson, C. Perkins, and J. Arkko, "Mobility Support in IPv6," IETF RFC 3775, June 2004.

[20] R. Koodli, "Fast Handovers for Mobile IPv6," IETF RFC 4068, July 2005.

Topologies and Coding Considerations for the Provision of Network-Coded Services via Shared Satellite Channels

Ulrich Speidel, Lei Qian
The University of Auckland
Auckland, New Zealand
ulrich@cs.auckland.ac.nz
lqia012@aucklanduni.ac.nz

'Etuate Cocker
Spark Digital NZ Ltd.
Auckland, New Zealand
Etuate.Cocker@spark.co.nz

Muriel Médard
RLE, MIT
Cambridge, MA, USA
medard@mit.edu

Péter Vingelmann, Janus Heide
Steinwurf ApS
Aalborg, Denmark
{peter|janus}@steinwurf.com

***Abstract*—Network traffic across shared bottleneck satellite channels using the Transmission Control Protocol (TCP) can suffer significant impairment due to TCP queue oscillation. In TCP queue oscillation, the input queue to the satellite uplink alternates between overflow and packet loss and subsequent exponential back-off. During back-off, the queue can drain completely and leave the link capacity idle and underused. Coding of such network traffic across multiple Internet Protocol (IP) packets allows packet loss to be masked from the senders to a certain degree. This lets TCP senders maintain larger congestion windows for longer, resulting in higher goodput rates. We argue that the concept of tunneling coded traffic across a satellite link is a flexible one and does not necessarily rely on a one-size-fits-all solution. This paper discusses a number of network topologies for the deployment of coding, from the perspective of satellite providers, Internet service providers (ISPs), end users and third-party entities, and looks at considerations surrounding code design, timing, and experiment methodology.**

Keywords*–*TCP; network coding; satellite Internet; queue oscillation

I. Introduction

The present paper is an extended version of [1], which investigates possible deployment scenarios for network-coded tunnel solutions to bridge the bottleneck given by the following scenario: An Internet Service Provider (ISP) on a small Pacific island receives its international connectivity via a geostationary (GEO) or medium earth orbit (MEO) satellite service. The capacity provisioned is in the range of several Mbps to several hundred Mbps, but always well below that of the networks connected at either end (assumed to be 1 Gbps or faster). The ISP services users on the island. The number of concurrently active client devices could be anywhere from a few dozen to a couple of thousand, and the ISP might observe up to a few thousand simultaneous TCP [2] flows. For the purposes of this paper, a TCP flow is a set of TCP packets travelling in one direction and is characterised by a unique combination of source and destination IP addresses and ports. Each flow belongs to a single TCP connection (i.e., a connection typically consists of two flows in opposite directions).

The flows across the link will typically be a heavily skewed mix: Most flows on the link will contain at most a few hundred bytes and will be too small and short to have their rate controlled by TCP flow control (also known as congestion control). Long flows, which are subject to flow control, contribute the majority of bytes on the link, however.

Satellite links of this type present a significant challenge to TCP: The long latency bottleneck makes it difficult for the TCP senders of sufficiently long flows to determine the correct congestion window [3], [4], [5], [6]. The root cause of this effect is the ACK-based feedback mechanism in TCP: A TCP sender interprets arriving / lost ACK packets as absence / evidence of congestion. However, in satellites, this feedback typically arrives with delays of over 500 ms on GEO and over 120 ms on current MEO links (at the time of writing, only a single MEO vendor existed, O3b, now part of SES [7], with orbital altitudes of around 8,000 km).

This delay gives each sender a rather outdated view of the current situation at the entrance to the bottleneck – the input queue at the satellite gateway for the uplink. In consequence, a sender may be encouraged by returning ACKs to increase its congestion window even though the input queue has since filled and is overflowing, and will now drop most additional packet arrivals from the sender. Similarly, a sender may be waiting for ACKs corresponding to data packets that were lost to a queue overflow event that has since resolved, and may needlessly reduce its congestion window. As the reduction in congestion window is an exponential back-off, multiple missing ACKs can quite radically reduce the goodput a sender is able to deliver.

Moreover, in our scenario, the link in question is *shared*, which means that a large number of simultaneous connections face exactly the same congestion situation and their packet round-trip-times (RTT) are dominated by the same latency. This causes all participating TCP senders to act more or less in unison when adjusting their congestion windows. Note that this is quite different from the situation at a "typical" Internet router, which sees connections with a wide mix of RTT values and senders that adjust their windows in either direction at any one time.

This effect on satellite links is known as *global synchronisation* [8], [9], [10] and can lead to *TCP queue oscillation*, where the input queue to the satellite link oscillates frequently between empty and overflow, causing link underutilisation when the queue is empty. Fig. 1 shows the effect of TCP queue oscillation on the queue sojourn time of `ping` [11] packets sent at 100 ms intervals into a 120 kB input byte queue of a simulated 16 Mbps GEO link. The queue sojourn time is a measure of queue length and reflects the fast filling and draining of the queue. A well-dimensioned queue drains completely at regular intervals but does not remain empty for extended period of time. Similarly, the queue should not overflow for extended periods of time. The 120 kB queue deployed here meets this requirement reasonably well.

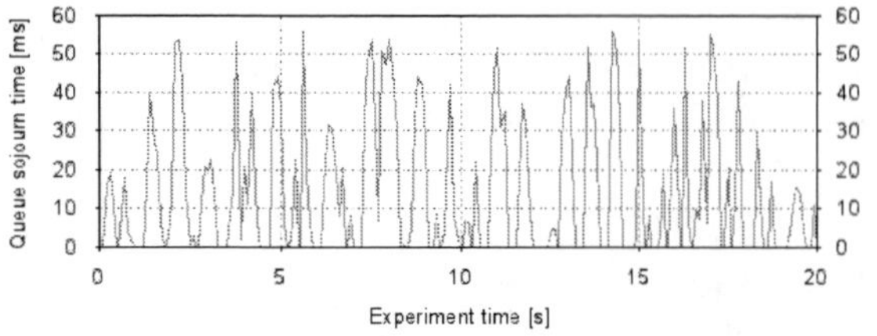

Figure 1. Queue sojourn time experienced by ICMP ping packets transmitted in 100 ms intervals across a simulated 16 Mbps GEO link experiencing TCP queue oscillation. Note the rapid rise and fall in queue sojourn time at regular intervals, which corresponds to the filling and draining of the link's input queue.

In addition to the work presented in [1], the present paper considers how tunnel solutions are constrained from a coding perspective, and how they may be evaluated experimentally. Section II provides a brief overview of related work. Section III explains the basic workings of the tunnel in a scenario where the ISP on the island provides the tunnel endpoint and where the coded traffic between the tunnel endpoints travels in the payload of UDP packets. On this basis, Section IV discusses the question as to where the off-island endpoint could be located and presents a case for having multiple endpoints. Section V describes a scenario in which a third-party entity operates the tunnel endpoint on the island. In Section VI, we look at the advantages and drawbacks of offering coding-as-a-service tunnels to individual end users on an island. Section VII then looks at various options for non-UDP communication between the tunnel endpoints. In extension of [1], Section VIII uses observations from real and simulated satellite links to explore criteria that the code design must meet. Section IX then looks at experimental approaches and introduces the Auckland Satellite Simulator facility, followed by our conclusion.

II. Related Work

The performance problem resulting from TCP queue oscillation has been studied in the context of satellite links for over two decades (see, e.g., [12], [13]) and remains essentially unsolved, despite the emergence of active queue management (AQM) techniques and improvements in the TCP congestion control algorithm itself [14], [15], [16].

In large parts, this is due to the fact that in our scenario, the senders overload the queue based on feedback from the receivers that is already enroute by the time that the queue shows signs of filling. Any feedback from explicit congestion notification (and even more so from random early drops) simply arrives too late to be useful. It is worth noting in this context that island ISPs do not normally control the TCP version used by the hosts on the island, and have no control whatsoever over versions used by senders on the rest of the Internet.

Network coding [17] offers a potential part-remedy here: By error-correcting packet losses that occur at the input queue, it is possible to prevent premature back-off by the TCP senders, allowing some of the lost capacity to be reclaimed. In order to do so, the packets that one wishes to protect by error correction coding must be encoded *before* the input queue: The conventional forward error correction that is a standard feature in many satellite terminals happens at the time of transmission to the satellite and can only code packets that have already made it into the queue – its function is to protect against errors from noise and fading. TCP performance under network coding has been investigated by other authors before [18], [19], but not in the context of satellite links. Similarly, network coding has been studied experimentally on satellite links, but not in the context of TCP [20].

The basic topology investigated in this paper is a tunnel [21], which operates across the link and both satellite input queues at either end. It accepts and delivers IP packets regardless of transport layer protocol involved, such that the end-to-end principle always remains intact. We have already demonstrated [21], [22] that such a tunnel solution can improve goodput for individual TCP connections, even in the presence of a majority of legacy TCP traffic on the same link.

III. Coded Tunnels

We begin our tour of the basic tunnel model (Fig. 2) by introducing our players and our components and following what happens during a TCP connection from an island end user client to a server off-island that the user wants to access:

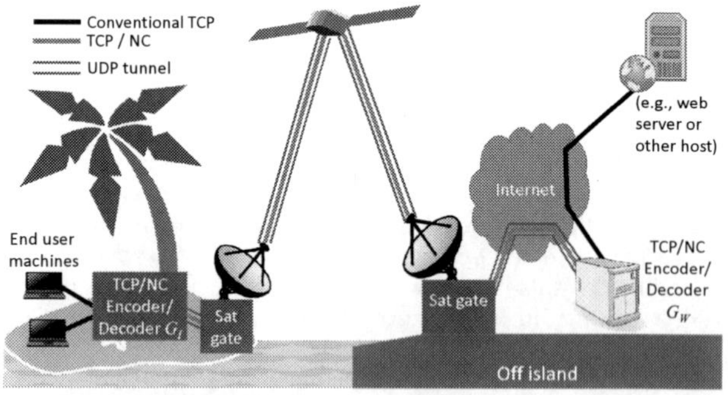

Figure 2. TCP/NC network topology in a scenario where the on-island ISP operates the local encoder/decoder. The off-island encoder/decoder may be at an arbitrary off-island location on the Internet.

The connection begins at an end user machine on the island. In most scenarios, we will assume that we have no control over this machine, i.e., that we cannot assume anything beyond the existence of a TCP/IP stack and some TCP client program on the machine. It means in particular that we cannot install software on the machine and that we cannot get the user to change settings on the machine. It is this machine that initiates the connection by sending a TCP packet to the off-island server, with the SYN flag set. The TCP/IP stack encapsulates this packet inside an IP packet whose source address is that of the client machine. Its destination address is that of the off-island server.

On its way to the world, IP initially forwards the packet to a local gateway router on the island, and from there possibly along further gateway routers in the direction of the on-island satellite gateway. In our case, we replace one of these gateway routers by our on-island encoder/decoder G_I. Since our packet is heading off-island, we use its encoder functionality here.

The encoding works as follows: G_I captures the original IP packet and prevents it from travelling further. Instead, G_I forms sets of n successive IP packets it has captured. Each such set is called a *generation* and n is the *generation size*. In random linear network coding (RLNC), G_I now creates $n + \omega$ byte-wise linear combinations of all packets $p_1, p_2, \ldots, p_n$ in the generation, using randomly chosen coefficients $c_{i1}, c_{i2}, \ldots, c_{in}$. That is, the i'th linear combination r_i that G_I produces is given by:

$$c_{i1}p_1 + c_{i2}p_2 + \ldots + c_{in}p_n = r_i. \quad (1)$$

The $n + \omega$ combinations thus produced form an overdetermined system of linear equations whose solution is the set of original packets $p_1, p_2, \ldots, p_n$. In doing so, G_I codes all bytes of the incoming packets, including the headers with the IP addresses of the island and off-island end hosts involved. Note that in pure RLNC, the length of r_i is that of the largest of the packets $p_1, p_2, \ldots, p_n$.

G_I now communicates this system, one equation at a time, to the decoder G_W, located somewhere on the Internet on the off-island side of the satellite link. For this purpose, G_I sends $n + \omega$ UDP packets to G_I, with its own IP address as source address and the IP address of G_W as destination address. Each UDP packet contains the equation for a particular i in the form of the $c_{i1}, c_{i2}, \ldots, c_{in}$ and r_i. In pure RLNC, this makes each UDP packet a little larger than the largest of the original packets – one of the reasons to use systematic coding, which we will discuss in Section VIII-E.

These UDP packets now travel via the satellite link and the off-island Internet to G_W, which solves the system of linear equations. The solution consists of the original packets $p_1, p_2, \ldots, p_n$, of course, which G_W then forwards to their off-island destinations. Note that G_W generally only needs any n of the $n+\omega$ UDP packets in order to decode the $p_1, p_2, \ldots, p_n$. The remaining ω UDP packets are not required and can safely be dropped along the way – for example, at the input queue to the satellite gateway. The important point here is that we can leave it up to the input queue to decide which packets to drop.

Our SYN packet has now arrived at its off-island server destination, and the server wishes to send a SYN+ACK in response. At this point, the network topology becomes critical: In most island scenarios, all island hosts including the satellite gateways at either end of the link belong to a single IP subnet. From the world's perspective, the off-island satellite gateway is also the IP gateway to this subnet. In this scenario, the SYN+ACK response from the server (and any subsequent packets from the server) are routed straight to the off-island satellite gateway, entirely bypassing G_W. This is unacceptable, of course, since most data flows in the direction to the island and it is important that we encode this direction in particular.

The solution is to split the subnet: End hosts in the islands become part of a new subnet A (this could also be several subnets), whereas the on-island satellite gateway is placed in a disjoint subnet B. One then configures routing such that traffic to A is routed to G_W as gateway, whereas traffic to B is routed to the off-island satellite gateway.

In this scenario, the off-island server receives the SYN packet with a source address from network A, and thus responds by forwarding the SYN+ACK to G_W. There, G_W encodes the packet in the same way G_I encodes packets in the opposite direction. It then forwards the coded packets inside UDP to G_I for decoding and release to the island end user machine, which completes the round-trip handshake. Further packets between the hosts follow the same path. That is, the packets travel trough a coded UDP *tunnel* between G_I and G_W and vice versa.

This scenario requires the ISP on the island to either operate G_W off the island, or contract an off-island entity to operate G_W on their behalf. In many cases, it will also be desirable to make at least network A an autonomous system (AS) for routing purposes, in which case G_W needs to be duplicated for redundancy. The current experimental software that we have been working with is capable of supporting two instances of G_W.

In the next sections, we will consider variations of this base scenario.

IV. Tunnel Endpoints and Their Locations

Our basic tunnel scenario above assumes that G_W is located at an arbitrary location on the Internet. As long as the tunnel that it spans with G_I covers the satellite link, it can fulfill its purpose of masking packet loss at the satellite gateway input queues. There are however good reasons to consider the placement of G_W carefully. The following options may deserve consideration:

- G_W could be placed in the path between the Internet at the off-island satellite gateway (Fig. 3), or even be a part of the satellite gateway hardware itself. In this case, network B could use private IP addresses, and G_W simply acts as a gateway for network A as in the previous scenario. That is, all machines on the island could be in the same subnet of an upstream provider's network, save the off-island facing interface of the on-island satellite gateway. For the ISP and/or their upstream provider, this removes the cost of maintaining a separate block of public IP addresses or even a separate AS.
  However, a placement at the satellite gateway requires the competent cooperation of whichever party controls the off-island satellite gateway: They need to install and assist in commissioning G_W or permit VSAT terminals with equivalent built-in functionality to be installed. In practice, one encounters a variety of scenarios, however: One ISP owns and controls both satellite gateways, another ISP owns and operates the island side only and contracts to a satellite provider

and upstream ISP off-island, and yet another buys a turnkey solution from a satellite provider who also controls and services the on-island satellite gateway. We note in this context that especially in the latter case, satellite providers often provide WAN accelerators with network memory, parity packets and various other optimisation functions – inserting G_W as part of such a solution would thus not be without precedent.

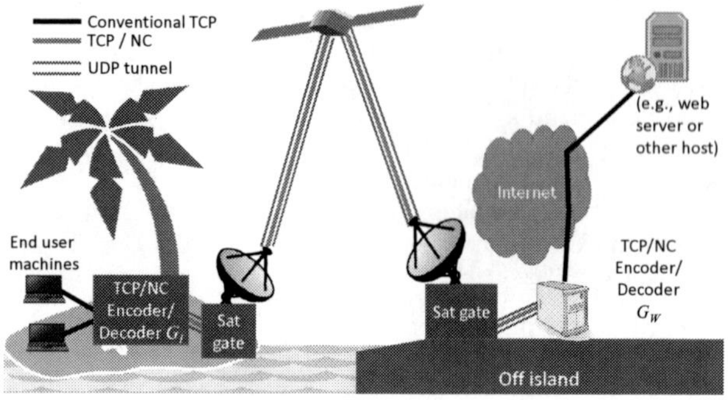

Figure 3. TCP/NC network topology in a scenario where the on-island ISP operates the local encoder/decoder, and the off-island encoder/decoder is inserted in the path between off-island satellite gateway and the Internet.

- G_W (or several instances thereof, labelled G_{W1}, G_{W2}, etc.) could be placed close to the known primary sources of bulk data content sought by island clients (Fig. 4). The advantage of such a placement would be that it would protect a longer portion of the paths between servers and clients by coding and bridge other potential sources of loss. However, there is an obvious drawback: G_W is no ordinary server – it needs a significant amount of network configuration in its environment to work. For example, the network that G_W is placed in has to advertise a route to network A in order to draw traffic for subnet A from the bulk data content sources. Hence, placing G_W in such a site potentially far away from both ISP and satellite provider premises requires the cooperation of a third party that is not only able to host G_W, but also able to arrange for its routing needs. Such partners could potentially be difficult to recruit for an ISP based on a remote island.
- G_W could be placed at the premises of a specialised off-island provider, who could also own and operate the device and sell its encoding/decoding services to the ISP on the island. An obvious advantage of this model is that it allows a provider to specialise in this type of service and host the G_W for multiple island installations, achieving some economies of scale. A potential disadvantage is added latency: The latency between off-island satellite gateway, G_W and off-island data sources may be much higher than that between data sources and satellite gateway alone. N.B.: This problem can be exacerbated by a failure to peer near the off-island satellite gateway. The authors are aware of a Pacific Island ISP whose off-island gateway is located in Hawaii. While the island has close cultural and economic links to New Zealand, lack of peering in Hawaii at the time of writing meant that all traffic between the island and New Zealand also has to travel between Hawaii and the U.S. mainland and back.

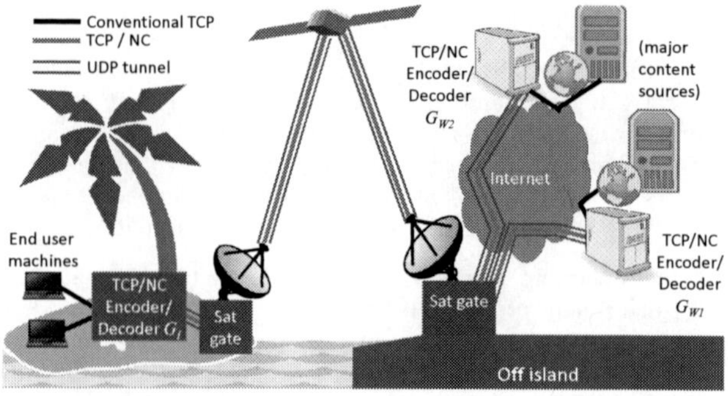

Figure 4. TCP/NC network topology in a scenario where the on-island ISP operates the local encoder/decoder, and off-island encoders/decoders are placed close to the servers on the Internet from which most of the download content originates.

V. Tunnels not Involving ISPs

In all our scenarios so far, the island ISP has played a core role as the operator of G_I, if not G_W. However, in principle there is no reason why G_I cannot be operated by another party on the island. Assuming for the moment that the ISP and satellite provider will pass UDP in both directions, any of the ISP customers within the island network can operate a G_I to tunnel to some G_W located off-island. This customer can then spawn their own network (Fig. 5) or – in the case of individual rather than institutional customers – simply run G_I on their own host or local NAT box.

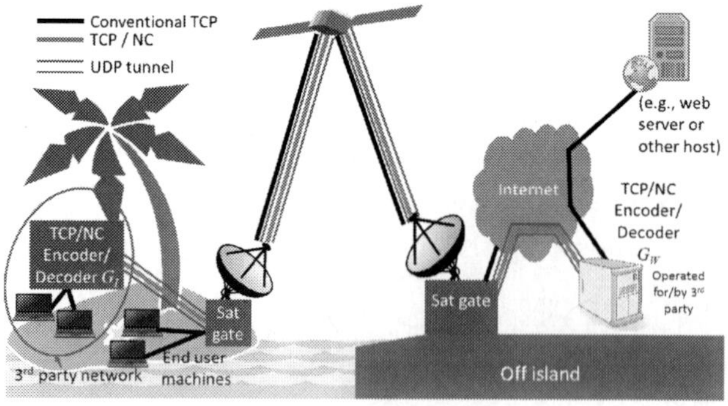

Figure 5. TCP/NC network topology in a scenario where an on-island encoder/decoder and the off-island encoder/decoder on the Internet are operated by third parties.

In the case of institutional customers, the corresponding G_W could be located at an organisation's off-island data centre or at the premises of a specialised third party off-island provider as discussed in the previous section. In the case of individuals, there could also be the option of G_W being provided on a subscription or pay-as-you-go basis by an off-island entity – an option that the next section explores.

Any such arrangement has a number of drawbacks, however. Firstly, it almost inevitably means that only some of the traffic on the link will be coded traffic, with the remainder being (mostly) conventional TCP. This residual uncoded traffic may still cause queue oscillation. While the coded traffic would be – at least to an extent – be protected from the associated packet loss and slow-down, the coding scheme involved would nevertheless have to provision sufficient overhead in order to cope with the potentially lengthy burst errors that queue oscillation causes. This would further increase to the load on the link.

Secondly, any overhead transmitted or received by a G_I under customer control increases that customer's data usage. In cases where the ISP on the island applies volume charges (a very common scenario in the Pacific), this results in additional cost for the customer. This may however be outweighed by data volume savings at the application layer as customers have to repeat fewer unsuccessful downloads.

VI. Coding-as-a-Service Tunnels

Another possible scenario is to absorb G_I into a virtual network interface on the end user machine and provision G_W off-island on a subscription or pay-per-coded-volume basis (Fig. 6). In this case, the end user would download an application which implements the client-side solution with G_I and interfaces with G_W off-island. The end user machine would then use two IP addresses: that assigned by the ISP, which appears in the header of the UDP packets between the machine and G_W, and an IP address assigned by the off-island provider of G_W, which belongs to the off-island provider's network and is not visible on the island to any host except G_I (which of course operates on the machine itself). This address is the source of IP packets departing G_W in the direction of off-island servers on behalf of the end user machine, and the destination of any packets that these servers send in response. In this respect, the service operates in a very similar fashion to a tunnelled VPN connection, except that the traffic across the tunnel is encoded rather than encrypted (it may of course also be encrypted in addition to the encoding).

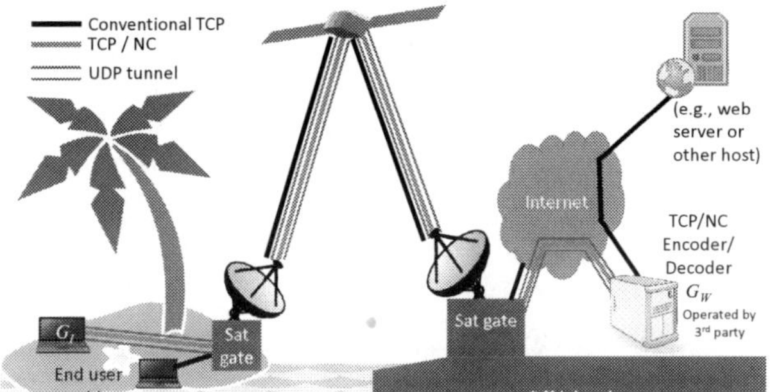

Figure 6. TCP/NC network topology in a scenario where an on-island encoder/decoder is integrated into an end user machine on the island, and the off-island encoder/decoder is provided by a third party on the Internet as a service, e.g., for a fee.

An obvious advantage of this approach is that there is no need for dedicated on-island infrastructure, the ISP does not have to expend or upskill personnel resources (or even be aware of the tunnel operation), and there is no need for equipment or personnel to be sent to the island to install or support the system. These are significant factors as many Pacific islands with satellite connection are difficult to reach – air services may be infrequent or non-existent, and intervals between ship visits may be lengthy and freight is expensive. Similarly, many island ISPs struggle to hire and retain qualified personnel.

Naturally, there are also a number of drawbacks, which start with those discussed in the previous section. In addition, there is now an additional challenge from the location perspective: As discussed in Section IV, the latency between satellite gateway, G_W and data sources may be significantly higher than the latency between satellite gateway and data sources alone. If the specialised off-island provider of G_W implements a coding-as-a-service scenario at scale, it will inevitably find its client software used in multiple island locations, with satellite gateways in geographically dispersed locations: An island in the western Pacific can have its off-island GEO gateway in Canada, whereas an island in French Polynesia might opt for space segment terminating in Australia.

A further challenge is the diversity in consumer operating systems. To be able to serve a large majority of users, the off-island provider would need to supply the application implementing G_I on multiple popular operating systems such as Windows, MacOS, IOS and Android. This represents significant additional effort compared to a tunnel application on a single operating system of the implementor's choice. It also carries the risk of leaving the end user machine disconnected: The software needs to modify the network configuration of the machine. There could be unintended consequences if, in doing so, the software interferes with any of the myriad of network configuration managers, tools and utilities which commonly inhabit these ecosystems. Given that the off-island provider has no control over what else may be installed on the end user's machine, this risk could be substantial. Another question that arises in this context is how an island user would pay the off-island provider: Not every islander has access to a credit card.

VII. Connecting the Tunnel Endpoints

On many islands, ISPs and/or satellite providers block UDP to keep traffic off their satellite link that does not back off under congestion. This can backfire, however, as many applications that have higher bandwidth efficiency using UDP do sense congestion and will switch to less efficient TCP when UDP is blocked. It is worth noting in this context that the UDP carrying our coded packets *will* back off as well: If too many packets of a generation are lost, the generation as a whole will become undecodable and the TCP packets it contains are lost as well, causing the contributing TCP senders to back off, too.

However, the communication between G_I and G_W need not rely on UDP. There are several options for this, two of which are discussed below:

A. Spoofing TCP

One option is to pass the coded combinations as TCP packets without actually running TCP at G_I or G_W. The only differences to the UDP variant are as follows:

- The packets carry a TCP header instead of a UDP header, with nominal sequence and acknowledgment numbers
- G_I and G_W acknowledge any packet received but do not attempt to retransmit any packets not received (and in fact ignore any ACK received)
- The first and second packet from G_I to G_W have their SYN and SYN+ACK flags set, respectively, and the first packet G_W to G_I correspondingly has SYN+ACK set.
- Either end ignores flags and ACK numbers upon receipt and concentrates on the packet payload instead.

To an outside observer, such flows are almost indistinguishable from genuine TCP and practically impossible to detect or block on a firewall with stateful inspection. Even in a real TCP connection, an observer somewhere along the path may not get to see all packets of the connection due to load balancing and asymmetric paths. The disadvantage of this approach is that it is a hack and, from the ISP's perspective, could be considered improper use.

B. Multiple TCP Connections

Another option would be to open multiple TCP connections between G_I and G_W at the outset and communicate only a small number of linear combinations (or even just one) per generation as data across each connection.

In scenarios where G_I and G_W are the only significant users on the satellite link, this has the advantage of replacing what would otherwise be a mix of TCP flows of varying lengths by a fixed number of TCP flows with infinite length and more or less equal data rate. Since the arrival of each combination is now ensured by TCP, one could also set $\omega = 0$ and thus reduce overhead to zero. However, TCP also adds its own overhead. It is also possible to use TCP variants optimised for long latency networks, such as Hybla [14] or H-TCP [15].

One potentially significant problem occurs at G_W (and possibly G_I, too), however: In the UDP or spoofed TCP scenarios, data arrives at G_W at full Gbps network rates and leaves in the direction of the sat gate at the same high rate in encoded form. So G_W does not need to buffer or concern itself with keeping any form of state once the coded packets of a generation have left. If we connect G_W and G_I via TCP, we transfer at least a significant part of the sat link bottleneck and its associated queue to G_W. Since TCP sockets cannot queue drop, G_W would need to implement this functionality *before* the linear combinations are written to the TCP connections with G_I.

VIII. CODING CONSIDERATIONS

The scenarios presented thus far do not consider under which circumstances one might achieve a goodput gain from coding. This section discusses a number of basic constraints that a scenario needs to satisfy in order to result in a gain.

A. Shared high latency bottlenecks

For TCP queue oscillation to occur at the satellite link, the link must represent a high latency bottleneck. If the link bandwidth does not represent a bottleneck, no queue can form at the input. Similarly, the fact that the satellite latency is shared between all flows is an essential ingredient for queue oscillation: It ensures that *all* senders respond with a significant minimum delay. Note that queues and queue drops also occur as part of normal TCP operation in terrestrial networks with links of varying latencies and bandwidths. However, where there are bottlenecks, there is often no significant latency that all flows share, and TCP senders accelerate and back off with a distribution of response times governed by network latency *away* from the bottleneck. Where there is significant latency, such as on transoceanic submarine fibre cables, there is often no bottleneck.

B. Flow size distribution

Real Internet traffic is highly heterogeneous. As a rule of thumb, most flows carry only a few packets' worth of bytes, as shown in Fig. 7, but most bytes in transit are found in large flows that contain many packets, as shown in Fig. 8. The beneficial effect from coding mostly accrues to TCP flows whose congestion windows can remain open wider for longer. This means that such flows must be long enough in order to see ACKs from the receiver arrive before their last packets have left the sender. Large TCP flows already slow down significantly at packet loss level of around 0.1% – a level at which only a fraction of small flows would be affected at all. Expending coding overhead on very small flows takes up capacity but yields no tangible benefit at all.

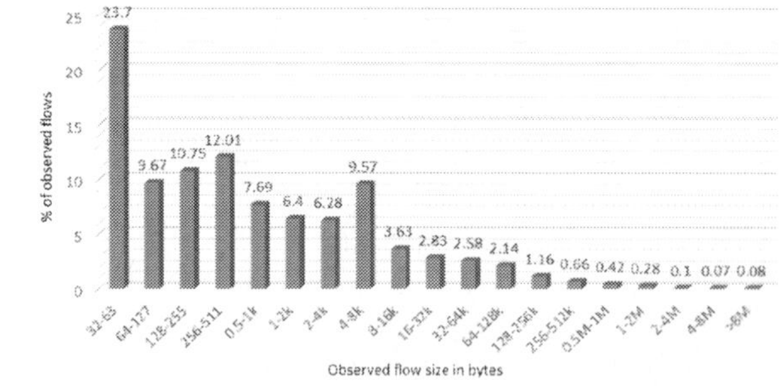

Figure 7. Percentage of flows of certain size classes in TCP traffic, observed on a real MEO link to Rarotonga, Cook Islands.

A typical default congestion window size in Linux is 10. At a maximum transmission unit (MTU) of 1500 bytes, this lets the sender transmit up to 15,000 bytes without having to wait for a first ACK. This rules out between 86 and 90% of all flows, but less than 3% of bytes on the link shown in Fig. 7 and Fig. 8.

One would thus expect coding to work best in situations where the share of large flows in the flow size distribution is high. Alternatively, it would be desirable to aim coding exclusively at large flows. However, this would require identifying such flows in advance, e.g., based on IP address and TCP port combinations known to produce large flows.

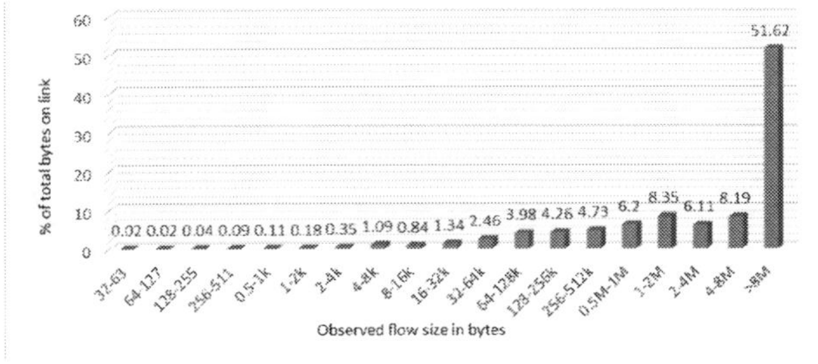

Figure 8. Distribution of bytes across flows of certain size classes in TCP traffic, observed on a real MEO link to Rarotonga, Cook Islands.

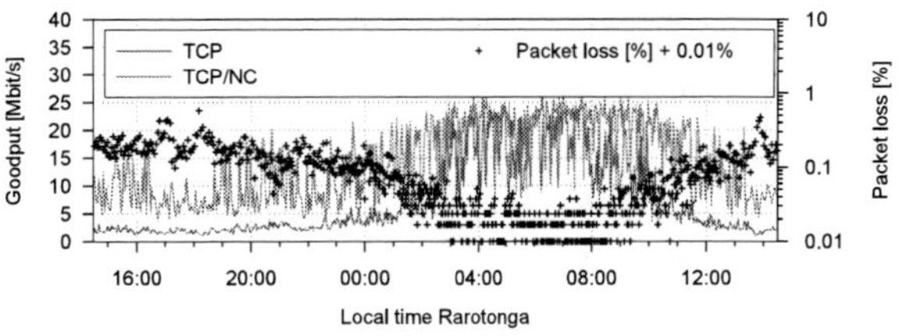

Figure 9. Goodput of uncoded (blue) and coded (red) TCP transfers between Auckland (New Zealand) and Rarotonga (Cook Islands) via a real MEO satellite link. Note that the goodput is quite comparable during the low demand hours (late night and early morning) with low packet loss from queue oscillation. During peak times, coded goodput significantly exceeds uncoded goodput. Peak link utilisation on this link was around 50%.

C. Demand considerations

A less obvious ingredient in TCP queue oscillation is the demand that is placed on the link. A TCP sender increases its congestion window when it receives ACKs from the receiver. The latencies involved on a satellite link make for a rather slow growth in congestion window. Consider a link whose queue is currently empty. If the number of flows simultaneously trying to increase their congestion windows across this link is small, the queue grows slowly as well: Each flow's contribution to the increase in arrival rate is small; their number limits the compound effect on the arrival rate. A slowly growing queue overflows more slowly, allowing for a more graceful back-off by the senders. Coding makes little sense in this context as most of the link underutilisation is a result of lack of demand rather than unreasonably harsh back-off.

As the number of competing large flows increases, their compound effect even under slow window growth results in fast queue fill. Similarly, the concerted back-off response of these flows results in a drastic drop in queue arrival rate. This is the demand region in which we expect coding to yield benefits, and where we have been able to observe significantly better goodput in practice. Fig. 9 shows a comparison between the goodput rate of coded and uncoded 20 MB TCP transfers via the otherwise uncoded MEO link above over a 24 hour period in 2015. The comparison shows that low TCP goodput and coding gain correlate with packet loss, which in turn has a strong diurnal pattern governed by demand. Even at peak demand times, the average link utilisation was only around 50% – a typical symptom of TCP queue oscillation. On this occasion, packet loss was determined by sending a sequence of large UDP packets, followed by a standard TCP transfer and then the coded TCP transfer, with whichever background traffic happened to be present.

At even higher demand, the rate at which new flows appear that have yet to engage with flow control can grow so large that packets from such flows alone can maintain a full queue. Large flows thus experience packet loss, no matter how much they back off, and consequently slow to a crawl. Fig. 10 shows this effect on a simulated 16 Mbps link using the flow size distribution above: As load grows, the link saturates with goodput from small flows. However, the long transfer cannot exploit the spare capacity; its goodput rate drops to about 2 Mbps at a load of 60 simultaneously active client sockets, even though the link still has over 6 Mbps of spare capacity. The fact that the transfer is able to achieve 8 Mbps at a low demand level shows that this is not a TCP slow start effect.

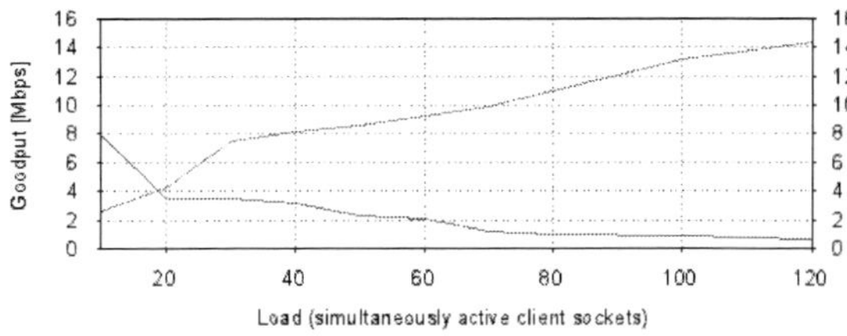

Figure 10. Goodput of uncoded TCP at different demand levels on a simulated 16 Mbps GEO link. The red curve shows the average goodput rate achieved by all flows on the link combined (red), the blue curve shows the goodput rate achieved by a single 40 MB transfer.

In the high demand regime, coding can at best displace some of the new flows but has no spare capacity on the link that could accommodate overhead and coding gains for all flows on the link. The authors of this study observed such a scenario on an (at the time) 8 Mbps GEO link into Niue, where high link utilisation simply saw coded TCP flows eat into the capacity taken up by conventional TCP traffic. The only benefit that coding yields at this demand level is that it can prevent individual large coded transfers from stalling – at a price.

D. Accommodating the overhead and gains

In principle, the more overhead ω we add, the larger the packet loss that we can tolerate. However, any overhead that makes it into an otherwise unmanaged input queue not only contributes to filling the queue, but subsequently makes it onto the link, and thus reduces spare capacity there. Compared to the uncoded case, the link's spare capacity must be able to accommodate both this overhead and the goodput gain we hope to achieve from coding [23]. There is thus a limit on how much overhead can be deployed before it starts to displace any goodput gains made. Quite where this point lies is a matter of ongoing research, especially as the question is further complicated by the timing issues discussed below, as well as by the type of tunnel.

Consider coding only a (small) subset of the (sufficiently large) TCP flows across a satellite link, as is the case for satellite links with tunnels that do not involve ISPs or do not aim at coding all such flows, e.g., in the coding-as-a-service scenario. Then this subset of flows has, in principle, the link's entire spare capacity to expand into. In such cases, one can use comparatively large amounts of overhead and still accommodate potentially substantial gain over the base performance of these flows. In fact, this is what we have been able to observe in our actual island experiments, which coded only a small part of the traffic.

On the other hand, if the tunnel handles all (suitable) flows on the link, the link's spare capacity must be shared between the flows. All else being equal, we are now dealing with more flows, so the total capacity occupied by the associated overhead is larger, and the spare capacity available for gain per flow is smaller. However, because coded flows are less prone to rapid TCP queue oscillation, a scenario that codes all flows may require less overhead per protected flow volume.

E. Timing issues

In our scenarios, we can still expect the vast majority of packets to make it into the queue and subsequently reach the receiver. Using entirely random c_{ij} means that we need to collect all n incoming IP packets at the encoder before we can send our first coded UDP packet to the decoder, i.e., we have a decoding delay that is more or less proportional to n. Therefore, our coding approach does not choose all c_{ij} randomly. Rather, it uses *systematic coding*, which for $i, j \leq n$ sets $c_{ij} = 1$ if $i = j$ and $c_{ij} = 0$ if $i \neq j$. This allows the first UDP packet to be sent immediately after the first IP packet arrives at the encoder. Only the c_{ij} for $i > n$ are randomly chosen.

One may thus think of the first n UDP packets (*systematic packets*) as being merely encapsulated original packets, while the remaining ω UDP packets (*coded packets*) carry coded "spares" in case any of the first n packets are lost.

1) Coding and decoding delay: In this context, we need to remember that TCP itself also provisions such "spares" in the form of retransmissions after ACK timeouts. Coding gain is only possible if the spares from coding arrive at the receiver before any retransmissions. As retransmissions will not arrive for at least one RTT, any coded packet that arrives within about one RTT after the original packet(s) represents an improvement over TCP's own mechanism.

We also generally want the coded packets to contain redundancy for all of our n packets, i.e., we want only non-zero c_{ij} for $i > n$. This prevents us from sending coded packets until all n incoming packets of the generation have been received. This means that the first systematic packet and the first coded packet are at least n packets apart, and the associated delay is the time between the arrival of the first and the last packet of the generation at the encoder. As we need this delay to be below one RTT, this imposes a limit on n.

Similarly, we also have a limit on ω arising from the fact that the last coded packet would be useless if it took longer to arrive than any TCP retransmission for the last of the systematic packets.

2) Overhead timing: While the coded packets must be delivered within a certain maximum time limit, it is also important that they are not delivered too quickly. The only occasion when the decoder needs the coded packets is when systematic packets are lost during a queue overflow event. If we transmit the coded packets immediately after the last systematic packet, we risk losing them to the queue overflow as well.

Another consideration in this context applies to links with particularly low transmission rates, especially in the scenario where the encoder G_W sits between the Internet and the off-island satellite gateway and has a Gigabit Ethernet (GbE) connection to the latter. Here, we need to consider that IP traffic headed to the gateway will generally have data rates *in the same order of magnitude* as the transmission rate of the link. However, this may still be one or two orders of magnitude below the GbE rate at which G_W can send overhead. A well-dimensioned queue at the satellite gateway will be designed to buffer at arrival rates in the order of the link rate. If we let G_W fire its overhead at the satellite gateway at GbE rates, we risk almost instantaneous queue overflow.

The following "all-of-island coding" experiment illustrates this: Consider sending a 32 Mbps UDP data stream into an encoder with $n = 60$ and $\omega = 10$. The encoder thus outputs around 37 Mbps, which is fed into a simulated 16 Mbps satellite link with 120 kB input queue capacity, i.e., overloading the link by a factor of at least 2.3. Note that this implies a permanently full queue at the satellite gateway. The ratio between systematically coded packets and overhead packets as they leave the encoder is n/ω, i.e., 6:1 in this case, and all overhead follows the systematically coded packets without delay on a Gigabit Ethernet link. On the other side of the link, the statistics collected by the decoder record the number of packets received of each of the two types.

One may now naively assume that the decoder should also see six times as many systematically coded packets as overhead packets. However, in the actual experiment, this was not so: The ratio between the packet types observed at the decoder was approximately 56:1. This demonstrates that overhead packets hitting the queue at a 1000 Mbps rate were largely dropped, with only a few getting the chance to fill whatever occasional spare capacity there may have been in the queue. When the experiment was repeated at rates below the link rate instead of at 37 Mbps, it did not overload the queue and all packets arrived.

F. Sizing n and ω – and choosing what to code

Beyond the timing considerations above, the choice of n and ω has other implications. For the same fraction ω/n of overhead, larger n provide higher robustness against the burst losses from queue overflow events. However, this carries a cost in terms of decoding complexity and decoding delay, as solving an $n \times n$ system of linear equations is $O(n^3)$. Systematic coding mitigates somewhat against this but still leaves an $O(\omega^3)$ residual complexity.

Larger ω add robustness but also contribute towards the development of standing queues at the input to the satellite link. Last but not least, it pays to remember that one should not attempt to correct for *all* packet losses at the input queue.

This would simply lead large flows to open their congestion windows to the point where the *average* data rate of the flow becomes unsustainable given the link capacity. Packet loss at queues is a necessary feature of TCP. The only goal of coding can be to delay the onset of packet losses at the receiver and to aid in the recovery from loss events where a large RTT prevents this from occurring in a more timely fashion.

The topologies presented in this paper open up several choices when it comes to deciding *what* to code. The choice in principle is between coding individual flows and coding all flows together. In the first case, all n packets of each generation belong to the same TCP flow. In the second case, a generation usually contains packets from multiple flows.

Coding individual flows requires the encoder and decoder to maintain state, i.e., they must be able to detect when a TCP flow starts (SYN or SYN+ACK packet) and when it ends (FIN, FIN+ACK, or as a result of a variety of timeouts), which adds complexity. It also implies that a generation of n packets will typically cover a larger time interval. With traffic naturally interleaved, it requires the encoder and decoder to maintain as many active generations as there are active flows. However, as all flows contribute to the packet loss during a queue overflow event, this limits the number of packets an individual flow loses – and this number determines sensible values for ω. Our observations in Rarotonga (shown above) and Tuvalu confirm that this approach can work even if all other flows on the link remain uncoded.

Coding all flows together means that the encoder and decoder only need to maintain one active generation at a given time, at least in principle, and do not need to maintain flow state. Generations fill faster, but burst losses from queue overflow now generally require more overhead per generation to correct, because the losses now no longer spread across multiple generations for multiple flows. Note however that a lost generation in this scenario generally still only translates into a small number of lost packets per flow, so the damage done to the flow's congestion window remains limited. Systematic coding further reduces this problem as systematically coded packets received do not require the presence of a whole generation of n coded packets to decode.

IX. Experimental Options

When investigating coding techniques over satellite links, one has the choice between four approaches:

1) Physical on-site experiments with a real production link. The authors of this paper used this approach in four Pacific Island locations [21], [22], and were able to obtain very encouraging results when coding small numbers of mostly large flows. The advantage of this approach is that the link uses real equipment, carries real traffic, and is subject to all phenomena a real link encounters. There are a number of disadvantages, too: Working on site is expensive, time-consuming, and logistically complex. Some of this can be addressed by only deploying equipment and working remotely, but this depends on the cooperation of locals who may need to assist in troubleshooting. Another challenge is that most islands of interest will only have one satellite link, which is often their only real-time link to the outside world. Loading this link with measurement traffic (e.g., TCP transfers for timing purposes or UDP streams for determination of packet loss) comes at an expense to the locals. Similarly, inserting an encoder/decoder into the path on either side of all-of-island coding requires reconfiguration and a (brief) service disruption, an operation with considerable commercial and health & safety risk: Typically, at a minimum, the local hospital, bank(s), airline(s) and government rely on the link.
2) Laboratory experiments using dedicated actual space segment. This option is the most costly, especially if one wants to be able to investigate all types of satellite links one encounters in practice. Another challenge here is to generate appropriate load.
3) Software-based simulation. The authors of this paper used this approach in [22], but it became apparent pretty quickly that it had serious drawbacks. Both TCP queue oscillation and coding are time-sensitive processes. Software network simulators can generally not simulate the networks of interest here in real time, so questions arise as to how the simulators handle the parallel generation of traffic, the chaotic interleaving of traffic before it arrives at the satellite gateway queue, TCP timeouts etc. Another question is how to integrate coding software written for a real TCP stack into a simulator. Even if this is all taken care of, simulating many hundreds of TCP clients and a large number of servers simply takes a very long time.
4) Hardware-based simulation/emulation: This is the approach we currently take.

Figure 11. The Auckland Satellite TCP/IP Traffic Simulator at the University of Auckland. The two racks on the left contain the "island" machines, the next rack to the right accommodates (from bottom) capture servers, copper taps, the satellite chain, and "world" servers on the top. The rack on the right holds the remaining "world" servers, a spare, and a special purpose server.

Fig. 11 shows the current setup of our simulator [24]. It uses 96 Raspberry Pis and 10 Intel NUCs to simulate up to several thousand "island clients", which are served with data from 22 "off-island" Super Micro servers operating with a variety of "terrestrial" latencies. A dedicated Super Micro server emulates the satellite link itself with its input queues, delays and bandwidth constraints. Two further servers operate as encoders/decoders; two more can run performance-enhancing proxies such as PEPsal [25] or TCPEP [19], and two standalone capture servers give passive listening access to any part of the network. Two further Raspberry Pis and another server are used for signaling and active measurements during experiments, and a central command, control and storage server orchestrates the other machines, wherever possible via an external, independent harness network. This approach has several advantages: It is real-time, uses real components (except for the satellite link itself), and by serving TCP data that follows a real size distribution, it is possible to control the load via the number of simultaneously active client sockets. The simulations shown in this paper in Fig. 1 and Fig. 10 were produced with the previous version of this simulator.

X. Conclusion

Network-coded tunnels carrying TCP/IP traffic in coded form across lossy bottlenecks in satellite networks have been shown to be able to improve goodput under TCP queue oscillation conditions even in the presence of a majority of flows using legacy TCP. The core insight that underpins the tunnel concept is that packet losses occur by queue drop at the input queue to the satellite link. As long as one can protect traffic against data loss at this location, the remaining system topology is a question of who will or can provide the tunnel service, how cooperative the local ISP and satellite provider are, and how much gain one requires from the coding to make the effort worthwhile.

As a general rule, topologies in which these two players are not involved (or even actively oppose the use of coded tunnels) should be less effective: The presence of legacy TCP connections forces coded traffic to use more overhead, so any parties on the island with coded traffic consume more data and bandwidth than necessary. Those not using coding are also put at a potential disadvantage as this may eat into their bandwidth as well. Active involvement of satellite providers and/or local ISPs thus seems advantageous.

On the other hand, coding all traffic for an ISP poses a number of additional challenges: One needs a more careful code design, goodput gains distribute over a larger number of flows, and timing of overhead is more critical. Avoiding the coding of small and inflexible flows becomes more important.

At the time of writing, only experimental implementations of coded tunnels are available. These are based on a Debian/Ubuntu Linux kernel module. While they do not cater for the subscription model discussed in Section VI at this point in time, they nevertheless represent a proof of concept for the remaining scenarios.

Current work aims to demonstrate that the technology scales to whole-of-island coding. For this purpose, we have built the hardware-based Auckland Satellite TCP/IP Traffic Simulator, which is capable of running island scenarios with up to around 4000 simultaneously active client sockets.

Acknowledgment

The research reported on in this paper would not have been possible without the generous support of many parties: APNIC/ISIF Asia and Internet NZ supported our work with multiple grants, and Brian Carpenter kindly donated a large residual balance in his research account to us. The Pacific Chapter of the Internet Society have been strong supporters throughout, and none of the practical work in the islands would have been possible without Telecom Cook Islands (now Bluesky Cook Islands), Internet Niue, and Tuvalu Telecom opening their doors and equipment racks to us. Meitaki ma'ata, fakaue lahi, fakafetai, thank you!

References

[1] U. Speidel, 'E. Cocker, M. Médard, Janus Heide, and Péter Vingelmann, "Topologies for the Provision of Network-Coded Services via Shared Satellite Channels", Ninth International Conference on Advances in Satellite and Space Communications (SPACOMM2017), Venice, Italy, 2017.

[2] J. Postel, "Transmission Control Protocol", RFC793, 1981, https://tools.ietf.org/html/rfc793 (accessed 24 November 2017).

[3] V. Jacobson and R. Braden, "TCP Extensions for Long-Delay Paths", RFC1072, 1988, https://tools.ietf.org/html/rfc1072 (accessed 24 November 2017).

[4] V. Jacobson, R. Braden and D. Borman, "TCP Extensions for High Performance", RFC1323, 1992, https://tools.ietf.org/html/rfc1323 (accessed 24 November 2017).

[5] D. Borman, R. Braden, V. Jacobson, and R. Scheffenegger, "TCP Extensions for High Performance", RFC7323, 2014, https://tools.ietf.org/html/rfc7323 (accessed 24 November 2017).

[6] M. Mathis, J. Mahdavi, S. Floyd, and A. Romanow, "TCP Selective Acknowledgment Options", RFC2018, 1996, https://tools.ietf.org/html/rfc2018 (accessed 24 November 2017).

[7] –, SES web site, https://www.ses.com (accessed 24 November 2017).

[8] B. Braden et al., "Recommendations on Queue Management and Congestion Avoidance in the Internet", RFC2309, 1998, https://tools.ietf.org/html/rfc2309 (accessed 24 November 2017).

[9] B. Briscoe and J. Manner, "Byte and Packet Congestion Notification", RFC7147, 2014, https://tools.ietf.org/html/rfc7147 (accessed 24 November 2017).

[10] F. Baker and G. Fairhurst, "IETF Recommendations Regarding Active Queue Management", RFC7567, 2015, https://tools.ietf.org/html/rfc7567 (accessed 24 November 2017).

[11] J. Postel, "Internet Control Message Protocol", RFC792, 1981, https://tools.ietf.org/html/rfc792 (accessed 24 November 2017).

[12] J.-M Jouanigot et al., "CHEOPS dataset protocol: an efficient protocol for large disk-based dataset transfer on the Olympus satellite", International Conference on the Results of the Olympus Utilisation Programme, Sevilla, CERN CN/93/6, 1993.

[13] J. Kim and I. Yeom, "Reducing Queue Oscillation at a Congested Link", IEEE Transactions on Parallel and Distributed Systems, 19(3), 394–407, 2008.

[14] C. Caini and R. Firrincieli, "TCP Hybla: a TCP enhancement for heterogeneous networks", Int. J. of Satellite Communications and Networks, 22, 547–566, 2004.

[15] D. Leith, "H-TCP: TCP Congestion Control for High Bandwidth-Delay Product Paths", Internet Draft, IETF, April 7, 2008. https://tools.ietf.org/html/draft-leith-tcp-htcp-06 (accessed 24 November 2017).

[16] S. Ha, I. Rhee, and L. Xu, "CUBIC: A New TCP-Friendly High-Speed TCP Variant", ACM SIGOPS Operating System Review, 42(5), 64–74, 2008.

[17] J. K. Sundararajan, D. Shah, M. Médard, S. Jakubczak, M. Mitzenmacher, and J. Barros, "Network Coding Meets TCP: Theory and Implementation", Proc. IEEE, 99(3), 490–512, 2011.

[18] J. Hansen, J. Krigslund, D.E. Lucani, and F.H.P. Fitzek, "Sub-Transport Layer Coding: A Simple Network Coding Shim for IP Traffic", IEEE VTS Vehicular Technology Conference (VTC), 1–5, 2014.

[19] G. Delannoy, "Design and Implementation of a Performance-Enhancing Proxy for connections over 3G networks", Dublin City University, May 27, 2013, https://github.com/GregoireDelannoy/TCPeP/blob/master/Final_Report.pdf (accessed 24 November 2017).

[20] H. Bischl, H. Brandt, and F. Rossetto, "An experimental demonstration of Network Coding for satellite networks", CEAS Space Journal 2.1-4, 75–83, 2011.

[21] U. Speidel, 'E. Cocker, P. Vingelmann, J. Heide, and M. Médard, "Can network coding bridge the digital divide in the Pacific?", International Symposium on Network Coding (NetCod), Sydney, Australia, 86–90, 2015

[22] U. Speidel, L. Qian, 'E. Cocker, P. Vingelmann, J. Heide, and M. Médard, "Can Network Coding Mitigate TCP-induced Queue Oscillation on Narrowband Satellite Links?", International Conference on Wireless and Satellite Systems, Springer International Publishing, 301–314, 2015.

[23] U. Speidel, S. Puchinger, and M. Bossert, "Constraints for coded tunnels across long latency bottlenecks with ARQ-based congestion control", IEEE International Symposium on Information Theory, Aachen, Germany, 271–275, 2017.

[24] Auckland Satellite TCP/IP Traffic Simulator, The University of Auckland, https://sde.blogs.auckland.ac.nz/ (accessed 24 November 2017).

[25] C. Caini, R. Firrincieli, and D. Lacamera, "PEPsal: a Performance Enhancing Proxy designed for TCP satellite connections", IEEE 63rd Vehicular Technology Conference, pp. 2607–2611, 2006.

Joint Beamforming, Terminal Scheduling, and Adaptive Modulation with Imperfect CSIT in Rice Fading Correlated Channels with non-persistent Co-channel Interference

Ramiro Sámano-Robles

Research Centre in Real-time and Embedded Computing Systems
Instituto Politécnico do Porto, Porto, Portugal
Email: rasro@isep.ipp.pt

***Abstract*—This paper presents a resource allocation algorithm for multi-user wireless networks with non-persistent co-channel interference. The analysis considers a network with one base station (BS) that employs an N multiple antenna transmitter (beamformer) to schedule (in a time-division format) a set of J one-antenna terminals in the presence of K non-persistent interferers. The transmitter is assumed to employ Maximum-Ratio Combining (MRC) beamforming with spatially-correlated branches and channel envelopes modelled as Rice-distributed processes. The BS has access to an imperfect (outdated) copy of the instantaneous Channel State Information (CSI) of each terminal. Based on this CSI at the transmitter side (CSIT), the BS proceeds to select (at each time interval or time-slot) the terminal with the highest measured channel strength. This imperfect CSIT is also used to calculate the coefficients of the beamformer that will be used to transmit information towards the scheduled terminal, as well as for selecting the most appropriate modulation format (via threshold-based decision). The main merits of this work are the following: 1) joint analysis of MRC-based beamforming, terminal scheduling based on maximum channel strength, and modulation assignment, and 2) impact analysis of spatial correlation, line-of-sight (LOS), co-channel interference, and imperfect CSIT. Results suggest that maximum channel strength scheduling helps in rejecting co-channel interference and the degrading effects of imperfect CSIT (due to multi-user diversity gains). Spatial correlation could some times lead to better performance than the uncorrelated case, particularly in the low SNR (Signal-to-Noise Ratio) regime. Conversely, uncorrelated branches always outperform the correlated case in the high SNR regime. Spatial correlation tends to accumulate over the antenna array thus leading to a more noticeable performance degradation and more allocation errors due to the outdated CSIT assumption. The LOS channel component is found to contribute to a better reception in general, but it also reduces the ability to counteract the degrading effects of imperfect CSIT due to the lack of diversity combining gains.**

Keywords–Beamforming; Scheduling; Resource allocation; Imperfect CSIT; Maximum Ratio Combining (MRC).

I. INTRODUCTION

Multiple antenna systems (also known as MIMO or Multiple-Input Multiple-Output systems) are expected to proliferate in the coming years, particularly in the context of 5G or fifth-generation of wireless systems [1][2]. The growing demand for wireless connectivity, the limited transmission resources, and the outdated spectrum allocation paradigm have created the need for more efficient, scalable and higher capacity transmission systems. MIMO technology offers considerable capacity growth that escalates with the number of transmit-receive antenna pairs (see [3] for an overview of capacity in MIMO channels). MIMO also offers improved energetic efficiency and reduced interference with minimum spectrum expenditure.

From the many different types of multiple antenna systems, perhaps *beamforming* technology represents the option with higher potential for commercial implementation, mainly due to its maturity, flexible implementation, and low computational costs (in comparison with other MIMO solutions). Beamforming refers to the ability to dynamically steer the phases of an antenna array and change the directionality properties of the resulting radiation beams. This enables a wide set of applications in multi-user settings, such as: interference rejection/management [4], spatial multiplexing [5], and more recently (with a few modifications) 3D beamforming with massive MIMO in 5G [6], beam-division multiple access [7], and interference alignment [8]. Other works in beamforming can be found in [9]-[11]. In future networks, beamforming will be key for efficiently organizing spectrum resources in dense cooperative small cells, as well as minimizing energy expenditure, reducing leakage and/or interference to adjacent cells or terminals, and also for improving security against potential attacks of signal jamming or eavesdropping in the network.

All these advances in the PHYsical (PHY) layer of multiple antenna systems need to be integrated/optimised with upper-layer algorithms, particularly with radio resource management (see [12]-[18]). This has opened several issues regarding the cross-layer design and optimization of beamforming and in general multiple-antenna systems. One particularly important topic in this field is the modelling of the underlying multiple antenna signal processing tools to be used in resource allocation and system-level evaluation frameworks. In large network set ups with tens or hundreds of BSs and hundreds or thousands of terminals, all the parameters of the PHY-layer cannot be usually included in full detail in the analysis or system-level simulation loop. Therefore, a trade-off must be found between the accuracy of the model that represents the underlying PHY-layer and its flexibility for purposes of resource allocation and optimisation at the system-level.

This paper attempts to partially fill these gaps by addressing the link-layer interface modelling in Rice fading correlated channels of an *adaptive wireless multi-user network using Maximum-Ratio Combining (MRC) beamforming and terminal scheduling based on limited (outdated) feedback*. The transmitter selects the most adequate Modulation and Coding Schemes (MCSs) and beamforming vectors based on an estimated Channel State Information (CSI). This imperfect CSI at the transmitter side (i.e., CSIT) is assumed to have been initially collected by the receiver (perfect estimation), and subsequently reported back to the transmitter via a feedback channel affected by delay (outdated information). This paper presents the analysis of the statistics of correct reception process conditional on the decision made by the transmitter (*modulation format selection, beamforming and scheduling*) based on the inaccurate CSIT. Link-layer throughput is evaluated by means of an *interface model* based on an instantaneous Signal-to-Interference-plus-Noise Ratio (SINR) adaptive switching threshold scheme for modulation assignment. This model aims to provide an accurate but flexible representation of the underlying PHY-layer suitable for upper-layer design. In the proposed model, a packet transmission using a given MCS is considered as correctly received with given values of BLock-Error Rate (BLER) and spectral efficiency whenever the instantaneous SINR exceeds the reception threshold of the selected MCS. The reception parameters of each MCS are obtained from Look-Up-Tables (LUTs) previously calculated via *off-line PHY-layer simulation*. The main contribution of this work is the joint analysis of spatial correlation, imperfect CSIT and non-persistent co-channel interference in link adaptation and terminal scheduling for MRC-based multiple antenna beamforming systems. This paper constitutes an extension of the work in the conference paper in [1] from Rayleigh channel to include a line-of-sight (LOS) channel component, i.e., Rice channel assumption. This paper also extends the conference paper from persistent channel interferers to non-persistent ones, which matches better real life settings where co-channel systems operate under randomized traffic distributions.

This paper is organized as follows. Section II describes previous works and the achievements of this paper with respect to the state of the art. Section III describes the system model and the assumptions of the paper. Section IV presents the link-layer interface model. Section V deals with the statistics of the estimated SNR and the instantaneous SINR. Section VI presents analytic results and sketches of the statistics of packet reception using different network assumptions. Finally, Section VII presents the conclusions of this paper.

II. Previous works

In theory, the simplest multiple antenna system is the MRC transceiver, which provides a relatively flexible framework for statistical analysis, interface modelling, and resource management. The literature of MRC transceivers has focused on the derivation of outage and bit error probability distributions (see [19]-[27]). The effects of imperfect channel knowledge on the performance of MRC receivers in Rayleigh fading correlated channels can be found in [19]-[20] following the analysis with perfect channel estimation presented in [21]. A series expansion of the statistics of MRC systems with correlated Rician channels is given in [22]. A unified approach for analysis of two-stage MRC systems with hybrid selection in generalized Rice correlated channels was proposed in [23]. Extensions to the case of co-channel interference are given in [24]-[27].

The present work considers the extension of outage probability analysis of MRC transmitters (beamformers) to the study of Adaptive Modulation and Coding (AMC) in Rice fading correlated channels with imperfect/outdated CSIT and no-persistent co-channel interference. To the best of our knowledge, this is the first attempt in the literature that addresses these issues under the same framework. This work attempts to extend the analysis of MRC systems towards including resource allocation aspects which are typical of upper layer design (radio resource management). In addition, network design and in particular resource allocation for multiple antenna systems is usually conducted under the assumption perfect CSIT. Imperfect CSIT has been addressed in [28] for distributed systems and in [29] for energy efficient MIMO link adaptation. In comparison with these works, which are focused on numerical evaluation of imperfect CSIT, this work provides an analytic framework for obtaining the statistics of errors in MCS assignment for correlated MRC transmitters.

The work in [30] provides a review of the state of the art of limited feedback in adaptation schemes for MIMO systems. The work in [31] presents the analysis of adaptive modulation for two-antenna beam-formers considering mean CSI at the transmitter side. The work in [32] addressed the impact of outdated feedback on AMC and user selection diversity systems for MIMO systems in Rayleigh uncorrelated channels. Other works with limited feedback for different types of system can be found in [34]-[36]. All these previous works consider uncorrelated MIMO channels. This work goes beyond this assumption searching for a joint analysis of limited feedback and spatial correlation for adaptive MRC transmitters with non-persistent co-channel interference.

Notation: Bold lower case letters (e.g., $\mathbf{x}$) denote vector variables, bold upper case letters (e.g., $\mathbf{A}$) denote matrices, $(\cdot)^T$ is the vector transpose operator, $(\cdot)^H$ is the Hermitian transpose operator, $E[\cdot]$ is the statistical average operator, $(\cdot)^*$ is the complex conjugate operator, f_z, F_z and $\bar{F}_z$ denote, respectively, the Probability Density Function (PDF), Cumulative Density Function (CDF) and Complementary Cumulative Density Function (CCDF) of any random variable z, $Re(\cdot)$ denotes the real part operator, and $\left(\begin{array}{c} J-1 \\ \mathbf{l} \end{array}\right) = \left(\begin{array}{c} J-1 \\ l_0, l_1, \ldots l_L \end{array}\right) = \frac{(J-1)!}{l_0! l_1! \ldots l_L}$ is the multinomial combinatorial number of $J-1$ and $L+1$ coefficients $l_0, l_1, \ldots l_L$ arranged in the vector $\mathbf{l} = [l_0, l_1, \ldots, l_L]^T$.

III. System model and assumptions

Consider the network depicted in Figure 1 with one Base Station (BS) scheduling transmissions (in a time-division fashion) towards J terminals , each one with one receiving antenna, and a set of K non-persistent single-antenna interferers. The BS uses an N-antenna Maximum-Ratio Combining (MRC) beamformer that is used to transmit information to a given terminal at specific time slots. The channel vector between the BS and the jth terminal is denoted by $\mathbf{h}_j = [h_j(1), h_j(2), \ldots h_j(N)]^T$. All instantaneous channel variables will be modelled as non-zero-mean complex circular Gaussian random variables with variance γ and mean ν: $h_j(n) \sim \mathcal{CN}(\nu, \gamma)$. The estimated channel variable available at the transmitter side is given by $\hat{\mathbf{h}}_j = [\hat{h}_j(1), \hat{h}_j(2), \ldots \hat{h}_j(N)]^T$. This information is used by the BS for purposes of beamforming, terminal scheduling and resource allocation (modulation format assignment). The channel between the interferer k towards terminal j is denoted by $h_{k,j}$ and is also modelled as a non-zero-mean complex circular Gaussian random variable with variance λ: $h_{k,j} \sim \mathcal{CN}(\xi, \lambda)$. It is assumed that the transmissions of the interferers are controlled by a binary Bernoulli random process δ_k described by the parameter p: $p = \Pr\{\delta_k = 1\}$.

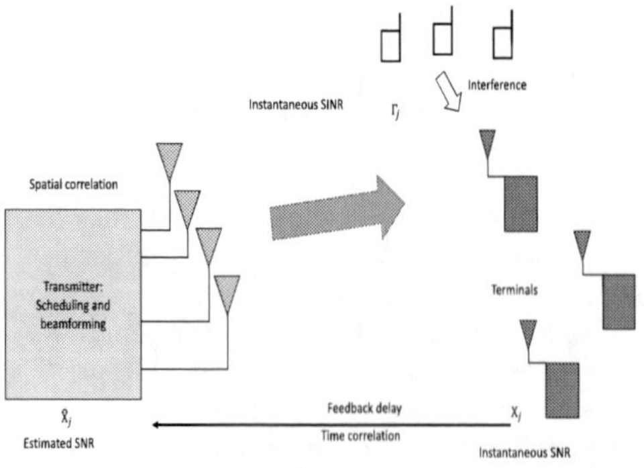

Figure 1. Wireless network with one transmitter using imperfect CSIT for scheduling, modulation assignment and beamforming information to a set of terminals in the presence of co-channel interference.

For each terminal, the BS selects one of M modulation formats, which are arranged in increasing order according to their target Signal-to-Interference plus Noise Ratio (SINR). The target SINR of the mth MCS will be denoted by β_m. The variables θ_m and η_m will denote, respectively, the BLER and spectral efficiency (in bps/Hz) considering operation at the target SINR of the mth MCS. It is assumed that the receiver monitors the quality of the channel and reports it back to the transmitter. Based on this collected Channel State Information (CSI), the transmitter selects the most appropriate MCS using a correction for the decision thresholds denoted here by $\hat{\beta}_m$. This paper considers perfect channel estimation at the receiver side and imperfect channel state information at the transmitter side (CSIT). Imperfect CSIT is assumed to be mainly due to a feedback channel affected by delay. The beamforming vector is denoted by $\mathbf{w}_j = [w_j(1), w_j(2), \ldots, w_j(N)]^T$, which using the MRC criterion is given by $\mathbf{w}_j = \mathbf{h}_j^*$. Therefore, the signal received by the scheduled terminal can be mathematically written as follows

$$r_j = \mathbf{w}_j^T \mathbf{h}_j s_j + \sum_{k=1}^{K} \delta_k h_{k,j} \check{s}_k + v_j, \qquad (1)$$

where s_j is the information symbol transmitted towards terminal j, $\check{s}_k$ is the symbol transmitted by interferer k, δ_k is the binary random variable that controls the transmissions of the non-persistent interferers ($p = \Pr\{\delta_k = 1\}$), and v_j is the additive white Gaussian noise experienced by terminal j with variance σ_v^2: $v_j \sim \mathcal{CN}(0, \sigma_v^2)$. Considering the symbol transmit power constraint $E[s_j^* s_j] = P$, the estimated SNR at the transmitter side from (1) is given by:

$$\hat{X}_j = \frac{\hat{\mathbf{h}}_j^H \hat{\mathbf{h}}_j E[s_j^* s_j]}{\sigma_v^2} = \frac{\sum_{n=1}^{N} P|\hat{h}_j(n)|^2}{\sigma_v^2}. \qquad (2)$$

Note that in this paper it is assumed that an estimate of interference $I_j = \sum_{k=1}^{K} \delta_k h_{k,j} \check{s}_k$ in (1) is not available at the transmitter. Therefore, all decisions will be based on an estimate of the SNR in (2). The estimated channels will be generated using the following linear correlation model:

$$\hat{h}_j(n) = \nu + \sqrt{1-\rho} Z_j(n) + \sqrt{\rho} G_j = \nu + \hat{\phi}_j(n), \qquad (3)$$

where ρ is the spatial correlation coefficient and the terms $Z_j(n)$ and G_j are the zero-mean complex circular Gaussian variables with variance γ. Considering that $h_j(n) = \nu_j + \phi_j(n)$, the correlation model complies with $E[\hat{\phi}_j(n)^* \hat{\phi}_j(\tilde{n})] = \rho\gamma$, $n \neq \tilde{n}$, and $E[\hat{\phi}_j(n)^* \hat{\phi}_j(n)] = \gamma$. This correlation model constitutes an approximation of real-life settings by assuming that all elements experience the same correlation with each other. In real-life systems, antennas farther apart from each other experience less correlation than contiguous elements. The correlation model for imperfect CSIT is given by:

$$h_j(n) = \nu + \phi_j(n) = \nu + \rho_c \hat{\phi}_j(n) + \sqrt{1-\rho_c^2} Y_j(n), \qquad (4)$$

where ρ_c is the temporal correlation coefficient that describes the accuracy of the CSIT. This correlation model complies with $E[\hat{\phi}_j(n)^* \phi_j(n)] = \rho_c \gamma$. The instantaneous SINR is given by:

$$\Gamma_j = \frac{Re(P \hat{\mathbf{h}}_j^H \mathbf{h}_j)}{I_j + \sigma_v^2}, \qquad (5)$$

where $I_j = \sum_{k=1}^{K} P|\delta_k h_{k,j}|^2$ is the interference created by K co-channel non-persistent interferers. Table I presents a list of the main variables used throughout this paper.

TABLE I. LIST OF VARIABLES.

Variable	Meaning
N	Number of antennas at the transmitter side
ρ	Spatial correlation coefficient
ρ_c	Temporal correlation coefficient
P	Transmit power
σ_v^2	Noise variance
γ	Channel variance
λ	Interferer channel variance
J	Number of terminals
M	Number of modulation formats
$\mathbf{h}_j$	Channel vector of terminal j
$\mathbf{w}_j$	Beamforming vector for terminal j
$\hat{\mathbf{h}}_j$	Estimated channel vector
$\hat{X}_j$	Estimated SNR for terminal j
Γ_j	Instantaneous SINR of terminal j
I_j	Interference experienced by terminal j
$h_{k,j}$	Channel between interferer k and terminal j
ν	Line of sight component main link
ξ	Line of sight component interfere link
K	Number of non-persistent interferers
s_j	Symbol transmitted towards terminal j
$\check{s}_k$	Symbol transmitted by interferer k
β_m	Reception SINR target threshold for modulation format m
θ_m	BLER for modulation format m @ β_m
η_m	Spectral efficiency of modulation format m @ β_m
T	Link Layer throughput
$\hat{\beta}_m$	Selection SNR threshold of modulation format m
δ_k	transmission binary control variable for interferer k
p	Interferer random transmission persistent factor

IV. LINK LAYER MODEL

The probability of selection of a modulation format m is given by the probability that the estimated SNR $\hat{X}_j$ at the transmitter side lies within the interval $[\hat{\beta}_m, \hat{\beta}_{m+1}]$:

$$\Pr\{\hat{\beta}_m \leq \hat{X}_j < \hat{\beta}_{m+1}\}. \quad (6)$$

Link-layer throughput (denoted by T) will be expressed as a linear contribution of all possible MCSs with their respective selection probabilities from (6) and conditional reception probabilities, each one weighted by their conditional throughput performance (T_m):

$$T = \sum_{m=1}^{M} E_{\Gamma_{j^*}}[T_m(\Gamma_{j^*}) | \hat{\beta}_m \leq \hat{X}_{j^*} < \hat{\beta}_{m+1}]$$

$$\Pr\{\hat{\beta}_m \leq \hat{X}_{j^*} < \hat{\beta}_{m+1}\} \Pr\{j^* = \arg\max_j \hat{X}_j\}, \quad (7)$$

where $T_m(\Gamma_j)$ indicates of the link-layer throughput of terminal j when using the mth MCS conditional on a given value of the operational SINR Γ_j in (5) of the selected terminal. In this paper, we consider a simplification of this expression, by assuming that the term $T_m(\Gamma)$ in (7) is a step function defined by a switching SINR threshold β_m above which all packet transmissions are assumed to be correctly received with a given BLER θ_m and spectral efficiency η_m. The simplification can be expressed as follows:

$$T = \sum_{m=1}^{M} \Delta_B W \eta_m (1-\theta_m) \Pr\{\Gamma_{j^*} \geq \beta_m | \hat{\beta}_m \leq \hat{X}_{j^*} < \hat{\beta}_{m+1}\}$$

$$\Pr\{\hat{\beta}_m \leq \hat{X}_{j^*} < \hat{\beta}_{m+1}\} \Pr\{j^* = \arg\max_j \hat{X}_j\} \quad (8)$$

where Δ_{BW} is the operational bandwidth in Hz, $\Pr\{j^* = \arg\max_j(\hat{X}_j)\}$ is the probability of terminal to experience the highest estimated SNR and therefore being scheduled for transmission by the BS, and $\Pr\{\Gamma_{j^*} \geq \beta_m | \hat{\beta}_m \leq \hat{X}_{j^*} < \hat{\beta}_{m+1}\}$ is the probability of the instantaneous SINR Γ_{j^*} to surpass the threshold β_m provided the estimated SNR $\hat{X}_{j^*}$ (used for MCS selection and terminal scheduling) lies in the range $[\hat{\beta}_m, \hat{\beta}_{m+1}]$.

Note that this last conditional probability term captures the effects of imperfect CSIT on the performance of the beamforming, scheduling and adaptation scheme. In the case of perfect CSIT ($\rho_c \to 0$), correct reception occurs with probability one. Also, note that the link-layer throughput expression in (8) represents only an approximation (compression) of the real performance of the system. The simplified model in (8) assumes packets are erroneous when the instantaneous SINR drops below the reception threshold β_m, when in practice there might be some cases where correct reception can still occur. Conversely, some cases with higher instantaneous SNR than the reception threshold could also lead to erroneous packet transmissions. This type of compression/abstraction model as in (8) has been proved accurate for system-level simulation of networks with considerable excursions of path-loss values, which are typical of cellular systems where terminals lie at different distances from the access point.

V. PERFORMANCE ANALYSIS

The following subsections present the derivation of analytic expressions of the different terms of the link-layer throughput model in (8). For convenience, it is useful to derive the statistics of the estimated SNR (presented in Section V-A) and then deal with the statistics of the instantaneous SINR (presented in Section V-C) conditional on the MCS selection, terminal scheduling, and beamforming processes.

A. Statistics of estimated SNR

Let us now substitute the correlation model described by (3) in the expression of the estimated SNR in (2), which yields:

$$\hat{X}_j = \frac{\sum_{n=1}^{N} P|\hat{h}_j(n)|^2}{\sigma_v^2} =$$

$$= \sum_{n=1}^{N} \frac{P|\nu + \sqrt{1-\rho} Z_j(n) + \sqrt{\rho} G_j|^2}{\sigma_v^2}. \quad (9)$$

The statistics of the estimated SNR have been investigated in our previous work in [37]. The sub-index j is dropped in subsequent derivations due to the symmetrical network assumption. The conditional characteristic function (CF) of $\hat{X}$ can be thus written as [39]:

$$\Psi_{\hat{X}|G}(i\omega) = (1 - i\omega\tilde{\gamma})^{-N} e^{\frac{i\omega\alpha|\tilde{\nu}+G|^2}{1-i\omega\tilde{\gamma}}}, \quad (10)$$

where $\tilde{\gamma} = \frac{P(1-\rho)\gamma}{\sigma_v^2}$, $i = \sqrt{-1}$, ω is the frequency domain variable, $\tilde{\nu} = \nu/\sqrt{\rho}$, $\alpha = \frac{PN\rho}{\sigma_v^2}$, and $\Psi_{X|Y}$ denotes the CF of random variable X conditional on an instance of random variable Y, for any X and Y random variables. By using the following change of variable $x = |\tilde{\nu} + G|^2$, the expression in (10) becomes:

$$\Psi_{\hat{X}|x}(i\omega) = (1 - i\omega\tilde{\gamma})^{-N} e^{\frac{i\omega\alpha x}{1-i\omega\tilde{\gamma}}}. \quad (11)$$

The unconditional CF of the estimated SNR can be now obtained by averaging the previous expression over the probability density function (PDF) of x, which under the Rice fading assumption is given by $f_x(x) = \sum_{q=0}^{\infty} C_q x^q e^{-\frac{x}{\gamma}}$, where $C_q = \frac{\kappa^q}{\gamma^{q+1}(q!)^2} e^{-\kappa}$ $\kappa = \frac{|\tilde{\nu}|^2}{\gamma}$ is the Rice factor. Therefore, the unconditional CF of the estimated SNR can be obtained as follows:

$$\Psi_{\hat{X}}(i\omega) = \int_0^{\infty} (1 - i\omega\tilde{\gamma})^{-N} e^{\frac{i\omega\alpha x}{1-i\omega\tilde{\gamma}}} \sum_{q=0}^{\infty} C_q x^q e^{-\frac{x}{\gamma}} dx, \quad (12)$$

which after the integration (see Appendix) becomes:

$$\Psi_{\hat{X}}(i\omega) = \sum_{q=0}^{\infty} \tilde{C}_q (1 - i\omega\breve{\gamma})^{-1-q} (1 - i\omega\tilde{\gamma})^{1+q-N}, \quad (13)$$

where $\tilde{C}_q = q! C_q \gamma^{q+1}$, $\breve{\gamma} = \alpha\gamma + \tilde{\gamma}$. The expression in (13) can be rewritten using partial fraction expansion (PFE):

$$\Psi_{\hat{X}}(i\omega) = \sum_{q=1}^{N-1} \frac{B_q}{(1 - i\omega\tilde{\gamma})^q} + \sum_{q=1}^{\infty} \frac{A_q}{(1 - i\omega\breve{\gamma})^q}. \quad (14)$$

where

$$A_q = \begin{cases} \sum_{n=1}^{N-1-q} A_{m,q}, & q \le N-1 \\ \breve{C}_q, & q > N-1 \end{cases}, \tag{15}$$

$$B_q = \sum_{n=0}^{N-2} B_{n,q}, \tag{16}$$

$$\breve{C}_q = \sum_{w=q}^{q+N} \tilde{C}_w \sum_{t=w-q}^{N} \sum_{u=0}^{t} \binom{1+w-N}{t} \left(\frac{\tilde{\gamma}}{\breve{\gamma}}\right)^t \tag{17}$$

$$\times (-1)^{u+1} \binom{t}{u} \tag{18}$$

$$A_{q,m} = \binom{N-1-q}{m} \frac{\tilde{C}_q(-\breve{\gamma})^{-1-q+m}(-\tilde{\gamma})^{1+q-N}}{(\breve{\gamma}^{-1}-\tilde{\gamma}^{-1})^m}, \tag{19}$$

$$B_{q,n} = \binom{1+q}{n} \frac{\tilde{C}_q(-\breve{\gamma})^{-1-q}(-\tilde{\gamma})^{1+q-N+n}}{(\tilde{\gamma}^{-1}-\breve{\gamma}^{-1})^n}. \tag{20}$$

See the Appendix for details of the derivation of these expressions. The probability density function (PDF) and complementary cumulative distribution function (CCDF) are thus given, respectively, by:

$$f_{\hat{X}}(y) = e^{-\frac{y}{\tilde{\gamma}}} \sum_{q=1}^{N-1} \frac{A_q y^{q-1}}{\tilde{\gamma}^q (q-1)!} + e^{-\frac{y}{\breve{\gamma}}} \sum_{q=1}^{\infty} \frac{B_q y^{q-1}}{\breve{\gamma}^q (q-1)!}, \tag{21}$$

and

$$\bar{F}_{\hat{X}}(y) = e^{-\frac{y}{\tilde{\gamma}}} \sum_{q=1}^{N-1} \sum_{m=0}^{q-1} \frac{A_q y^m}{\tilde{\gamma}^m m!} + e^{-\frac{y}{\breve{\gamma}}} \sum_{q=1}^{\infty} \sum_{n=0}^{q-1} \frac{B_q y^n}{\breve{\gamma}^n n!},$$

which can be rewritten, for convenience, as follows:

$$\bar{F}_{\hat{X}}(y) = e^{-\frac{y}{\tilde{\gamma}}} \sum_{q=1}^{N-1} \tilde{A}_q y^{q-1} + e^{-\frac{y}{\breve{\gamma}}} \sum_{q=1}^{\infty} \tilde{B}_q y^{q-1}, \tag{22}$$

where $\tilde{A}_q = \sum_{t=q}^{N-1} \frac{A_t}{\tilde{\gamma}^{q-1}(q-1)!}$ and $\tilde{B}_q = \sum_{t=q}^{\infty} \frac{B_t}{\breve{\gamma}^{q-1}(q-1)!}$.

B. Order statistics of estimated SNR

The effects of terminal scheduling on the statistics of the estimated SNR will be obtained via the theory of order statistics. The statistics of the random variable with maximum value are given by the following formula [38]:

$$f_{\hat{X}^{max}}(y) = J f_{\hat{X}}(y) F_{\hat{X}}(y)^{J-1}. \tag{23}$$

By substituting the expressions for the PDF and CDF of $\hat{X}^*$ in (23) and using the formula for multinomial theorem we obtain the following expression:

$$f_{\hat{X}^{max}}(y) = \sum_{\mathbf{l}; \sum_t l_t = J-1, q<N-1} \tilde{\alpha}_{\mathbf{l},q} e^{-y\tilde{\mu}_{\mathbf{l}}} y^{\tilde{\tau}_{\mathbf{l},q}}$$

$$+ \sum_{\mathbf{l}; \sum_t l_t = J-1, q>0} \alpha_{\mathbf{l},q} e^{-y\mu_{\mathbf{l}}} y^{\tau_{\mathbf{l},q}}, \tag{24}$$

where

$$\tilde{\alpha}_{\mathbf{l},q} = \alpha_{\mathbf{l}} \frac{\tilde{A}_q}{\tilde{\gamma}^q (q-1)!}, \tag{25}$$

$$\alpha_{\mathbf{l},q} = \alpha_{\mathbf{l}} \frac{\tilde{B}_q}{\breve{\gamma}^q (q-1)!}, \tag{26}$$

$$\alpha_{\mathbf{l}} = J \binom{J-1}{\mathbf{l}} \prod_{t=1}^{N} \left(-\tilde{A}_t\right)^{l_t} \prod_{t=N+1} \left(-\tilde{B}_{t-N+1}\right)^{l_t}, \tag{27}$$

$$\tilde{\mu}_{\mathbf{l}} = \frac{\sum_{t=1}^{N-1} l_t + 1}{\tilde{\gamma}} + \frac{\sum_{t=N} l_t}{\breve{\gamma}}, \tag{28}$$

$$\tau_{\mathbf{l},q} = \sum_{t=1}^{N-1} t l_t + q - 1 + \sum_{t=N} (t-N) l_t, \tag{29}$$

$$\mu_{\mathbf{l}} = \frac{\sum_{t=1}^{N-1} l_t}{\tilde{\gamma}} + \frac{\sum_{t=N} l_t + 1}{\breve{\gamma}}, \tag{30}$$

$$\tilde{\tau}_{\mathbf{l},q} = \sum_{t=1}^{N-1} (t-1) l_t + q - 1 + \sum_{t=N} (t-N) l_t. \tag{31}$$

The vector $\mathbf{l} = [l_1, l_2, \dots l_t, \dots]^T$ contains the exponents l_t of the elements of the multinomial term $F_{\hat{X}}(y)^{J-1}$. For details of this derivation please see the Appendix.

C. Statistics of instantaneous SINR

Let us now substitute the correlation model described by (4) into the expression of the instantaneous SINR in (5):

$$\Gamma_j = \frac{P\rho_c \hat{\mathbf{h}}_j^H \hat{\mathbf{h}}_j + Re[P \sum_{n=1}^{N} \hat{h}_j(n)^* \Phi_j(n)]}{I_j + \sigma_v^2}, \tag{32}$$

where $\Phi_j(n) = \nu(1-\rho_c) + \sqrt{1-\rho_c^2} Y_j(n)$. Since we are interested in the reception probability term $\Pr\{\Gamma_j > \beta_m\}$ we can use (32) to express the term $\Pr\{\Gamma_j > \beta_m\}$as follows:

$$\Pr\{\Gamma_j > \beta_m\} =$$

$$\Pr\left\{ \frac{P\rho_c \hat{\mathbf{h}}_j^H \hat{\mathbf{h}}_j + Re[P \sum_{n=1}^{N} \hat{h}_j(n)^* \Phi_j(n)]}{I_j + \sigma_v^2} > \beta_m \right\}.$$

By rearranging the terms of the inequality we obtain:

$$\Pr\{\Gamma_j > \beta_m\} =$$

$$\Pr\{P\rho_c \hat{\mathbf{h}}_j^H \hat{\mathbf{h}}_j + Re[P \sum_{n=1}^{N} \hat{h}_j(n)^* \Phi_j(n)] - \beta_m I_j$$

$$> \beta_m \sigma_v^2\} = \Pr\{\psi_j > \sigma_v^2\}.$$

The characteristic function of ψ_j conditionally on a particular value of $\hat{\mathbf{h}}_j$ is the addition of two random variables: a Gaussian process with mean $P\rho_c X_j + \nu(1-\rho_c)$ and variance $P(1-\rho_c)X_j = \breve{\gamma} X_j$ and a non-central chi-square random variable with K degrees of freedom, and parameters $-\beta_m \lambda$ and ξ. This can be mathematically written as follows:

$$\Psi_{\psi_j|\mathbf{h}_j,k}(i\omega) = \frac{e^{i(P\rho_c X_j + \nu(1-\rho_c)) + \omega^2 \breve{\gamma} X_j}}{(1 + i\omega\beta_m \lambda)^K} e^{\frac{i\omega\xi^2}{1+i\omega\beta_m\lambda}}.$$

The CF conditional on the decision made by the transmitter can be obtained as follows:

$$\Psi_{\psi_j|\hat{\beta}_m<X^{max}<\hat{\beta}_{m+1},k}(i\omega) = \int_{\hat{\beta}_m}^{\hat{\beta}_{m+1}} \Psi_{\psi_j|X^*}(i\omega) f(X^{max}) dX.$$

This operation yields:

$$\Psi_{\psi_j|\hat{\beta}_m<X^{max}<\hat{\beta}_{m+1}}(i\omega) =$$

$$\sum_{1;\sum_t l_t=J-1;q<N-1} \frac{\tilde{\alpha}_{1,q}}{(i\rho_c P + \tilde{\mu}_1 + \omega^2\check{\gamma})^{\tilde{\tau}_{1,q}+1}(1+i\omega\beta_m\lambda)^K}$$

$$\times e^{\frac{Ni\omega\xi^2}{1+i\omega\beta_m\lambda}} e^{i(1-\rho_c)\nu}$$

$$+ \sum_{1;\sum_t l_t=J-1,q>0} \frac{\alpha_{1,q}}{(i\rho_c P + \mu_1 + \omega^2\check{\gamma})^{\tau_{1,q}+1}(1+i\omega\beta_m\lambda)^K}$$

$$\times e^{\frac{Ni\omega\xi^2}{1+i\omega\beta_m\lambda}} e^{i(1-\rho_c)\nu}$$

The back transform is obtained numerically thus leading to the desired statistics of instantaneous SINR

VI. RESULTS

This section presents graphical results of the statistics of the MRC beamformer with adaptive modulation, scheduling and co-channel interference with imperfect CSIT. Figure 2 displays the results of the Cumulative Distribution Function (CDF) of the SNR of the scheduler conditional on the decision made by the transmitter based on imperfect CSIT using a hypothetical MCS selection threshold equal to ($\hat{\beta} = 2$). The results in Figure 2 have been obtained using fixed transmit power settings ($P\gamma/\sigma_v^2 = 1$) assuming no interference with different numbers of antennas ($N = 2, N = 4$), Rice factor $\kappa = -10$ dB, persistent factor $p = 0.7$, and different values of correlation coefficients ($\rho = 0.2$, $\rho = 0.95$, $\rho_c = 0.2$ and $\rho_c = 0.95$).

Figure 3 shows the results for the CDF of the SNR using the same settings as in the previous example, except for the transmit power which is now set to $P\gamma/\sigma_v^2 = 5$. The objective of investigating the conditional CDF is to observe the effects of imperfect CSIT on the instantaneous SNR experienced by the scheduled terminals. The results show the heavy influence of imperfect CSIT on the characteristics of the CDF. Low values of the correlation coefficient $\rho \to 0$, see a considerable degradation on the probability of correct reception. Note that all curves of the CDF depart from the hypothetical decision threshold set to $\hat{\beta} = 2$. This departure to the left-hand side of the figure is a measure of the incorrect reception due to imperfect CSIT. All the curves at the top left of the figure are indeed the curves with worse CSIT conditions. It is observed that spatial correlation degrades performance at high values of SNR, but it could be beneficial in the low SNR regime. In some cases, spatial diversity provided by higher numbers of antennas can even compensate for the effects of imperfect CSIT, particularly at with low values of spatial correlation. In all cases in both figures, it is observed that the performance of the CDF is superior with higher numbers of terminals in the scheduler, but this gain is more noticeable in channels with low spatial correlation. It can be also observed that user scheduling reduces the effects of spatial correlation. Spatial correlation reduces the diversity gains of the combining beamformer, and it can be accumulated over the several antennas resulting in a more noticeable performance reduction. User scheduling provides extra diversity gains that can compensate this reduction. The results can also be compared to the Rayleigh fading case presented in our previous conference publication in [1]. All the curves seem to be more straight in the vertical direction, which is an indication of the effect of line of sight.This "straightening" effect has consequences in different aspects of the protocol. First of all, it helps to reduce the likelihood of missing the SINR threshold for values near the threshold. However, it can also contribute to having difficulties in achieving such threshold, particularly with low values of the temporal correlation coefficient.

TABLE II. SINR(dB) vs BLER FOR WiMAX MODULATION AND CODING SCHEMES [40].

QPSK 1/3		QPSK 1/2		QPSK 2/3	
SINR	BLER	SINR	BLER	SINR	BLER
-1.14	4.10e-3	1.32	4.13e-3	3.47	6.50e-3
QPSK 3/4		**QPSK 4/5**		**16 QAM 1/3**	
SINR	BLER	SINR	BLER	SINR	BLER
4.78	3.30e-3	5.46	4.97e-3	3.66	7.15e-3
16 QAM 1/2		**16 QAM 2/3**		**16 QAM 3/4**	
SINR	BLER	SINR	BLER	SINR	BLER
6.52	5.70e-3	9.37	3.80e-3	10.98	1.57e-3

The results presented in Figure 3 and Figure 4 have been obtained using the same settings used in the previous two examples, except for the interference assumption. The channel power settings of the $K = 2$ persistent interferers were all set to $\lambda/\gamma = 0.1$. The results show the CDF of the instantaneous SINR instead of the SNR. The CDF results show how affected the system becomes by the presence of interference. It becomes evident that the presence of interference affects also how the spatial correlation plays a role on the performance of the system. This will become more evident in the results of throughput presented in the following figures.

To test the performance of the algorithm in a full wireless transmission system with different modulation formats, we have used the settings of the WiMAX standard and its different modulation schemes (see Table II). The results in Figure 4 and Figure 5 present the overall throughput for a network with different numbers of users included in the scheduler versus different values of transmit average SNR. Figure 4 shows the results with no interference, while Figure 5 shows the results with $K = 2$ interferers using set to $\lambda/\gamma = 0.1$. The results with interference show several changing patterns due to the complex relation between interference and the received signal by the terminals. Surprisingly at high values of transmit SNR some of the curves with low spatial correlation tend to perform worse that the correlated cases, which can only be explained by the increased importance of the interference term and the parameters of the modulation formats used in the simulation.

VII. CONCLUSIONS

This paper has presented an analytical framework for the study of joint MRC beamforming, terminal scheduling and resource allocation (modulation assignment) algorithms for multiuser networks in the presence of persistent co-channel interference. The results show that co-channel interference can

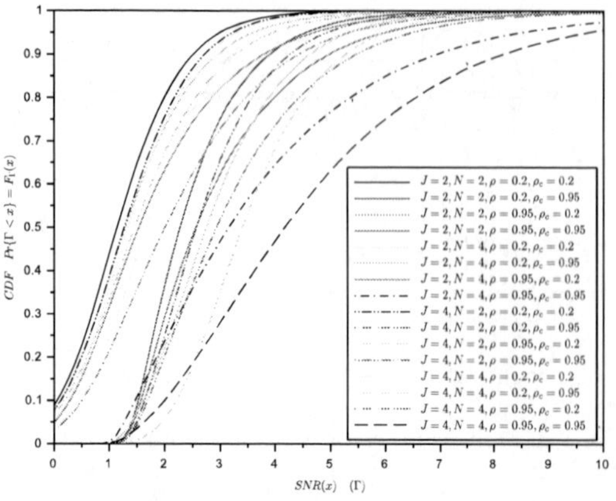

Figure 2. CDF of instantaneous SNR conditional on the estimated SNR being above the threshold $\hat{\beta} = 2$ with fixed Tx power settings $(P\gamma/\sigma_v^2) = 5)$ without interference, $\kappa = -10$ dB and different vales of antennas and correlation coefficients.

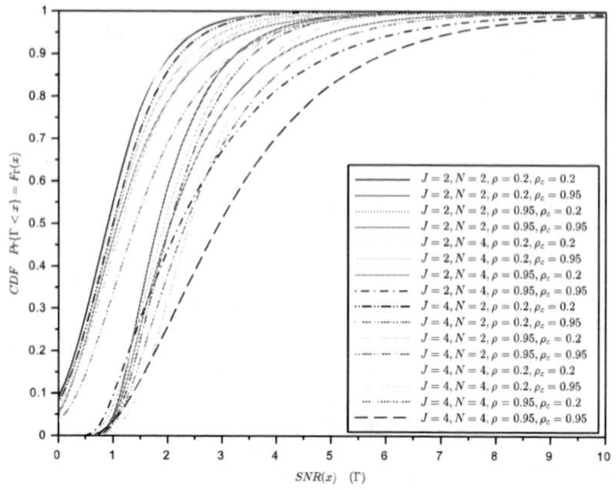

Figure 4. CDF of instantaneous SINR conditional on the estimated SNR being above the threshold $\hat{\beta} = 2$ with fixed Tx power settings $(P\gamma/\sigma_v^2) = 1)$ in the presence of cochannel interference $(K = 2, \lambda/\gamma = 0.1)$, $\kappa = -10$ dB, $p = 0.7$ and different vales of antennas and correlation coefficients.

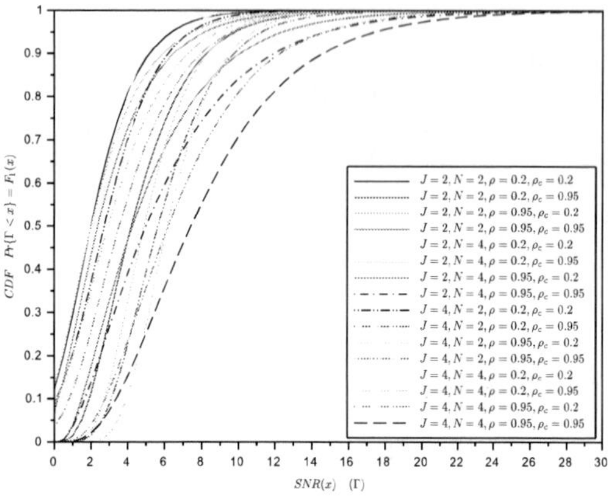

Figure 3. CDF of instantaneous SNR conditional on the estimated SNR being above the threshold $\hat{\beta} = 2$ with fixed Tx power settings $(P\gamma/\sigma_v^2) = 5)$ without interference,$\kappa = -10$ dB, and different vales of antennas and correlation coefficients.

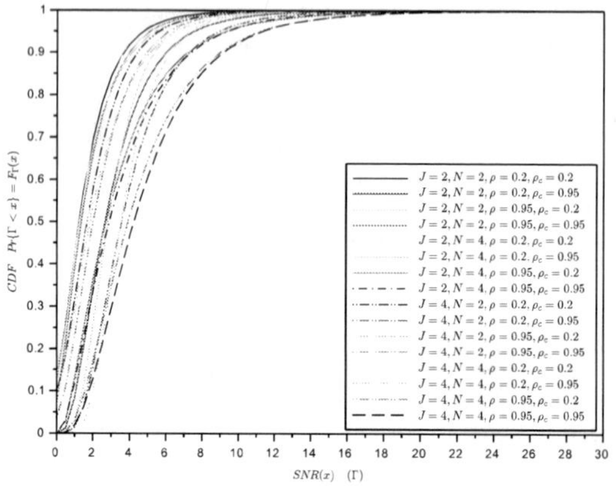

Figure 5. CDF of instantaneous SINR conditional on the estimated SNR being above the threshold $\hat{\beta} = 2$ with fixed Tx power settings $(P\gamma/\sigma_v^2) = 5)$ in the presence of co-channel interference $(K = 2, \lambda/\gamma = 0.1)$, $\kappa = -10$ dB, $p = 0.7$ and different vales of antennas and correlation coefficients.

considerably affect the performance of beamforming, being counteracted by the effects of scheduling and higher degree of accuracy of channel state information at the transmitter side. The number of antennas tends to reduce the effects of imperfect CSIT and interference. However, channel correlation can affect these gains, particularly in the high SNR regime. Conversely, in the low SNR regime it seems that channel correlation can outperform the case on uncorrelated channels. Spatial correlation effects tend to be accumulated when the number of antennas increases and, therefore, its effects will be more clearly observed in the high SNR regime. The line-of-sight component analyzed in this paper tends to improve reception for high values of temporal correlation, but it seems that when the quality of the information used for resource allocation, it contributes to reduce the diversity combining effects that can be used to overcome the errors due to imperfect CSIT.

ACKNOWLEDGMENTS

This work has received funding from project SCOTT (www.scottproject.eu) within the Electronic Component Systems for European Leadership Joint Undertaking under grant agreement No 737422. This Joint Undertaking receives support from the European Unions Horizon 2020 research and innovation programme and Austria, Spain, Finland, Ireland,

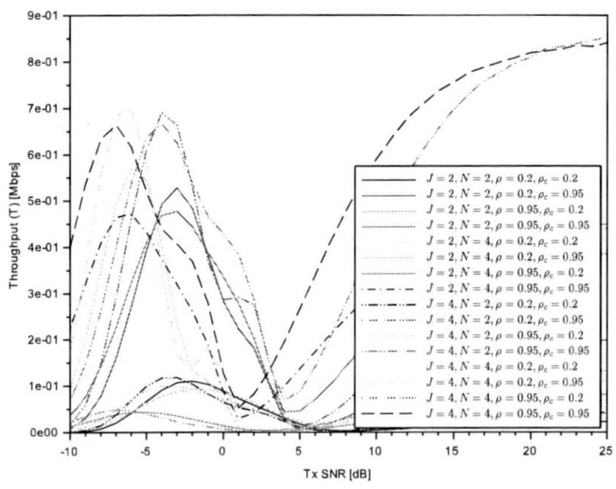

Figure 6. Throughput vs. transmit SNR for the MRC beamforming, scheduling and resource allocation algorithm without interference, $\kappa = -10$ dB and different vales of antennas and correlation coefficients.

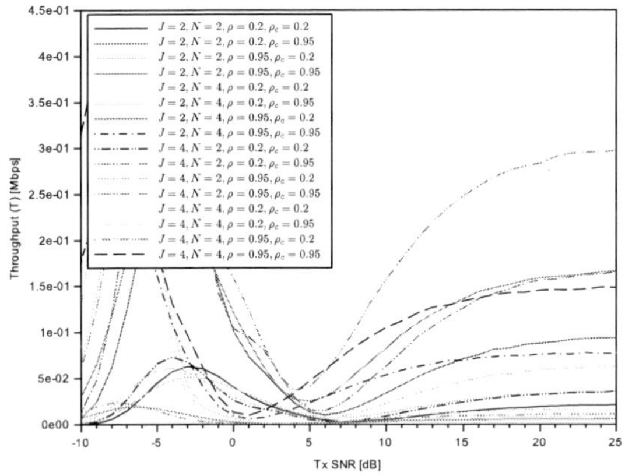

Figure 7. Throughput vs. transmit SNR for the MRC beamforming, scheduling and resource allocation algorithm in the presence of cochannel interference ($K = 2$, $\lambda/\gamma = 0.1$), $\kappa = -10$ dB, $p = 0.7$ and different vales of antennas, numbers of terminals and correlation coefficients.

Sweden, Germany, Poland, Portugal, Netherlands, Belgium, Norway. Funded also by FCT/MEC (Fundacão para a Ciência e a Tecnologia), ERDF (European Regional Development Fund) under PT2020, and by CISTER Research Unit (CEC/04234) .

APPENDIX

A. Derivation of the unconditional CF of $\hat{X}$ in (13)

Consider the following modification of (12):

$$\Psi_{\hat{X}}(i\omega) = \int_0^\infty (1-i\omega\tilde{\gamma})^{-N} \sum_{q=0}^{\infty} C_q x^q e^{-x\left(\frac{1-i\omega(\alpha\gamma+\tilde{\gamma})}{\gamma(1-i\omega\tilde{\gamma})}\right)} dx. \tag{33}$$

By using the following changes of variable $u = x\left(\frac{1-i\omega(\alpha\gamma+\tilde{\gamma})}{\gamma(1-i\omega\tilde{\gamma})}\right)$, $\breve{\gamma} = \alpha\gamma + \tilde{\gamma}$ and $du = dx\left(\frac{1-i\omega(\alpha\gamma+\tilde{\gamma})}{\gamma(1-i\omega\tilde{\gamma})}\right)$ the previous integral becomes:

$$\int_0^\infty \sum_{q=0}^{\infty} C_q \gamma^{q+1} (1-i\omega\tilde{\gamma})^{q+1-N} (1-i\omega\breve{\gamma})^{-1-q} u^q e^{-u} du.$$

The results of the above integration ($\int_{u=0}^{\infty} u^q e^{-u} du = q!$) yields the expression in (13).

B. Derivation of the partial fraction expansion of the CF of $\hat{X}$ in (14)

For convenience we rewrite the expression in (13) as follows:

$$\begin{aligned}
\Psi_{\hat{X}}(i\omega) &= \sum_{q=0}^{\infty} \tilde{C}_q (1-i\omega\breve{\gamma})^{-1-q} (1-i\omega\tilde{\gamma})^{1+q-N} \\
&= \sum_{q=0}^{N-2} \frac{\tilde{C}_q}{(1-i\omega\breve{\gamma})^{1+q}(1-i\omega\tilde{\gamma})^{N-1-q}} \\
&\quad + \sum_{q=N-1}^{\infty} \frac{\tilde{C}_q (1-i\omega\tilde{\gamma})^{1+q-N}}{(1-i\omega\breve{\gamma})^{1+q}},
\end{aligned} \tag{34}$$

The first term of this expression can be expanded in partial fractions as follows:

$$\frac{\tilde{C}_q}{(1-i\omega\breve{\gamma})^{1+q}(1-i\omega\tilde{\gamma})^{N-1-q}} = \sum_{m=1}^{1+q} \frac{A_{q,m}}{(1-i\omega\breve{\gamma})^m} + \sum_{n=1}^{N-1-q} \frac{B_{q,n}}{(1-i\omega\tilde{\gamma})^n},$$

where $A_{q,m} = \binom{N-1-q}{m} \frac{\tilde{C}_q (-\breve{\gamma})^{-1-q+m} (-\tilde{\gamma})^{1+q-N}}{(\breve{\gamma}^{-1}-\tilde{\gamma}^{-1})^m}$ and $B_{q,n} = \binom{1+q}{n} \frac{\tilde{C}_q (-\breve{\gamma})^{-1-q} (-\tilde{\gamma})^{1+q-N+n}}{(\tilde{\gamma}^{-1}-\breve{\gamma}^{-1})^n}$. The second term of the expression in (34) can be rewritten as follows:

$$\sum_{q=N-1}^{\infty} \frac{\tilde{C}_q (1-i\omega\tilde{\gamma})^{1+q-N}}{(1-i\omega\breve{\gamma})^{1+q}} = \sum_{q=N-1}^{\infty} \sum_{t=0}^{1+q-N} \binom{1+q-N}{t} \frac{\tilde{C}_q (-i\omega\tilde{\gamma})^t}{(1-i\omega\breve{\gamma})^{1+q}},$$

which can be rewritten as

$$\begin{aligned}
&\sum_{q=N-1}^{\infty} \sum_{t=0}^{1+q-N} \binom{1+q-N}{t} \sum_{u=0}^{t} \binom{t}{u} \\
&\qquad \times \frac{\tilde{C}_q (\tilde{\gamma}/\breve{\gamma})^t (-1)^{u+1}}{(1-i\omega\breve{\gamma})^{1+q-u}} \\
&= \sum_{q=N-1}^{\infty} \frac{\breve{C}_q}{(1-i\omega\breve{\gamma})^{1+q}},
\end{aligned}$$

where

$$\breve{C}_q = \sum_{w=q}^{q+N} \tilde{C}_w \sum_{t=w-q}^{N} \sum_{u=0}^{t} \binom{1+w-N}{t} \left(\frac{\tilde{\gamma}}{\breve{\gamma}}\right)^t \times (-1)^{u+1} \binom{t}{u}.$$

By substituting the results back in (34), we obtain:

$$\Psi_{\hat{X}}(i\omega) = \sum_{q=0}^{N-2} \left\{ \sum_{m=1}^{1+q} \frac{A_{q,m}}{(1 - i\omega\breve{\gamma})^m} + \sum_{n=1}^{N-1-q} \frac{B_{q,n}}{(1 - i\omega\tilde{\gamma})^n} \right\}$$

$$+ \sum_{q=N-1}^{\infty} \frac{\breve{C}_q}{(1 - i\omega\breve{\gamma})^{1+q}},$$

which can be rewritten as

$$\Psi_{\hat{X}}(i\omega) = \sum_{q=1}^{N-1} \frac{B_q}{(1 - i\omega\tilde{\gamma})^q} + \sum_{q=1}^{\infty} \frac{A_q}{(1 - i\omega\breve{\gamma})^q},$$

where: $A_q = \begin{cases} \sum_{n=1}^{N-1-q} A_{m,q}, & q \leq N-1 \\ \breve{C}_q, & q > N-1 \end{cases}$, and $B_q = \sum_{n=0}^{N-2} B_{n,q}$,

C. Derivation of order statistics of estimated SNR in from (2)

Using the multinomial theorem, it is possible to obtain a formula for the term $F_{\hat{X}}(y)^{J-1}$ considering the expression in (22) as follows:

$$F_{\hat{X}}(y)^{J-1} = \sum_{\sum_t l_t = J-1} \binom{J-1}{\mathbf{l}} \prod_{t=1}^{N-1} \left(-\tilde{A}_t y^{t-1} e^{-\frac{y}{\breve{\gamma}}}\right)^{l_t}$$

$$\times \prod_{t=N} \left(-\tilde{B}_{t-N+1} y^{t-N} e^{-\frac{y}{\tilde{\gamma}}}\right)^{l_t}$$

where l_t is the exponent index of the t-th element of the multinomial expression$(x_0 + x_1 + x_2 + \ldots x_t + x_{t+1} \ldots)^{J-1}$, considering that $x_0 = 1$, $x_t = -\tilde{A}_t y^{t-1} e^{-\frac{y}{\breve{\gamma}}}$, $1 \leq t \leq N-1$, $x_t = -\tilde{B}_{t-N+1} y^{t-N} e^{-\frac{y}{\tilde{\gamma}}}$, $N \leq t$,. The vector $\mathbf{l} = [l_1, l_2, \ldots l_t, \ldots]^T$ contains the exponents l_t of the elements of the multinomial term $F_{\hat{X}}(y)^{J-1}$. The previous expression can be reorganized as follows:

$$F_{\hat{X}}(y)^{J-1} = \sum_{\sum_t l_t = J-1} \binom{J-1}{\mathbf{l}}$$

$$\times e^{-y\left(\frac{\sum_{t=1}^{N-1} l_t}{\breve{\gamma}} + \frac{\sum_{t=N} l_t}{\tilde{\gamma}}\right)} y^{\sum_{t=1}^{N-1}(t-1)l_t + \sum_{t=N}(t-N)l_t}$$

$$\times \prod_{t=1}^{N} \left(-\tilde{A}_t\right)^{l_t} \prod_{t=N+1} \left(-\tilde{B}_{t-N+1}\right)^{l_t}$$

By substituting the previous expression back in (23) we then obtain:

$$f_{\hat{X}^{max}}(y) = \sum_{\sum_t l_t = J-1} \binom{J-1}{\mathbf{l}}$$

$$\times e^{-y\left(\frac{\sum_{t=1}^{N-1} l_t}{\breve{\gamma}} + \frac{\sum_{t=N} l_t}{\tilde{\gamma}}\right)} y^{\sum_{t=1}^{N-1}(t-1)l_t + \sum_{t=N}(t-N)l_t}$$

$$\times \prod_{t=1}^{N} \left(-\tilde{A}_t\right)^{l_t} \prod_{t=N+1} \left(-\tilde{B}_{t-N+1}\right)^{l_t}$$

$$\times \left(e^{-\frac{y}{\tilde{\gamma}}} \sum_{q=1}^{N-1} \frac{\tilde{A}_q y^{q-1}}{\tilde{\gamma}^q (q-1)!} + e^{-\frac{y}{\breve{\gamma}}} \sum_{q=1}^{\infty} \frac{\tilde{B}_q y^{q-1}}{\breve{\gamma}^q (q-1)!} \right),$$

which can be rewritten as follows

$$f_{\hat{X}^{max}}(y) = \sum_{\sum_t l_t = J-1} \alpha_{\mathbf{l}} e^{-y\left(\frac{\sum_{t=1}^{N-1} l_t}{\breve{\gamma}} + \frac{\sum_{t=N} l_t}{\tilde{\gamma}}\right)}$$

$$\times y^{\sum_{t=1}^{N-1}(t-1)l_t + \sum_{t=N}(t-N)l_t}$$

$$\times \left(e^{-\frac{y}{\tilde{\gamma}}} \sum_{q=1}^{N-1} \frac{\tilde{A}_q y^{q-1}}{\tilde{\gamma}^q (q-1)!} + e^{-\frac{y}{\breve{\gamma}}} \sum_{q=1}^{\infty} \frac{\tilde{B}_q y^{q-1}}{\breve{\gamma}^q (q-1)!} \right)$$

where

$$\alpha_{\mathbf{l}} = J \binom{J-1}{\mathbf{l}} \prod_{t=1}^{N} \left(-\tilde{A}_t\right)^{l_t} \prod_{t=N+1} \left(-\tilde{B}_{t-N+1}\right)^{l_t}.$$

A further modification of this expression leads to:

$$f_{\hat{X}^{max}}(y) =$$

$$\sum_{\mathbf{l};\sum_t l_t = J-1} \sum_{q=1}^{N-1} \tilde{\alpha}_{\mathbf{l},q} e^{-y\left(\frac{\sum_{t=1}^{N-1} l_t + 1}{\tilde{\gamma}} + \frac{\sum_{t=N} l_t}{\breve{\gamma}}\right)}$$

$$\times y^{\sum_{t=1}^{N-1}(t-1)l_t + q - 1 + \sum_{t=N}(t-N)l_t}$$

$$+ \sum_{\mathbf{l};\sum_t l_t = J-1} \sum_{q=1}^{\infty} \alpha_{\mathbf{l},q} e^{-y\left(\frac{\sum_{t=1}^{N-1} l_t}{\tilde{\gamma}} + \frac{\sum_{t=N} l_t}{\breve{\gamma}}\right)}$$

$$\times y^{\sum_{t=1}^{N-1} t l_t + \sum_{t=N}(t-N)l_t + q - 1}$$

where

$$\tilde{\alpha}_{\mathbf{l},q} = \alpha_{\mathbf{l}} \frac{\tilde{A}_q}{\tilde{\gamma}^q (q-1)!},$$

and

$$\alpha_{\mathbf{l},q} = \alpha_{\mathbf{l}} \frac{\tilde{B}_q}{\breve{\gamma}^q (q-1)!}.$$

This can be rewritten as the intended expression in (24), which finalizes the derivation.

REFERENCES

[1] R. Samano-Robles, "Joint Beamforming, Terminal Scheduling, and Adaptive Modulation with Imperfect CSIT in Rayleigh Fading Correlated Channels with Co-channel Interference," *The Second International Conference on Advances in Signal, Image and Video Processing - from Sensing to Applications (SIGNAL 2017)*. 21-25 May 2017, 5GSIGNAL-WAVE. Barcelona, Spain.

[2] H. Kim, "Coding and modulation techniques for high spectral efficiency transmission in 5G and Satcom," *23rd European Signal Processing Conference (EUSIPCO)* Nice, France, pp. 2746-2750, 31 Aug.-4 Sept. 2015, DOI: 10.1109/EUSIPCO.2015.7362884

[3] A. Goldsmith, S. A. Jafar, N. Jindal, and S. Vishwanath, "Capacity limits of MIMO channels," *IEEE Journal on Selected Areas in Communications*, vol. 21, no. 5, pp. 684-702, June 2003, DOI: 10.1109/JSAC.2003.810294

[4] W. Ge, J. Zhang, and G. Xue, "MIMO-Pipe Modeling and Scheduling for Efficient Interference Management in Multihop MIMO Networks," *IEEE Transactions on Vehicular Technology*, vol. 59, no. 8, pp. 3966-3978, Oct. 2010, DOI: 10.1109/TVT.2010.2060376

[5] R. Smano-Robles and A. Gameiro, "Joint Scheduling, link adaptation and space division multiplexing for distributed antenna systems," *TELFOR (Telecommunications Forum)* Belgrade, Serbia, 2012.

[6] D. Soldani and A. Mazalini, "On the 5G Operating System for a True Digital Society," *IEEE Vehicular Technology Magazine. 2015* March, pp. 32-42. DOI: 10.1109/MVT.2014.2380581

[7] A. Sasi and P. Santhiva, "Quantum internet using 5G NanoCore with Beam Division Multiple Access," *International Conference on Advanced Computing and Communication Systems*, Jan. 2015, Coimbatore, India, 2015.

[8] H. J. Yang,W.-Y. Shin, B. C. Jung, C. Suh, and A. Paulraj, "Opportunistic Downlink Interference Alignment for Multi-Cell MIMO Networks," *IEEE Transactions on Wireless Communications.* vol. 16, no. 3, pp. 1533 - 1548, March 2017, DOI: 10.1109/TWC.2017.2647942

[9] F. Rashid, K. J. Ray Liu, and L. Tassiulas, "Transmit beamforming and power control for cellular wireless systems," *IEEE Journal on Selected Areas in Communications,* vol. 16, no. 8, pp. 1437-1450, Oct. 1998, DOI: 10.1109/49.730452

[10] H. Dahrouj and W. Yu. "Coordinated beamforming for the multi-cell multi-antenna wireless system," *IEEE Transactions on Wireless Communications,* vol. 9, no. 5, pp. 1748-1759, May 2010, DOI: 10.1109/TWC.2010.05.090936.

[11] Y. Huang, G. Zheng, M. Bengtsson, K. Wong, L. Yang, and B. Ottersten, "Distributed Multicell Beamforming With Limited Intercell Coordination," *IEEE Transactions on Signal Processing,* vol. 59, no. 2, pp. 728-738, Feb. 2011, DOI: 10.1109/TSP.2010.2089621

[12] Deliverable D5.1: System level evaluation metrics and interfacing, "FP7 CODIV: Enhanced Wireless Communication Systems Employing COoperative DIVersity,", Available at: http://www.ict-codiv.eu/ Last Accessed November 2017.

[13] Deliverable D5.4: Final report on link level and system level channel models, "FP7 WINNER: Wireless World Initiative New Radio,", Available at: http://www.ist-winner.org Last Accessed November 2017.

[14] Deliverable D7.1: System level interfacing, metrics and simulation scenarios, "FP7 FUTON: Fibre-Optic Networks for Distributed Extendible Heterogeneous Radio Architectures and Service,", Available at: http://www.ict-futon.eu/ Last Accessed November 2017.

[15] K. Brueninghaus, et al., "Link performance model models for system level simulations of broadband radio access systems," *Proceedings IEEE International Symposium on Personal, Indoor and Mobile Radio Communications*, vol. 4, pp. 2306-2311, March 2005.

[16] J. Murkovic, G. Orfanos, and H. J. Reumermann, "MIMO link modeling for system-level simulations," *The 17th annual IEEE International Symposium on Personal, Indoor and Mobile Radio Communications, PMRC,* , vol. 4, pp. 1-6, 2006.

[17] M. Wrulich and M. Rupp, "Efficient link measurement model for system-level simulations of Alamouti encoded MIMO HSDPA transmissions," *2008 ITG Workshop on smart antennas* pp. 351-355.

[18] A. Perez-Niera and M Campalans, "Cross-Layer Resource Allocation in Wireless Communications: Techniques and Models from PHY and MAC Layer Interaction," *Academic Press, Oxford, 2010*

[19] F. A. Dietrich and W. Utschick, "Maximum ratio combining of correlated Rayleigh fading channels with imperfect channel knowledge," *IEEE Communications Letters*, vol. 7, no. 9, pp. 419-421, Sept. 2003, DOI: 10.1109/LCOMM.2003.817299.

[20] Y. Ma, R. Schober, and S. Pasupathy, "Effect of channel estimation errors on MRC diversity in Rician fading channels," *IEEE Trans. on Vehicular Technologies*, vol. 54, no. 6, pp. 2137-2142, November 2005, DOI: 10.1109/TVT.2005.853454.

[21] Y. Ma, "Impact of correlated diversity branches in Rician fading channels," *IEEE International Conference on Communications (ICC)*, vol. 1, pp. 473-477, 2005.

[22] H. T. Hui, "The performance of the maximum ratio combining method in correlated Rician-Fading channels for antenna-diversity signal combining," *IEEE Trans. on Antennas and Propagation*, vol. 53, no. 3, pp. 958-964, March 2005, DOI: 10.1109/TAP.2004.842649.

[23] P. Loskot and N.C. Beaulieu, "A unified approach to computing error probabilities of diversity combining schemes over correlated fading channels," *IEEE Transactions on Communications*, vol. 57, no. 7, pp. 2031-2041, 2009.

[24] N.C. Beauliu and X. Zhang, "On selecting the number of receiver diversity antennas in Ricean fading cochannel interference," *IEEE Global Telecommunications Conference (Globecom) 2006*, pp. 1-6.

[25] N.C. Beauliu and X. Zhang, "On the maximum number of receiver diversity antennas that can be usefully deployed in a cochannel interference dominated environment," *IEEE Transactions on Signal Processing*, vol. 55, no. 7, pp. 3349-3359, July 2007, DOI: 10.1109/TSP.2007.894395.

[26] N.C. Beauliu and X. Zhang, "On the maximum useful number of receiver antennas for MRC diversity in cochannel interference and noise," *IEEE International Conference on Communications (ICC)*,pp. 5103-5108.

[27] K. S. Ahn and R.W. Heath, "Performance analysis of maximum ratio combining with imperfect channel estimation in the presence of cochannel interferences," *IEEE Transactions on Wireless Communications*, vol. 8, no. 3, pp. 1080-1085, March 2009, DOI: 10.1109/TWC.2009.080114.

[28] R. Samano-Robles and A. Gameiro, "Joint Spectrum Selection and Radio Resource Management for Distributed Antenna Systems with Cognitive Radio and Space Division Multiplexing," *Workshop on Smart Antennas, Stuttgart, Germany,* 2013.

[29] L.Chen, Y. Yang, X. Chen, and G. Wei, "Energy-Efficient Link Adaptation on Rayleigh Fading Channel for OSTBC MIMO System With Imperfect CSIT," *IEEE Transactions on Vehicular Technology*, vol. 62, no. 4, pp. 1577-1585, May 2013, DOI: 10.1109/TVT.2012.2234155.

[30] A. E. Ekpenyong and Y.F. Huang, "Feedback Constraints for Adaptive Transmission," *IEEE Signal Processing Magazine*, vol. 24, no. 3, pp. 69-78, May 2007, DOI: 10.1109/MSP.2007.361603.

[31] S.i Zhou and G. B. Giannakis, "Adaptive Modulation for Multi-antenna Transmissions With Channel Mean Feedback," *IEEE Transactions on Wireless Communications*, vol. 3, no. 5, pp. 1626-36, Sept. 2004, DOI: 10.1109/TWC.2004.833411.

[32] M. Torabi and J.F. Frigon, "Impact of Outdated Feedback on the Performance of M-QAM Adaptive Modulation in User Selection Diversity Systems with OSTBC over MIMO Rayleigh Fading Channel," *IEEE Vehicular Technology Conference,* 3-6 Sept. 2012, Canada.

[33] P. Yang, Y. Xiao, Y. Yu, L. Li, Q. Tang, and S. Li, "Simplied Adaptive Spatial Modulation for Limited-Feedback MIMO Systems," *IEEE Signal Processing Magazine*, vol. 62, no. 6, pp. 2656 - 2666, July 2013, DOI: 10.1109/TVT.2013.2242502.

[34] P. Xia, S. Zhou, and G. B. Giannakis, "Multiantenna Adaptive Modulation With Beamforming Based on Bandwidth Constrained Feedback," *IEEE Transactions on Communications* vol. 53, no. 3, pp. 526 - 536, March 2005, DOI: 10.1109/TCOMM.2005.843431.

[35] Z. Bouida, A. Ghrayeb, and K. A. Qaraqe, "Adaptive Spatial Modulation for Spectrum Sharing Systems With Limited Feedback," *IEEE Transactions on Communications,* vol. 63, no. 6, pp. 2001-2014, June 2015, DOI: 10.1109/TCOMM.2015.2420567.

[36] Z. Bouida, A. Ghrayeb, and K. A. Qaraqe, "Joint Adaptive Spatial Modulation and Power Adaptation for Spectrum Sharing Systems with Limited feedback," *IEEE Wireless Communications and Networking Conference (WCNC 2015)*

[37] R. Samano Robles, E. Lavendelis, and E. Tovar, "Performance Analysis of MRC Receivers with Adaptive Modulation and Coding in Rayleigh Fading Correlated Channels with Imperfect CSIT," *Wireless Communications and Mobile Computing*, Volume 2017 (2017), Article ID 6940368,.

[38] http://mathworld.wolfram.com/OrderStatistic.html

[39] J. Proakis, *Digital Communications,* McGraw-Hill, 4th edition 2001.

[40] WiMAX Forum Standard,"*WiMAX system level evaluation methodology, V.0.0.1,*" 2006.

iaria journals

www.iariajournals.org

International Journal On Advances in Intelligent Systems
issn: 1942-2679

International Journal On Advances in Internet Technology
issn: 1942-2652

International Journal On Advances in Life Sciences
issn: 1942-2660

International Journal On Advances in Networks and Services
issn: 1942-2644

International Journal On Advances in Security
issn: 1942-2636

International Journal On Advances in Software
issn: 1942-2628

International Journal On Advances in Systems and Measurements
issn: 1942-261x

International Journal On Advances in Telecommunications
issn: 1942-2601